Victims in the War on Crime

CRITICAL AMERICA

General Editors: Richard Delgado and Jean Stefancic

White by Law: The Legal Construction of Race
Ian F. Haney López

Cultivating Intelligence: Power, Law, and the Politics of Teaching
Louise Harmon and Deborah W. Post

Privilege Revealed: How Invisible Preference Undermines America
Stephanie M. Wildman with Margalynne Armstrong,
Adrienne D. Davis, and Trina Grillo

*Does the Law Morally Bind the Poor? or What Good's the Constitution
When You Can't Afford a Loaf of Bread?*
R. George Wright

Hybrid: Bisexuals, Multiracials, and Other Misfits under American Law
Ruth Colker

Critical Race Feminism: A Reader
Edited by Adrien Katherine Wing

*Immigrants Out! The New Nativism and the Anti-Immigrant Impulse
in the United States*
Edited by Juan F. Perea

Taxing America
Edited by Karen B. Brown and Mary Louise Fellows

Notes of a Racial Caste Baby: Color Blindness and the End of Affirmative Action
Bryan K. Fair

*Please Don't Wish Me a Merry Christmas: A Critical History of the
Separation of Church and State*
Stephen M. Feldman

To Be an American: Cultural Pluralism and the Rhetoric of Assimilation
Bill Ong Hing

Negrophobia and Reasonable Racism: The Hidden Costs of Being Black in America
Jody David Armour

Black and Brown in America: The Case for Cooperation
Bill Piatt

Black Rage Confronts the Law
Paul Harris

Selling Words: Free Speech in a Commercial Culture
R. George Wright

The Color of Crime: Racial Hoaxes, White Fear, Black Protectionism, Police Harassment, and Other Macroaggressions
Katheryn R. Russell

The Smart Culture: Society, Intelligence, and Law
Robert L. Hayman, Jr.

Was Blind, But Now I See: White Consciousness and the Law
Barbara J. Flagg

The Gender Line: Men, Women, and the Law
Nancy Levit

Heretics in the Temple: Americans Who Reject the Nation's Legal Faith
David Ray Papke

The Empire Strikes Back: Outsiders and the Struggle over Legal Education
Arthur Austin

Interracial Justice: Conflict and Reconciliation in Post–Civil Rights America
Eric K. Yamamoto

Black Men on Race, Gender, and Sexuality: A Critical Reader
Edited by Devon Carbado

When Sorry Isn't Enough: The Controversy over Apologies and Reparations for Human Injustice
Edited by Roy L. Brooks

Disoriented: Asian Americans, Law, and the Nation State
Robert S. Chang

Rape and the Culture of the Courtroom
Andrew E. Taslitz

The Passions of Law
Edited by Susan A. Bandes

Global Critical Race Feminism: An International Reader
Edited by Adrien Katherine Wing

Victims in the War on Crime

The Use and Abuse of Victims' Rights

Markus Dirk Dubber

NEW YORK UNIVERSITY PRESS

New York and London

NEW YORK UNIVERSITY PRESS
New York and London
www.nyupress.org

First published in paperback in 2006.

Library of Congress Cataloging-in-Publication Data
Dubber, Markus Dirk.
Victims in the war on crime : the use and abuse of victims' rights /
Markus Dirk Dubber.
p. cm. — (Critical America)
Includes bibliographicical references and index.
ISBN-13: 0-8147-1928-7 (cloth : alk. paper)
ISBN-10: 978-0-8147-1928-2 (cloth : alk. paper)
ISBN-13: 0-8147-1929-5 (pbk : alk. paper)
ISBN-10: 978-0-8147-1929-9 (pbk : alk. paper)
1. Victims of crimes—United States. 2. Victims of crimes—Legal status,
laws, etc.—United States. 3. Crime—Government policy—United States.
4. Crimes without victims—Government policy—United States. 5. Criminal
justice, Administration of—United States. 6. Criminal law—United States.
I. Title. II. Series.
HV6250.3.U5 D82 2002
362.88'0973—dc21   2002001436

New York University Press books are printed on acid-free paper,
and their binding materials are chosen for strength and durability.

Manufactured in the United States of America
c 10 9 8 7 6 5 4 3 2 1
p 10 9 8 7 6 5 4 3 2 1

To my parents

Contents

Acknowledgments

Many people and institutions helped me write this book. Much of the work on it was done at the Institute for Legal Philosophy in Munich, where Bernd Schünemann was the perfect host in 2000–2001. This memorable year was made possible by the generosity of the Humboldt Foundation, the flexibility of Dean Nils Olsen, and the support of my family, including my parents, my wife, and my kids. The German-American Academic Council and SUNY Buffalo Law School deserve thanks for funding a research project on victims' rights, which first got me thinking seriously about the subject. This project, undertaken jointly with Bernd Schünemann, resulted, among other things, in a stimulating German-American conference on victims' rights, held at the Buffalo Criminal Law Center in the fall of 1998. I learned a lot from the participants in this conference, and I am deeply grateful to them. (The conference papers were published in "Victims and the Criminal Law: American and German Perspectives," 3 Buff. Crim. L. Rev. no.1 [1999].)

Thanks are also due to the participants in seminars at the Institute for Criminal Law in Frankfurt and the Institute for Legal Philosophy in Munich, where I presented parts of the book in early 2001. For statistical information on possession offenses in New York State, I am grateful to the New York State Division of Criminal Justice Services and to Simon Singer. Lots of people allowed me to bend their ears about this book over the past couple of years; many of them were kind enough to read all or part of the manuscript. At the risk of leaving someone out, these good samaritans included Guyora Binder, Hanoch Dagan, Teresa Faherty, Shubha Ghosh, Sam Gross, Klaus Günther, Phil Halpern, George Hezel, Tatjana Hörnle, Jerry Israel, Klaus Lüderssen, Errol Meidinger, Wolfgang Naucke, Cornelius Nestler, Cornelius Prittwitz, Mathias Reimann, Lorenz Schulz, Rob Steinfeld, Bob Weisberg, Peter Westen, Jim Whitman, Jim Wooten, Leo Zaibert, and Sara Faherty, who is not only my wife, but also knows a lot more about victims' rights than I do. Clara, Dora, and Maura didn't read much of the manuscript but still managed to help in their own special way.

Earlier versions of portions of this book appeared as "Policing Possession: The War on Crime and the End of Criminal Law," 91 J. Crim. L. & Criminology no.3 (2001), and "The Victim in American Penal Law: A Systematic Overview," 3 Buff. Crim. L. Rev. no.1 (1999). Any previously published material is used with permission.

Introduction

Two phenomena have shaped American criminal law for the past thirty years: the war on crime and the victims' rights movement. These two political programs are related. The war on crime has been waged on behalf of victims against offenders; to pursue criminals has meant to pursue victims' rights. To be pro-victim was to be anticrime, and vice versa.

The very first "victims' bill of rights," inserted into the California constitution by popular referendum in 1982, made explicit the connection between victims' rights and the war on crime. Victims' rights, so the preamble, encompassed the "expectation that persons who commit felonious acts causing injury to innocent victims will be appropriately detained in custody, tried by the courts, and sufficiently punished so that the public safety is protected and encouraged as a goal of highest importance."[1]

The California victims' bill of rights then went on to list three rights: a "right to restitution," a "right to safe schools," and a "right to truth-in-evidence." It also announced that "[p]ublic safety shall be the primary consideration" in bail hearings. Finally, it declared that prior felony convictions "shall subsequently be used without limitation for purposes of impeachment or enhancement of sentence in any criminal proceeding." The right to restitution is self-explanatory, and the right to safe schools purely declamatory ("All students and staff of public primary, elementary, junior high and senior high schools have the inalienable right to attend campuses which are safe, secure and peaceful."). The right to truth in evidence was meant to force the introduction of relevant but otherwise inadmissible incriminating evidence and thereby to close a legal loophole through which too many guilty offenders had escaped their just punishment. Other parts of the referendum included a then-draconian mandatory habitual criminal statute intended to maximally incapacitate repeat offenders and a prohibition against plea bargaining intended to prevent prosecutors from giving felons a break in punishment in exchange for saving them the trouble of having to prove guilt at trial.[2]

The first victims' right, in other words, was the right not to be a victim in the first place. The second was the right to see the state bring the wrath of the criminal law down upon whoever violated the first. The war on crime systematically and successfully vindicated these rights through a prolonged campaign of mass incapacitation, which after three decades left more than two million Americans in prison or jail and another four million under noncarceral penal control.

This association with the war on crime has given victims' rights a bad name in some circles, and an excellent one in others. The condemnation of the victims' rights movement among academic commentators is almost universal.[3] At the same time, its anticrime connection has gained the victims' rights movement almost universal approval among American politicians. These two diametrically opposed camps agree on one point, and one point only: that anticrime and pro-victim stands are two sides of the same coin.

And they are both right, of course. As a matter of political reality, the victims' rights movement is but one plank, though surely an important one, in the platform of the war on crime. So closely linked are the war on crime and victims' rights in fact that any effort to disentangle the two may appear hopeless. After the recent history of American criminal law, what could be more pointless than trying to find a notion of victims' rights apart from a war on offenders' rights?

Yet that's precisely what this book sets out to do: to salvage the project of vindicating victims' rights for its own sake, rather than as a weapon in the war against criminals. What's more, I believe that it's not only *possible* to excavate a legitimate core of the victims' rights movement from underneath the layers of bellicose rhetoric. It's also *necessary* if we want to build a system of American criminal law for the time after the hateful frenzy of the war on crime has died down, and die down it will.

The victims' rights movement has a legitimate core that, once properly excavated, can point the way to the much needed revision of the fundamental principles of American criminal law. Placed in a broader historical context, the war on crime is but the latest and the most systematic manifestation of a mode of governance that views criminal law as the protection of the state by the state. In this type of criminal law as criminal administration, the individual person has no room, except as the facilitator of state control (the "victim") or its object (the "offender").

American lawmakers and commentators took this statist, apersonal model from England, where the sovereign had long been recognized as the ultimate victim of any criminal act, which was cast as a direct personal affront on the dignity of the king. After bumbling beginnings, American criminal law was transformed into an ever more sophisticated system for the control of antisocial activity, or, in the words of California's victims' bill of rights, of anyone or anything that threatened a "serious disruption of people's lives." By the early decades of the twentieth century, punishment became rehabilitative or incapacitative treatment and criminal law a branch of public health policy. Eventually, rehabilitative treatment gave way to incapacitative treatment. This was the time of the war on crime.

The war on crime has sought the extermination of criminal deviance in all its myriad forms and manifestations. In pursuit of its ambitious incapacitative mission, the crime war dramatically expanded and refined the state's web of criminal norms and, at the same time, made the consequences of their violation more severe. That way, more potential sources of "serious disruption" could be extinguished more completely.

The victims' rights movement provided a convenient cover for this mass incapacitation campaign. The state transformed its constituents into a community of potential victims who identified with the sympathetic sufferers of criminal violence. That community of potential and actual victims, "us," was pitted against the lot of potential and actual offenders, "them." This struggle between victims and offenders, between good and evil, had a familiar ring to it: it reflected and barely concealed long-standing socioeconomic divisions within American society. Minorities, once again, found themselves on the outside looking in, corralled behind the ever more impenetrable walls of warehouse prisons that sprang up all over the country.

But, to be politically effective, the victims' rights movement had to hold up an image of the victim with which people could identify. The victims of the victims' rights movement had to matter, and they had to be victims of crimes that mattered. They could not be apersonal institutions or "social interests" or "the state," they could not be victims of trivial crimes, and they most certainly could not be victims of victimless crimes.

In other words, in order to cover the state's expansion of its system of criminal administration, the victims' rights movement had to operate with a very narrow concept of criminal law. In order to shield the state's apersonal system of hazard management through ever vaguer, wider, and harsher incapacitative directives from public scrutiny, the victims' rights movement had to portray the criminal law as the state's response to serious interpersonal crime.

And this is the legitimate core of the victims' rights movement: its implicit understanding of criminal law as limited to the most egregious forms of violence that one person can inflict on another. The second part of this book is an extended attempt, first, to make this conception of criminal law explicit and, second, to expand it into a broader account of what crime is and how the state is to employ law, including criminal law, to deal with it.

By defining crime as interpersonal violence, the victims' rights movement has hit upon a view of criminal law that is far more consistent with the American commitment to the protection of the rights of persons than is the state-centered, preconstitutional approach to criminal law imported from England. More specifically, it has put the person back where it belongs in the criminal law of a democratic republic dedicated to the equal worth of persons, rather than the protection of superior sovereign power: at the center.

For too long, American criminal law has been run by the state in the name of ill-defined "public interests" or even "public safety." For too long, American criminal law has been regarded as a matter of administration, rather than law, of regulation, rather than right. Crime is not a public health issue but a traumatic experience shared by two persons, the offender and the victim. The state has an important role to play in responding to this often catastrophic event, but it has no role in the event itself. The state is not the victim in criminal law; the person is. By transferring her right of punishment to the state, the victim does not transfer her victimhood.

In addition to reminding us of the personal foundation of criminal law, the victims' rights movement also highlighted two central, and related, features of the phenomenology of crime that any system of criminal law ignores at its peril. First, the victims' rights movement demonstrated the crucial role of *identification* in criminal law. The political power of the victims' rights movement stemmed from the public's identification with the victims of violent crime as new cultural icons. Narratives of the suffering of actual victims allowed the mass of potential victims to experience that suffering as their own, through identification. Having vicariously experienced the pain of crime, the public then could vicariously experience the victim's cry for revenge. Thus consolidated into a community of vengeful victims, the public turned to the state for the manifestation of its communal hatred.

No legitimate system of law can be built on this communal reflex triggered by identification. Yet identification as a process of judgment does have an important role to play in a new law of crime that gives persons their due. The victims' rights movement was right to insist that we identify with victims of crime. Without that identification, the state loses its connection to the suffering of persons and criminal law becomes a means of state self-protection. But that insight must be expanded to encompass not only victims but other persons, as well, including offenders. Rather than substitute identification with victims for identification with offenders, as the victims' rights movement urged, we must recognize that the only legitimate point of identification *in a system of law* is not the victim, or the offender, or the fellow New Yorker, or the fellow Caucasian, or the fellow male, or the fellow thirty-something, but the person. And that's what all the participants in the criminal process are, be they victims, judges, jurors, or even offenders.

So identification is crucial, but only if it's *interpersonal* identification. As crime, so its judgment in the eyes of the law is a matter between persons.

Second, the victims' rights movement illustrated the enormous power of emotional responses to victimization. The identification with victims of serious interpersonal crime induces a profound feeling of empathy for the victim, as well as, and this is the difference between flood victims and murder victims, a strong desire to lash out against the person responsible for the victim's suffering, the offender. Through identification with the victim, the offender's attack on the victim is experienced as an attack on oneself and triggers a communal reflex of self-defense.

A stable system of criminal law must acknowledge and address these punitive emotions. Rather than exploit them for political gain—where political is understood in the sense of a struggle between friend and foe[4]—they must be integrated into a rational legal response to the catastrophe of crime. Empathy for crime victims is crucial if the transfer of the right to punishment from victim to state is not to result in communal apathy and the immunization of criminal behavior. Yet the desire to punish the offender may easily develop into a desire to eliminate him, to treat him as an alien threat, rather than to punish him as a person. Without that respect for his person, however, whatever action the state might take against the offender will be illegitimate, no matter how gratifying that action might be to the community of victims, potential and actual, or even to the state whose dignity the offender has dared to challenge by violating its criminal norms. This is the fundamental, and revolutionary, insight that separates American law from its English origins. It may limit the power to punish, but it also provides it with a legitimacy that it never had before.

But to reveal these important contributions that the victims' rights movement can make to a new law of crime, we first must extricate victims' rights from their political context, the war on crime. This, in turn, requires a better understanding of the inner workings of the war on crime than we have at this point. A close analysis of the war on crime in action reveals that, all victims rhetoric aside, the war on crime is fought primarily with victimless crimes.

As we see in the first part of this book, the war on crime employs a panoply of possession offenses to do much of its incapacitative dirty work. Possession offenses are ideal tools of mass incapacitation because they are easy to detect and easy to prove and have tremendous incapacitative potential, either in conjunction with other offenses or standing alone, all the way up to life imprisonment without the possibility of parole.

In the smooth day-to-day operation of the crime war, victims are simply a hindrance. The efficient identification and disposal of dangerous elements has no room for victims' rights. Possession offenses are detected by state officials (police), proved and adjudicated by state officials (prosecutors and judges), and punished by state officials (wardens), without any involvement of "lay" persons, be it as victim, witness, or juror.

This hazard control system involves no persons of any kind, not as offenders, not as victims. It's a matter of the state identifying and eliminating, or at least containing, hazards that happen to be human beings. In principle, there's no distinction between a criminal and a piece of hazardous waste, a vicious dog, or even an oncoming hurricane. In the face of these ever present dangers, the state must act quickly and decisively. Individual victims are only in the way.

Still, the state's war on crime needs victims. It's the very real suffering of personal victims of violent crime that justifies the state's usurpation of ever greater powers of investigation and control. The detection and proof of possession must be simplified because the state can't afford to leave dangerous people who possess dangerous objects—such as drugs or guns—on the street, since they are bound to use these objects to murder, maim, and rape innocent victims. For the same reason, once these dangerous possessors have been found, through a collaborative policing effort by officers from local, state, and national police agencies using undercover agents, informers, wiretaps, video cameras, trackers, and various and sundry detection devices (to measure heat, radiation, and even "fluctuations in the earth's magnetic field")[5], they must be neutralized for as long as possible, preferably permanently. Hence the urgent need for increased punishment.

And it's the drama of violent interpersonal crime that attracts the attention of the public, played out in elaborate trials complete with witnesses and jurors. Under the cover of this process, as grandiose as it is atypical, the war on crime goes about its incapacitative business with the help of an expedited disposal mechanism, plea bargaining, that involves neither trial nor murder nor any victim other than the state itself.

But not only the *image* of real-life victims seeking justice in our country's courtrooms plays an important role in the war on crime. So do the victims themselves. Understanding the power of interpersonal identification, politicians surround themselves with victims of violent crime, or their surviving relatives, when the time has come to re-pledge their commitment to the war on crime.

The instrumental political significance of victims in the dogged pursuit of their rights becomes clear when one searches for the voices of victims who hesitate to join the communal anticrime chorus. An anticrime politician (and who isn't nowadays?) has no more use for a victim who doesn't call for more draconian punishments of offenders generally speaking than a death penalty prosecutor has for the mother of a murder victim uninterested in venting her hatred for a specific offender in a capital sentencing hearing.[6]

The time has come to free victims' rights from their use as a tool for the achievement, maintenance, and expansion of state power. The time has come to turn the pursuit of victims' rights from a weapon in the war on crime into a cause worth pursuing for its own sake.

To imagine a notion of victims' rights without a war on crime, a pro-victim agenda disconnected from an anticrime crusade, it's helpful to go back to the days before the crime war. Victims of crime first received serious attention in the mid-1960s, with the establishment of victim compensation programs, beginning in California in 1965. By 1970, when the war on crime was still very much in its infancy, New York, Hawaii, Massachusetts, Maryland, and the Virgin Islands had followed suit. Today, compensation programs can be found in every state of the Union.[7]

The idea, and the practice, of victim compensation is an idea of the American welfare state. It has nothing to do with the suppression of crime or the incapacitation of criminals. Crime victims deserved compensation for their own sake. State intervention on behalf of crime victims took the form of distributing palpable and direct financial benefits to crime victims, rather than of symbolic pronouncements of victims' rights or the infliction of palpable and direct punitive pain on offenders. Victim compensation addressed victims first, and offenders not at all.

Victim compensation provides a fresh perspective on the question of crime victims' rights not only because it takes us back to a time when vindicating victims' rights didn't mean waging war on crime. It also places U.S. law into a larger international context and thereby may help stem the recent trend toward an American punitive exceptionalism. New Zealand set up the first compensation fund in 1963, followed by Britain a year later, and then by several Australian states and Canadian provinces. Civil law countries, like Germany, began compensating victims of crime at around the same time.[8]

The close nexus between the fight for victims and the fight against criminals exists in none of these countries. Except in the United States, the call for greater recognition of victims' interests instead has been associated with *constraints* on the state's power to punish, rather than with an all-out war on crime by any means necessary. For instance, one of the central demands of victims' rights advocates in other countries is that victims should have the option of receiving restitution from the offender on the basis of victim-offender meetings, *in lieu of* state-imposed and -inflicted punishment.[9]

Despite the existence of victim compensation programs throughout the United States, victim compensation has played no role in what has come to be known as the victims' rights movement. That movement instead has fought for victims' rights indirectly by assisting the crime war effort. By the time of California's victims' bill of rights, California crime victims had been receiving compensation from the state for more than fifteen years. The victims' rights movement wanted more than compensation. It wanted to express the victims' hatred for the offender in anticrime measures and thereby to use the state's power to punish the offender, rather than to assist the victim. The indirect benefit to the victim came in the form of an emotional release with questionable therapeutic effects, rather than as financial support. Direct victim support smacked of the welfare state and was therefore incompatible with the conservative tenets held by crime warriors, who nonetheless wholeheartedly supported the dramatic expansion of the state's *punitive* power during the war on crime.

Victim compensation law deserves more attention than it has gotten during the victims' rights era. Using the victims' rights movement's notion of crime as one person's violent assault upon another as our point of departure, we find in the law of compensation a rich analysis of the legal significance of crime for the victim. The tools for this analysis have been developed over thirty years of legislative activity and judicial interpretation, which add up to a complex body of victim jurisprudence, a veritable law of victimhood.

Our tour of the law of victimhood reveals it as the mirror image of the law of offenderhood, better known as substantive criminal law. Compensation law and punishment law provide a legal analysis of crime from the perspectives of the two persons who constitute it: the victim and the offender. One seeks to determine the compensability of a "claimant," the other the punishability of a "defendant." Along the way, they struggle with identical issues from diametrically opposed, yet complementary, viewpoints, beginning with the question of jurisdiction and ending with that of responsibility, that is, of (victim) innocence or (offender) guilt.

It turns out that the notion of victimhood that underlies the victims' rights movement also animates the law of victim compensation. A crime victim for purposes of crime victim compensation is not the state but a person, and more particularly a person who has suffered violence at the hands of another. Other victims may deserve to be made whole in other ways, but they are not entitled to state compensation as victims of crime.

Reflecting this narrow vision of crime from the victim's standpoint back onto the law of offenderhood allows us to peel off the superfluous layers of doctrine that have obscured the core of criminal law: violent interpersonal crime as the ultimate violation of one person's autonomy by another. By focusing on the experience of victimization captured in the rhetoric of the victims' rights movement and in the law of victim compensation, we are led to reassess much of the law of punishment, including the imposition of *criminal* liability for victimless crimes, nonintentional offenses, and attempts and upon nonpersonal entities (e.g., corporations).

Taking victims seriously, as persons and on their own account, thus may result in less, rather than more, punishment for the offender.[10] That victims may *mitigate* the offender's criminal liability is nothing new but is easily forgotten at a time when the victims cause is enlisted in the war on crime. Victims who attack or provoke the offender, give their consent to the offender's conduct, negligently or intentionally aggravate the harm inflicted by the offender, or assume the risk of suffering criminal harm have long prevented, or at least lessened, the offender's criminal liability.

In the end, compensation and punishment, the law of victimhood and the law of offenderhood, emerge as complementary responses by the state through law to the fact of crime. In any given case of crime, the crucial question is which, if any, of these responses is appropriate. Sometimes compensation may be sufficient; other times, punishment may be necessary, as well. And, often, no state response of any kind is called for, because the persons who constitute the crime are perfectly capable of dealing with its effects on their own, as persons possessed with the power of self-determination who require the state's assistance only in extraordinary cases where that very power has been compromised or destroyed altogether.

PART I

The War on Victimless Crime

1

Waging the War on Crime

The essential paradox of the war on crime is that it has everything and nothing to do with victims and their rights. On its face, the war on crime has been fought on behalf of victims' rights, including their most important right, the right not to become crime victims in the first place. Under the surface, however, the war on crime has been a war on *victimless* crime, fought by the state for the state, rather than for personal victims. The first part of this book is devoted to exposing the inner workings of the war on victimless crime, which reduces its professed beneficiaries, victims, to instrumental significance at best and transforms them into enemies at worst.

The second part of this book is about the other, more visible, prong of the paradox, the war on crime as the protector of victims' rights. Part II takes the war on crime, and its victims' rights movement, at face value, amplifying its legitimate core of crime as a traumatic interpersonal event into a law of victimhood.

Part I, by contrast, has little occasion to mention victims or their rights. And that's exactly the point: victims have no part to play in the actual operation of the crime war, other than as cover or as nuisance. That's why the nexus between victims' rights and the war on crime is so perverse, and why the vindication of victims' rights will remain an illusion as long as it persists.

For some thirty years, American criminal law has waged a war on crime. From Robert Kennedy's war on organized crime[1] and Lyndon Johnson's war on poverty, crime, and disorder[2] to Richard Nixon's war of "the peace forces" against "the criminal forces," "the enemy within,"[3] the war on crime evolved into an extended comprehensive police action to exterminate crime by incapacitating criminals.[4] As wars go, the crime war has been unusual, and unusually successful, in that its casualties have also been its success stories; it has managed to incapacitate millions, most through imprisonment, some through death, most temporarily, some permanently. In 1970, the American prison and jail population stood at around three hundred thousand. Today, it tops two million, with another four million or so under various forms of noncarceral control, including parole and probation, for a total of more than six million people, or 3 percent of American adults, under state penal control.[5]

The war on crime has been fought on many fronts, and with many weapons. Most dramatically, it has brought us the resurgence of capital punishment as a measure for the permanent incapacitation of violent predators. Less dramatically, but more pervasively, ever harsher laws combating the plague of violent recidivism have pursued a similar incapacitative strategy.[6]

As a war on violent criminals, the crime war has attracted a great deal of attention. Over decades, the media have eagerly recorded its campaigns and initiatives, kicked off with great fanfare by generations of state officials (and would-be state officials) eager to incorporate the tough-on-crime plank into their political platforms. The crime war's failures have made for particularly and persistently good news, as criminal violence has continued even in the face of an all-out campaign to eradicate it. These failures have led to calls not for the abandonment of the campaign but for its expansion and more rigorous prosecution.

To understand the war on crime, however, one must go beneath the sensational and well-covered surface of crimes of violence suffered by innocent victims at the hands of murderers, rapists, robbers, kidnappers, and other assorted miscreants. There, in the murky depths of criminal law in action, one finds the everyday business of the war on crime: the quiet and efficient disposal of millions of dangerous undesirables for offenses with no human victim whatsoever. To analyze this disposal regime is the main goal of this part.

The war on crime, though ostensibly waged on behalf of crime victims, has been first and foremost a war on *victimless* crime. The paradigmatic crime of the war on crime is not murder but possession; its sanction not punishment but forfeiture; its process not the jury trial but plea bargaining; its mode of disposition not conviction but commitment; and its typical sentencing factor not victim impact, but offender dangerousness as "evinced" by a criminal record. Our prisons and jails (which we persist in calling "correctional" institutions) are filled not with two million murderers, nor are the additional four million probationers and parolees superpredators. No, our comprehensive effort to control the dangerous by any means necessary reaches "possessors" along with "distributors," "manufacturers," "importers," and other transgressors caught in an ever wider and ever finer web of state norms designed for one purpose: to police human threats.

Policing human threats is different from punishing persons. A police regime doesn't punish.[7] It seeks to eliminate threats if possible and to minimize them if necessary. Instead of punishing, a police regime disposes. It resembles environmental regulations of hazardous waste more than it does the criminal law of punishment.

In a sense, the current regime of penal police marks the end of criminal law as we know it. It's no more about *crimes* than it is about *law*, as these concepts have come to be understood. Crimes, as serious violations of another's rights, are of incidental significance to a system of threat control. By the time a crime has been committed, the system of threat identification and elimination has failed. Law, as a state-run system of interpersonal conflict resolution, is likewise irrelevant. Persons matter neither as the source nor as the target of threats. Penal police is a matter between the state and threats.[8]

A penal police regime may *look* like traditional criminal law. But this appearance is deceiving. A crime consists no longer in the infliction of harm but in the threat of harm. Harm itself turns out to be the threat of harm. So to punish crime means to eliminate—or at least to minimize—the threat of the threat of harm.

The effort to disguise itself as bread-and-butter criminal law is an important component of a modern police regime.[9] The camouflage is crucial to its success because nonnegligible public resistance would interfere with the state's effort to eliminate as many threats as efficiently and as permanently as possible. It's therefore in the interest of a police regime both to retain traces of traditional criminal law and to infiltrate traditional criminal law by manipulating its established doctrines, rather than to do away with it altogether.

To illustrate the inner workings of the war on crime, I carefully analyze the theory and practice of possession offenses, the new paradigm of criminal law as threat police. Possession offenses have not attracted much attention.[10] Yet they are everywhere in modern American criminal law, on the books and in action. They fill our statute books, our arrest statistics, and, eventually, our prisons. By last count, New York law recognized no fewer than 153 possession offenses; one in every five prison or jail sentences handed out by New York courts in 1998 was imposed for a possession offense.[11] That same year, possession offenses accounted for more than one hundred thousand arrests in New York State, while *drug* possession offenses alone resulted in over 1.2 million arrests nationwide.[12]

The dominant role of possession offenses in the war on crime is also reflected in the criminal jurisprudence of the U.S. Supreme Court. They are the common thread that connects the Court's sprawling and discombobulated criminal procedure jurisprudence of the past thirty years. As we will see, virtually every major search and seizure case before the Court, from 1968's *Terry v. Ohio*[13] (which relaxed Fourth Amendment requirements for so-called *Terry* stops and frisks) to *Illinois v. Wardlow*[14] (which further relaxed *Terry*'s already relaxed requirements in "high crime areas").

Possession offenses also figure prominently in scores of Supreme Court opinions on *substantive* criminal law. What do the defendants in the following Supreme Court cases have in common: *Pinkerton v. United States* (which gave the infamous *Pinkerton* conspiracy rule its name),[15] *United States v. Bass* (the Court's leading lenity case),[16] *Stone v. Powell* (one of the Court's key habeas corpus cases),[17] *McMillan v. Pennsylvania* (the case that laid the foundation for one of the key doctrinal strategies of the war on crime, the shifting of proof elements from the guilt phase to the sentencing hearing and therefore from the jury to the judge),[18] *Harmelin v. Michigan* (one of the Court's leading cases on the principle of proportionate punishment),[19] and *Lopez v. United States* (the Court's unanticipated 1995 attack on federal commerce clause jurisdiction)?[20] They were all convicted of possession offenses. And, last but not least, there's *Apprendi v. New Jersey*, 2000's big hate-crimes case. Charles Apprendi had fired several rifle shots into the home of a black family that lived in his otherwise all-white neighborhood. What was Apprendi sentenced for, after a guilty plea? Three counts of possession.[21]

So broad is the reach of possession offenses, and so easy are they to detect and then to prove, that possession has replaced vagrancy as the sweep offense of choice. Unlike vagrancy, however, possession offenses promise more than a slap on the wrist.[22] Backed by a wide range of penalties, they can remove undesirables for extended periods of time, even for life. Also unlike vagrancy, possession offenses so far have been insulated against constitutional attack, even though they too break virtually every law in the book of cherished criminal law principles.

To better understand the workings of policing through possession and of the crime war in general, part I of this book develops a kind of phenomenology of possession. We come to appreciate the many and complex uses of possession as a policing tool, some direct, others indirect, some foundational, others supplemental. And we see how possession has managed to escape the serious scrutiny of courts and commentators.

Like its prototypical policing tool, the war on crime hasn't attracted much scholarly attention, at least as the comprehensive penal regime that it is.[23] Much has been written about the war on drugs. The drug war certainly has been an important part of the war on crime, but it's a mistake to conflate the two. The war on crime is a general strategy of state governance that uses various tools to achieve its goal of eliminating threats, above all threats to the state itself. The war on drugs is but one prong in the war on crime's widespread assault on anyone and anything the state perceives as a threat. To treat the war on crime as synonymous with the war on drugs is to underestimate the significance of the war on crime as a phenomenon of governance.

Only by widening one's focus of inquiry from the war on drugs to the war on crime can one appreciate the comprehensive strategy of governance by possession. While drug possession is a popular and extremely powerful policing tool, other possession offenses also make significant contributions to the crime war effort. *Terry* and *Wardlow*, for example, were gun possession cases; so was *Apprendi*. The most recent national effort to incapacitate human hazards, Project Exile, likewise employs tough federal statutes that criminalize the possession of guns by felons and during violent or drug-related crimes.[24] And as we will see, other possession offenses often come in handy, as well.

We desperately need a detailed account of the war on crime. Without understanding how it came about, how it works, and what it has accomplished, we cannot hope to move beyond it. But move beyond it we must, as the crisis of crime that triggered the war on crime already has begun to subside.[25] The crime war will go the way of crime hysteria.

Rebuilding American criminal law, however, isn't simply a matter of undoing the damage caused by the war on crime. The war on crime could not have succeeded as easily as it did if it hadn't found fertile soil in the reigning orthodoxy of American criminal law: treatmentism. All the war on crime had to do was flip over the treatmentist coin from its benign rehabilitative to its unsavory incapacitative side.[26] It stands as a powerful reminder of the uncomfortable fact that treatmentism, once celebrated as the progressive reform of the atavistic practice of punishment, always allowed for incapacitative "treatment" for incorrigible criminal types.

The war on crime once and for all dashed the naïve hope that the incapacitative arm of treatmentism would simply whither away as criminal policy became increasingly enlightened. When push came to shove, it was the rehabilitative wing of treatmentism that buckled and eventually broke under the pressure of a crisis of crime, where it mattered not whether the crisis was real, imagined, or even artificially generated for political gain. For the victims of the war on crime, it was real enough.

The analysis of the war on crime in this, the first, part of the book proceeds as follows. Chapter 1 lays out three of the basic characteristics of the war on crime as a system of controlling threats, rather than of punishing persons. The war on crime is *preventive* in that it focuses on the threat, rather than on the occurrence, of harm. It's *communitarian* in that it seeks to eliminate threats not to persons but to communities of one sort or another. And it's *authoritarian* insofar as the community it protects against outside threats ultimately turns out to be the state.

Chapter 2 then presents the phenomenology of possession as the crime war's penal policing tool of choice. Through the analysis of statutes, doctrine, Supreme Court jurisprudence, and statistics, we see just how and why possession has proved uniquely useful in the identification and incapacitation of criminal threats and has emerged as the new and improved vagrancy.

Finally, in chapter 3 this in-depth analysis of possession is placed within the broader context of the war on crime as state nuisance control. Here we see how the state depersonalizes criminal law by turning to crimes both victim- and offenderless to maintain its authority in the name of conveniently vague concepts like "public welfare" and "social interests." The war on crime, in the end, reveals itself not as an aberration from the principled path of Anglo-American criminal law but as the culmination of the progressive project to reform the barbaric practice of punishment in light of ill-considered social science. This project can be traced back to the early decades of this century and found its most influential manifestation in the Model Penal Code.

Penal police is about the elimination, or at least the minimization, of threats. But threats to what, or whom? This question is rarely posed, not to mention answered. In an important sense, posing it already is to misunderstand the point of penal police. If you need to ask, you don't need to know; if you don't feel threatened by something or someone, you may well be a threat yourself. The need to police threats requires no justification. And threats are, by their very nature, vague. A threat is the unfulfilled risk that something bad may happen. What that something might be, or how likely it is that it will come about or that you may suffer from it, remains unclear. And that's a good thing, for the vagueness of threats equips their eliminators and minimizers—the state, through its representatives in the field—with the necessary flexibility to make those split-second decisions about what or who is or isn't a threat, that executive *discretion* so crucial to effective law enforcement, or, rather, threat police.

Still, to get at the structure of this deliberately unstructured phenomenon of penal police, we need to ask this question, however inappropriate it might seem: what or who is being threatened, exactly, by the threats that penal police seeks to eliminate? If nothing else, pondering this question is convenient for our expository purposes. For it turns out that the police regime established during the war on crime has three general functions, which roughly correspond to three objects of the threat it seeks to eliminate—or, in other words, to three possible answers to our question.

On the political surface, the war on crime aims to prevent violent interpersonal crime. The relevant threat here is to potential victims of interpersonal crime, that is, every person. This is the *preventive* function.

If we dig a little deeper—and turn to sociology for help—we find another function, related to prevention but distinct from it. This one might call the *communitarian* function.[27] What's threatened here is not injury to particular victims. Instead, the victim is the community itself. The identification and incapacitation of dangerous deviants thus serves to maintain the community's existence, not by preventing future offenses but by redefining the community in stark contradistinction to the deviant.

At the very bottom, however, we find not the community but the state as the ultimate object of the criminal threat. The *authoritarian* function of the police regime is the enforcement of obedience to state commands and the assertion of the state's authority as the sole and proper guardian of the common good. Unlike the previous two functions, authoritarianism has no interest in interpersonal crime, at least not for its own sake. Authoritarian policing pursues violations of state-issued commands as such. It prosecutes victimless crimes not for any indirect effect on the suppression of the crimes that matter, that is, victim*ful* crimes, and crimes of interpersonal violence in particular. In fact, under authoritarian policing, what was victimful is now victimless and what was victimless now victimful. Authoritarian policing takes so-called victimless crimes personally, very personally.

Prevention

The crime war wears crime prevention on its sleeve.[28] By "subject[ing] to public control persons whose conduct indicates that they are disposed to commit crimes,"[29] we also incapacitate those predisposed to commit *violent* crimes. Here the war on crime is fueled by images of the relatives of horrific crimes calling for swift and harsh punishment of "their" offender. Apart from allowing the victim in all of us to live out vengeance fantasies born of the powerlessness inherent in victimhood, these measures are said to prevent future violent crime by taking criminal predators off the street.[30]

The preventive aspect of the war on crime is the one most closely related to the rights of personal victims. In this preventive light, the war on crime subjects the dangerous classes to police supervision in order to prevent murders. Gun possession is criminalized to avoid "their potential harmful use" in crimes of interpersonal violence.[31] Similarly, gun possession is declared an inherently violent felony because of the "use or risk of violence" resulting from its "categorical nature."[32] And mandatory life imprisonment for simple drug possession is upheld because "(1) [a] drug user *may* commit crime because of drug-induced changes in physiological functions, cognitive ability, and mood; (2) [a] drug user *may* commit crime in order to obtain money to buy drugs; and (3) [a] violent crime *may* occur as part of the drug business or culture."[33]

The success of an incapacitationist regime in the name of prevention depends on how quickly it can intervene once dangerous deviance is diagnosed. Eager to eradicate threats, this regime always feels the pressure to intervene at the earliest possible moment, without awaiting the manifestation of the threat in the form of a criminal act. And the pressure increases with every failure to incapacitate, with every "false negative," in the words of incapacitationist criminology, which came to prominence in the 1970s and 1980s.[34] The goal of nipping every potential threat in the bud, combined with the impossibility of its achievement, sets in motion a continuing expansion of preventive measures, an infinite regress along the causal chain toward the origin of threats, the heart of darkness.

This expansion of the preventive police net proceeds along two lines, one focused on the offense, the other on the offender. On the abstract level of offense definitions and theories of criminal liability, incapacitation in the name of prevention tends to expand the number and reach of offenses the commission of which triggers a diagnosis of dangerousness and, therefore, police control. To return to the example of possession offenses, such a regime finds it expedient to criminalize the mere possession of burglary tools or, more broadly, of "instruments of crime,"[35] absent any evidence of use that would amount to even a *preparation*, which traditionally has remained beyond the reach of criminal law, never mind the more extensive use, coupled with criminal purpose, ordinarily required for conviction of *attempt*.[36]

Alternatively, instead of criminalizing possession outright, such a regime might establish a host of presumptions emanating backward and forward in time from a finding of possession, including a presumption of illegal manufacture or importation on the retrospective end of the spectrum and of illegal use or distribution on the prospective end.[37] In either case, possessors would have displayed sufficient criminal deviance—that all-important *disposition* to commit crimes—to warrant a conviction (which remains the formal prerequisite for penal, if not civil, incapacitation), provided they prove unable to rebut the presumption of criminality by giving a "satisfactory account" of themselves.[38]

Similarly, in such a system of preventive incapacitation, explicit endangerment offenses of all shapes and sizes would soon proliferate. Here one may find specific and abstract endangerment offenses, criminalizing either threats to a particular person or persons (specific) or criminalizing something that generally poses such a threat, though it needn't have posed it in the particular case (abstract). Reckless endangerment is an example of the former, speeding of the latter. Once again, the point of these offenses is the identification and neutralization of sources of danger, that is, threats of threats.

The secret of preventive policing is not only the seamlessness but also the flexibility and interconnectedness of its web. So the definition of offenses is intimately related to the diagnosis and treatment of offenders. Offenses simply lay the foundation for an assessment of dangerousness. In their very malleability lies their value. It's this malleability that makes room for the discretionary dangerousness assessments at the heart of the system.

A "speeder" may be neutralized as a source of danger by a simple fine, or even by a stern warning. Then again, it might take a more intrusive incapacitative sanction, like confiscation of his driver's license, and in some cases even imprisonment.[39] A similar range of measures is available to treat an "assailant" (or, in New York, a "menacer"[40]) who threatens, as opposed to harms, his victim. In both cases, and this is crucial, the state official in question (the police officer, the prosecutor, the judge, the warden) also always has the option of radically revising his dangerousness diagnosis upward. Once a potential source of danger has been caught in the web of preventive police, for one reason or another, he has subjected himself to a dangerousness analysis whose scope and intensity depend entirely on the discretion of the state ("law enforcement") official he happens to run across. As hundreds of thousands, perhaps millions, of prisoners have learned over the past thirty years, a simple traffic stop can soon balloon into a full cavity search of person and car and a simple speeding ticket mushroom into a lengthy term of imprisonment.[41] The car is pulled over for a defective tail light and the passenger looks "suspicious" (not necessarily in that order), the driver has no driver's license, a consensual search of the car reveals drugs in the glove compartment, a search incident to arrest turns up an unregistered gun in the passenger's pants pocket, and within ten minutes another source of danger has been temporarily, or perhaps even permanently, extinguished.[42]

As we have seen, the definition of offenses under a preventive regime of incapacitation is simply a means of giving state officials the opportunity for a dangerousness assessment. At the level of offenders, rather than of offenses, a preventive police regime dedicated to the elimination of crime is forced to act on ever less concrete evidence of dangerousness, resulting in the control of ever more sources of threats and *potential* threats. As the pressure to identify human hazards mounts with every undiagnosed danger that slips through the police net, the system comes to rely increasingly on the discretionary diagnoses of ever more and ever less well trained state officials. Given the current mass of regulations that governs every aspect of modern life, only a minuscule portion of which can be enforced, the most important diagnostician of criminal predisposition is not the expert psychiatrist but the police officer on the beat, aided by a network of informers, anonymous or not, who supply him with indicia of dangerousness.[43]

With such a vast area of discretion enjoyed by such a vast number of often poorly trained state officials often working under conditions of extreme stress and fear, the factors that influence police discretion are as crucial as they are unknown and unreviewed. They lie even further beyond the reach of analysis and supervision than the notoriously unspecifiable "hunch" that leads a police officer to suspect that a given person has committed a specific offense. Consciously and unconsciously shaping a police officer's discretion, these factors never enter the record for one reason or another, though they occasionally emerge, like a sudden break in the clouds, from enforcement statistics or transcripts of intrapolice communications.[44]

These occasional insights into an otherwise hazy world, often intentionally obscured, suggest that police officers' discretion operates in much the same unreflected way as that of the public at large. Police officers' discretion simply brings into sharp relief the unreflected judgments all of us make. Police officers, after all, have the power—and the obligation—to act on their discretion, whereas the rest of us can sit idly by as we (pre)judge this person or that. And whatever conscious or unconscious communal identifications guide our judgment are magnified a thousandfold in the case of police officers who actually fight the war on crime we simply observe with varying degrees of attention. To a police officer, the "enemies of society"[45] that we, fully aware of our powerlessness, vilify in mind and word are not mere chimeras: they are his personal enemies in the war on crime.

Communitarianism

The communal aspect of the war on crime is undeniable.[46] A focus on the preventive aspect of the war on crime at the expense of its communal significance fails to capture its essence. In fact, as we shall see, these two components mutually reinforce each other. In the end, those who are incapacitated for the purpose of preventing violent interpersonal crime are often those who attract communal hatred as deviant outsiders, and vice versa.

There they stand, side by side, united in common hatred, the murder victim's father and the prosecutor. And their communal experience is replicated vicariously by many others, even millions, thanks to the miracle of modern media. In a society uncertain about its commonalities, divided on many constitutive issues, the common and deeply felt differentiation from sources of danger or evil is a welcome opportunity to feel as one, to be part of something bigger.[47] And, after the collapse of continuously publicized external threats, all of which were traceable to the ultimate source of danger and uncertainty, the Evil Empire itself, the criminal predator suggests itself as a convenient focus for the maintenance of an otherwise disparate community.

The fact of this prolonged episode of communal feeling is as troubling as it is plain. It is troubling because it subjugates the designated scapegoat to serve the "community's" need for self-preservation. To serve his proper community-enhancing function, the object of communal hatred must first be excluded from the community. In theory, this exclusion occurs at the moment of conviction. In fact, it happens much earlier. Already the "suspect" and certainly the "defendant" finds herself differentiated from the community and therefore the target of exclusionary, and consolidating, communal sentiment.

And the moment of exclusion can be moved back even further. The offender excludes himself from the community through his deviant act. That self-exclusion finds formal or informal recognition only later on, through suspicion, arrest, indictment, and conviction, or, in the more forthright days of Anglo-Saxon law, the act of outlawry.[48]

But that is not all. So far we have assumed that the exclusion from the political community occurs through an act of some kind. In fact, so far we have assumed that the offender's deviant status derives from an "exclusion," which presupposes that he has been a member of the community at some point in the past. Deviant status, however, need not result from a deviant act. Deviance, instead, may be just that, deviance.

In this case, the act that triggers exclusion is merely symptomatic of a preexisting condition of deviance. There's no need to exclude the offender, that is, the deviant, from the community because he didn't belong in the first place. Depending on the nature and origin of his deviance, the offender may never have belonged to the community at all; he may have been an outsider by birth. Then again, perhaps deviants acquire their condition only later on, perhaps as a result of losing or failing to develop their empathic capacity "through," in the words of John Rawls, "no fault of their own: through illness or accident, or from experiencing such a deprivation of affection in their childhood that their capacity for the natural attitudes has not developed properly."[49]

Most troubling, of course, is the case where a person is subjected to exclusionary sentiments merely on account of his status, especially if that criminogenic status is for one reason or another permanent. According to the essentialist tendencies that underlie the current incapacitative police regime, offenders must be incapacitated because they are presumptively incorrigible. They are presumptively incorrigible because they are essentially dangerous. They are essentially dangerous because they are genetically predisposed to commit crimes, because they are by nature evil, because they are black, because they are Hispanic, because they are poor, because they have a low IQ, or all of these at once. The particular nature of their essential dangerousness is of no interest. Unlike the rehabilitationist penologists before them, who prided themselves in their complex nosology of criminal pathology and insisted on careful and prolonged scientific study of the particular symptoms of a specific individual deviant, the modern incapacitationists have no patience for subtleties of this sort. What matters is that there is danger and evil out there that needs to be eliminated, or at least minimized.

In the communitarian approach to the question of police control, the battle lines are clearly drawn. On one side is the community of potential victims, the insiders. On the other side is the community of potential offenders, the outsiders. The boundaries of these communities are not fluid. One belongs either to one or to the other. And it is the duty of the community of potential victims to identify those aliens who have infiltrated its borders so that they may be expelled and controlled and their essential threat thereby neutralized.

This clear demarcation is very convenient. It eliminates the need to disassociate oneself from the object of hatred. Whatever inclination one might have had to identify oneself with the offender is overcome by the realization that, from the beginning, the offender had merely passed as "one of us." There is also no need to question oneself, in particular whether one might oneself be "disposed to commit crimes."[50] As a member of a community defined by its absence of criminal tendencies, one can be sure that doubts of this nature are entirely misplaced. There is no need to blame oneself, either. Shared responsibility for the offender's act is out of the question; as a deviant, the offender displayed criminal behavior that was rooted incorrigibly in his nature. And, finally, distancing oneself from the offender enormously simplifies the process of disposal. Since moral judgments are inappropriate in the case of a predatory animal, an efficiency analysis will do. There is no need to understand why and how this could have happened. The only question is why it didn't happen sooner.

The current police regime put in place during the war on crime combines preventive and communitarian elements. On the surface, it seeks to protect potential victims of violent crime by incapacitating dangerous criminals. A closer look, however, reveals that the potential victims who enjoy the protection are predominantly middle-class whites with political power and that the potential offenders who suffer the incapacitation are predominantly poor blacks with no political power whatever.[51] This is so despite the facts that most victims of violent crime are poor blacks and that middle-class whites face not crime but the threat of crime and that they, perhaps driven by a bourgeois obsession with the wondrous complexities of their inner lives, seek not freedom from crime but freedom from the fear of crime,[52] or, simply, "freedom from fear."[53]

And this last point is crucial: the war on crime, to the extent that it is fought on behalf of white middle-class victims of violent crime, is purely a symbolic matter, for two reasons. First, there are relatively few middle-class victims of violent crime, and, second, the *fear* of violent crime is best met with symbolic action: adopt a victims' rights amendment here, pass a law solemnly granting victims the right to make victim impact statements at sentencing there, and, most important, express great concern about the high levels of crime, while at the same time expressing satisfaction at the success of the war on crime in the face of steadily falling crime rates.[54]

Authoritarianism

The war on crime, though ostensibly fought on behalf of victims, has very little to do with victims, and everything to do with the state. What's more, it has very little to do with persons of any kind. It treats offenders as mere sources of danger, to be policed along with other threats, animate and inanimate alike, from rabid dogs to noxious fumes. And it treats victims as mere nuisances themselves, annoying sources of inefficiency in a system built to incapacitate the greatest number of source individuals for the longest possible time with the least effort. In the end, crime victims got their wish. All they wanted was "to be treated like criminals."[55] And that they were. In the war on crime, offenders and victims alike are irrelevant nuisances, grains of sand in the great machine of state risk management.

The true victim in the war on crime is not a person, not even "the community," but simply the state itself. Surrounded by pesky nuisances in the form of hordes of persons, be they offenders or victims, it maintains its authority and enforces that obedience which is due its commands. From the state's perspective, victimless crimes thus are not victimless after all. They're victimless only in the sense that they're missing a *personal* victim. Any violation of the state's missives, any disruption of its administrative scheme, perhaps even of its very foundation—unquestioning obedience to its carefully calibrated rules and regulations formulated by expert bureaucrats guided exclusively by the concern for the common good—victimizes the state. Contumacious conduct of this sort not only challenges the state's authority but also inflicts palpable emotional harm on its officials, who feel unappreciated and inconvenienced by the persistent and perplexing unwillingness of the commoners to comply with the very rules promulgated for their common well-being, their commonwealth.

The war on crime as a police action by the state against its objects easily makes room for the preventive and the communitarian police regimes just described. As the preventive model turned out to be driven by the same differentiating impulse that motivates the communitarian model, so the authoritarian, state-based model in turn accommodates the goals of prevention and of communitarianism. On the connection between preventive incapacitation and the enforcement of obedience to state commands, Roscoe Pound remarked as early as 1927 that modern "penal treatment" is best understood as "interference to prevent disobedience," rather than as punishment.[56] Other than to prevent disobedience against the state, criminal law had for its province not the protection of individual right against interference but, on the contrary, "the securing of social interests regarded directly as such, that is, disassociated from any immediate individual interests with which they may be identified."[57] And the objects of this preventive interference in the form of penal treatment were "well recognized types of anti-social individuals and of anti-social conduct."[58]

In one sense, the preventive-communitarian-authoritarian police regime of the war on crime is simply the full-scale adoption of Pound's approach, an approach that removes the person from the criminal law in every respect, as offender and as victim. The offender becomes the manifestation of a "type" of "antisocial individual." This disappearance of the person from punishment in the name of scientific penology has often been remarked upon, so often, in fact, that it contributed significantly to the demise of rehabilitation as a purpose of punishment.[59]

What does need emphasis, however, is that the person of the victim, and not merely that of the offender, disappears entirely and emphatically. It is replaced with a new, amorphous, victim, "society," whose "social interests" are protected against that "antisocial conduct" one expects from "antisocial individuals." The victim's "individual interests" are of no interest to the criminal law. In fact, the criminal law is defined in terms of its exclusive focus not on individual but on social interests.

A few years later, in an article that continues to be cited as the authoritative study of the rise and scope of so-called public welfare offenses, Francis Sayre followed and developed Pound's lead when he commented on "the trend . . . away from nineteenth century individualism toward a new sense of the importance of collective interests" and again on "the shift of emphasis from the protection of individual interests which marked nineteenth century criminal administration to the protection of public and social interests. . . ."[60]

The victim as a person is so irrelevant to this new system of "criminal administration" designed to protect social interests "from those with dangerous and peculiar idiosyncracies"[61] that the "individual interests" said to have found such extensive protection in nineteenth-century criminal law are the interests of the *offender* (or rather the defendant), not those of the *victim*. The following passage is worth quoting at length for its remarkable, even astonishing, clarity and foresight:

> During the nineteenth century it was the individual interest which held the stage; *the criminal law machinery was overburdened with innumerable checks to prevent possible injustice to individual defendants.* The scales were weighted heavily in his favor, and, as we have found to our sorrow, the public welfare often suffered. In the twentieth century came reaction. We are thinking today more of the protection of social and public interest; and coincident with the swinging of the pendulum in the field of legal administration in this direction modern criminologists are teaching the objective underlying correctional treatment should *change from the barren aim of punishing human beings to the fruitful one of protecting social interests.*[62]

In other words, criminal law does not concern itself with interpersonal crimes and so neither punishes nor protects human beings but instead protects social interests against whatever threat they may face. The paradigmatic offense of this modern criminal law is Sayre's "public welfare offense." In this regulatory scheme of danger police, the offender is stripped of his personhood and reduced to a threat, a source of danger. As an apersonal threat whose personhood is immaterial, his "guilt" is immaterial as well: "the modern conception of criminality . . . seems to be shifting from a basis of individual guilt to one of social danger."[63] How can a threat be guilty, and even if it could, what difference would that make? The distinguishing feature of Sayre's public welfare offenses is, after all, that they do away with the requirement of mens rea of any kind. All that matters is that, one way or another, through an act or a failure to act, intentionally or not, some social interest or other (the "public welfare") has been threatened. So important are social interests that they required the utmost protection, against whomever or whatever. Under these circumstances, the police regime, of course, cannot await the actual interference with these paramount interests. No, early interference is called for; the mere risk of interference, the mere threat, is more than enough. Naturally, the efficient policing of dangers of this sort requires the abandonment of all "defenses based upon lack of a blameworthy mind, such as insanity, infancy, compulsion and the like."[64] Since guilt is irrelevant, guiltlessness is irrelevant as well.

At the same time, the *victim* as a person also has no place in this regulatory scheme. It's the *public* welfare that needs protection against all threats, not the individual's. And it's the vague concept of public *welfare*, or rather the social *interests* that the state in its wisdom might fit into that concept, that must be safeguarded at all costs, not the person's concrete rights to life, liberty, and property.

Sayre's article, in the end, is a veritable blueprint for the twentieth-century depersonalization of American criminal law and its transformation into a state regulatory scheme, which culminated and found its most perverse manifestation in the war on crime of the last quarter of that century. Here we find all the ingredients for a streamlined "criminal administration" in substance and procedure. The central concept is flexibility. It is this flexibility that gives state officials—experts all—the discretion necessary to determine not only which social interests require protection but also how they are best protected, in general as well as in particular instances.

Once these interests are identified, the state determines the most efficient means of protecting them. Here convenience is key. Substance is driven by enforcement. So offenses are defined to minimize inconvenient proof requirements, most important mens rea, thus relieving prosecutors of the inconvenient burden of establishing each and every offender's mental state. Similarly, the requirement of blameworthiness, or guilt, is jettisoned, thus eliminating the time wasted on defenses such as mistake, ignorance, insanity, infancy, duress, or entrapment. Then, the process itself is streamlined. The jury is abandoned and the decision assigned to a professional judge, either after a bench trial or, preferably and far more frequently, after a plea agreement. Whenever possible, the matter is to be turned over to "some form of administrative control which will prove quick, objective and comprehensive."[65]

The precise definition of offenses is of secondary importance. All offenses spring from a single source, the state's duty to guard the public welfare against social dangers. All specific public welfare offenses, therefore, are nothing more than specifications of a single, all-encompassing offense, or, rather, command, which instructs everyone (and everything) not to interfere with the public welfare. The details and particular applications of this general injunction are to be worked out by expert state officials at all levels of government. So Sayre's list of categories of public welfare offenses (not a list of the offenses themselves, mind you) is not meant to be exhaustive but is subject to continuous revision (meaning expansion), the only limits to which are set by the regulatory inventiveness of state officials. Still, Sayre's list is worth reproducing, since it, though framed as a mere snapshot in the history of American criminal administration, so nicely—some anachronisms notwithstanding—charts the course of what was to come in the decades ahead, while at the same time placing recent developments—including the war on crime—in a broader historical context:

1. Illegal sales of intoxicating liquor;
2. Sales of impure or adulterated food or drugs;
3. Sales of misbranded articles;
4. Violations of antinarcotic acts;
5. Criminal nuisances;
6. Violations of traffic regulations;
7. Violations of motor-vehicle laws;
8. Violations of general police regulations, passed for the safety, health, or well-being of the community[66]

Offenses that fall under these categories today account for the vast majority of matters of "criminal administration." Offenses in categories (4), (6), and (7) alone easily account for most offenses committed, prosecuted, and sanctioned.

Certainly, things have changed since Sayre's 1933 article. The state has shown considerable imagination in making use of the flexibility it needed to discharge its duty to safeguard the "public welfare." The scope of public welfare offenses has been expanded, the sanctions for their commission enhanced, and their enforcement simplified and accelerated. This general development culminated in and was dramatically accelerated by the war on crime. Regulatory offenses provided the ideal means for incapacitating large numbers of undesirables quickly and, eventually, for long periods of time. Among the offenses on Sayre's list, violations of antinarcotics law (no. 4) proved to be a particularly popular weapon in the police campaign against crime. The penalties for drug violations today include every punishment short of death, including life imprisonment without parole. In 1993, the number of drug offenders in American prisons reached 350,000, almost twice the *total* number of prison inmates in the early 1960s. The tripling of the *federal* prison population since the 1970s is largely attributable to the expansion and the increasing harshness of federal drug criminal law, with the number of federal drug offenders increasing eighteenfold, from three thousand to more than fifty thousand, or 60 percent of federal prisoners.

But other offense categories have proved useful, as well. Weapons offenses, which qualify as violations of "general police regulations, passed for the safety, health, or well-being of the community" (no. 8), also allow police officers to take dangerous elements off the streets in large numbers, and with little effort. And, thanks to unprecedented cooperation between state and federal law enforcement agencies, weapons offenders can now be incapacitated for extended periods of time. "Project Exile" makes use of the harsh federal weapons laws, literally, to "exile" offenders from their local communities by committing them to faraway federal prisons. In a typical case, a Philadelphia police officer, while "frisking [a] suspect near a drug area," happened to find a loaded gun in the suspect's waistband. Instead of the probationary sentence the man might have gotten in city court, he was sentenced to five and a half years in a federal prison. As the officer explained in an interview, "[a]nd that's not just local jail where the family can come visit him, or come see him and visit him. They're sent anywhere in the country, so they're separated from their families and there's no probation or parole under the federal guidelines, so they're doing their complete sentence."[67]

2

Policing Possession

In general, the offense of possession—whether of drugs, of guns, or of anything else—has emerged as the policing device of choice in the war on crime. Most straightforwardly, and now also most commonly, possession operates directly as possession *qua* possession, an offense in and of itself. Or it functions indirectly, through some other offense, either as a springboard to another offense, through retrospective and prospective presumptions, or as an upgrade for another offense, through sentence enhancements. Since possession has achieved the status of the crime war's paradigmatic police offense, it deserves a closer look. By focusing on possession, we also get a sense of the marvelously integrated operation of the regulatory machine that is the war on crime. Possession, after all, achieved its favored status partly because it is flexible, yet durable enough to fit so nicely into the policing process as a whole.

Simply Possession

Operating below the radars of policy pundits and academic commentators, as well as the Constitution, possession offenses do the crime war's dirty work. Possession has replaced vagrancy as the most convenient gateway into the criminal justice system. Possession shares the central advantages of vagrancy as a policing tool: flexibility and convenience. Yet, as we shall see, it is in the end a far more formidable weapon in the war on crime: it expands the scope of policing into the home, it results in far harsher penalties and therefore has a far greater incapacitative potential, and it is far less vulnerable to legal challenges.

Millions of people commit one of its variants every day, from possessing firearms and all sorts of other weapons, dangerous weapons, instruments, appliances, or substances,[1] including toy guns,[2] air pistols and rifles,[3] tear gas,[4] ammunition,[5] body vests,[6] and antisecurity items,[7] to burglary tools[8] or stolen property,[9] and, of course, drugs[10] and everything associated with them, including drug paraphernalia,[11] drug precursors,[12] not to mention instruments of crime,[13] graffiti instruments,[14] computer-related material,[15] counterfeit trademarks,[16] unauthorized recordings of a performance,[17] public benefit cards,[18] forged instruments,[19] forgery devices,[20] embossing machines (to forge credit cards),[21] slugs,[22] vehicle identification numbers,[23] vehicle titles without complete assignment,[24] gambling devices,[25] gambling records,[26] usurious loan records,[27] inside information,[28] prison contraband,[29] obscene material,[30] obscene sexual performances by a child,[31] "premises which [one] knows are being used for prostitution purposes,"[32] eavesdropping devices,[33] fireworks,[34] noxious materials,[35] and taximeter accelerating devices (in New York),[36] spearfishing equipment (in Florida),[37] undersized catfish (in Louisiana)[38]—and the list could go on and on.

And that's the first prerequisite for a sweeping offense. Lots of people must be guilty of it. Thanks to the erosion of constitutional constraints on police behavior in the state-declared emergency of the war on crime, possession is easy to detect. Every physical or merely visual search, every frisk, every patdown, is also always a search for possession. Like vagrancy (and pornography), then, police officers know possession when they see it. Unlike vagrancy, they also know it when they feel it.

Police officers have become experts at detecting "bulges" in various articles of clothing, each signaling an item that may be illegally possessed. Similarly, police officers and the judges who occasionally review their actions have long been particularly imaginative in their interpretation of the particular nature of these bulges, when the time has come to confirm one's visual suspicion with a physical frisk. Here the search for one illegally possessed item—say a concealed weapon—may actually bear fruit in the form of the discovery of another illegally possessed item—say a gram of cocaine. Possession offenses in this way manage to bootstrap themselves, each giving the other a helping hand.

Moreover, the case for a possession offense begins and ends with a search, no matter whether it was a search for a possession offense or for some other crime. If it's a search in connection with some other crime, the police officer may well stumble upon evidence of illegal possession. This may come in handy if no evidence of the other crime is found or if that evidence doesn't stick for one reason or another, say because it's not sufficiently corroborated by other evidence or because some defense or other applies (like self-defense, perhaps). If it *is* a search for a possession offense, however, the scope of the search is virtually unlimited, given that items possessed come in all shapes and sizes (especially drugs) and can be hidden in the smallest cavity, bodily or not.

Thanks to an expansive reading of possession statutes—which includes the inapplicability of many defenses—possession is easy to prove. In fact, there won't be any need to prove anything, to anyone, judge or jury. Virtually all defendants in possession cases see the writing on the wall and plead guilty. And, thanks to penalty enhancements for prior convictions and—most recently—the innovative collaboration of federal and state law enforcement, possession once proved can send a possessor to prison for a long time, even for life without the possibility of parole.

So, in a recent New York case, a defendant was relieved to find himself acquitted of several serious burglary charges on what we now like to call a "technicality." Unfortunately for him, he *was* convicted of possessing stolen property—the loot of the very burglary of which he had been acquitted. What's more, the judge sentenced him to twenty-five years to life on the possession count alone. As a professional burglar, he was a "scourge to the community."[39]

In 1998, possession offenses accounted for 106,565, or 17.9 percent, of all arrests made in New York State.[40] Of these cases, 295 (or 0.27 percent) resulted in a verdict (by a judge or a jury), a whopping 129 (0.12 percent) in an acquittal. Of those originally arrested for possession, 33,219 (31.2 percent) went to prison or jail. New York boasts no fewer than 115 felony possession offenses, all of which require a minimum of one year in prison; eleven of them provide for a maximum sentence of life imprisonment.

Possession has become the paradigmatic offense in the current campaign to stamp out crime by incapacitating as many criminals as we can get our hands on. Every minute of every day, police pull over cars and sweep neighborhoods looking for, or just happening upon, "possessors" of one thing or another. Prosecutors throw in a possession count for good measure or, if nothing else sticks, make do with possession itself. As one Michigan prosecutor remarked before the U.S. Supreme Court, why bother charging more involved offenses if you can get life imprisonment without parole for a possession conviction?[41]

In many cases, possession statutes also save prosecutors the trouble of proving that other major ingredient of criminal liability in American criminal law, mens rea, or a guilty mind. This means that many possession statutes, particularly in the drug area—where some of the harshest campaigns of the war on crime have been prosecuted—are so-called strict liability crimes. In other words, you can be convicted of them if you don't know that you are "possessing" a drug of any kind, what drug you are "possessing," how much of it you've got, or—in some states—even that you are possessing anything at all, drug or no drug.[42]

This much we might have expected from Sayre's theory of "public welfare offenses." Possession, however, also does away with the traditional requirement that criminal liability must be predicated on an actus reus, an affirmative act or at least a failure to act (rather than a status, like being in possession of something). So, even if some sort of intent (or at least negligence) is required for conviction, there is no need to worry about the actus reus.

Plus, it turns out that other defenses also don't apply to possession offenses. We've already seen that, in Sayre's scheme, culpability and responsibility defenses have no place in a possession case. But what about other defenses, such as self-defense or necessity?

Say you're riding in the back seat of your friend's car as a couple of men try to jack the car, guns drawn. You notice a gun under the driver seat, bend down and grab it, and then shoot one of the men in the leg. You're cleared of the assault on grounds of self-defense. Still, since you weren't licensed to carry the gun, you're liable for possessing it illegally. This is so because, technically, the defense of self-defense applies only to the use but not to the possession of the gun.[43]

As a final example, consider the so-called agency defense. It turns out that this defense applies to the sale, but not to the simple possession, of narcotics.[44] To understand why, we need to take a closer look at the menu of possession offenses available to the modern legislator. We can distinguish between two types of possession offenses, *simple* possession and possession with intent, or *compound* possession. Simple possession itself can, but need not, require proof of actual or constructive awareness— that you knew or should have known that you possessed the object in question. If it doesn't, it's called a strict liability offense. Possession with intent is by definition not a strict liability offense, since it requires proof of intent.

It may be helpful to view the varieties of possession along a continuum from dangerousness at the one end to its manifestation at the other. At the end of pure dangerousness is simple possession. Here we are farthest removed from the harm that the use of the object may cause. And, in the strict liability variety of simple possession, the inference from the dangerousness of the item possessed to its possessor is most tenuous—since she by definition is not even aware of her possession. Next is compound possession, which still inflicts no harm since the possession itself is harmless, but at least we have the intent to use the item possessed in a way that may or may not be harmful. Moving further along the continuum, we encounter the *preparation* to use the item possessed in some particular way. This preparation, as distinct from an attempt, is not criminalized.

Next comes the *attempt* to use the object possessed, which is a preparation that has almost, but not quite, borne fruit. And, eventually, there is the use of the possessed item. In the case of drugs, that use may come in the form of a sale, as in the popular and often severely punished offense of possession with intent to distribute. Of course, the distribution itself is also entirely harmless. It's another kind of use, which may or may not follow the distribution, that renders drugs harmful, namely their consumption. But the harmfulness of the use is not an element of a compound possession offense criminalizing possession with intent to distribute. There is no offense of possession with intent to consume. In fact, some jurisdictions recognize possession with intent to consume as a *mitigating* rather than an aggravating factor, especially when the drug possessed is marijuana (possession of quantities for personal use).[45]

Now courts have held that the agency defense does not reach the simple possession of drugs because someone who merely possesses drugs, without the intent to sell, does not—and in fact cannot—act as the agent of the ultimate buyer, and her possession therefore cannot be merely incidental to the purchase.[46] She doesn't *act* at all; she merely possesses. The mere *fact* of possession is enough for conviction, no matter what the reason or who the eventual beneficiary. This arrangement, once again, has the convenient effect—for the prosecutor—of ensuring him of a conviction for simple possession, in cases where the agency defense would block convictions of possession with intent to sell, or even the sale itself.

By now, you may not be surprised to learn, in our carjacking example, that you didn't even have to pick up the gun to be guilty of possessing it illegally. Again in New York—but in many other jurisdictions as well—you may well have "constructively" possessed the weapon simply by having been in the car at the same time. To possess something in the eye of the criminal law doesn't mean you owned it, nor does it mean you physically possessed it. It's generally enough that you *could have* brought it within your physical possession or at least kept others from bringing it within theirs. (Technically, you constructively possessed the gun if you "exercise[d] dominion or control over" it.)[47]

And as though proving possession isn't easy enough, the law of possession also teems with evidentiary presumptions. Not only can you constructively possess something you don't have in your hands or on your person; you can also be *presumed* to constructively possess it. In our example, this means that it will be up to you to prove to the jury—should you be among the minuscule percentage of possession defendants who make it to a jury trial—that you did not in fact possess the gun, constructively, which is a tough row to hoe, given what we just learned about how little it takes to establish possession.

The most popular choice among legislators eager to further reduce prosecutorial inconvenience associated with the enforcement of possession offenses is to establish the rule that mere presence constitutes presumptive possession. The more eager the state is to get certain possessors off the street, the more dangerous these possessors have revealed themselves to be through their possession, and the more dangerous the item possessed, the greater the temptation will be to do away with evidentiary requirements and thereby to accelerate the incapacitation process. Small wonder that these presumptions from presence to possession pop up in gun and drug possession cases.[48]

In the New York Penal Law, for example, merely being around drugs not only amounts to presumptively possessing them. It further simplifies the prosecutor's incapacitative task by also establishing a presumption of "knowing" possession.[49] So, from evidence of your being in a car or room with a controlled substance, the prosecutor, without additional evidence, gets to jump to the conclusion that you possessed the drugs, and knew that you did. And, as we just saw, this conclusion will stand, unless you convince the fact finder otherwise. And that fact finder is, in virtually every possession case, none other than the prosecutor himself, who offers you a reduced sentence in exchange for a guilty plea.

The use of mere presence as a foundation of criminal liability has an additional benefit. Presence not only simplifies the prosecutorial task of connecting a given object with a particular possessor. Presence can with one fell swoop ensnare not just one but several persons in the web of possession liability that emanates from a piece of contraband at its center. Presence-to-possession has this useful feature thanks to a generous interpretation of possession that makes room for nonexclusive possession of chattels, notwithstanding that "real" is supposed to differ from "movable" property precisely in that nonexclusive possession is possible in the former but impossible in the latter: "if we concede possession to the one, we must almost of necessity deny it to the other."[50]

Presence-based liability of this sort points up another feature of possession offenses: the irrelevance of traditional distinctions among principals and accomplices. Nonexclusive possession combined with a presumption of possession based on mere presence brings anyone somehow "involved" with a dangerous object within the scope of police control. Careful doctrinal—that is, abstract—distinctions among different levels of "involvement" in the crime of possession would inconvenience state officials, mostly police officers, to whose discretion the diagnosis of dangerousness in particular cases is entrusted. And it makes sense that complicity analysis would be entirely inappropriate; since possession is not an act, the central question of complicity—can A's act be imputed to B— simply does not arise. What's at stake is not liability for an act, carefully calibrated by individual culpability, but the ascription of the label "possessor" (or, functionally, "dangerous individual") for the purpose of permitting police interference with possible punitive consequences.

Still, the complicity model turns out to be surprisingly useful in an analysis of possession offenses, as long as one frees oneself of the notion that complicity—or any other form of group criminality—requires at least two persons. Possession offenses, in a sense, treat anyone "involved" with the dangerous object as an accomplice. The interesting thing about possession offenses is that the principal is not a person but an inanimate object. In theory if not in function, the source of criminal liability is the object, not the possessor. Hence, criminal liability results from contact, however slight, with the object. The involvement with the object need only be substantial enough to allow its taint, its dangerousness, to come into contact with its possessor. By failing to disassociate himself from the dangerous object, the possessor has placed himself in a position where the object's dangerousness can be ascribed to him. He has revealed himself as sharing the object's dangerousness. He will be deemed its "possessor," as "exercising dominion or control over it," if he "was aware of his physical possession or control thereof for a sufficient period to have been able to terminate it."[51]

This imputation of an object's characteristics to its possessor is familiar from medieval law. There, each head of household was presumptively liable for damage caused by his possessions, animate and inanimate alike, unless he surrendered them to the victim's household immediately upon becoming aware of the damage they had done. If he didn't disassociate himself from the tainted piece of property in this way and instead continued to feed the offending slave or dog or used the blood-stained axe, he had to pay wergeld to the victim's household.[52] The only prerequisite for liability was causation of harm and possession. On the householder's part, no act was required.

While medieval law thus knew of transferring an object's taint onto its possessor and holding the possessor liable simply as possessor, it differed from contemporary possession liability in one important respect: it required harm, and therefore also a victim. Modern possession liability transfers the danger from an object to its possessor and holds him liable as a source of danger without the object's danger ever having manifested itself.

One difference between the two instances of ascribing characteristics from an object to its possessor is that the medieval example is centered on the possessor, whereas the contemporary one focuses on the object possessed. The medieval householder is liable for the harm caused by his possessions because they are *his* possessions. Today's nonexclusive constructive gun possessor is incapacitated because of his spatial association with the dangerous object. The medieval model extracts damages for the victim from the most obvious source, either in the form of the offending possession which the victim could use—or not use—at his discretion or of the householder's wergeld, traveling up the ladder of property relations from possessed to possessor. The modern model turns possession itself into the offense, without harm, to subject a presumptively dangerous individual to police investigation and control. In the medieval model, responsibility travels from the possessor to the possessed. In the modern model, with no harm and therefore no responsibility to be ascribed, dangerousness travels from the possessed to the possessor for its own sake, to label the possessor as dangerous.

The idea of complicity among objects and their human possessors, and of a transfer of characteristics from one to the other and back again, may appear odd. But it makes perfect sense in a police regime of threat elimination and minimization. In such a regime, characteristics apparently limited to persons—such as mens rea, or culpability—turn out to be nothing more than general, though cryptic, references to dangerousness. So a person acting with mens rea, or "malice," reveals herself to be abnormally dangerous. The "higher" the mens rea, the higher the level of dangerousness. So the *purposeful* actor is most dangerous (because of her evil disposition and her likelihood of success), followed by the actor who acts with *knowledge* that she will cause harm, rather than the intent to do so, followed by the merely *reckless* actor, who knows that her conduct may cause harm but goes ahead with it anyway, followed by the *negligent* actor, who is simply dangerously clueless.

The connection between dangerousness and mens rea is so natural that courts slide back and forth between the two even in the analysis of the dangerousness of objects. So an object's "inherent dangerousness" became its "inherent *vice*" when the New York Court of Appeals struggled with the question whether rubber boots qualified as a "dangerous instrument" (they do: though themselves free of "inherent vice," they were used in a dangerous way, by stomping someone on the pavement).[53] In the end, not only can persons be noxious, but objects can be evil, as well.

Apersonal Hazard Control

From the perspective of threat management, no qualitative difference separates possessor from possessed. There simply are more or less serious threats, source individuals and danger carriers, with evil taints passing back and forth between them. It only makes sense, then, that possessors and possessed, in fact dangers of all shapes and sizes, be processed by a general hazard control system that begins with the identification of possible threats, proceeds to their diagnosis, and ends with their disposal.

The general contours of such an apersonal hazard management regime emerge if we superimpose various of its manifestations upon one another.[54] The identification and disposal of dangerous objects occurs in many contexts. In general, every object—or animal—the possession of which is criminal is subject to a parallel system of hazard control. This makes sense: even after the possessor is punished for possessing and deprived of his possession, the item possessed still needs to be disposed of.

The mere possession of certain highly hazardous (or "toxic") waste is prohibited.[55] And so environmental law deals, among others things, with the "management," that is, the identification and disposal, of "hazardous waste," or, more broadly, "substances hazardous or acutely hazardous to public health, safety, or the environment."[56]

Possessing dangerous dogs, at least without a license, also is a crime.[57] Supplementing this prohibition, animal laws (often awkwardly classified under laws that deal with agriculture)[58] handle the "control," that is, the identification and disposal, through "seizure," "confiscation,"[59] and "destruction," of "dangerous dogs" or "mischievous animals."[60]

Then, of course, there are the laws that track the criminal proscription of gun and drug possession. These "administrative provisions"[61] deal with the "[d]isposition of weapons and dangerous instruments, appliances, and substances"[62] and the "seizure," "forfeiture," and "disposition" of "controlled substances [and] imitation controlled substances."[63] And, of course, the entire law of in rem forfeiture, which has made such enormous strides in the war on crime, is based on the identification and disposal of objects (*rei*) that are dangerous in and of themselves.[64]

The general law of nuisances can be seen as the archetypal hazard control regime. (Many, but not all, of the more specific schemes make their connection to nuisance disposal explicit.)[65] Modern nuisance statutes are all about the identification and disposal of hazardous or otherwise "offending" objects, "declaring," "enjoining," "condemning," and "abating" nuisances.[66] There we also find the distinction between nuisances per se—inherently dangerous objects—and other nuisances—objects that are merely put to "noxious" use. Abatement of the former requires destruction (without compensation).[67] Abatement of the latter doesn't; putting the object to nonnoxious use is enough.

Hazard control schemes generally begin with a "declaration." Before an item can be subjected to the proper kind of control, it must first be determined *whether* it is a hazard at all and, if so, *what kind* of hazard it is. Only items "declared" to be a "nuisance" (or "dangerous") fall within the jurisdiction of a system of hazard administration or management.[68]

Among nuisances, a system of hazard management then roughly distinguishes between two types of threats, one incidental and curable, the other inherent and incurable. Depending on the type of hazard, its source is either forfeited and turned to good use or destroyed as a nuisance per se. Objects not inherently dangerous, that is, objects for which there is hope, are first subjected to a diagnosis that determines whether they in fact have been tainted through association with a dangerous person. These objects may include, for example, "vehicles, vessels, and aircraft used to transport or conceal gambling records,"[69] family cars used to solicit prostitutes,[70] and anything somehow associated with a drug offense, from cars, to houses, to yachts, and even exercise equipment.[71]

If the objects have been tainted, and it is upon the possessor to rebut the presumption that they have, then they are forfeited. This means that they are temporarily or permanently brought under state control—and thereby also taken out of the control of their tainted possessor, thus removing the taint. State officials decide in their discretion the duration of the period of control. In cases of temporary control, an object is eventually released to the general public by public sale.[72] Alternatively, state officials may decide to subject the objects to permanent control. They may "retain such seized property for the official use of their office or department."[73] (This provision has brought substantial income to police departments throughout the country and has provided an important incentive to pursue the war on crime with great vigor.)

Inherently dangerous objects, the incurably vicious, such as guns and drugs, are permanently incapacitated. Weapons, for instance, are "destroyed" or otherwise "rendered ineffective and useless for [their] intended purpose and harmless to human life."[74] Dangerous dogs similarly are "euthanized immediately" or "confine[d] securely [and] permanently."[75]

Interestingly, the New York weapons disposal statute provides for two exceptions to this general rule of permanent incapacitation. One is within the discretion of a judge or a prosecutor: "a judge or justice of a court of record, or a district attorney, shall file with the official a certificate that the non-destruction thereof is necessary or proper to *serve the ends of justice*." The other is up to the designated disposal official himself: "the official directs that the same be retained in any laboratory conducted by any police or sheriff's department *for the purpose of research*, comparison, identification or other endeavor toward the prevention and detection of crime."[76]

The parallels between this fairly complex scheme for the identification and disposal of nonhuman threats, animate or inanimate, and modern criminal administration are apparent. As we saw earlier, these hazard control schemes apply to objects the possession of which is criminal; that is, they apply to contraband. But not only is the possession of noxious objects criminal, the possessors themselves are noxious objects. In a comprehensive hazard control regime, the distinction between possessor and possessed, between person and property, is as insignificant as the distinction among hazards generally speaking. A person is "declared an enemy of the state,"[77] while property is "declared a public nuisance."[78]

Possessor and possessed are lumped together into a hazard cluster that must be neutralized. That one is a person and the other isn't makes no difference. In the face of such danger, very personal considerations of mens rea are out of place. The possessor's mens rea matters as much as the possessed's: the fact of dangerousness *is* the mens rea, the viciousness, that requires state interference. To say that the possession of hazardous objects is a typical strict liability offense therefore is only half right.[79] It's the connection to a hazard that substitutes for mens rea. The liability isn't strict; it's grounded in dangerousness.

In the end, possessors are punished not only for possessing nuisances but for *being* nuisances themselves. A "dangerous dog" is "any dog which (a) without justification attacks a person and causes physical injury or death, or (b) poses a serious and unjustified imminent threat of harm to one or more persons."[80] Similarly, offenders are persons who, in the words of the Model Penal Code, (a) engage in "conduct that unjustifiably and inexcusably inflicts or threatens substantial harm to individual or public interests"[81] or (b) "whose conduct indicates that they are disposed to commit crimes."[82] Dangerous dogs are identified and controlled.[83] Dangerous humans are identified and then subjected to "public control."[84]

The control of human hazards can be temporary or permanent, depending on their classification as an incidental or an inherent danger. Corrigible human threats are subjected to rehabilitative treatment, a cleansing process in social control institutions (i.e., prisons). Incorrigible ones suffer incapacitative treatment, possibly through permanent warehousing under a life sentence, with an additional element of enlisting inmates in the service of the state. Consider here the use of inmates in prison industries. Note, also, that the Thirteenth Amendment, which prohibits slavery, explicitly excludes prisoners[85] and that even enlightened reformers like Cesare Beccaria viewed (and advocated) imprisonment as a form of state slavery.[86]

Alternatively, incorrigible human threats are destroyed through execution. It's no accident that the modern method for eliminating human hazards closely resembles that for the elimination of dangerous dogs. Conversely, the New York dangerous dog law provides that "'[e]uthanize' means to bring about death by a humane [!] method."[87]

Even the exceptional retention of inherently dangerous objects marked for neutralization finds a parallel in the realm of human hazards. Consider, for instance, the frequent retention of otherwise dispensable offenders as witnesses in the disposal processes of other human hazards, and more generally the practice of granting leniency in exchange for testimony. In either case, "nondestruction" of the human hazard can be deemed "necessary or proper to serve the ends of justice." Today, prisoners are no longer forced to subject themselves to scientific experiments, though they may submit to them voluntarily, or as voluntarily as one can submit to them under the conditions in many prisons.[88]

What's more, some nonhuman hazard control regimes provide not only a definition of offenses familiar from criminal codes. They go on to lay out defenses to an allegation of dangerousness analogous to the defenses recognized in criminal law. For instance, New York's statute governing the "Licensing, Identification and Control of Dogs"[89] is dedicated to "the protection of persons, property, domestic animals and deer from dog attack and damage."[90] A dog reveals itself as dangerous if it "attack[s] any person who is peaceably conducting himself in any place where he may lawfully be"[91] or if it "attack[s], chase[s] or worr[ies] any domestic animal . . . while such animal is in any place where it may lawfully be."[92] So the actual infliction of harm isn't a prerequisite. When the victim is a domestic animal, "chasing" will do.

So much for the special part of this dangerous dog code. But what about defenses? Several are available:

> A dog shall not be declared dangerous if the court determines the conduct of the dog
>
> (a) was justified because the threat, injury or damage was sustained by a person who at the time was committing a crime or offense upon the owner or custodian or upon the property of the owner or custodian of the dog, or
>
> (b) was justified because the injured person was tormenting, abusing or assaulting the dog or has in the past tormented, abused or assaulted the dog; or
>
> (c) was responding to pain or injury, or was protecting itself, its kennels or its offspring.[93]

The facially dangerous dog thus has at least four defenses at its disposal. All of these defenses qualify as "justifications." Recall that already in the definition of "dangerous dog," we find a limitation to attacks "without justification" and "unjustified" threats. First, and more general, the dog can raise a general justification defense by claiming that its victim, in the case of a person, was not "peaceably conducting himself" or was not "in [a] place where he may lawfully be"[94] or, in the case of a domestic animal, that it was not "in [a] place where *it* may lawfully be."[95] This first line of defense finds a rough analogue in the Model Penal Code's general justification defense (choice of evils), which provides that "[c]onduct that the actor believes to be necessary to avoid a harm or evil to himself or to another is justifiable, provided that . . . the harm or evil sought to be avoided by such conduct is greater than that sought to be prevented by the law defining the offense charged. . . ."[96] Here it would seem that the New York legislature has determined that the balance of evils weighs against the victim of a dog attack if she (or it) wasn't engaging in lawful conduct at the time of the attack, either by not peaceably conducting herself (or itself) or by not being where she (or it) may lawfully be.

Alternatively, this implicit, general justification defense is simply fleshed out by the three defenses laid out in the passage quoted earlier. Again, these defenses are familiar from the Model Penal Code—and from traditional criminal law. Defense (a) is analogous to the Code provisions on "use of force for the protection of other persons" (defense of others)[97] and "use of force for the protection of property" (defense of property).[98] Defenses (b) and (c) parallel the Code defenses "use of force in self-protection" (self-defense),[99] "extreme mental or emotional disturbance" (provocation), and, once again, defense of others.[100] If anything, the canine versions of these defenses are more generous than the human ones.[101] The Code—and traditional criminal law—limits the defense of provocation to homicide cases.

By encompassing and connecting human and nonhuman threats as possessors and possessed, the concept of possession helps to make this apersonal system of hazard control, where hazards are identified and eliminated regardless of who or what they might be, possible. By providing state officials with a flexible doctrinal framework for their discretionary analyses of dangerousness, possession offenses quietly supplement a growing system for the explicit assessment of human dangerousness, which includes pretrial detention hearings, sentencing hearings, and, most recently, sexual predator ratings, as well as parole hearings.[102] They introduce dangerousness considerations into an area of criminal law that, on its face, follows the traditional approach of matching behavior to definitions of proscribed conduct in criminal statutes. Dressed up like an ordinary criminal statute replete with conduct element ("possesses"), attendant circumstances ("three kilos of powder cocaine"), perhaps even mens rea ("with intent to distribute"), a possession offense in reality is a carte blanche for police control of undesirables, through initial investigation and eventual incapacitation.

Given the flexibility of their conception and the convenience of their enforcement, possession offenses alone can quickly and easily incapacitate large numbers of undesirables for long periods of time. Possession, however, unfolds its full potential as a threat elimination device when used in conjunction with other broad-sweeping police offenses.

The most potent combination of modern policing is the traffic offense and possession. Every day, millions of cars are stopped for alleged violation of one of the myriad regulations that govern our use of public streets. As soon as you get into your car, even before you turn the ignition key, you have subjected yourself to intense police scrutiny. So dense is the modern web of motor vehicle regulations that every motorist is likely to get caught in it every time he drives to the grocery store. The good news is that the gap between regulation and enforcement of the traffic laws is enormous. Unfortunately, that's also the bad news. It is by the good graces, or the inattention, of a police officer that you escape a traffic stop and a ticket, or worse.

Penalties for traffic violations are often astonishingly high, including short-term incarceration even for a first offense, but they are irrelevant in the large, incapacitative, scheme of things.[103] The war on crime uses traffic stops not to hand out tickets or even ten-day jail sentences. In the war on crime, traffic stops are a convenient opportunity to identify and eliminate threats. The identification begins with general observation, continues with a glance inside the car, and ends with a full-fledged search of the car and its occupants. The elimination takes the form of the one-two punch of traffic violation and possession offense. Untold times each and every day, traffic stops reveal evidence of possession at some stage of the identification process, be it the gun protruding from under the passenger seat, the rounds of ammunition rolling around on the floor, the marijuana paraphernalia sticking out from under a blanket on the back seat, or the vial of crack cocaine found during the search incident to arrest for driving without a registration. One moment the driver of the "late-model sedan" is cruising down I-95. The next moment he finds himself charged with a possession felony of one kind or another, or both, as in the "variety of narcotics and weapons offenses" familiar from Supreme Court opinions.[104]

In the end, it really makes little difference exactly why a particular person attracts the attention of a police officer. What matters is that, once he has been identified as a potential threat, possession offenses are a convenient way to get him off the streets, either in conjunction with another offense or, increasingly, all by themselves. The connection between evidence of possession and possession is instantaneous, and evidence of possession is easily found.

To see just how easy, let's take a closer look at some of the ways in which police can happen upon "contraband," in the specific sense of "the very things the possession of which was the crime charged."[105] We needn't look far for illustrations of the convenience of possession policing. The Supreme Court's criminal procedure opinions are filled with them. Given that only successful possession searches make it before any court, that only a small portion of these cases then make it before an appellate court, and that only a minuscule fraction of these in turn make it to the Supreme Court, we can only guess how often the policing practices considered by the Court are used "in the field."

Possession in the Supreme Court

A glance at the Supreme Court's possession-related opinions reveals the significance of possession police in all its marvelous variety. We also see how willing the Court has been to accommodate the needs of law enforcement in its effort to incapacitate undesirables by connecting them to one or more of the offenses in their possession grab bag. In fact, it turns out that much of the Supreme Court's recent criminal procedure jurisprudence has been made with possession cases. From *Carroll* to *Terry* to *Wardlow*, possession offenses have inspired the Court to loosen constitutional protections in the service of more effective policing and, most recently, of the war on crime.

Police officers are likely to stumble upon possession evidence anytime they make an arrest. This makes sense. Early on, police were entitled to search any area in the arrestee's possession, so evidence *of* possession was found *within* an arrestee's possession. For instance, in *United States v. Rabinowitz*,[106] the search incident to Rabinowitz's arrest revealed a plate "from which a similitude of a United States obligation had been printed" and possession of which was illegal.

This connection between possession and possession was muddled when the Court overruled *Rabinowitz* some twenty years later, in *Chimel v. California*.[107] Since *Chimel*, the scope of the search incident to an arrest is defined by the arrestee's "armspan."[108] That way, police are not supposed to be able to search areas within the arrestee's possession but not within his reach. This doesn't mean, of course, that police no longer find evidence of (illegal) possession during a "search incident." On the contrary. For one thing, the armspan area is merely a subset of the area within the arrestee's possession. For another, since the 1990 decision in *Maryland v. Buie*,[109] police can do a much broader "protective sweep"—as opposed to a search—of surrounding areas far beyond the arrestee's armspan, as well as beyond the area within his actual possession. As Justice Brennan explained in his *Buie* dissent, "a protective sweep would bring within police purview virtually all personal possessions within the house not hidden from view in a small enclosed space."[110] He's right, of course, and, from the perspective of possession police, that's a good thing. "Personal possessions" obviously—and conveniently—include not only evidence of the crime underlying the arrest but evidence of the standard possession offenses, as well.

As one might expect, the combination of search incident to arrest and traffic stops has been a fruitful one for the detection of items illegally possessed and for the incapacitation of those who possess them. The Supreme Court expanded a passenger's "armspan" to the interior of a car in *New York v. Belton*.[111] Belton had been a passenger in a car whose driver had been pulled over for speeding. He ended up convicted of cocaine possession. The trooper had smelled and then found marijuana in the car, which led him to put everyone in the car, including Belton, under arrest for marijuana possession. Incident to that arrest for possession offense number 1, the trooper then searched the entire car. It was then and there that he found cocaine in a zipped pocket of Belton's jacket on the back seat. Hence Belton's connection to the second, and far more serious, possession offense.

It doesn't take a full-blown arrest, however, to generate possession evidence—and therefore possession convictions. Mini-arrests called *Terry* stops will do. In 1968, the Supreme Court permitted police officers to detain suspects, however briefly, without probable cause—never mind a warrant.[112] That case was *Terry v. Ohio*. *Terry* was a possession case, though a quaint one compared with today's possession proliferation. Terry and two others had been "stopped and frisked"—to use the Court's technical description of their mini-arrest and search—by a police officer on the beat who suspected they were casing a store for a burglary or a robbery. The "frisk" turned up guns on Terry and another of the men. They were convicted, not of attempted burglary but of carrying a concealed weapon, "and sentenced to the statutorily prescribed term of one to three years in the penitentiary." Such a convenient method of incapacitation was sure to catch on in the war on crime.

And it did. Soon officers en masse were discovering suspicious bulges in the "outer garments" of *Terry* friskees. In *Terry*, Police Detective Martin

McFadden at least had found what he was looking for, a gun. But once a frisking officer is patting down a suspect, there's no telling what contraband she might come across. So the exploration of bulges in search of "weapon-like objects" soon began turning up not only weapons but a panoply of other illegally possessed items, including drugs (of course)[113] and lottery slips, in New Jersey.[114]

And, just like full-fledged arrests, *Terry* mini-arrests work well with traffic stops that don't blossom into "custodial arrests," as they did in *Belton*. The seminal case of *Pennsylvania v. Mimms* nicely illustrates the familiar chain of events leading from traffic stop to bulge to frisk to gun possession to a prison sentence.[115] The Supreme Court's rendition is too full of the standard technical lingo to pass up:

> While on routine patrol, two Philadelphia police officers observed respondent Harry Mimms driving an automobile with an expired license plate. The officers stopped the vehicle for the purpose of issuing a traffic summons. One of the officers approached and asked respondent to step out of the car and produce his owner's card and operator's license. Respondent alighted, whereupon the officer noticed a large bulge under respondent's sports jacket. Fearing that the bulge might be a weapon, the officer frisked respondent and discovered in his waistband a .38-caliber revolver loaded with five rounds of ammunition. The other occupant of the car was carrying a .32-caliber revolver. Respondent was immediately arrested and subsequently indicted for *carrying a concealed deadly weapon* and for unlawfully *carrying a firearm without a license.* [116]

"Armspans" play a role in frisks incident to stops as they do in searches incident to arrests. And, once again, the Court has found a way to extend that span to include the interior of cars in traffic stops. In *Michigan v. Long*,[117] decided six years after *Mimms*, the Court applied *Terry* to the following connection between possession—in this case, of drugs—and a routine traffic violation—in this case, speeding. Once again, here is the Court's account of the chain of events, culminating in Long's conviction for marijuana possession:

> Deputies Howell and Lewis were on patrol in a rural area one evening when, shortly after midnight, they observed a car traveling erratically and at excessive speed. The officers observed the car turning down a side road, where it swerved off into a shallow ditch. The officers stopped to investigate. . . . After another repeated request [to produce his registration], Long, who Howell thought "appeared to be under the influence of something,"

turned from the officers and began walking toward the open door of the vehicle. The officers followed Long and both observed a large hunting knife on the floorboard of the driver's side of the car. The officers then stopped Long's progress and subjected him to a *Terry* protective patdown, which revealed no weapons. Long and Deputy Lewis then stood by the rear of the vehicle while Deputy Howell shined his flashlight into the interior of the vehicle, but did not actually enter it. The purpose of Howell's action was "to search for other weapons." The officer noticed that something was protruding from under the armrest on the front seat. He knelt in the vehicle and lifted the armrest. He saw an open pouch on the front seat, and upon flashing his light on the pouch, determined that it contained what appeared to be marihuana. After Deputy Howell showed the pouch and its contents to Deputy Lewis, Long was arrested for *possession of marihuana*. A further search of the interior of the vehicle, including the glovebox, revealed neither more contraband nor the vehicle registration. The officers decided to impound the vehicle. Deputy Howell opened the trunk, which did not have a lock, and discovered inside it approximately 75 pounds of marihuana.[118]

Long got away with a sentence of two years' probation, a fine of $750, and court costs of $300.[119] That was in 1978, in a Michigan state court. In today's coordinated federal-state police regime, possession offenses carry a much heavier incapacitative stick. In federal court, possession of seventy-five pounds of marijuana would get him between thirty-one and forty-one months of real prison time, without parole, assuming he had a clean record.[120] But federal intervention wouldn't have been necessary. In Michigan state court today, he would face "imprisonment for not more than 7 years or a fine of not more than $500,000.00, or both."[121] Michigan, after all, is the land of *Harmelin*, the case in which the Supreme Court upheld a mandatory sentence of life imprisonment without the possibility of parole for simple drug possession.[122]

Police understand the connection among traffic violations, *Terry*, and possession offenses very well. Long before *Terry*, the Supreme Court aided another war on possession—of liquor—by carving out the automobile exception to the Fourth Amendment's warrant requirement. In the 1925 case of *Carroll v. United States*,[123] the Court was so impressed with the mobility of the "automobile" that it did away with the requirement that a police officer get a warrant to search a car he thought might contain contraband, to wit, liquor; by the time he showed up with the warrant, the car—unlike the more familiar, and stationary, houses—might be long gone. Carroll was suspected, and convicted, of "transportation or possession of liquor."

Seventy-five years later, police are not limited to pulling over and searching cars they suspect of containing evidence of illegal possession. Instead, they are just as likely to pull over cars for something entirely different and then bootstrap themselves into a search of the car for that all-important possession evidence. The officer in *Carroll*, after all, still needed probable cause to search the car for liquor. The automobile exception is an exception to the warrant requirement, not to the Fourth Amendment altogether.

As a result, the car search–possession jurisprudence of the war on crime often has been about everything but possession. It has been about broken tail lights, expired registration stickers, touched divider lines, rolled-through stop signs, improperly signaled turns, and, of course, speeding. There are many possession offenses. And there are many who commit possession offenses every day. But there are even more traffic offenses, and millions of them are committed every minute.

Nothing's easier than cruising down the street or staking out a highway and developing probable cause that someone has committed a traffic infraction. Armed with that probable cause, a police officer can stop a car and eventually search its occupants and the car itself, happening upon possession offense evidence along the way.

But that's not all. Since 1968, the police don't need probable cause that an offense—including a traffic infraction—has been committed. Since *Terry*, "reasonable suspicion" will do. And, once stopped, cars and their occupants have a tendency to be searched and to yield possession evidence.

More recently, the Supreme Court has made the leap from car stop to possession evidence even easier. In 1976, the Court began authorizing police officers to stop cars without any suspicion of any kind, not reasonable suspicion, not probable cause, as long as the stop qualifies as a "roadblock" for routine checks of this or that—illegal aliens,[124] driver's licenses,[125] registrations,[126] DWI.[127]

No matter how the initial stop (or arrest) occurs, the so-called plain view exception comes in handy in order to transform this encounter between police and citizen into an instance of possession police. If a police officer has a right to be where she is, she has a right to see what she sees—and feel what she feels,[128] hear what she hears,[129] or smell what she smells.[130] In the case of a traffic stop, what she sees often enough is evidence of illegal possession. The plain view exception was first recognized in 1971, in a murder case.[131] But it was significantly expanded for use in the crime war in 1983, in yet another possession case. In *Texas v.*

Brown,[132] the Court did away with the requirement that the criminal nature of the item seized in plain view be immediately apparent. Since *Brown*, the police merely need probable cause to believe that the item is contraband. Brown had been stopped at "a routine driver's license checkpoint" in Fort Worth, "[s]hortly before midnight." When the officer shone the ever present flashlight[133] into Brown's car, he noticed "between the two middle fingers of the hand . . . an opaque, green party balloon, knotted about one-half inch from the tip," which turned out to contain heroin. Brown pled nolo contendere to heroin possession and received four years in prison "pursuant to a negotiated plea bargain."[134]

It makes no difference whether the police officer used the traffic violation as a mere pretext to find evidence of some other offense, and possession offenses in particular. The police officer's subjective intent is irrelevant. In 1996, the Supreme Court removed any doubt on this issue in another possession case, *Whren v. United States*.[135] There plainclothes members of a drug task force developed a serious interest in traffic enforcement when they noticed that a car whose occupants they suspected of possessing drugs was driving off at an "unreasonable speed." Their hunch turned out to be correct—it always does in court opinions—and the driver and passenger were convicted of drug possession.

Terry has proved enormously useful to the war on crime as a war on possession. It authorizes police officers to put their hands on suspects without probable cause. And this laying on of hands is enough to provide conclusive evidence of possession, even if nothing else sticks. Without *Terry*, possession wouldn't be the universal velcro charge it is today, one that sticks when nothing else will.

As a final example, take the recent case of *Illinois v. Wardlow*.[136] There the Supreme Court decided that behavior in a "high crime area" may give rise to the reasonable suspicion required for a *Terry* stop even if the same behavior wouldn't have been suspicious elsewhere. This decision was warmly welcomed by police organizations and heavily criticized by civil rights groups. In the melee, the fact that Wardlow was convicted of a possession offense received scant attention. It didn't help that the Supreme Court reported that Wardlow had been convicted of *using* a weapon. The Illinois statute in question, though entitled "unlawful use or possession of weapons by felons . . . ," actually criminalizes the mere possession of a weapon, without more.[137]

Wardlow nicely illustrates the potential of possession as a sweep offense, as the favored incapacitation broom of the war on crime. Police officers descend on "high crime areas," either in coordinated raids or in casual cruise-throughs, in the hope of finding evidence of possession offenses. In the case of a raid, that evidence emerges in the course of the execution of a search warrant or an arrest warrant, with the inevitable search incident. In the case of a regular patrol, it reveals itself through personal observation ("bulges"), informer tips, or frisks incident to *Terry* stops. The items illegally possessed tend to be drugs or guns (as in *Wardlow*), or both; drug and gun possession offenses pack the greatest incapacitative punch. And in a "high crime area," they aren't hard to come by. In New York City alone, the number of illegal guns is estimated at between one and two million.[138]

Still, for searches incident to arrests and frisks incident to stops, police officers need to be able to articulate some (legitimate) reason for focusing their investigative attention on a particular person: probable cause and reasonable suspicion, respectively—except, of course, if their initial stop is part of a "roadblock." There's no need for this type of rationalization in another common source of possession evidence: consensual searches. The Supreme Court approved suspicionless consent searches in 1973, in *Schneckloth v. Bustamonte*, holding that officers asking for consent didn't have to tell suspects that they had the right to say no.[139] *Schneckloth* was another possession case. And the possession evidence was found after another "routine" traffic stop, this time for a burned-out headlight and license plate light. Only the type of possession offense differed from the run-of-the-mill drug-cum-gun possession case. What the police found "[w]added up under the left rear seat" were three *checks*. And what Bustamonte was convicted of was "possessing a check with intent to defraud."

Needless to say, in the decades since *Schneckloth*, police officers have been finding more than stolen checks during their consent searches. In Supreme Court cases, as well as presumably in real life, they tended to find drugs and guns, and especially drugs.[140] That's not to say, however, that *only* illegally possessed drugs and guns turned up. The variety of possession offenses available to the modern police officer ensured that, even among the small sample of Supreme Court cases, there's also a case of illegal possession of *stolen mail*.[141]

That possession case from 1976, *United States v. Watson*, made its own significant contribution to the war on crime. There the Supreme Court for the first time declared that the Fourth Amendment didn't stand in the way of public arrests without a warrant. In and of itself, that authority is a convenient weapon in the hands of police officers ferreting out crime. As we've seen, however, it also has the indirect advantage of justifying searches incident to warrantless street arrests: every arrest is also an armspan search—plus a "protective sweep." And "searches incident" have a tendency to reveal evidence of possession offenses, especially since the Court has taken an expansive view of what an arrestee's arm might reach.

After *Watson*, police officers once again were more likely to stumble upon drugs than stolen mail in their search incident to a warrantless public arrest. In *United States v. Santana*,[142] for example, they arrested a suspect on the "curtilage" of her home without a warrant. The search incident produced, among other things, "two bundles of glazed paper packets with a white powder." Santana was convicted of possession of heroin with intent to distribute.

But possession evidence doesn't just happen to crop up incident to arrests or stops for other offenses, traffic or not. Although it's very effective as a piggyback offense, possession is much more than that. It can itself be the offense that justifies the initial police intervention. The myriad possession offenses therefore also mean that police officers have myriad justifications for approaching, stopping, or arresting a suspect.

That's what happened in *Watson*, for example. An informer had told a postal inspector that Watson, a mailman, was in the midst of committing a possession offense, specifically that he "was in possession of a stolen credit card." That's also what happened in the recent case of *Florida v. J. L.*, where an anonymous informer called the Miami police department to report that "a young black male standing at a particular bus stop and wearing a plaid shirt was carrying a gun." J. L. was *Terry*-stopped and frisked and charged with "carrying a concealed firearm without a license and possessing a firearm while under the age of 18."[143]

No Supreme Court case, however, better illustrates the initial justificatory, and the indirect piggyback, function of possession offenses in the war on crime, as well as the interplay between different possession offenses, than 1972's *Adams v. Williams*. An informer—there tend to be lots of informers in victimless possession cases—had told a police officer on patrol that "an individual seated in a nearby vehicle was carrying narcotics and had a gun at his waist," that is, that he was engaging in two possession offenses at the same time, drug possession and gun possession. Here's what happened next:

> After calling for assistance on his car radio, Sgt. Connolly approached the vehicle to investigate the informant's report. Connolly tapped on the car

window and asked the occupant, Robert Williams, to open the door. When Williams rolled down the window instead, the sergeant reached into the car and removed a fully loaded revolver from Williams' waistband. The gun had not been visible to Connolly from outside the car, but it was in precisely the place indicated by the informant. Williams was then arrested by Connolly for unlawful possession of the pistol. A search incident to that arrest was conducted after other officers arrived. They found substantial quantities of heroin on Williams' person and in the car, and they found a machete and a second revolver hidden in the automobile.[144]

After a bench trial, Williams was convicted of one drug and two gun possession offenses: "having narcotic drugs in his control," "carrying a pistol on his person without a permit," and "knowingly having a weapon in a vehicle owned, operated or occupied by him."[145] The evidence for the gun possession counts stemmed from the initial *Terry* stop-and-frisk. And the evidence for the drug possession count turned up during the search incident to arrest based on the results of that frisk.

Searches that result from investigations into ongoing possession offenses can, of course, produce evidence not only of other possession offenses but of any other offense. Finding evidence of possession offenses is simply more convenient. It's self-evident, whereas other evidence is merely circumstantial. And the chances of finding other possession evidence are so much greater than those of finding evidence of other crimes. As the courts, including the Supreme Court, are fond of pointing out, drug and gun possession tend to go hand-in-hand. Whoever has drugs is likely to have a gun, and—at least in so-called high-crime areas—vice versa. As the Court explained in *Wardlow*, "it [is] common for there to be weapons in the near vicinity of narcotics transactions." That's why the officers in *Wardlow* found a gun, even though they were ostensibly looking for drugs, or, rather, "converging on an area known for heavy narcotics trafficking in order to investigate drug transactions."[146]

Either way, as the boot or the strap, possession offenses are particularly convenient policing instruments because they are continuous, across space and time. As we see in greater detail later in this chapter, possession offenses are continuous across space in that they can be committed in public or in private. As a result, they have always justified state intrusion into the private sanctuary of the home-castle. But they're also continuous across time. The whole point of carrying a gun, for instance, or keeping it at home or in the car is to have it around when the need might arise. Gun possession, therefore, can continue for hours, days, even weeks, months, years, or decades, depending on how insecure the possessor is without her possession. And, at any time during this period, the illegal possessor exposes herself to police intervention of various levels of intrusiveness, culminating in an arrest, with its inevitable search incident. She is a constant policing target, subject to incapacitation at any moment, day or night.

As we can see from our brief survey of possession police in the Supreme Court, the Court's criminal procedure jurisprudence since *Terry* represents an increasingly explicit effort to tap the full potential of possession as a general policing tool. With remarkable frequency, the Court has found ways to legitimize possession searches and seizures in an ever increasing variety of circumstances.

But the frequency of possession offenses as factors in decisions that have loosened constitutional safeguards in the interest of crime control is not the only remarkable aspect of this jurisprudence; another is the sheer number of possession cases that have found their way before the Court, hinting at the frequency of possession cases in criminal courts throughout the country. In the thirty-odd years since *Terry*, the Supreme Court has written opinions in scores of cases that involved one possession offense or another, in one way or another. Among these opinions are not only most of the Court's important Fourth Amendment opinions but also several significant opinions in other doctrinal areas, not only in criminal procedure but elsewhere, as well.

As the investigatory tool par excellence, possession has left its greatest mark on the constitutional law of police investigation. The list of Fourth Amendment/possession cases since *Terry* reads like a who's who of search and seizure law:

Terry v. Ohio, 392 U.S. 1 (1968)
Sibron v. New York, 392 U.S. 40 (1968)
Vale v. Louisiana, 399 U.S. 30 (1970)
Hill v. California, 401 U.S. 797 (1971)
United States v. Harris, 403 U.S. 573 (1971)
Adams v. Williams, 407 U.S. 143 (1972)
Schneckloth v. Bustamonte, 412 U.S. 218 (1973)
United States v. Robinson, 414 U.S. 218 (1973)
Gustafson v. Florida, 414 U.S. 260 (1973)
United States v. Watson, 423 U.S. 411 (1976)

United States v. Miller, 425 U.S. 435 (1976)
United States v. Santana, 427 U.S. 38 (1976)
Stone v. Powell, 428 U.S. 465 (1976)
South Dakota v. Opperman, 428 U.S. 364 (1978)
Connally v. Georgia, 429 U.S. 245 (1977)
United States v. Ramsey, 431 U.S. 606 (1977)
United States v. Chadwick, 433 US 1 (1977)
Pennsylvania v. Mimms, 434 U.S. 106 (1977)
Rakas v. Illinois, 439 U.S. 128 (1978)
Delaware v. Prouse, 440 U.S. 648 (1979)
Dalia v. United States, 441 U.S. 238 (1979)
Arkansas v. Sanders, 442 U.S. 753 (1979)
Michigan v. DeFillippo, 443 U.S. 31 (1979)
Ybarra v. Illinois, 444 U.S. 85 (1979)
United States v. Mendenhall, 446 U.S. 544 (1980)
United States v. Havens, 446 U.S. 620 (1980)
United States v. Salvucci, 448 U.S. 83 (1980)
Rawlings v. Kentucky, 448 U.S. 98 (1980)
Reid v. Georgia, 448 U.S. 438 (1980)
Steagald v. United States, 451 U.S. 204 (1981)
Michigan v. Summers, 452 U.S. 692 (1981)
New York v. Belton, 453 U.S. 454 (1981)
Washington v. Chrisman, 455 U.S. 1 (1982)
United States v. Ross, 456 U.S. 798 (1982)
Michigan v. Thomas, 458 U.S. 259 (1982)
Florida v. Royer, 460 U.S. 491 (1983)
Texas v. Brown, 460 U.S. 730 (1983)
Illinois v. Gates, 462 U.S. 213 (1983)
United States v. Villamonte-Marquez, 462 U.S. 579 (1983)
Illinois v. Lafayette, 462 U.S. 640 (1983)
United States v. Place, 462 U.S. 696 (1983)
Illinois v. Andreas, 463 U.S. 765 (1983)
Michigan v. Long, 463 U.S. 1032 (1983)
United States v. Jacobsen, 466 U.S. 109 (1984)
New York v. Quarles, 467 U.S. 649 (1984)
United States v. Karo, 468 U.S. 705 (1984)
Segura v. United States, 468 U.S. 796 (1984)
United States v. Leon, 468 U.S. 897 (1984)

Florida v. Rodriguez, 469 U.S. 1 (1984)
United States v. Hensley, 469 U.S. 221 (1985)
New Jersey v. T. L. O., 469 U.S. 325 (1985)
United States v. Johns, 469 U.S. 478 (1985)
United States v. Sharpe, 470 U.S. 675 (1985)
United States v. Montoya de Hernandez, 473 U.S. 531 (1985)
United States v. Sharpe, 470 U.S. 675 (1985)
California v. Carney, 471 U.S. 386 (1985)
New York v. Class, 475 U.S. 106 (1986)
Colorado v. Bertine, 479 U.S. 367 (1987)
United States v. Dunn, 480 U.S. 294 (1987)
New York v. Burger, 482 U.S. 691 (1987)
Griffin v. Wisconsin, 483 U.S. 868 (1987)
California v. Greenwood, 486 U.S. 35 (1988)
Michigan v. Chesternut, 486 U.S. 567 (1988)
Murray v. United States, 487 U.S. 533 (1988)
Florida v. Riley, 488 U.S. 445 (1988)
United States v. Sokolow, 490 U.S. 1 (1989)
Florida v. Wells, 495 U.S. 1 (1990)
Alabama v. White, 496 U.S. 325 (1990)
Illinois v. Rodriguez, 497 U.S. 177 (1990)
California v. Hodari D., 499 U.S. 621 (1991)
Florida v. Jimeno, 500 U.S. 248 (1991)
California v. Acevedo, 500 U.S. 565 (1991)
United States v. Padilla, 508 U.S. 77 (1993)
Minnesota v. Dickerson, 508 U.S. 366 (1993)
Arizona v. Evans, 514 U.S. 1 (1995)
Wilson v. Arkansas, 514 U.S. 927 (1995)
Ornelas v. United States, 517 U.S. 690 (1996)
Whren v. United States, 517 U.S. 806 (1996)
Ohio v. Robinette, 519 U.S. 33 (1997)
Maryland v. Wilson, 519 U.S. 408 (1997)
Richards v. Wisconsin, 520 U.S. 385 (1997)
United States v. Ramirez, 523 U.S. 65 (1998)
Bousley v. United States, 523 U.S. 614 (1998)
Muscarello v. United States, 524 U.S. 125 (1998)
Caron v. United States, 524 U.S. 308 (1998
Pennsylvania Bd. of Probation & Parole v. Scott, 524 U.S. 357 (1998)

Minnesota v. Carter, 525 U.S. 83 (1998)
Knowles v. Iowa, 525 U.S. 113 (1998)
Illinois v. Wardlow, 528 U.S. 119 (2000)
Florida v. J.L., 120 S. Ct. 1375 (2000)
Bond v. United States, 120 S. Ct. 1462 (2000)

The list of possession-related Fourth Amendment classics is complete once we look past *Terry* and back to *Carroll*, the 1925 opinion that established the automobile exception in a liquor possession case. Although the fifty-plus years between *Carroll* and *Terry* produced "only" fifty-plus Supreme Court opinions in possession-related cases, foundational opinions like *Mapp* (applying the exclusionary rule to the states) and *Aguilar* (the first half of the *Aguilar-Spinelli* test, to be undone some twenty years later in *Gates*, another possession case) remind us that the war on crime didn't invent possession offenses; it just used them to greater effect. Here are some of the Fourth Amendment chestnuts of the pre-*Terry* era:[147]

Carroll v. United States, 267 U.S. 132 (1925)
Steele v. United States, 267 U.S. 498 (1925)
Dumbra v. United States, 268 U.S. 435 (1925)
Agnello v. United States, 269 U.S. 20 (1925)
Byars v. United States, 273 U.S. 28 (1927)
McGuire v. United States, 273 U.S. 95 (1927)
Segurola v. United States, 275 U.S. 106 (1927)
Marron v. United States, 275 U.S. 192 (1927)
Olmstead v. United States, 277 U.S. 438 (1928)
Go-Bart Co. v. United States, 282 U.S. 344 (1931)
Husty v. United States, 282 U.S. 694 (1931)
United States v. Lefkowitz, 285 U.S. 452 (1932)
Taylor v. United States, 286 U.S. 1 (1932)
Grau v. United States, 287 U.S. 124 (1932)
Sgro v. United States, 287 U.S. 206 (1932)
Nathanson v. United States, 290 U.S. 41 (1933)
Scher v. United States, 305 U.S. 251 (1938)
Davis v. United States, 328 U.S. 582 (1946)
Harris v. United States, 331 U.S. 145 (1947)
United States v. Di Re, 332 U.S. 581 (1948)
Johnson v. United States, 333 U.S. 10 (1948)

Trupiano v. United States, 334 U.S. 699 (1948)
United States v. Rabinowitz, 339 U.S. 56 (1950)
United States v. Jeffers, 342 U.S. 48 (1951)
Rochin v. California, 342 U.S. 165 (1952)
Walder v. United States, 347 U.S. 62 (1954)
Rea v. United States, 350 U.S. 214 (1956)
Benanti v. United States, 355 U.S. 96 (1957)
Jones v. United States, 357 U.S. 493 (1958)
Giordenello v. United States, 357 U.S. 480 (1958)
Draper v. United States, 358 U.S. 307 (1959)
Henry v. United States, 361 U.S. 98 (1959)
Jones v. United States, 362 U.S. 27 (1960)
Elkins v. United States, 364 U.S. 206 (1960)
Rios v. United States, 364 U.S. 253 (1960)
Mapp v. Ohio, 367 U.S. 643 (1961)
Wong Sun v. United States, 371 U.S. 471 (1963)
Ker v. California, 374 U.S. 23 (1963)
Aguilar v. Texas, 378 U.S. 108 (1964)
Beck v. Ohio, 379 U.S. 89 (1964)
Stanford v. Texas, 379 U.S. 476 (1965)
United States v. Ventresca, 380 U.S. 102 (1965)
Angelet v. Fay, 381 U.S. 654 (1965)
One 1958 Plymouth Sedan v. Pennsylvania, 380 U.S. 693 (1965)
McCray v. Illinois, 386 U.S. 300 (1967)

Although possession offenses were most likely to crop up in Fourth Amendment cases, their ubiquity ensured that they also appeared in other constitutional and nonconstitutional contexts. Non–Fourth Amendment cases involving possession included:

Yee Hem v. United States, 268 U.S. 178 (1925) (presumptions; drug possession)
Lanzetta v. New Jersey, 306 U.S. 451 (1939) (vagueness; gun possession)
Pinkerton v. United States, 328 U.S. 640 (1946) (conspiracy; possession of liquor)
Roviaro v. United States, 353 U.S. 53 (1957) (presumptions; drug possession)

Harris v. United States, 359 U.S. 19 (1959) (double jeopardy; drug possession)

Smith v. California, 361 U.S. 147 (1959) (1st Am. (mens rea); possession of obscene matter)

Massiah v. United States, 377 U.S. 201 (1964) (5th & 6th Am.; drug possession)

Leary v. United States, 395 U.S. 6 (1969) (presumptions; drug possession)

Turner v. United States, 396 U.S. 398 (1970) (presumptions; drug possession)

United States v. Bass, 404 U.S. 336 (1971) (lenity; gun possession)

Davis v. Alaska, 415 U.S. 308 (1974) (evidence (confrontation); gun possession)

Stone v. Powell, 428 U.S. 465 (1976) (habeas corpus; gun possession)

County Court of Ulster Cty. v. Allen, 442 U.S. 140 (1979) (presumption (due process); gun possession)

McMillan v. Pennsylvania, 477 U.S. 79 (1986) (sentence enhancement; gun possession)

Kuhlmann v. Wilson, 477 U.S. 436 (1986) (habeas corpus; gun possession)

Arizona v. Fulminante, 499 U.S. 279 (1991) (confession; gun possession)

Harmelin v. Michigan, 501 U.S. 957 (1991) (8th Am.; drug possession)

Williams v. United States, 503 U.S. 193 (1992) (sentencing; gun possession)

Wright v. West, 505 U.S. 277 (1992) (habeas corpus; possession of stolen property as presumptive evidence of larceny)

Withrow v. Williams, 507 U.S. 680 (1993) (habeas corpus; gun possession)

Stinson v. United States, 508 U.S. 36 (1993) (sentencing guidelines; gun possession)

Deal v. United States, 508 U.S. 129 (1993) (statutory construction; gun possession)

United States v. Alvarez-Sanchez, 511 U.S. 350 (1994) (confession; possession of counterfeit currency)

Custis v. United States, 511 U.S. 485 (1994) (sentencing; gun possession)

Staples v. United States, 511 U.S. 600 (1994) (mens rea; gun possession)

Shannon v. United States, 512 U.S. 573 (1994) (insanity; gun possession)

United States v. Lopez, 514 U.S. 549 (1995) (commerce clause; gun possession)

Bailey v. United States, 516 U.S. 137 (1995) (statutory intrepretation ("uses"); gun possession)

Neal v. United States, 516 U.S. 284 (1996) (sentencing guidelines; drug possession)

United States v. Watts, 519 U.S. 148 (1997) (sentencing guidelines; drug & gun possession)

United States v. Gonzales, 520 U.S. 1 (1997) (concurrent state-federal sentence; drug & gun possession)

United States v. Labonte, 520 U.S. 751 (1997) (sentencing guidelines; drug possession)

Gilbert v. Homar, 520 U.S. 924 (1997) (suspension; drug possession)

Rogers v. United States, 522 U.S. 252 (1998) (mens rea; gun possession)

Spencer v. Kemna, 523 U.S. 1 (1998) (parole conditions; drug & gun possession)

Muscarello v. United States, 524 U.S. 125 (1998) (statutory interpretation ("carries"); gun possession)

Caron v. United States, 524 U.S. 308 (1998) (statutory interpretation (felon-in-possession); gun possession)

Monge v. California, 524 U.S. 721 (1998) (double jeopardy; drug possession)

Jones v. United States, 526 U.S. 227 (1999) (sentencing enhancement vs. offense element; gun possession)

United States v. Martinez-Salazar, 120 S. Ct. 774 (2000) (jury selection; drug possession)

United States v. Johnson, 120 S. Ct. 1114 (2000) (ex post facto; drug & gun possession)

Portuondo v. Agard, 120 S. Ct. 1119 (2000) (prosecutorial argument; gun possession)

Apprendi v. New Jersey, 120 S. Ct. 2348 (2000) (sentencing enhancement vs. offense element; gun & bomb possession)

In roughly chronological order, possession offenses thus appeared in opinions dealing with, in addition to the never-ending issues raised by the Fourth Amendment, evidentiary presumptions (due process), vagueness (due process), conspiracy (substantive criminal law), the First Amendment, burden of proof (due process), right to a jury trial (Sixth Amendment), statutory interpretation (substantive criminal law), habeas corpus (federal courts), the Fifth Amendment (due process and self-incrimination), the Sixth Amendment (right to counsel), the Eighth Amendment (cruel and unusual punishment), mens rea (substantive criminal law), insanity (substantive criminal law), the commerce clause (constitutional law), sentencing guidelines (substantive criminal law), lenity (constitutional law), parole conditions (law of punishment), double jeopardy (constitutional law), ex post facto (constitutional law), and prosecutorial argument (law of evidence).

That a possession offense appears in an opinion, no matter what its official subject matter, is significant for two reasons. De facto, it illustrates the ubiquity of possession offenses and their frequent and varied use. De jure, it may tell us something about *why* this is so, why there are so many possession offenses and why they are so popular as policing tools.

Not only the number but also the variety of possession-related cases is impressive. As one might expect, most cases involve the possession of drugs and related "paraphernalia" (or of liquor, during Prohibition), followed by gun possession. But other cases provide glimpses of other offenses in the possession grab bag that have been available to American police at a particular time in American history, including, in chronological order, possession of

gasoline ration coupons;[148]
draft cards;[149]
counterfeiting stamps;[150]
stolen property;[151]
obscene matter;[152]
lottery slips;[153]
"books, records, pamphlets, cards, receipts, lists, memoranda, pictures, recordings and other written instruments concerning the Communist Party of Texas, and the operations of the Communist Party in Texas";[154]

foodstamps;[155] and
counterfeit currency.[156]

When we look more closely at the Court's possession opinions, we can detect the function and the impact of possession offenses for various policing efforts throughout the twentieth century, culminating in their extensive use during the war on crime. The 1939 *Lanzetta* case, for instance, reveals the usefulness of possession offenses as a device for identifying and incapacitating undesirables.[157] The statute at issue in this classic vagueness case was very explicit about its incapacitative aim:[158]

1. A gangster is hereby declared to be an enemy of the State.
2. Any person in whose *possession* is found a machine gun or a submachine gun is declared to be a gangster: *provided, however,* that nothing in this section contained shall be construed to apply to any member of the military of naval forces of this State, or to any police officer of the State or of any country or municipality thereof, while engaged in his official duties.
3. Any person, having no lawful occupation, who is apprehended while *carrying* a deadly weapon, without a permit so to do, and who has been convicted at least three times of being a disorderly person, or who has been convicted of any crime, in this or in any other State, is declared to be a gangster.
4. Any person, not engaged in any lawful occupation, known to be a member of any gang consisting of two or more persons, who has been convicted at least three times of being a disorderly person, or who has been convicted of any crime, in this or in any other State, is declared to be a gangster; *provided, however,* that nothing in this section contained shall in any wise be construed to include any participant or sympathizer in any labor dispute.
5. Any person convicted of being a gangster under the provisions of this act shall be guilty of a high misdemeanor, and shall be punished by a fine not exceeding ten thousand dollars ($10,000.00), or by imprisonment not exceeding twenty years, or both.

The *Lanzetta* statute was a classic instrument for the neutralization of perceived threats, "enemies of the state." And possession offenses, coupled with classic vagrancy (of the "disorderly persons" variety),[159] fit the bill. Quickly detected, easily proved, and harshly punished, gun possession was the ideal weapon against those "declared to be a gangster."

Pinkerton illustrates the sort of disrespect for the constraints of legality that was to characterize the crime extermination campaign of the war on crime.[160] In this infamous conspiracy case from 1946, the Court turned a blind eye to the sweeping use of conspiracy law for the purpose of destroying criminal enterprises. By holding every "member" of a conspiracy liable for the substantive crimes of any other member, the Court equipped law enforcement officials combating underground criminal conspiracies with a powerful weapon to strike at the very heart of their enemy. Minor players could now be held vicariously liable for the acts of major ones. Facing serious punishment for acts they hadn't committed, the former could be turned against the latter, enabling police to crack the group.

Possession offenses spring from the same eagerness to suppress crime by any means necessary, born of a perception of criminal law as the struggle against an alien threat. Possession provides state officials with a flexible policing tool and flouts almost every principle of criminal law along the way, including the act requirement, the prohibition against status offenses, the general resistance to omission liability, the mens rea requirement, and the principle of personal—as opposed to group—liability.[161]

Combining conspiracy and possession, as in *Pinkerton*, produces a formidable policing tool. Conspiracy is an inchoate crime, that is, a crime that inflicts no harm. So is possession. A conspiracy to possess thus is an inchoate inchoate crime. Specifically, it is a plan to engage in a nonharmful nonact, or to share in a state, that of possessing something that may be used in a harmful way.

Like conspiracy, possession offenses also have been used to impose liability on entire groups of people. Whereas the law of complicity has long been careful to remind itself that mere presence does not an accomplice make, the law of possession has had no difficulty imposing liability on that very basis. We've already noted that being in the presence of contraband is enough to establish a presumption of possession.[162] Possession therefore often becomes a group affair, with everyone in a room, or everyone in a car, being found in possession of a gun, or a bag of marijuana.

Lanzetta and *Pinkerton* illustrate the use of possession offenses to police groups perceived as threatening to the state, gangsters and "conspiracies," respectively. The 1965 case of *Stanford v. Texas* shows how possession offenses can be employed against a particular type of group, a political party. By criminalizing the possession of "books, records, pamphlets, cards, receipts, lists, memoranda, pictures, recordings and other written instruments concerning the Communist Party of Texas, and the operations of the Communist Party in Texas,"[163] Texas authorized state officials to rummage through the homes of suspected sympathizers in order to nip the Communist threat in the bud. The mere possession of this explosive literature represented the first step along a continuum that was sure to lead from distribution to agitation and, eventually, to revolution.

It's no surprise, then, that so-called profiles should play such an important role in policing possession. Possession offenses are committed by certain people who fit a certain image. An item that is perfectly harmless in the hands of a decent member of society becomes a threat to the survival of that society in the hands of an outsider. In this respect, it's the possessor who makes the possession criminal. And possession merely provides the formal justification, the pretext, for the harassment of persons who arouse suspicion because of their membership in some group that remains ill defined precisely because its distinguishing characteristic is its difference from the ingroup, the society whose safety the state is charged with protecting against outside threats. Profiles are a post hoc attempt to justify an ad hoc suspicion whose true basis remains hidden, often even to the person harboring it. Nonetheless, the Supreme Court has not stood in the way of the widespread use of profiles in the crime war effort.[164]

The war on crime would have been impossible without a dramatic expansion of federal criminal law. Begun as a presidential police action, the war on crime became a national crime suppression campaign through a remarkable expansion of federal criminal law and the close coordination of federal and state criminal law. The possession cases before the Supreme Court bear witness to both phenomena. On the subject of expanding federal criminal law, the Court has proved remarkably reticent. For instance, much of its (nonconstitutional) jurisprudence on mens rea (and ignorance of law) can be found in opinions that narrowly construe federal possession statutes, and gun possession statutes in particular.[165] Again and again, the Court was surprisingly receptive to the argument that a statute that criminalized "knowing" possession of a weapon required the prosecution to prove not only that the possessor knew he was possessing a certain gun (a mens rea issue) but also that he knew that knowingly possessing that particular gun was illegal (an ignorance-of-law issue). In the face of the age-old common law maxim that ignorance of the law is no excuse, this receptivity may well reflect a general uneasiness with the federal government's assumption of criminal lawmaking powers traditionally reserved for the states. In its uneasiness, the Court even found itself invoking the principle of lenity, which provides that ambiguous criminal statutes are to be interpreted in favor of the defendant, a principle it had no difficulty ignoring on other occasions.[166] Quiet discomfort recently turned into open obstruction when the Court dusted off the commerce clause to *strike down* a federal statute that criminalized gun possession, in this case gun possession near a school.[167]

Still, the Court's occasional resistance to the expansion of *federal* criminal law, and of federal criminal possession law in particular, should not be mistaken for unwillingness to further the crime war effort in general. The war on crime, after all, is not being fought with federal law alone, and even the federal arsenal of possession offenses is hardly depleted by the loss of an offense as inconsequential as the prohibition of gun possession near a school. Who needs a federal offense like that if a state offense of simple drug possession, anywhere and anytime, calls for a mandatory life sentence without the possibility of parole?[168]

And if the state sentence is not enough, the coordination of state and federal crime suppression, combined with the inapplicability of double jeopardy to punishment by separate sovereigns, allows for the extension of incapacitation, if necessary. The Court has done its share to facilitate this coordination, as illustrated by the recent case of *United States v. Gonzales*.[169] A popular federal statute, 18 U.S.C. § 924(c), provides that "any person who, during and in relation to any crime of violence or drug trafficking crime, . . . uses or carries a firearm . . . shall, in addition to the punishment provided for such crime of violence or drug trafficking crime, . . . be sentenced to a term of imprisonment of not less than 5 years. . . ."[170] The statute further provides that "no term of imprisonment imposed on a person under this subsection shall run concurrently with any other term of imprisonment imposed on the person."

Gonzales and two others had been sentenced in state court to prison terms of from thirteen to seventeen years for drug offenses and for having pulled guns on undercover officers during a "drug sting operation." While in state prison, they were indicted in federal court for the same conduct and convicted, once more, of drug offenses, including possession, and of "using firearms during and in relation" to those crimes in violation of § 924(c). There they "received sentences ranging from 120 to 147 months in prison, of which 60 months reflected the mandatory sentence required for their firearms convictions." The Tenth Circuit held that the sixty months for the firearms offenses could run concurrently, not consecutively, with the defendants' state and federal sentences for the drug offenses.[171]

The Supreme Court reversed, however, deciding that Congress meant what it said when it provided that "a prison sentence under 18 U.S.C. § 924(c) shall [not] . . . run concurrently with any other term of imprisonment," whether imposed by a state or a federal court. As a result, the federal-state collaboration in this case resulted in an additional five-year period of incapacitation for three "drug offenders" who had threatened federal officers.

Gonzales and his partners in crime, however, got off easy. In its current form, section 924(c) mandates not only a five-year minimum sentence for gun possession during a drug or violent crime but also a *twenty-five year* minimum sentence for "a second or subsequent conviction under this subsection."[172] That second conviction, however, can result from the same plea agreement (or trial, should there be one). Enterprising Assistant U.S. Attorneys fighting the war on crime therefore can dramatically expand 924(c)'s incapacitative potential—sixfold, from five to thirty years—by tying the possession of a single weapon to different counts arising out of a single drug transaction, such as distribution and possession. The first five years would be for possessing a gun in connection with the drug offense of *distribution*, and the second twenty-five for possessing the same gun in connection with the drug offense of *possession*. And that mandatory thirty-year sentence would be tacked onto whatever other sentence the court imposed for the two drug offenses (distribution and possession), on top of any state sentence imposed for the same offenses, as Gonzales found out. In a recent case out of Rochester, New York, this multiple possession bootstrapping strategy (from drug possession to gun possession to second gun possession of the same gun) netted the prosecutor a sentence of 477 months, or roughly forty years.[173]

When the Supreme Court does resolve an issue in a way that might be perceived as interfering with the executive flexibility required for an effective anticrime campaign, Congress steps in to iron out the wrinkles. In *Gonzales*, the drug offenders were charged with "using" a gun. In an earlier case, *Bailey v. United States*, the Supreme Court had decided, quite sensibly but against several circuits, that "mere" possession didn't amount to "use" for purposes of § 924(c).[174] Congress quickly corrected this misunderstanding by amending § 924(c) explicitly to include "any person who, during and in relation to any crime of violence or drug trafficking crime . . . , in furtherance of any such crime, *possesses a firearm*," thus at the same time reelevating possession to its proper status in the war on crime and rendering the old "uses or carries" clause superfluous.[175]

The declaration that "possession" wasn't "use" under § 924(c) didn't mean that possession alone wouldn't result in a higher sentence. This two-track approach to the significance of gun possession in drug offenses, denying it on the one hand while affirming it on the other, was made possible by another important prong of the war on crime, the federal sentencing guidelines, which helped coordinate the crime war, both within the federal system and without, and gave its incapacitative measures the necessary bite. For, already at the time of *Bailey*, the relevant sentencing guideline provided for a two-level enhancement for drug offenses, including possession with intent and simple possession, "[i]f a dangerous weapon (including a firearm) was possessed."[176]

The mandatory federal sentencing guidelines made a comprehensive federal war on crime possible by keeping in line federal judges, some of whom might have been tempted to blunt the incapacitative blow of particular provisions. And the Supreme Court significantly enhanced the guidelines' coordinating potential, by first upholding the guidelines against a host of constitutional attacks and then declaring their every word, from guidelines to policy statements to commentary, to constitute binding authority on the federal courts.[177]

The federal guidelines, however, also contributed to the war effort beyond the borders of federal criminal law. They helped initiate and, backed by federal grants, significantly shaped a national move toward determinate sentencing. Even if the federal guidelines themselves could not be exported to the states for the simple reason that federal law differed from state law, their concept of controlling judicial sentencing authority could be, and was. As a result, not only the federal government but also state governments could implement their crime war initiatives without undue interference, no matter how timid and sporadic, from the judiciary.

The federal guidelines, however, were not only mandatory. They also were draconian. The elimination of parole alone—under the heading of "honesty in sentencing"—dramatically expanded the incapacitative potential of existing criminal law. The guidelines created a criminal law behind or, rather, beneath the criminal law, a system of punishment that operated beyond constitutional constraints. They reflected a general shift from the law of crimes to the law of punishments, from conviction to sentencing. In this system, the precise nature of the offense of conviction mattered less and less, and sentence enhancements mattered more and more. What a defendant was convicted of became less important than *that* he was convicted of something, which then marked him for incapacitation to the greatest extent possible. That extent, in turn, was determined by sentence enhancements, chief among them enhancements for gun possession.

Possession Plus

Section 924(c), the federal sentence premium for gun possession in furtherance of a "drug trafficking crime" (including possession) as well as of "any crime of violence," merely illustrates a more general incapacitative strategy of using possession *indirectly* to increase the incapacitative potential of a given conviction. In this indirect use, gun possession in particular ensures that dangerous offenders will stay off the street longer than they otherwise would have.

As we have seen, the versatility of possession as an instrument of threat suppression is remarkable. So far we have focussed on one application of possession offenses, their *direct* use as the offense of arrest and conviction, even if only as the fallback velcro charge that always sticks, for the simple reason that possession is as easy to detect as it is to prove. Possession, however, has many indirect uses, as well.

Aggravation

The most obvious *indirect* use of possession is as an aggravating or predicate element in another offense or as a sentence premium, which amounts to the same thing: the fact of possession increases the incapacitative potential of the underlying offense. This technique is particularly popular in the case of gun possession. Our modern statute books overflow with offenses whose severity is enhanced by the addition of proof—either at trial or at sentencing—of gun possession. For instance, the original federal carjacking statute was defined in terms of gun possession: "Whoever, possessing a firearm . . . , takes a motor vehicle . . ."[178] In New York, one variety of first-degree trespass is defined as "[p]ossess[ing], or know[ing] that another participant in the crime possesses, an explosive or a deadly weapon."[179] Felon in possession of a firearm, a federal felony, is among the predicate offenses that can add up to a RICO violation.[180]

And the federal sentencing guidelines provide for harsher sentences in cases of minor assault ("if a dangerous weapon (including a firearm) was possessed and its use was threatened"[181]) and stalking ("possession, or threatened use, of a dangerous weapon"[182]).

In general, legislatures prefer to use gun possession as a sentence enhancement, rather than as an offense element. That way, the prosecutor can make full use of the incapacitative potential of possession without having to establish it under the burden of proof at trial (beyond a reasonable doubt), should there be a trial. Instead, the judge can enhance the sentence after the conviction or, more likely, the guilty plea, upon a showing of possession by a mere preponderance of the evidence. In 1986, the Supreme Court explicitly endorsed this circumvention of constitutional constraints on criminal lawmaking, in *McMillan v. Pennsylvania*,[183] showing remarkable deference to the legislature's classification of gun possession as a sentencing factor, rather than as an offense element, in the process.

Possession offenses serve to extend—or replenish—the incapacitative potential of convictions (which, of course, may be for possession offenses themselves, as in the case of drug possession under § 924(c)) not only at sentencing but also at later points in the life of a person who has been marked as a threat to society. Most immediately, possession offenses are used to police and, if possible, to further incapacitate persons under supervised release (parole and probation), four million by last count. Federal law, for instance, mandates the revocation of supervised release if a "defendant . . . possesses a controlled substance . . . [or] possesses a firearm . . . in violation of Federal law, or otherwise violates a condition of supervised release prohibiting the defendant from possessing a firearm. . . ."[184]

Next, and most intrusively, possession offenses play an important role in the policing of the roughly two million people under supervised *non*-release, prison inmates. In prison, the prohibition of possession, as a matter of prison discipline, helps complete the incapacitation of human threats during their period of incarceration and, if necessary, allows the extension of that period as a matter of criminal law. Prisoners are considered so dangerous that they are presumptively prohibited from possessing anything. In the hands of a prison inmate, anything is a dangerous weapon. A prison inmate cannot be trusted to possess the most innocuous items, including toothbrushes, coat hangers, and radio antennas. (Possessing telescoping radio antennas, for example, is forbidden "because they might be turned into 'zip guns.' By inserting a bullet into the base of an extended antenna and then quickly compressing it, an inmate could fire the inaccurate but still potentially deadly gun.")[185] Anything in the possession of a prison inmate, through mere association with this human threat, becomes tainted. That taint can be removed only by an affirmative license granted by the administrator of the prison, the prison police.

Prison management is threat management. And the first line of defense against prisoner threats is the prohibition of possession, except as permitted by the prison police. As Ted Conover reports, prisoners at Sing Sing

> couldn't possess clothing in any of the colors reserved for officers: gray, black, blue, and orange. They couldn't possess cash, cassette players with a record function, toiletries containing alcohol, sneakers worth more than fifty dollars, or more than fourteen newspapers. The list was very long—so long, in fact, that the authors of the *Standards of Inmate Behavior* found it easier to define what *was* permitted than what wasn't. Contraband was simply "*any article that is not authorized by the Superintendent or [his] designee.*"[186]

Like their analogues in the outside world, however, these prison possession prohibitions are violated every minute of every day. In fact, the more categorical a possession prohibition gets—and it can't get any more categorical than that applied to prisoners—the less categorical its enforcement tends to become. In Sing Sing, for example, where Conover worked as a prison guard, guards were as likely to violate the possession prohibitions that applied to them as prisoners were to violate their own. In prison, guards were barred from possessing "glass containers, chewing gum, pocket knives with blades longer than two inches, newspapers, magazines, beepers, cell phones, or . . . our own pistols or other weapons."[187] The reason for this prohibition was, once again, the constant threat personified by the *prisoners*, rather than by the guards themselves: "A glass container, such as a bottle of juice, might be salvaged from the trash by an inmate and turned into shards for weapons."[188] Smoking, whether by inmates or guards, was prohibited indoors. But, according to Conover, officers didn't pay much attention to these rules: "[P]lenty of officers smoked indoors. Many chewed gum. The trash cans of wall towers were stuffed with newspapers and magazines."[189]

Needless to say, prisoners found it even more difficult, if not downright impossible, to comply with the far stricter possession rules that applied to them. Again, Conover learned that contraband, in "its most obvious forms—weapons, drugs, and alcohol—could all be found fairly readily inside prison."[190] As a result, enforcing the possession prohibition against inmates became a matter of discretion. Guards knew that they could write up any prisoner for illegal possession of one item or another any time they decided to "look[] for contraband during pat-frisks of inmates and during random cell searches."[191] Possession violations thus became a convenient and flexible way of enforcing discipline, a trump card that could be drawn when needed to recommend to the "adjustment committee"[192] that an obstreperous inmate receive more intensive incapacitative treatment, perhaps by transferring him to the "special housing unit."

If necessary or convenient, possession violations could blossom into possession offenses. Possession of certain items by a prisoner is, after all, not merely a matter of prison discipline but also a matter of criminal law, an issue not only for the adjustment committee but also for a criminal court. Possession of a dangerous weapon by a prisoner is a serious offense; so is drug possession; as one might expect, prisoners are not among the privileged, or licensed, few who are exempted from the general prohibition against possessing such dangerous items. Some prison guards are.[193] Possession of weapons or drugs therefore can not only land a prisoner in solitary. It can also extend his stay in prison.[194]

Control by the possession police, however, doesn't end with the period of penal supervision, carceral or not. Certain possession offenders, in particular those labeled "felons," will find themselves back in prison even after their supervised release—or nonrelease—has ended. These felon-in-possession offenses have proved particularly powerful and popular possession police devices. They extend the period of possession police far beyond the period of punishment. Once a person has been marked a danger, a felon, he will be subject to police through possession no matter where he might be, and no matter how unsupervised he might be in theory.

We saw earlier how the federal-state war on crime, under the code name "Project Exile," uses the draconian federal felon-in-possession statute to take released felons back off the streets.[195] With the right felony priors, mere possession of a firearm will land a "felon" (as opposed to an "ex-felon") in prison for at least fifteen years.[196] And, thanks to "honesty in sentencing," a fifteen-year sentence in federal prison means what it says. Finding felons in possession, however, can be as easy as pulling someone over for rolling through a stop sign. The felon-in-possession statute gives the police terrific incapacitative bang for their investigative buck. There is something chillingly simple about the operation of possession police. As the slogan of Project Exile, prominently displayed on city bus shelters, explains "You + Illegal Gun = Federal Jail."[197]

Presumption

But possession, indirectly employed, does more than aggravate the incapacitative treatment of those marked as "convicts"; it also facilitates the marking itself. We've already seen how possession can be established with the help of evidentiary presumptions, which shift the burden of proof onto the alleged possessor. So presence quickly transforms itself into possession, unless the person present comes forward with a satisfactory explanation of his presence that blocks the transformation.[198]

But possession itself may function as presumptive evidence of another offense: it can be the source, as well as the target, of a presumptive inference. This presumption can either be explicit or implicit, and either backward or forward looking.

Among the explicit variety are retrospective presumptions of illegal acquisition, including importation, manufacture, transfer, even larceny.[199] Moving ahead in time, possession may be taken concurrently as presumptive evidence of knowing possession (knowing that and knowing what),[200] and then prospectively as presumptive evidence of possession with intent to use, where the nature of the use may or may not be further specified,[201] and in some cases both at the same time.[202] Presumptions of this sort are underhanded attempts to reduce simple possession offenses to strict liability offenses and compound possession offenses to simple possession offenses, or both.

Possession presumptions have become less significant since legislatures figured out that they could get away with criminalizing possession outright and punishing it severely. In that case, there would be no reason to have the prosecutor waste time establishing both possession and some ultimate fact that could be presumed from the possession, especially when the Supreme Court has scrutinized possession-based presumptions but not the outright proscription of possession.[203]

The more interesting case of possession as presumption, as opposed to possession as presumed, is that of an *implicit* presumption. This phenomenon goes to the heart of possession offenses for two reasons. First, it brings out the inchoate nature of possession. One way of thinking of possession offenses is to view them as criminalized presumptions of some other offense. In criminalizing possession, the legislature *really* criminalizes import, manufacture, purchase. Or, looking forward, the legislature *really* criminalizes use, sale, or export. In the latter variety, the prospective presumption resembles an implicit inchoate offense. So possession *really* is an attempt to use, sell, or export, or, more precisely, possession is an attempt to attempt to use, sell, or export, that is, an inchoate inchoate offense. Some courts have even recognized the offenses of attempted possession[204] and conspiracy to possess,[205] which adds an explicit inchoacy layer to the two implicit ones inherent in the concept of possession, resulting in an inchoate inchoate inchoate offense, a triple inchoacy.

Second, the implicit presumption inherent in the concept of a possession offense reveals the modus operandi of possession, the secret of its success as a policing tool beyond legal scrutiny. Possession succeeds because it removes all potentially troublesome features to the level of legislative or executive discretion, an area that is notoriously difficult to scrutinize. In its design and its application, possession is, in doctrinal terms, a doubly inchoate offense, one step farther from the actual infliction of personal harm than ordinary inchoate offenses such as attempt. In practical terms, it is an offense designed and applied to remove dangerous individuals even before they have had an opportunity to manifest their dangerousness in an ordinary inchoate offense. On its face, however, it does not look like an inchoate offense, nor does it look like a threat reduction measure that targets particular types of individuals.

The New Vagrancy

It is this sub rosa quality of possession that helps set it apart from its predecessor, vagrancy. Prior to the advent of possession police, vagrancy laws fulfilled a similar sweeping function. Yet, in comparison to possession, vagrancy laws are the blunt tools of oppression wielded by a state unsophisticated in the science of police control as public hygiene. Blessed with all the definitional flexibility and executory convenience of vagrancy, possession is superior to vagrancy in at least three respects.

Reach: Privacy! What Privacy?

Possession's first advantage is that is not a public offense; unlike vagrancy, possession can be committed in private, as well as in public. This means that the state, through a suspicion of possession, gains entry into the home of suspected danger sources or, while there, can detect evidence of possession. As we have seen, police officers are very good at finding illegally possessed items "in plain view" whenever they enter a residence or get a look inside a car for one reason or another.

This is the beauty of possession as a police instrument: anyone *can* possess anything anywhere anytime and *does* possess something anywhere anytime. Especially if one expansively defines possession to include constructive possession, the criminalization of possession presumptively criminalizes everyone everywhere. The ideal police environment, therefore, is the prison, where the possession of anything is presumptively forbidden and where, not by accident, the private sphere no longer exists.[206]

So far, the First Amendment appears to be the only constitutional barrier to a comprehensive possession police crossing the traditional—and traditionally impenetrable—border between public and private, the wall surrounding the proverbial home that is also my castle. In 1969, the Supreme Court declared categorically that the "private possession of obscene material may not be punished."[207] But, as the Court made very clear, that doesn't mean that there is anything wrong with "mak[ing] the [private or public] possession of other items, such as narcotics, firearms, or stolen goods, a crime," because "[n]o First Amendment rights are involved in most statutes making mere possession criminal." So, when in 1986 the Supreme Court upheld Georgia's criminal sodomy statute, it made no difference that the statute proscribed private, as well as public, conduct: "Victimless crimes, such as the possession and use of illegal drugs, do not escape the law where they are committed at home."[208]

The use of possession offenses to extend police regimes into the private sphere has a long tradition. Already the first English Metropolitan Police Courts Act of 1839 included not only several possession offenses, such as the possession of "instruments for unlawfully procuring and carrying away wine"[209] and of loaded guns on ships,[210] but also authorized police officers to enter and search private homes "in case of information given that there is reasonable cause for suspecting that any stolen goods are concealed in a dwelling house."[211] At about the same time in the American South, white slave patrols were authorized to rummage through the houses of blacks in search of illegally possessed weapons.[212] A few years later, American prohibitionary legislation backed up its criminalization of the possession of liquor by equipping local law enforcement officers with extensive powers to search private homes and confiscate illegally possessed liquor.[213]

In the contemporary United States, the irrelevance of privacy in the policing of possession as an incapacitation strategy generally remains a hidden, and therefore all the more convenient, feature of the war on crime. Occasionally, however, a legislature makes it explicit. So in the year 2000, a Connecticut law authorized police to enter private homes to seize *legally* possessed guns on the basis of a finding that the possessor might be "dangerous" to himself or others. Searches and confiscations under the law are based not on the commission of an offense of any kind but on other evidence of dangerousness. So, in one recent case, a Connecticut man found his mother's home searched and his legally possessed guns seized on the basis of allegations by two of his neighbors "that they'd had disputes with him and had observed him with a gun at his side."[214]

Convenience and Permanence: The Velcro Offense

Possession offenses also are far more efficient than the clunky, toothless vagrancy statutes of old; they give law enforcement officials much more bang for their buck. Penalties for vagrancy paled in comparison to those for possession. Although vagrants might be imprisoned for short terms, vagrancy laws were most important in low-level and continuous police harassment of undesirables. Already in colonial Virginia, we learn that "[v]ery few cases appear in the County Court records of Virginia of persons brought in solely for vagrancy. . . . But when a person was brought before the County Court for some other offense—a petty theft, for example—the fact that he was a vagabond might make the punishment a little more severe; or it might serve as an excuse for administering a whipping in case the other charge could not be completely proved."[215] And Christopher Tiedeman colorfully describes how vagrancy laws were used in late-nineteenth-century America to harass, and "warn out," the dangerous classes:

> A very large part of the duties of the police in all civilized countries is the supervision and control of the criminal classes, even when there are no specific charges of crime lodged against them. A suspicious character appears in some city, and is discovered by the police detectives. He bears upon his countenance the indelible stamp of criminal propensity, and he is arrested. There is no charge of crime against him. He may never have committed a crime, but he is arrested on the charge of vagrancy, and since by

the ordinary vagrant acts the burden is thrown upon the defendant to dis-prove the accusation, it is not difficult in most cases to fasten on him the offense of vagrancy, particularly as such characters will usually prefer to plead guilty, in order to avoid, if possible, a too critical examination into their mode of life. But to punish him for vagrancy is not the object of his arrest. The police authorities had, with an accuracy of judgment only to be acquired by a long experience with the criminal classes, determined that he was a dangerous character; and the magistrate, in order to rid the town of his presence, threatens to send him to jail for vagrancy if he does not leave the place within twenty-four hours. In most cases, the person thus sum-marily dealt with has been already convicted of some crime, is known as a confirmed criminal, and his photograph has a place in the "rogues' gallery."[216]

Equipped with an arsenal of possession offenses, today's law enforce-ment official has no reason to confine herself to expelling dangerous ele-ments, knowing full well that they may soon find their way back into town. Now she can incapacitate them through substantial prison terms, after a summary process that will take little more of her time. Today's possessor faces not the choice between a short stay in jail and hitting the road. Instead, he finds himself choosing between pleading to a five-year prison term and taking the chance of spending the rest of his life behind bars after a jury trial, where the deck is stacked decisively in the state's favor.[217]

Impunity: The Teflon Offense

Most important, possession is far less susceptible to legal challenges than vagrancy. Vagrancy had been the police sweep offense of choice for centuries until vagrancy statutes began to run into constitutional trouble in the 1960s. Vagrancy statutes were too explicit in their criminalization of status without any particular criminal act and in their delegation of in-terpretive discretion to frontline police officers. So courts began to strike down vagrancy statutes that targeted "disorderly persons" or even "suspi-cious persons" and thus gave free rein to police officers and their fellow "criminal administrators," sympathetic local magistrates and justices of the peace, to cleanse their community of undesirables, among whom one could find a disproportionate percentage of racial minorities, poor peo-ple, and other outsiders.

Historically, twentieth-century American vagrancy laws had replaced even more obvious and oppressive attempts to dispose of undesirables.

While, according to a study by Eric Foner, "most provisions" of the Black Codes passed by southern legislatures immediately after emancipation "were quickly voided by the army or Freemen's Bureau, or invalidated by the Civil Rights Act of 1866," the vagrancy statutes remained in force, presumably because they were racially neutral, at least on their face. Thus immunized from legal challenges, they could fulfill their function of policing newly freed blacks in the field. As Foner points out,

> [w]hat is critical is the manner of their enforcement, and in the South of 1865 and 1866, with judicial and police authority in the hands of the planter class and its friends, impartial administration was an impossibility. Many southern vagrancy laws, in fact, contained no reference to race. But as John W. DuBose, the Alabama planter and Democratic politico later remarked, "the vagrant contemplated was the plantation negro."[218]

The vagrancy laws' immunity survived for another hundred years, when they themselves fell prey to judges who were willing to look behind the abstract letter of the law to its meaning on the streets. Possession offenses represent the next generation of general police measures. They make no reference to race or any other suspect classification. In fact, they make no explicit reference to any sort of status. By contrast, vagrancy statutes brimmed with descriptions of types, rather than of acts, which—given the act requirement in criminal law—invited scrutiny. Their objective was to define not vagrant acts but vagrants. Those who fit the definition were not convicted of vagrancy but "deemed vagrants." Take, for example, the Florida vagrancy statute eventually invalidated by the Supreme Court in the 1972 case of *Papachristou v. City of Jacksonville*:

> Rogues and vagabonds, or dissolute persons who go about begging, common gamblers, persons who use juggling or unlawful games or plays, common drunkards, common night walkers, thieves, pilferers or pickpockets, traders in stolen property, lewd, wanton and lascivious persons, keepers of gambling places, common railers and brawlers, persons wandering or strolling around from place to place without any lawful purpose or object, habitual loafers, disorderly persons, persons neglecting all lawful business and habitually spending their time by frequenting houses of ill fame, gaming houses, or places where alcoholic beverages are sold or served, persons able to work but habitually living upon the earnings of their wives or minor children shall be deemed vagrants. . . .[219]

A statute as broad and rambling as this, straining to capture the image of disagreeable people, even looks like the sweep it is obviously designed to facilitate. It bespeaks the very irrationality and arbitrariness it attempts to justify.

It didn't help matters that the pedigree of these statutes was fraught with arbitrary and thinly veiled oppression. This history extended past the post–Civil War Black Codes through colonial America and the complex English system of poor police of the sixteenth, seventeenth, and eighteenth centuries and eventually to the first English poor laws of the fourteenth century. The new colonies took up the task of policing vagrants almost immediately. The establishment and refinement of the vagrancy regime in colonial Virginia may serve as an illustration:

> In 1672 the Assembly found it necessary to order that the English laws against vagrants should be strictly enforced. The chief of these laws was the 39 Eliz., chapter 4 (1597), which permitted the erection of houses of correction in any county, and directed that rogues and vagabonds were to be whipped by order of a justice, constable, or tithingman, and sent to their own parishes, there to be put in the house of correction until employment was found for them, or until they were banished. The law of 1 James I, chapter 7 (1604), provided that incorrigible and dangerous rogues might by order of the justices be branded with the letter R. . . . The English statute 17 Geo. II, chapter 5, repealed the earlier laws on vagrancy, and went on to provide for the punishment of idle and disorderly persons, vagabonds, and incorrigible rogues. It was from this statute that the Assembly copied extensively in 1748. . . . The law defined vagabonds, and provided that they were to be taken by warrant before a justice, who might order them whipped from constable to constable like runaways, until they reached the parish in which their families last resided. At that point the local justices were to take a bond that the delinquents would find work. Failing this, the next County Court might bind such persons to work for a year.[220]

Efforts to control this dangerous class continued uninterrupted and virtually unchanged through the nineteenth century and were by no means confined to the South, as an opinion of the Ohio Supreme Court upholding a vagrancy statute in the year 1900 makes very clear:

> The act in question undertakes to define a tramp, or vagrant, by stating what acts shall constitute such character. It is, in the main, the old method of describing a vagrant, and vagrancy, time out of mind, has been deemed a condition calling for special statutory provisions, i.e., such as may tend to suppress the mischief and protect society. These provisions rest upon the economic truth that industry is necessary for the preservation of society, and that he who, being able to work, and not able otherwise to support

himself, deliberately plans to exist by the labor of others, is an *enemy to society* and to the commonwealth.[221]

Possession offenses not only avoid explicitly criminalizing types but they also steer clear of criminalizing facially innocent conduct, such as the "wandering or strolling around from place to place without any lawful purpose or object," which drew such derision from the Supreme Court in *Papachristou*.[222]

Compared to the bumbling vagrancy laws, which, on their face, looked as suspicious as the types they described, possession offenses look very much like modern criminal statutes. On their face, one finds no description of types and no reference to status, no awkward definition of facially innocent conduct, in fact no definition of conduct of any kind.

So possession is, on the face of it, neither status offense nor conduct offense. As a result, it is immune against all challenges. It is the phantom offense of modern American criminal law, everywhere yet nowhere, an offense so flexible that it no longer is an offense but a scheme, a means of surreptitiously expanding the reach of existing criminal prohibitions, of transforming them into instruments of incapacitation. Neither fish nor foul, possession is sui generis, the general part of criminal law as police control of undesirables, the paradigmatic modern police offense.

To appreciate its function and the complexity of its operation, one must scratch the surface of this apparently bland, yet ubiquitous and potent offense. So far we have taken the first step toward understanding possession by identifying it as a phenomenon. Normally, the offense goes about its work unnoticed as it disappears in its myriad particular manifestations. So discussions of the "legalization" of drugs as a rule ignore the technique by which drugs are "criminalized." But the criminalization of drugs means the criminalization of their possession. Similarly, any debate about gun "control" always also is a debate about gun possession.

Once the teflon layer has been stripped away, possession emerges as an offense that closely resembles its predecessor, vagrancy, in substance if not in form. Possession does what vagrancy did, only better and behind a legitimate façade.

Behind the Façade

Let us begin with the obvious. It is true that possession is not a conduct offense. As commentators have pointed out for centuries, possession is not an act; it is a state of being, a status.[223] To possess something is to *be* in possession of it.

To dismiss possession simply on the ground that it violates the so-called act requirement of Anglo-American criminal law, however, would be premature. The act requirement, from the outset, applied to common law offenses only, that is, to offenses that traced their origins back through a grand chain of common law precedents, rather than to a specific statute that created a new offense. Certainly, the concept of common law offenses was malleable, so judges had some discretion in treating a particular offense as a common law or as a statutory offense. That's not the point here, however. The point is that English judges, from very early on, threw out possession indictments as violative of the act requirement only if they alleged a *common law* offense of possession, rather than invoking a *statutory* possession provision. Once it was settled that the possession indictment was brought under one of the increasing number of possession statutes, the common law's act requirement was no longer an issue.[224] The act requirement was as irrelevant to statutory possession as the mens rea requirement was to "statutory" rape.[225]

The common law's act requirement, therefore, does not stand in the way of modern possession statutes. And the thin slice of the act requirement constitutionalized by the U.S. Supreme Court in the (decidedly pre-crime war) 1962 case of *Robinson v. California*[226] also can do little, by itself, to challenge possession offenses. The constitutional act requirement merely prohibits the criminalization of addiction in particular, and of sickness in general (or at least "having a common cold").[227] Possession doesn't criminalize an illness, at least not directly. The Supreme Court in *Robinson* went out of its way to reassure legislatures that they remained free to "impose criminal sanctions . . . against the unauthorized manufacture, prescription, sale, purchase, or *possession* of narcotics."[228]

Then there is the general uneasiness regarding omission offenses characteristic of American criminal law. Absent a clear duty to act, the failure to act is not criminal. If possession isn't an act, perhaps one should think of it as an omission, the omission to get rid of the item one possesses.[229] But what is the duty that compels me to drop the shiny new pistol my friend has just bought himself at the local gun store, or to toss out the baggie of cocaine I noticed in the glove compartment of my rental car? If one looked hard enough, perhaps one could find such a duty nestled in the criminalization of a possession that is defined as the failure to end it. But the point of requiring a specific duty for omission liability, the significance of the general unwillingness to criminalize omission, is precisely to reject omission liability absent specific and unambiguous provisions to the contrary. Still, by itself, the disfavored status of omissions does not imply rejecting possession liability.

And the same could be said about the abandonment of another ironclad principle of Anglo-American criminal law, mens rea. Some possession offenses, after all, do away not only with the—even more iron clad—requirement of an actus reus but also with the requirement of criminal intent.[230] If this absence of mens rea alone would condemn possession offenses to illegitimacy, the bulk of modern American criminal law would suffer the same fate.

Finally, as discussed earlier, one might try to domesticate possession offenses by categorizing them as a kind of inchoate offense. To pick a familiar example, the simple possession of certain large quantities of drugs can be seen as an attempt to sell them. Possession in this case would be a kind of inchoate inchoate offense, an attempted attempt, perhaps. Inchoate liability, however, much like omission liability, is disfavored in traditional Anglo-American law and therefore limited to cases where the offender acted with the specific intent to bring about the proscribed harm. But, by definition, that intent is missing in a simple possession offense, as opposed to a compound possession offense, which requires proof of an intent to use the object possessed in one way or another. Punishing simple possession as a quasi-inchoate offense, therefore, would violate the general rule that inchoate liability requires specific intent. As nineteenth-century cases emphasized again and again, in terms reminiscent of the theory of attempt liability, it was the *intent* to use the objects in a proscribed way that justified criminalizing compound possession, *not* the possession itself: "The offense consists not in the possession of [adulterated] milk . . . but in the *intent* to sell or exchange" it.[231] Lacking this all-important intent element, the prohibition of simple possession obviously could not avail itself of this justification.

The point of this litany of difficulties is not to suggest that any or each of them taken individually exposes the illegitimacy of possession offenses. Instead, we learn two things from this quick diagnosis. First, we come to recognize that possession is sui generis and therefore subject neither to traditional categories of criminal liability nor to traditional avenues of critique. Second, and more important, we come to appreciate just how anxious the modern state is to pursue its incapacitative mission, so eager, in fact, that it is willing to enlist the services of an offense that runs afoul of most, if not all, of the fundamental tenets of traditional American criminal law.

What's more, it is the very fact that possession ignores so many of the basic rules, even bedrock principles, of traditional American criminal law that turns it into such an attractive weapon in the war on crime. This is so because every substantive principle has its procedural analogue. Without actus reus, no act needs to be proved. Without mens rea, no evidence of intent is required. Without omission, there's no need to establish a duty. Without inchoacy, the prosecutor can do without proving specific intent. Possession is unclassifiable; it is everything and nothing, an unspecifiable offense for a task best left unspecified: the control of undesirables.

It is this control function of possession that is most troubling, not its tensions with established principles of criminal law doctrine. Possession offenses are wolves in sheep's skin, highly efficient instruments of oppression and discrimination that have been camouflaged as run-of-the-mill criminal offenses and thereby protected against legal challenges and shielded from public scrutiny.

It is true that, on the surface, possession offenses don't stand out among the offense definitions in the special part of our modern criminal codes. They are professionally short and to the point, in welcome contrast to vagrancy's amateurishly rambling laundry lists of suspicious types. But, as soon as one looks beyond the definition of a core possession offense like "criminal possession of a weapon,"[232] one finds lists, lists of types! These lists take one of two forms: they are either lists of the policed[233] or lists of the police.[234] The former are modern versions of the lists of those "deemed to be vagrants," the latter of those who do the deeming. "Whoever" fits a type on the first list may not possess a gun. "Whoever" fits a type on the second list is not only entitled to possess a gun but is exempt from the law criminalizing its possession. The former cannot legally possess a gun; the latter cannot illegally possess one.

It turns out that, instead of replacing vagrancy's list of types, a gun possession statute like the one in the New York Penal Law simply removes the list from the definition of the offense to another, subsidiary part of the statute. This strategy of burying the troubling aspect of a criminal statute in the fine print has proved popular in the war on crime. So legislatures have been fond of classifying aggravating factors—including, as we saw earlier, gun possession—as sentencing considerations, thereby insulating these provisions from constitutional attack and, thanks to the lower burden of proof at sentencing, simplifying their application, all at once.

Two types appear again and again on the list of dangerous characters prohibited categorically from possessing a gun: convicted felons[235] and aliens.[236] The justification for inclusion of the former is explicitly based on dangerousness considerations: convicted felons are "persons who, by their actions, have demonstrated that they are dangerous, or that they may become dangerous. Stated simply, they may not be trusted to possess a firearm without becoming a threat to society."[237] Presumably, aliens too are potential threats to society simply on account of their outsider status.

"Convicted felons" and "aliens" thus resemble the targets of vagrancy laws, who too were considered far too dangerous to possess a gun.[238] "The vagrant," as one commentator remarked in 1886, "has been very appropriately described as the chrysalis of every species of criminal."[239] Vagrants were members of a permanent underclass who, by moving about the land without attachment to a recognized unit of social control, such as a household, an employer, a school, or a prison, were by their very nature disobedient, disorderly, and therefore dangerous. Congregating under bridges and in other hidden places, they constituted a constant conspiracy against innocent and hardworking citizens who knew their place in orderly society. They were a breeding ground of criminality, a menace to society.

The point is not simply that vagrants, like convicted felons and aliens today, were not allowed to possess guns. The larger point is that members of these groups are considered by their nature to be dangerous simply on account of that membership, without any need to assess their dangerousness individually. The prohibition of gun possession is merely symptomatic of this general classification by type. Those deemed to be "felons," "aliens," or "vagrants" are inherently dangerous and therefore cannot be trusted to possess a gun without putting it to harmful use. Once a felon, always a felon.

To prohibit not merely possession but possession by a certain type of person is to create a double status offense. To *be* in possession is a status. And to *be* a felon, or alien, or youth, or insane person in possession is another status. So a felon in possession is punished for the status of being a "felon" and of being "in possession." This makes "Felon in Possession of a Firearm . . . the prototypical status offense," as a federal court recently put it.[240]

Lumping together felons and aliens in this way may seem odd, but it is not unusual. Aliens and felons also share other disqualifications, including the prohibition against voting,[241] holding elected office,[242] and serving on juries[243] or as judges, prosecutors, police officers, prison guards, or wardens.[244] In other words, since felons and aliens have no say in the making, application, or enforcement of police regulations or the criminal law, for that matter, they consistently find themselves among the policed, rather than the police, among the objects, rather than the subjects of police. They are by their nature excluded from the political community, outsiders by definition.

One way of thinking about the list of classes whose members are bound to wreak havoc with a gun is to recognize it as establishing an irrebuttable presumption that anyone who matches the type is not of "good character" and cannot give a "good account of himself." From this perspective, two key characteristics of possession offenses clearly emerge, each of which highlights the similarities between possession- and vagrancy-based police regimes: their incorporation into a comprehensive policing scheme driven by the discretion of state officials and their heavy reliance on presumptions of dangerousness, general and specific.

By the eighteenth century, English vagrancy laws belonged to a complex scheme for the control of deviants, which began with sureties and ended with whipping and imprisonment. According to Blackstone, sureties for keeping the peace or for good behavior were "intended merely for prevention, without any crime actually committed by the party, but arising only from a probable suspicion, that some crime is intended or likely to happen. . . ."[245] Any justice of the peace could demand such a guarantee on his own discretion or at the request of any person upon "due cause."[246] If the bound person violated the conditions of his bond (to keep the peace or to show good behavior), he forfeited to the king the amount posted. Most interesting for our purposes, the recognizance for good behavior "towards the king and his people" applied to "all them that be not of good fame." Just who fell in this category was up to the individual justice of the peace:

> Under the general words of this expression, that be not of good fame, it is holden that a man may be bound to his good behaviour for causes of scandal, contra bonos mores, as well as contra pacem; as, for haunting bawdy houses with women of bad fame; or of keeping such women in his own house; or for words tending to scandalize the government; or in abuse of the officers of justice, especially in the execution of their office. Thus also a justice may bind over all night-walkers; eaves-droppers; such as keep suspicious company, or are reported to be pilferers or robbers; such as sleep in the day, and wake on the night; common drunkards; whoremasters; the

putative fathers of bastards; cheats; idle vagabonds; and other persons, whose misbehaviour may reasonably bring them within the general words of the statute. . . .[247]

There was, in other words, substantial overlap between those subject to regulation by sureties and those in danger of being classified as vagrants; "idle vagabonds" were explicitly listed as in need of control through sureties of the peace. In fact, the vagrancy laws can be see as a fall-back option, should the sureties prove unsuccessful. By the eighteenth century, vagrancy laws grouped vagrants into three categories:[248] "idle and disorderly persons" (punished by one month's imprisonment), "rogues and vagabonds" (whipping and imprisonment up to six months); and "incorrigible rogues" (whipping and imprisonment up to two years). The severity of the sanction increased as the amenability to treatment decreased. While the least serious type of vagrant retained the title of a "person" with the incidental qualities of being "idle and disorderly," the more serious types were defined exclusively by their deviant status: they were "rogues and vagabonds," rather than persons. Any hope for a reclassification as a person was lost in the case of the most aggravated type of vagrant, the "incorrigible rogue."

All of these vagrants posed a threat simply through their existence. They were, in Blackstone's words, "offenders against the good order, and blemishes in the government, of any kingdom."[249] As blemishes, they had to be removed, through reeducation or, if inherently and unalterably deviant, incapacitation.

The dangerous classes, then, were subject to a three-step police regime. First came the surety bond, designed to avert the manifestation of the threat by tying it to conditional financial loss. Next, for threats so substantial as not to be amenable to such inducements for self-correction, came the forced correction through fines, whipping, infamous punishments, or imprisonment. And, finally, for the incorrigible rogues beyond all hope of reintegration, there was the prospect of incapacitation through prolonged and repeated imprisonment. At each level, a presumption of dangerousness attached upon an initial suspicion of "being not of good fame" or "being idle or disorderly," which could be rebutted by proof to a justice of peace who enjoyed wide discretion, assuming of course that one's initial attempt to remove the suspicion of the police officer (or concerned citizen), who enjoyed even wider discretion, proved unsuccessful.

In the case of gun possession offenses, a modern possession police regime like New York's operates much like a full-fledged vagrancy regime. The criminalization of possession essentially sets up two presumptions of dangerousness, one rebuttable, the other not. Gun possession is presumptively illegal.[250] It is up to the state, in its discretion, to grant licenses to those whom it deems insufficiently dangerous in general and insufficiently likely to use a gun to harm others. The state is not required to issue a gun license to anyone. Gun possession is a matter not of right but of grace.[251] For this reason, an applicant for a gun license also is not entitled to an administrative hearing, though the state may grant him one, again in its discretion.[252] The presumption of dangerousness becomes irrebuttable when the individual has revealed himself to be inherently dangerous, as in the case of "felons."

But how can an applicant for a gun license remove the presumption of dangerousness? By convincing a "licensing officer," in large cities a member of the police department's license division, that he is "of good moral character."[253] And, like the English justice of the peace, the state licensing officer enjoys virtually unlimited discretion in deciding whether the applicant is "not of good fame."[254] Felons are by definition not "of good character"; that's what it means to *be* a felon. And so are aliens who, also by definition, have not been found to be "a person of good moral character, attached to the principles of the Constitution of the United States, and well disposed to the good order and happiness of the United States."[255]

The use of presumptions, however, is not limited to gun possession offenses. We already have discussed at some length the specific evidentiary presumptions that emanate from and point toward possession.[256] The very concept of possession liability is based on the presumption that the possession of certain items by certain people is inherently dangerous and therefore worthy of police investigation, if not of outright interference by seizing the possessors and the item possessed for incapacitative purposes. Ill-defined presumptions granting ill-defined discretion to police officials have accompanied possession offenses at least since the late eighteenth century, when the state began to tap the police potential of possession offenses. For example, the English Frauds by Workmen Act of 1777 defined the following new possession offense: "having in his or her possession any materials suspected to be purloined or embezzled, and not producing the party or parties being duly intitled [*sic*] to dispose of the same, of whom he or she bought or received the same, nor *giving a satisfactory ac-*

count how he or she came by the same."[257] Similarly, the 1851 Act for the Better Prevention of Offences imposed a prison sentence of up to three years on anyone "found by Night having in his Possession *without lawful Excuse* (the Proof of which Excuse shall lie on such Person) any Picklock Key, Crow, Jack, Bit, or other Implement of Housebreaking."[258]

Not even the licensing scheme is unique to gun possession offenses. Drug possession offenses operate in much the same way.[259] Once again, the possession of certain "controlled" substances is presumptively illegal. A controlled substance is a substance subject to a license requirement. Possession is legal only to the extent authorized by the state. That authorization, that license, is granted to particular groups of persons.

Licensing is less important in the case of drug possession offenses simply because so few licenses are granted. As a result, drug possession is criminal for almost everyone. This means that, for all intents and purposes, the presumption of dangerousness is irrebuttable in drug possession cases. Everyone is presumed to be incapable of putting the inherently dangerous drug to harmless use. Given the addictive potential of drugs, their very dangerousness consists of their tendency to overcome their possessor's ability to prevent them from unfolding their dangerous potential. So strong is the power of drugs, and so weak the power of resistance of almost everyone, that their mere possession is so likely to result in not only use but harmful use that we are presumptively ill equipped to even possess these noxious substances.

Possession offenses, and particularly gun possession, therefore, are merely the punitive culmination of a policing process that begins with a licensing requirement. And what a sophisticated process it is! By requiring a license, the state kills several birds with one stone. First of all, it deters anyone from applying for a license who is not blessed with a "good moral character." Moreover, the requirement of a license itself very probably has a disproportionate effect on outsiders, who are far less likely to apply for a gun license in the first place precisely because they do not identify with the state and its institutions. In fact, they are unlikely to be inclined to comply with state licensing requirements of any kind, whether for dogs, cars, or guns, perhaps because they resent such obvious efforts to police them, perhaps because they don't expect much of a chance of actually being awarded a license, perhaps because their neighborhood is so inundated with unlicensed guns that the license requirement strikes them as entirely toothless—until, of course, they are stopped by a police officer who subjects them to a *Terry* frisk.

Anyone who does submit an application for a gun license thereby subjects herself and her character to the inquisitive eye and virtually limitless discretion of a licensing officer. Here those not "of good moral character" who had the audacity to apply can be weeded out. And, as yet another level of inquiry, the ones who slip through the cracks can later be subjected to license revocation proceedings, which in turn are backed up with criminal penalties. Furthermore, an additional inquiry into fitness and harmlessness will take place when the license comes up for renewal, perhaps as often as every other year.[260]

Of course, if a bad character doesn't apply for a license, and most don't, then the possession offenses come into play. Obviously, they apply to anyone who, like "felons" and "aliens," has revealed himself to be not "of good moral character" without further inquiry by the licensing officer. Not so obviously, possession offenses also capture those perfectly good characters who possess guns without licenses. Possession without a license is possession without a license, no matter who does the possessing.

This formal irrelevance of good moral character, of harmlessness, deserves emphasis. It suggests that the core of the possession offense is not the prevention of harm but the chastisement of disobedience. In this light, the immediate and very real victim of a possession offense is the state, as the origin of the command not to possess guns without specific authorization. Licensing is a regulatory technique of the modern state and assumes a state powerful and sophisticated enough to set the background condition against which a licensing regime can operate. That background condition is a universal presumption of dangerousness, which the state in its discretion permits its regulatory objects to rebut. Everyone is presumed dangerous, unless the state declares it to be otherwise under conditions defined and applied by the state.

Another way of looking at the possession licensing scheme is to regard the state as the original owner of all objects it deems dangerous. Having declared itself the owner of all contraband (all "controlled substances"), it is within the state's discretion to assign possession of this contraband to certain individuals. As the rightful owner, the state can also retake these objects into its possession anytime it pleases, and certainly anytime the conditions of its grant have been violated or someone has boldly taken possession of contraband without receiving permission from the state. As Justice Murphy explained in his dissent in *Harris v. United States*,[261] "certain objects, the possession of which is in some way illegal, may be seized on appropriate occasions without a search warrant. Such objects include stolen goods, property forfeited to the Government, property concealed to avoid payment of duties, counterfeit coins, burglar tools, gambling paraphernalia, illicit liquor and the like."

Under either view, and even without an explicit licensing mechanism, possession offenses are the sign of a powerful state. Possession is illegal, literally, because the state says so. Illegal (or "unlawful" or "criminal," in some possession offenses) means unauthorized, period. In the words of the New York Court of Appeals, "a person either possesses a weapon lawfully or he does not,"[262] and the conditions of lawful possession are exhaustively established by the state in the possession offense itself. Hence, there's no need to worry about such messy concepts as self-defense or, even worse, justification, which claims that a violation of a statute may be justified on the general ground that, though facially criminal, it was not unlawful in the grand scheme of things.[263] Possession offenses begin and end with the state. This is what makes them so simple and so useful to the state.

But this is also what makes them so troubling. To commit a possession offense is to interfere with the state's effort to regulate, to control, the possession of certain dangerous items, including not only certain guns and drugs but also, say, firecrackers.[264] In its heart of hearts, the illegal—that is, unauthorized—possession of guns or of drugs does not differ from the illegal—that is, unauthorized—possession of firecrackers. The essence of a possession offense is disobedience of state authority.

Authoritarian States and Fatherly Monarchs

Despite the central role of the modern state in possession-based policing, there are important structural similarities between the possession model and the original English vagrancy model. It is no accident that the theory of original state ownership of contraband generally resembles the theory of original royal ownership of land and, in fact, the entire system of delegation that traced the origin of all legal authority and entitlements to the king. Both models presume a strong central authority of governance charged with maintaining the well-being of the political community.

And both models spring from the police power of their respective sovereigns. In a passage much quoted by nineteenth-century American writers on police power and regulation, Blackstone explained, in 1769, that the king, as the "father" of his people[265] and "*pater-familias* of the nation,"[266] was charged with:

the public police and oeconomy[, i.e.,] the due regulation and domestic order of the kingdom: whereby the individuals of the state, like members of a well-governed family, are bound to conform their general behaviour to the rules of propriety, good neighbourhood, and good manners: and to be decent, industrious, and inoffensive in their respective stations.[267]

In the United States, the paternal (or parental, as John Locke insisted[268]) "police power" of the king eventually was taken over by the state as *parens patriae*, which—but ultimately, of course, also who—regulated the commonwealth and later on defined and protected the interests of the community as such.

It was this same quasi-paternal police power, proceeding from a quasi-familial hierarchy of policer and policed, of subject and object, that gave rise to the string of American vagrancy laws that began in the early days of colonial America, when the *parens patriae* was still the English king, and continued for more than three centuries, through the second half of the twentieth century. The American Revolution and the Civil War might have wrought fundamental changes in American law. They had no effect on vagrancy police, which was considered a necessary weapon in the arsenal of any government that took its task of preserving public order and welfare seriously. Only the civil rights era brought the downfall of this convenient police mechanism, as judges began to identify with the objects of this police regime, rather than only with its subjects.[269]

Still, something does distinguish the possession scheme from the tried but true and ultimately dismantled vagrancy police regime. Here I don't mean the many ways in which possession offenses are preferable to vagrancy statutes as instruments of social control, in particular their insulation against legal attack, at least on their face and in the abstract. I mean, instead, precisely the flip side of that process of abstraction which rendered possession police facially unassailable.

The fundamental difference between a vagrancy statute and a possession statute is that one is open about its discriminatory purpose, and the other isn't. In other words, vagrancy statutes apply only to vagrants; possession statutes apply to everyone.

Vagrancy laws were clearly a way, and clearly understood as a way, of policing the boundaries of a political community, which was neatly defined along socioeconomic and, not only in the South and not only immediately after the Civil War, especially along racial lines.[270] The same cannot be said for possession offenses and that's why they make the NRA so nervous.

When we marvel at the antiseptic, and apparently unassailable, neutrality of sleek modern possession offenses, it's good to remember that they weren't always so. They wore their now hidden connection to vagrancy laws right on their sleeves. Through the nineteenth century, the suppression of gun possession among blacks and other undesirable sources of threats to the governing group was a common, and very explicit, strategy of governance.[271] Before the Civil War, Slave Codes regularly prohibited free blacks and slaves from possessing guns.[272] Legislatures also already made full use of the intrusive potential of possession offenses. In 1825, Florida authorized slave patrols to "enter into all negro houses and suspected places, and search for arms and other offensive or improper weapons, and . . . lawfully seize and take away all such arms, weapons, and ammunition. . . ."[273] Eight years later, Florida reaffirmed the patrols' broad search authority and went on to provide that blacks unable to "give a plain and satisfactory account of the manner . . . they came possessed of" weapons found in their possession were to be "severally" and summarily punished.[274]

After the Civil War, Black Codes continued the general prohibition of gun possession by blacks, until the passage of the Civil Rights Act of 1866.[275] Thereafter, openly discriminatory gun possession statutes disappeared from the statute books.

That didn't mean that gun possession statutes in general were a thing of the past. On the contrary. As in the case of vagrancy statutes, the goal of racial oppression simply migrated underground, from the face of the statute into its increasingly unspoken intent. As in the case of now race-neutral vagrancy statutes, the race-neutral gun possession statutes applied only to blacks, and everybody knew it. Here is what a judge on the Florida Supreme Court, in 1941, had to say about the racist point of that state's race-neutral gun possession law:

> I know something of the history of this legislation. The original Act of 1893 was passed when there was a great influx of negro laborers in this State drawn here for the purpose of working in turpentine and lumber camps. The same condition existed when the Act was amended in 1901 and the Act was passed for the purpose of disarming the negro laborers. . . . *The statute was never intended to be applied to the white population and in practice has never been so applied.* We have no statistics available, but it is a safe guess to assume that

more than 80% of the white men living in the rural sections of Florida have violated this statute. It is also a safe guess to say that not more than 5% of the men in Florida who own pistols and repeating rifles have ever applied to the Board of County Commissioners for a permit to have the same in their possession and *there has never been, within my knowledge, any effort to enforce the provisions of this statute as to white people. . . .*[276]

Possession offenses and vagrancy statutes thus followed a similar trajectory from explicit to implicit oppression. What distinguishes possession from vagrancy is the subtlety with which possession discharged its oppressive function. Vagrancy statutes, even after their forced neutralization in the wake of the Civil War, never managed to shed their oppressive origins. Possession offenses did. Modern possession offenses on their face apply to anyone and everyone who possesses some object without the authorization required by the state. They apply, as modern criminal statutes do generally, to "whomever." By contrast, vagrancy statutes by their very nature singled out rogues, vagabonds, dissolute persons, common gamblers, jugglers, gamblers, common drunkards, common night walkers, thieves, pilferers, pickpockets, lewd, wanton and lascivious persons, common railers and brawlers, habitual loafers, disorderly persons, and even "persons wandering or strolling around from place to place without any lawful purpose or object." Singling out undesirable types, that is, vagrants, remained the explicit point of vagrancy statutes, while possession offenses managed to transform themselves into quasi-conduct offenses that could be committed by all types.

There *is* a list of types even in possession offenses, as we have seen, but that list is much shorter: felons and aliens. Other distinctions are irrelevant, except for one, and this is the crucial distinction for possession as a pure state obedience offense: the fundamental distinction between the state and everyone else. The state commands; everyone else obeys.

In this particular case, the state commands that anyone who wants to possess must apply for a license. This is so because everyone, not just those "deemed vagrants," is presumed to be dangerous and therefore incapable of possessing a gun without putting it to harmful use. The presumption of dangerousness has been expanded from vagrants to everyone. To rebut it, everyone must convince a state license officer of his "good character."

Anyone who fails to comply with these commands, and thereby to acknowledge the state's authority, is guilty of a weapons offense, no matter how good his character. And this is the problem, and the distinctive fea-

ture of possession offenses: the lines separating the policer and the policed are no longer clearly drawn. Those middle-class whites who could
be certain to escape classification as vagrants cannot rest assured that
they may not find themselves on the wrong side of the law of possession.

The anxiety about gun control, that is, the regulation of gun possession, arises from this tension, this uncertainty among those who once
clearly identified themselves with the policers in their effort to control
undesirables. Privileged members of the political community are ap-
palled to find themselves treated by the law, if not necessarily by its enforcers, as presumptively dangerous, and therefore as vagrants, felons,
aliens, and "negroes." Pointing to the Second Amendment, they challenge
the state's claim to original ownership of guns as dangerous instruments,
with possession to be delegated to those deemed worthy. Men of "good
moral character" balk at the requirement that they demonstrate their
moral fitness to a state official.

They are, in short, experiencing the very sense of powerlessness so familiar to the traditional objects of police control. Now they, too, are outsiders who find themselves confronted with the arbitrary discretion of a
superior power, the state. And this sense of alienation only grows when
these state-defined sources of danger realize that state officials are exempt
from the general prohibition against possession.

This, then, is the second list of types one finds in modern possession
offenses, to go along with the list of inherently dangerous characters like
felons and aliens: the list of types who are inherently harmless and therefore subject to an irrebuttable presumption of fitness to possess a
weapon, without further inquiry into their moral character. What follows
is a short excerpt from the New York exemption provision:

Section 265.20 Exemptions

a. Sections 265.01, 265.02, 265.03, 265.04, 265.05, 265.10, 265.11, 265.12,
   265.13, 265.15 and 270.05 [weapons offenses] shall not apply to:
   1. Possession of any of the weapons, instruments, appliances or sub-
      stances . . . by the following:
      (a) Persons in the military service of the state of New York . . .
      (b) Police officers . . .
      (c) Peace officers . . .
      (d) Persons in the military or other service of the United States . . .
      (e) Persons employed in fulfilling defense contracts with the gov-
          ernment of the United States . . .
      . . .

2. Possession of a machine-gun, firearm, switchblade knife, gravity knife, pilum ballistic knife, billy or blackjack by a warden, superintendent, headkeeper or deputy of a state prison, penitentiary, workhouse, county jail or other institution for the detention of persons . . .

. . .

11. Possession of a pistol or revolver by a police officer or sworn peace officer of another state while conducting official business within the state of New York.

. . .

b. Section 265.01 shall not apply to possession of that type of billy commonly known as a "police baton" which is twenty-four to twenty-six inches in length and no more than one and one-quarter inches in thickness by members of an auxiliary police force. . . .

But how is this reverse presumption possible? It is possible because the only relevant victim in modern criminal law (or, rather, administration) is the state, and state officials by definition cannot pose a threat to the state, no matter how dangerous the instruments they possess and no matter how prone to violence or how bad their character.[277] Only harm against the state counts; harm against anyone or anything else does not.

State officials are qualitatively different from the rest of us. They can do no relevant harm. They cannot illegally possess guns. And the communal boundary they police is that between the state and everyone else. They, and only they, do the policing. They, and only they, are the subjects of police. Everyone else is reduced to its object.

Or so it is in principle, if not in fact. In fact, the white middle class still has little to fear, the NRA's constant warnings notwithstanding. In fact, possession police draws the same socioeconomic lines familiar from the days of vagrancy, only more deeply, thanks to its vastly greater punitive potential. The devastating impact that the war on drug possession has had on poor blacks is well known. Poor blacks also are disproportionately represented among unlicensed gun possessors[278] and, more important, among "felons in possession." Weapons arrest rates are five times higher for blacks than for whites.[279]

And yet possession police is so much more than a hypercharged vagrancy police. For, in principle, if not in fact, the ingroup that protects itself against outside threats is the state itself, rather than this or that social, ethnic, or economic group or class. The ultimate victim in a regime of possession police is the state, and the ultimate offender the community at large, rather than a mere subset of it.

So far, possession police merely functions as a more sophisticated cover for the hidden oppression of those social groups that have always been oppressed in the open. The ever increasing facial neutrality of police measures has done little more than to insulate long-standing practices from legal attack. But the removal of distinguishing features from the definitions of state norms for the purpose of eliminating open discrimination not only has driven the same discrimination underground. It also has dramatically expanded the group of potential police objects from the well-recognized outsiders persecuted by old-style police measures like vagrancy statutes to everyone (and everything) whom (or that) the state, or rather a particular state official, perceives as a threat to its (or her) authority and therefore to the authority of the grand institution she represents, serves, and protects.

3

State Nuisance Control

By reducing everyone to a potential threat to the state, possession offenses are symptomatic of an apersonal regime of criminal administration in which persons have a role only as sources of inconvenience, as nuisances to be abated, as objects of regulation. This police regime is apersonal in three senses: First, it does without personal offenders. Second, it does without personal victims. And, third, its only victim is apersonal, namely the state itself considered as an abstraction, rather than as a group of persons.

In the end, everything and everyone is policed as a nuisance, an inconvenience to state officials who know best. Contraband is a nuisance; dogs are a nuisance; offenders are a nuisance; victims are a nuisance; and so is the cumbersome apparatus of traditional criminal law. So offenders are abated, victims rendered irrelevant or used as cover, and the principles of criminal law ignored or openly abandoned as anachronistic remnants of a time when the regulatory nature of criminal law had not revealed itself, when the criminal law was about personal rights, rather than social interests.

Offenderless Crimes

The irrelevance of the offender's personhood is obvious. We already have noted, prior to our exploration of the place of possession offenses in an apersonal police regime, that the "public welfare" takes "offense" as soon as it is threatened by, literally disturbed by, anyone and anything. The preventive measures of social control put in place for its protection will attach themselves to any threat, whether or not it emanates from a person. Hence, there is no need to worry about that peculiarly human question of "guilt." In similar fashion, the reluctance to criminalize the failure to act (something of which plants are capable) evaporates, status (namely that of being dangerous, again a familiar attribute of dogs, objects, and natural phenomena) is freely punished in open defiance of the venerable actus reus principle, mere presence (also something well within the capacity of inanimate objects) is enough for penal intervention, infancy and insanity defenses are irrelevant, and so on and so on.

We have seen how possession has been adapted to assist the state in its identification and then eradication of human sources of danger. Possession has proved very useful because it bears the form of a traditional offense, while it is in substance merely an instrument of nuisance control. Its form, therefore, is the only concession to the personhood of its objects. The state generally does not find it necessary to pour measures for the control of threats that emanate from animals, inanimate objects, or natural phenomena into the mold of a criminal statute, which at least on its face is addressed not only to state officials but also to those who might fall within the scope of its prohibition.

Victimless Crimes

Perhaps less obvious, this system of nuisance control also has no room for persons as *victims*. Once again, possession recommends itself as a useful tool, this time not because it's offenderless but because it's victimless. Take gun possession, for instance. *Possession* of a gun harms no one. Using it may, but we're not talking here about the many statutes that criminalize improper gun *use*, say to kill someone. We're talking about simply possessing, not using, not abusing,[1] not even owning, a gun. Conviction of a possession offense does not require the prosecution to show that the gun was used to harm anyone, or anything for that matter. Again, this doesn't mean that the gun might not in fact also have been used to cause some harm. This simply means that, even if it was, that result is not required for a conviction of possessing the gun. That's why possession works both individually and in conjunction with other charges. Depending on the case, a prosecutor can either go after the possession alone or can use the possession charge as a fallback in case the more serious offense—which involved the use, not the possession, of the gun—does not stick for one reason or another. Possession is the universal velcro offense.

The absence of a victim is convenient in two ways. First, it lightens the prosecution's burden of proof. It's always easier to prove possession than it is to prove its use against a particular victim in a particular way at a particular time. Why? Because use includes possession, so every use is also a possession but not every possession a use. In addition, we have seen how easy it is to prove possession.

Second, and most important, victims are a nuisance. They slow down the process. They forget things, lose evidence, misremember facts, change their stories. They miss appointments. They try to drop charges. They want harsher penalties, they want lower penalties. They just want their money back, or their hospital bills paid for. They require attention, even handholding. They may be annoying, greedy, poor. In fact, victims tend to resemble offenders in every socioeconomic category, including race, income, residence, gender, even age.[2]

Victims are in the way. They are a hindrance to the efficient disposal of dangers, which is what the war on crime, ostensibly fought on their behalf, is all about. And the recent creation of victims' rights measures to give victims more say in more aspects of the criminal process only makes things harder on the prosecutor who is just trying to do her part in the state's grand scheme of incapacitation.[3]

How much cleaner, faster, more convenient is a victimless crime like possession, with no victim to deal with—no victim to notify about court hearings, no trial dates, no negotiations with defense counsel, no victim to be consulted about charges, about plea arrangements, about trial strategy, about sentencing, about everything.

As a victimless regulatory offense, possession is a perfect creation of the state. Who is offended, whose interests violated, by gun possession? No one in particular, except the state. The only clear violation of a personal interest, and a heavily guarded personal interest at that, occurs not in the commission of a possession offense but in its punishment.

Property! What Property?

To put it more succinctly, the only personal victim of a possession offense is the person doing the possessing, or *being* the possessor. The punishment of possession directly interferes with the possessory interest of the person in possession of the thing in question. And, traditionally, that possessory interest has enjoyed extensive protection in American law. Interference with someone's possession gives rise to criminal liability (in the form of the crime of larceny) and civil liability (in the form of the tort of trespass).

In fact, courts have from early on enforced the possessory interest even of wrongful possessors. Since the crime of larceny protects possession per se, the thief can be the victim of another thief. This age-old doctrine has been interpreted as an attempt to deter the use of self-help, which in medieval English law was treated as contempt of the king, who claimed the monopoly of violence.[4] To engage in self-help, for example by using violence to retake stolen goods or land illegally possessed, drew into question the king's ability to maintain the peace of his realm by punishing the illegal possessor. At the same time, the universal prohibition of interference with possession also reflected the central significance assigned to the possessory interest itself. The violent retaking of stolen goods was prohibited for the same reason that the initial larceny was prohibited—it interfered with the current possessor's interest in the objects, even though the original possessor's *ownership* remained undisturbed.[5] It was larceny, since larceny was the interference with possession, period.

So close is the connection between larceny and possession that the history of the law of larceny is largely the history of the concept of possession. In this context, the concept of possession already displayed the considerable malleability that would allow it to play such an important role in the use of possession offenses as flexible policing tools. Interestingly, the judicial use of possession to expand the borders of larceny already had obvious policing overtones. This manipulation of larceny with the help of the invention of the concept of "constructive possession" occurred against the background of master-servant law, with the effect of dramatically expanding the servant's liability vis-à-vis the property of his lord. Originally, servants could not steal objects entrusted to them by their lord for the simple reason that they had thereby legally acquired possession of them. What they already possessed they couldn't steal, since larceny was interference with someone else's possession. This loophole was eventually closed to better protect the lord's property against disloyal, but not yet thieving, servants. So the courts invented the concept of constructive possession. The servant, it was decided in the eighteenth century, had only "custody" of the objects handed to him by his lord, while possession, *constructive* possession, remained with the master. Hence, when the servant ran away or otherwise misappropriated the objects constructively possessed by his lord, he committed larceny.[6]

That the possession of the object has been prohibited by the state makes no difference; it can still be stolen. Even the possessory interest in contraband is protected against interference by another. Again and again, the courts have upheld convictions for larceny of contraband, including intoxicating liquor[7] and gambling devices.[8]

Yet, it is an entirely different story when the *state*, rather than another person, interferes with the otherwise so strictly guarded possessory interest. A full discussion of this topic would take us too far afield, since it would require an investigation of the relationship between the power of eminent domain and the regulation of real property under the police power. A brief look at the state's authority to interfere with *personal* property, or chattel, will suffice for our purposes, especially since the privileged position of the state comes through loud and clear even in this limited context. This limitation also makes sense because larceny originally was limited to personal, as opposed to real, property, and the possession offenses that concern us here all prohibit the possession of personal, not real, property.

State officials enjoy very wide authority to commit acts that would constitute larceny if committed by a private person. Any seizure of property by a police officer, as opposed to a brief inspection, is technically speaking a theft; it permanently interferes with the possessory interest of a person. Notice that this theft occurs long before the state action that tends to receive the lion's share of attention, forfeiture. The disposal of forfeited property presumes a prior theft and constitutes an additional offense: destruction of property or criminal mischief.[9] Similarly, an arrest is on the face of it an assault[10] and false or unlawful imprisonment,[11] the mere entrance into a house to execute a search warrant a trespass;[12] imprisonment is, once again, false or unlawful imprisonment, and execution is prima facie murder.[13] In each case, what distinguishes one from the other is that one is justified and the other isn't.

But what provides this justification? The answer is, in a state-centered system of criminal law, the status of the actor as a state official. In fact, and increasingly also in law, the inquiry begins and ends with the question whether or not the putative thief was a police officer. So entrenched is the notion that status alone justifies in these situations that the very need to inquire into a justification is dismissed as preposterous. This was not always the case. In nineteenth-century America, trespass actions against police officers who entered private residences were not uncommon and not always unsuccessful.[14]

The point is not that no justifications would be available. In fact, larceny and each of the offenses listed—with the exception of assault and murder—often have justifications built into their very definition ("having no right to do so nor any reasonable ground to believe that he has such right,"[15] "not licensed or privileged,"[16] "unlawful,"[17] "false"[18]). The point is, instead, that these justifications are irrelevant, that no state official needs to avail himself of them. State officials are by their nature implicitly exempt; it is as though every criminal offense, no matter how serious, contained the following silent clause: "except if it is committed by a state official." A criminal code littered with this clause would drive home the point that the official (noncivilian) makers, appliers, and enforcers of penal norms lie beyond the reach of the relevant statutes.

This tacit exemption for state officials is rarely made explicit. This is why the lengthy and detailed list of "exemptions" from gun possession laws, which we encountered earlier on, is so remarkable. Imagine that every provision in every criminal code, in fact every criminal provision anywhere, were followed by an exemption provision like this:

> The prohibition of [insert name of crime here] shall not apply to:
> (a) Persons in the military service of the state,
> (b) Police officers,
> (c) Peace officers,
> (d) Persons in the military or other service of the United States,
> (e) Wardens,
> (f) Prison guards,
> (g) Members of any auxiliary police force.[19]

An exemption differs from a defense. While a defense exculpates someone who has engaged in facially criminal conduct, an exemption removes the conduct from the realm of crime. To defend oneself against an allegation of criminal behavior is to provide reasons for that behavior or to plead for mercy. To claim an exemption, by contrast, is to deny the need for a defense, an explanation, a plea for mercy. It is, instead, to claim that the general criminal laws do not apply to oneself for one reason or another.[20]

Status-based exemptions thus shield state officials from criminal liability under the laws they generate, apply, or enforce. They turn on a fundamental distinction between the subject and the object of governance. Laws are made for others, applied against others, and enforced on others. The legislator, the judge, the police officer never imagines herself as the object but rather always only as the subject of governance, the one doing the governing, rather than the one being governed.

Exemptions join the under-the-table immunity of state officials from criminal liability as testimony to the power of the state to protect its own.[21] As every state official knows, he is virtually immune against the sort of police measures the state uses to keep the rest of us under control. Few, if any, police officers, prosecutors, judges, and legislators receive speeding tickets. Especially police officers, who are so identified with the task of policing as to bear its name, are effectively exempted from the rules they apply.

Viewed in this light, the radical distinction between private and state interference with a person's possessory interest in personal property merely exemplifies a fundamental distinction between private and state action typical of contemporary criminal law. The contrast is nonetheless startling in its starkness, given that Anglo-American law so long has been so unyielding in its protection of possessory interests against private interference. At a time when the distinction between state and private larceny was not yet obvious to all, courts occasionally found themselves in the uncomfortable position of having to immunize the state while at the same time punishing a private person for the same act.

Take, for example, the 1923 case of *People v. Otis* from New York. Here, Mr. Otis argued against his larceny conviction for stealing whiskey on the perfectly reasonable—though by now hopeless—ground that he couldn't be convicted of taking possession of something from someone who had no right to possess it. Unfortunately for the New York Court of Appeals, it couldn't dismiss this argument, as many other courts had done before it and have done since, simply by referring to the old common law saw that stealing from someone who had no right to possess the item stolen, and who perhaps had stolen it himself, was still stealing. (Any other conclusion would mean "to discourage unlawful acquisition but encourage larceny," to quote a much trotted-out phrase.[22]) Otis's case was different because the New York legislature had, in its prohibitionary zeal, declared that "'no property rights shall exist' in liquor illegally possessed."[23]

But, the court went on, since "[t]here can be no larceny of property not subject to ownership . . . [h]ow then, it is asked, may there be larceny of such liquor?"[24] The answer was, simply, that the state was different. The purpose of the New York legislature's broad declaration was not to immunize private persons from larceny liability for dispossessing private persons of illegally possessed whiskey. No, the purpose was to immunize *the state* from criminal and, more important, tort liability for doing exactly the same thing. There was some cause for concern, since every wave of prohibitionary legislation in the nineteenth and twentieth centuries had brought with it a slew of tort suits and constitutional challenges by liquor owners who saw their inventory turn into contraband and their often substantial investments into (criminal) liabilities from one day to the next. And, unlike the courts in most other states, with the notable exception of Indiana, the New York courts had once proven receptive to these complaints.[25] The state, in short, meant to immunize itself, not anyone else. And, since Otis was anyone else, he was out of luck.

It was in the nineteenth-century challenges to liquor prohibition, that is, the prohibition of the simple possession of liquor, that American courts took their hardest and, so far, only look at the oppressive potential of possession offenses. The prohibition of liquor possession was a harbinger of things to come, also because it fit into a comprehensive police regime that began with a general licensing requirement. At the outset, liquor regulation looked in the nineteenth century much like it does today—and, as we'll see, generally resembled the regulation of guns. To sell liquor, one needed a license. Selling liquor without a license was a crime. According to William Novak, these penal provisions were "a constant feature of local law enforcement," at least in Plymouth County, Massachusetts.[26] A 1787 Massachusetts law provided that liquor licenses were to be granted by town selectmen only to applicants whom they found to be "person[s] of sober life and conversation."[27]

This license system was simple, but it was not strict enough for temperance enthusiasts. By the 1830s, outright prohibitions of liquor began to appear, culminating in a much copied Maine liquor law of 1851. Under this new regime, licenses were still granted, but they were restricted to "special municipal agents for medicinal and mechanical purposes."[28] Now, for the first time, the possession of liquor was criminalized. Liquor possessed in violation of these laws was subject to confiscation and summary abatement as a public nuisance, without compensation. Much of the litigation and commentary triggered by these new laws focused on their procedural aspect. So, for example, Massachusetts Chief Justice Lemuel Shaw was inspired to write an eloquent opinion on the demands of "due process," even in the case of the forfeiture and destruction of contraband liquor.[29] There was also much handwringing about the retroactive effect of the sudden condemnation of once valuable property held by businessmen, who at one time or another had been at least reputable enough to have passed the character test of a liquor licensing officer, perhaps more than once.

These musings, though often extensive, are of little interest to us, expect perhaps to point out, once again, the tendency of American jurists to

evade difficult substantive questions by delving into detailed, but secondary, procedural ones. Far more interesting are two now celebrated
cases in which courts addressed the substantive question of whether the
state may interfere with the property rights of liquor owners through
statutes that prohibited, among other things, the possession of liquor.

In *Beebe v. State*,[30] the Indiana Supreme Court struck down as an unjustified interference with the right to property an 1855 Indiana law that
provided that "no person shall manufacture, keep for sale, or sell" liquor.
Violations of the law were punished with confiscation and destruction of
the liquor and fine. Beebe had refused to pay the fine and landed in
prison. Technically, the case arose out of his habeas corpus petition to
win release from confinement. In essence, the court concluded that the
statute's radical interference with a person's right to property could not
be justified because the property in question was not inherently dangerous, or, in the court's words, because "the manufacture and sale and use
of liquors are not necessarily hurtful."[31] The criminalization of public
drunkenness was another question, for "[i]t is the abuse, and not the use,
of all these beverages that is hurtful."[32]

One year later, the New York Court of Appeals followed suit, but on
broader grounds. In *Wynehamer v. People*, the court invalidated the "Act
for the Prevention of Intemperance, Pauperism and Crime," also passed
in 1855, which prohibited the sale of liquor, as well as both its possession
with intent to sell and its simple possession.[33] In the court's view, the
statute confronted liquor possessors with an intolerable dilemma:

> Property is lost before the police are in motion, and, I may add, crime is
> committed without an act or even an intention. On the day the law took ef-
> fect, it was criminal to be in possession of intoxicating liquors, however in-
> nocently acquired the day before. It was criminal to sell them, and under
> the law, therefore, no alternative was left to the owner but their immediate
> destruction.[34]

The New York court based its decision on the simple, and sweeping,
proposition that the legislature was not justified in summarily destroying
liquor because liquor was private property, period. What was at stake was
nothing less than "a vindication of the sanctity of private property." Unlike their Indiana colleagues, the New York judges saw no need to investigate the dangers of alcohol. Since "all property is alike in the characteristic of inviolability," the only thing that mattered was that liquor was indeed property. "If the legislature has no power to confiscate and destroy

property in general," which it clearly had not, "it has no such power over any particular species." In the face of such categorical principles, a detailed analysis of the dangers of a particular type of property was not only unnecessary but positively dangerous:

> It may be said, it is true, that intoxicating drinks are a species of property which performs no beneficent part in the political, moral or social economy of the world. It may even be urged, and, I will admit, demonstrated with reasonable certainty, that the abuses to which it is liable are so great, that the people of this state can dispense with its very existence, not only without injury to their aggregate interests, but with absolute benefit. The same can be said, although, perhaps, upon less palpable grounds, of other descriptions of property. Intoxicating beverages are by no means the only article of admitted property and of lawful commerce in this state against which arguments of this sort may be directed. But if such arguments can be allowed to subvert the fundamental idea of property, then there is no private right entirely safe, because there is no limitation upon the absolute discretion of the legislature, and the guarantees of the constitution are a mere waste of words.[35]

Although the Indiana statute prohibited possession with intent to sell and the New York one possession with intent to sell as well as mere possession, neither court focused on that aspect of the statute before it. Beebe was convicted of manufacturing and selling liquor, Wynehamer of selling, and Toynbee, the other defendant in the New York case, of possession with intent to sell. The possession question didn't come up, simply because the courts found that the prohibition of manufacture and sale alone constituted an unjustified interference with the right of property. Their discussion applies with even greater force to the prohibition of possession, which, of course, is even more intrusive than the prohibition of the creation and alienation of the item possessed.

If the prohibition of possession was insignificant, so was the distinction between different kinds of possession, namely simple possession and possession with intent to sell. That distinction, however, played a crucial role in several later decisions that reviewed liquor statutes that contained possession clauses and other possession offenses. The prohibition of simple possession was struck down, and the prohibition with intent to sell was upheld, on the general ground that mere possession "neither produces nor threatens any harm to the public."[36] For example, an 1889 West Virginia case invalidated the 1887 amendment to the state liquor law that made it a crime to "keep [liquor] in his possession for another" on the ground that "[t]he keeping of liquors in his possession by a person, whether for himself or for another, unless he does so for the illegal sale of it, or for some other improper purpose, can by no possibility injure or affect the health, morals, or safety of the public; and, therefore, the statute prohibiting such keeping in possession is not a legitimate exertion of the police power."[37] We have already encountered the Rhode Island case that, in upholding an 1882 statute that made it a crime to "have in his possession adulterated milk, to wit, milk which contained more than eighty eight per cent. of watery fluids, and less than twelve per cent. of milk, with intent then and there to sell same," stressed that "[t]he offense consists not in the possession of [adulterated] milk ... but in the *intent* to sell or exchange such milk,"[38] implying that there would have been trouble had it prohibited mere possession.

As we have seen, the distinction between simple and compound possession has lost much of its significance because of implicit and explicit presumptions that, emanating backward and forward in time, could quickly generate upon prosecutorial demand not only the intent to sell but all manner of illegal acquisitions and alienations of the object simply possessed. The significance of these nineteenth-century cases, however, lies not in their recognition of the distinction between different types of possession but in their deep respect for the property rights of the possessor. Fine doctrinal distinctions, such as that between simple and compound possession, were carefully drawn precisely because the courts knew that they were entering a sensitive area when they were reviewing statutes that massively interfered with property rights, even to the point of prohibiting not only the acquisition and sale but even the mere possession of certain items of property, or, as the *Wynehamer* court put it, the existence of the thing itself.[39]

Today, this concern about the policing of contraband property has completely disappeared. Today's legislatures and courts don't think twice about the legitimacy of criminalizing not only the manufacture and sale (along with virtually every imaginable means of acquisition and alienation) but also the possession of certain items. In fact, contemporary criminal law punishes not only the possession with intent to sell, but simple possession. And it punishes not only simple possession but simple possession with no mens rea requirement of any kind. Today, the legitimacy of possession offenses is so far beyond the shadow of a doubt that we punish simple possession with life imprisonment without parole, which is a far cry from the modest fines imposed by the statutes that so incensed the *Beebe* and *Wyne-*

hamer courts. So oblivious are we to the otherwise so heavily guarded property rights at stake in possession offenses that we completely ignore that aspect of the property police that drew the harshest criticism from nineteenth-century courts: the automatic confiscation and destruction of contraband, supplemented by the widespread "forfeiture" (i.e., confiscation and disposal) of any property, real and personal, somehow connected to some criminal activity or other, which more often than not consists precisely in the possession of contraband, specifically drugs.

Opium, Chinese Immigrants, and the War on Crime

How did we get from there to here? The answer is dangerous drugs, dangerous outsiders, and a depersonalized criminal law as danger disposal, or, more simply, opium, Chinese immigrants, and the war on crime.

Possession offenses are a fairly recent invention in Anglo-American criminal law. We know already that the common law did not recognize any possession offenses, simple or compound, because "the bare possession is not an act."[40] To punish possession of "indecent, lewd, filthy, bawdy and obscene prints" with intent to publish, stamps that could impress the scepter on coin with intent to utter sixpences for half guineas, or counterfeit coin with intent to utter would amount to punishing a mens rea without an actus reus, "an intent without an act."[41] No one would have dreamed of punishing simple possession, without any intent, since then both mens rea and actus reus would be missing.

English *statutory* law had no similar compunction about criminalizing possession and, for that matter, simple possession directly. The crown was not shy about enlisting the extraordinary preventive potential of suppressing possession even before use. A good, and early, example is the treason statute 8 & 9 Will. 3 c. 26, which provided

> [t]hat whoever (other than the persons employed in the Mint) shall make or mend, or assist in the making or mending, &c. any puncheon, counter-puncheon, matrix, stamp, die, pattern or mould, of any materials whatsoever, in or upon which there shall be, or be made or impressed, or which will make or impress the figure, stamp, resemblance, or similitude, of both or either of the sides or flats of any gold or silver coin current within this kingdom . . . or *shall have in their houses, custody, or possession, any such puncheon, counter-puncheon, matrix, stamp, die, or other tool or instrument before-mentioned, shall be adjudged guilty of High Treason.*[42]

After early attempts to use gun possession to police blacks, the punishment of simple possession in American criminal law began in earnest when the western states, and Oregon in particular, decided it was high time to police two new serious threats to the well-being of the community, one an inherently dangerous object, opium, and the other an inherently dangerous race, the Chinese. The 1887 Oregon "Act to regulate the sale and gift of opium, morphine, eng-she or cooked opium, hydrate of chloral, or cocaine" provided that "[n]o person shall have in his or her possession or offer for sale" any of the drugs enumerated in the title "who has not previously obtained a license from the county clerk of the county in which he or she resides or does business."[43]

In *Ex parte Mon Luck*, a Chinese man who had been imprisoned under this new law filed a habeas corpus petition to regain his freedom, pointing out that courts had struck down statutes prohibiting the simple possession of liquor as unjustified uses of the police power. In response, the court explained that opium, unlike alcohol, was dangerous per se, and its use therefore necessarily constituted abuse. It was "admitted by all to be an insidious and demoralizing vice, injurious alike to the health, morals, and welfare of the public."[44]

But not only was opium qualitatively different from—and more dangerous than—alcohol, that traditional American beverage of choice. At least as important, the people who possessed it were likewise qualitatively different from—and more dangerous than—Americans. As the court explained, opium, again unlike alcohol, "has no place in the common experience or habits of the people of this country."[45] The well-being of the "public" was threatened by aliens, the Chinese, through their very presence, but in particular through their possession of an alien substance that, because of its inherent and mysterious dangerousness, was certain to drive "the weak and unwary . . . to their own physical and mental ruin."[46]

In other words, the dangerous Chinese must be prevented at all costs from using the dangerous opium to ruin the American—alcohol-drinking—community. Given the vital importance of this campaign of preventive communal self-protection for the very existence of the community, the legislature could not afford to detain itself with legal niceties. Quick and decisive action was called for. There simply was no time for luxuries such as qualms about the unconstitutionality of destroying property rights in an object by prohibiting its sale, and, if not its sale, then certainly its possession with intent to sell, and, if not its possession with intent to sell, then certainly its simple possession.

Such worries were entirely misplaced not only because the situation was so desperate and the threat to the American community so serious. They were also simply inappropriate given the object of the necessary police action: threats. It made no difference whether these threats emanated from the possessor or the item possessed, or, for that matter, from the interplay of the two. Possessor and possessed were relevant only as threats, and threats don't have constitutional rights.

In the end, the possessor and the possessed, and the respective threats they embodied, were indistinguishable. In particular, the perceived dangerousness of opium derived in large part from the perceived dangerousness of those who possessed it, particularly in the absence of scientific research into the constitution and the effect of opium, though in the end it mattered little whose dangerousness infected the other. This identification of possessor and possessed emerges clearly from a remarkably—and unusually—honest federal court opinion that upheld the constitutionality of a predecessor to the statute at issue in *Mon Luck*.[47] The 1885 statute at issue in *Ex parte Yung Jon*, "An act to regulate the sale of opium, and to suppress opium dens," prohibited the sale, and not yet the possession, of opium. In rejecting Yung Jon's habeas corpus petition, the court conceded that opium use was "now chiefly confined to the Chinese" and even that, in direct contradiction to the reasoning of the Oregon court in *Mon Luck* ten years later, "[s]moking opium is not a vice." But, more important, even stunning, was its conclusion: "therefore it may be that this legislation proceeds more from a desire to vex and annoy the 'Heathen Chinee' in this respect, than to protect the people [!] from the evil habit."[48] Perhaps even more remarkable was that the court, having just let the cat out of the bag, squeezed it right back in, on the ground of no less sweeping a principle of constitutional adjudication than that "the motives of legislators cannot be the subject of judicial investigation for the purpose of affecting the validity of their acts."[49]

Whether "to vex and annoy the 'Heathen Chinee'" or "to protect the people from the evil habit" of opium smoking, or both at the same time, Oregon's opium statute amounted to an allout war on the Chinese and opium, with the goal of extinguishing them as potential sources of threats to "the people" before they had a chance to manifest their inherent noxious potential. The opium possession statute thus must be seen as part of a comprehensive, two-pronged effort to eliminate the Chinese threat: by keeping them out by expelling them from the body politic and, if this proved impossible for some reason, by subjecting them to intensive police control through simple possession offenses. The possession offenses proved useful police tools for the now familiar reasons, including easy detection and easy proof, followed by incapacitation. In addition, conviction could result in the preferred means of policing: expulsion through deportation.

Although this police campaign emanated from the western states, it soon engulfed the entire nation. Federal interference prohibiting Chinese immigration was necessary. And a new administrative agency, the Immigration and Naturalization Service, was needed to police the influx of Chinese. This is not the place for a detailed recounting of the history of the growth of American immigration law as an anti-Chinese police measure, especially since this story has been told recently and with great success.[50] This discriminatory purpose also requires no great interpretative unearthing because it appears brazenly on the surface, for the entire world to see. The Chinese were so far beyond the pale, and everyone knew that they were, that a camouflage for racism was unnecessary. As the first Justice Harlan put it matter-of-factly in 1896, the same year the Oregon Supreme Court decided *Mon Luck*, in his dissent in *Plessy v. Ferguson*, now celebrated as a plea for the constitutional enforcement of racial equality: "There is a race so different from our own that we do not permit those belonging to it to become citizens of the United States. Persons belonging to it are, with few exceptions, absolutely excluded from our country. I allude to the Chinese race."[51] Harlan's point? The criminal prohibition against blacks riding in white-only railroad cars was patently irrational since the same prohibition did not apply to the Chinese who, as was common knowledge, were inferior to and even more despised than blacks.

A federal case from the same period—1892 to be exact, and thus falling between *Mon Luck* and *Yun Jong*—made the connection between containment of the dangerous Chinese and of their dangerous opium as police measures explicit. The question in this case out of Louisiana was whether the court had criminal jurisdiction over an illegal Chinese immigrant, Hing Quong Chow, who had been "found" in the United States in violation of a federal statute providing that "any Chinese person or person of Chinese descent . . . shall be adjudged to be unlawfully within the United States, unless such person shall establish by affirmative proof, to the satisfaction of such justice, judge, or commissioner, his lawful right to remain in the United States."

The court dismissed the indictment on the ground that the case involved a matter of preventive police, not of retrospective punishment. As such, it was something for an immigration commissioner, not a judge. Along the way, the judge gave a telling reading of the statute which he explained, "deals with the coming in of Chinese as a police matter, and is the re-enacting and continuing what might be termed a 'quarantine against Chinese.' They are treated as would-be infected merchandise, and the imprisonment is not a punishment for a crime, but a means of keeping a damaging individual safely till he can be sent away. In a summary manner, and as a political matter, this coming in is to be prevented."[52]

This being a police matter, then, rather than a punishment matter, the principles of substantive and procedural criminal law were suspended. As an object of police, rather than of punishment, as a danger to be eliminated, rather than a person guilty of a criminal act, the Chinese defendant was a threat carrier, a nuisance, and, thus depersonalized, enjoyed the same individual rights as "infected merchandise." There was no mens rea requirement, no actus reus, no inquiry into guilt, no conviction, no trial, no judge, no jury, no presumption of innocence, no burden of proof on the state, and, of course, no punishment:

> The matter is dealt with as political, not criminal. The words used are those which are ordinarily found in criminal statutes; but the intent of Congress is . . . unmistakable. What is termed "being convicted and adjudged" means "found," "decided" by the commissioner, representing not the criminal law, but the political department of the government. . . . A reversal of the presumption of conduct or presence being lawful might be introduced into procedures which were political in character, and assimilated to those relating to quarantine. . . . The whole proceeding of keeping out of the country a class of persons deemed by the sovereign to be injurious to the state, to be effective of its object, must be summary in its methods and political in its character.[53]

The mere fact that the statute provided for one year's imprisonment at hard labor didn't mean that it was a criminal law rather than a police measure any more than did its employment of terms "ordinarily found in criminal statutes." No, the imprisonment also was a matter of quarantine: "[H]e must keep from entering the community of the people of the United States, and therefore is to be imprisoned. To prevent expense to the government, and as a sanitary matter, he is to be made to work."[54]

Of course, the racist immigration policies against the Chinese fit into a comprehensive local and national effort in the nineteenth century to exclude and, if that proved unsuccessful, to police all immigrants. Like vagrants and tramps, immigrants as a group posed a dual threat to the "public welfare" as potential criminals or potential public charges. The constitutionality of this police regime was never seriously questioned. So, in *New York v. Miln*, the Supreme Court, in 1837, upheld a New York statute that required ship captains to post bond for each passenger to cover any expenses the port city might incur in poor relief as "a mere regulation of internal police": "We think it as competent and as necessary for a state to provide precautionary measures against the moral pestilence of paupers, vagabonds, and possibly convicts; as it is to guard against the physical pestilence, which may arise from unsound and infectious articles imported, or from a ship, the crew of which may be labouring under an infectious disease."[55]

Still, in their open racism and harshness, the anti-Chinese policies stood apart from this general discrimination against aliens in the name of social hygiene. Unlike other, particularly European, immigrants, the Chinese were not simply presumptively dangerous; they were dangerous per se. And so was opium, making it the paradigmatic Chinese drug. Unlike liquor, the intoxicant of choice among Americans and European immigrants alike, opium was inherently dangerous, so dangerous that only complete prohibition, even of its possession, would stand any chance of containing its noxious nature.

Eventually, the instrument of police through possession spread from opium to other dangerous drugs, and from the Chinese to other dangerous classes, and, ultimately, with the development of a state-centered criminal law, to the entire "public" as a giant dangerous class. In the end, the very public whose welfare originally was protected against outside threats finds itself transformed into an outside threat, this time to the interests of the state, all of course ostensibly in the interest of its own welfare. Through the use of facially neutral, abstract, police offenses like possession, camouflaged as traditional criminal statutes, the public ends up being policed by the state to protect it from itself.

In the area of drug police, the analogue to the general prohibition of gun possession without a state-issued license that on its face applies to the very people of "good morals" whom it is designed to protect, is the prohibition of marijuana possession. Designed in the early decades of the twentieth century along the lines of the earlier Chinese opium model as a campaign to police another class of dangerous aliens, Mexican immigrants, this prohibition fulfilled its regulatory function admirably, at least at first. It was an added benefit when marijuana use, and therefore the scope of its police through possession offenses, spread in the 1920s to another troublesome outgroup, urban blacks, and black jazz musicians in particular. It didn't hurt, either, that "'degenerate' bohemian subcultures" soon took up the drug, as well.[56]

The facially unlimited scope of marijuana possession offenses did not become apparent until the 1960s, when the chickens came home to roost. Having entrusted itself with the power to punish marijuana possession, the state began to apply that power against members of the very community whose integrity, whose order, these laws were, in practice though not on paper, designed to protect. Suddenly, the "sons and daughters of the middle class"[57] found themselves the objects of police, demoted to the status of a dangerous outgroup. And the enormous police potential of possession thereby revealed itself to those who had always thought of themselves as the policers, rather than the policed. As Richard Bonnie and Charles Whitebread pointed out in 1970, "[s]ince marijuana use has become so common, there are certain student and hippie communities in which the police could arrest nearly everyone. Here the problem of selective enforcement necessarily arises—the police arrest those they dislike for other reasons. . . ."[58] Substitute "gun or drug possession" for "marijuana use" and "urban blacks" for "certain student and hippie communities" and the statement captures an important aspect of the war on crime today.

To recapitulate, the right to property of possessors of contraband today is as irrelevant as their other personal rights simply because they are considered not as persons but as threats. Threats cannot have rights. They also can't be victims. The difference between the nineteenth-century cases that carefully reviewed, and in some cases overturned, statutes that interfered with the right to property in liquor and contemporary cases that uphold statutes that prohibit simple possession of drugs without any proof of mens rea, including negligence, is the difference between respectable white Americans who enjoy their occasional drink or who run a liquor-related business and opium-smoking Chinese immigrants or their contemporary analogue, the inner-city "drug fiend." Over time, the formally abstract but substantively discriminatory system of possession police showed its potential as a convenient means of state oppression not only of recognized outgroups but of those who fancied themselves members of the ingroup.

The State as Victim

With the irrelevance of the possessor himself, all potential personal victims of possession offenses have been eliminated. Only the state remains. And the state is defined precisely in contradistinction to a community of persons. The state is apersonal because it ostensibly, and simply, manifests the interests of the community it governs. It is a bureaucratic institution with no identity and no function, except the maintenance of "public welfare" through the protection of "social interests." It is that which stands above the particular groups that constitute the mass of people under its governance, (civil) society or the community at large.

Left without personal victims, the essence of a possession offense is reduced to disobedience of state authority. At bottom, the function of possession offenses is to control dangerous persons and things, that is, to eliminate or at least to minimize threats. Threats to what? To the "welfare" of the "public," the fundamental "social interest." The state defines both "public" and "welfare," "social" and "interest." Most often, the public is simply the dominant group in society, the ingroup. The state, however, may also come to identify itself with the public and may confuse the public's welfare with the state's. The first case results in intrasocial conflict, the second in consternation among members of the (normally) dominant social group who see the state as the extension of their community. Oppression occurs in both cases, either of outsiders by the dominant social group (via the state) or of the community at large by the state directly.

Both aspects of a state-centered criminal law, or rather police regime, are important. Not only is the state the only victim, but the state, as an abstraction, is an entirely apersonal victim. The first move eliminates all personal victims; the second move insulates the first from critique.

Once again, the notion of the state as the only victim is nothing new to modern American criminal law. Since the Middle Ages, English criminal law has been conceived of as a system of enforcing the king's peace. And the king's peace, in turn, was nothing other than the peace attached to every householder, his *griđ* or *mund*.[59] Since the king's household eventually covered the entire realm, rather than his court, any attack within the realm against one of *his* subjects (an odd, but all too common, oxymoron) also disturbed *his* peace. In Pollock and Maitland's words, "[b]reach of the king's peace was an act of personal disobedience," a personal affront, daring him to exercise his power to keep his house in order.[60]

And, yet again, the modern American state makes an entirely different victim than did the English king, much as it makes a different kind of *pater patriae*. The significant difference here lies in the fact that a breach of the king's peace amounted to a personal challenge to the king, as a person and not merely as an institution. Every man within the king's *mund* was beholden to him personally by an oath of fealty, as every man to his lord, ever since William the Conqueror "decree[d] that every freeman shall affirm by oath and compact that he will be loyal to king William both within and without England, that he will preserve with him his lands and honor with all fidelity and defend him against his enemies."[61]

The state, unlike the king, has no personal identity. As a total institution, not merely an abstraction but an abstraction precisely from particular persons and their conflicting interests, the state has only an institutional identity. So counterfeiting is not an offense against the king but "a contempt of and misdemeanor against the United States."[62]

Or so "it" would have us believe. In practice, though not in theory, the state, of course, is constituted by certain persons called officials, officers, ministers, judges, senators. Although a violation of state commands constitutes, technically speaking, an act of abstract disobedience against the state, as opposed to one of personal disobedience against the king, who it is always also an act of disobedience against the officials who constitute the state and one of *personal* disobedience against the particular official who is issuing the command or enforcing it. The modern American system of governance thus turns out to be just like the historical English one, except that it has no head, or, rather, its head is not a person but a deliberately apersonal abstraction. In the United States today, an act of disobedience against the state is an act of disobedience against a particular state official. In England, threats to judicial authority were always also threats to royal authority because all judges derived their power from a commission issued on the king's prerogative. As a "judicial officer," a judge represented royal authority to nonofficials. As a "ministerial" officer, however, he was a link in the chain of command that moved from the king through superior to inferior courts.[63] Unlike in England, the indignity of defiance or contempt in the United States does not travel up the ladder to the king, but remains with the state official who experiences it firsthand, since there is nothing at the top except a great abstraction called "the state."

So we find that the modern American state takes great pains to protect the authority, dignity, safety, and well-being, in the broadest sense, of "its" officials. Acts, even hints, of disobedience are punished severely, and acts of obedience rewarded. Any interference with the well-being of a state official, physical or otherwise, is likewise threatened with punishment. In general, the line between the state and everyone else, between the policers and the police, is guarded with great vigilance. So any behavior by the policed that is inconsistent with their inferior status, including the egregious attempt to assume the superior status of the state official on the other side of the line, is taken as a challenge to the line that separates the state from the rest and therefore represents a welcome opportunity to reinforce that all-important line by putting the disorderly and the contumacious in their proper place.

The protection of state officials is achieved through a variety of status-based provisions, sprinkled throughout modern American criminal codes. For example, in the New York Penal Law one finds not only a special "assault on a peace officer, police officer, fireman or emergency medical services professional,"[64] along with a special "aggravated assault on a police officer of peace officer,"[65] but also a special "assault against a peace officer, police officer, fireman, paramedic, or emergency medical technician . . . by means including releasing or failing to control an animal."[66] As in all modern American death penalty statutes, first-degree murder is elevated to capital murder if the victim is a police officer, peace officer, or employee of a correctional institution.[67] Even "killing or injuring a police *animal*" is covered in a special provision.[68]

At the same time, the authority and dignity of state officials is ensured by punishing disobedience and rewarding obedience. Most obvious are offenses that explicitly criminalize acts of disobedience, including, in the New York Penal Law, disorderly "conduct" by "congregat[ing] with other persons in a public place and refus[ing] to comply with a lawful order of the police to disperse"[69] (a watered-down version of the infamous English Riot Act, which criminalized disobedience of the order to disperse communicated by reading the Act),[70] resisting arrest,[71] refusing to aid a peace or police officer,[72] failing to respond to an appearance ticket,[73] and refusing to yield a party line.[74] In addition, there are extensive and comprehensive prohibitions of all manner of contempt, including criminal contempt in the first and second degrees,[75] which reaches "[d]isorderly, contemptuous, or insolent behavior, committed during the sitting of a court, in its immediate view and presence and directly tending to interrupt its proceedings or to impair the respect due to its authority,"[76] "intentional disobedience or resistance to the lawful process or other mandate of a court except in cases involving or growing out of labor disputes,"[77] "[c]ontumacious and unlawful refusal to be sworn as a witness in any court proceeding or, after being sworn, to answer any legal and proper interrogatory,"[78] "[i]ntentional failure to obey any mandate, process or notice, issued pursuant to . . . the judiciary law, or to rules adopted pursuant to any such statute or to any special statute establishing commissioners of jurors and prescribing their duties or who refuses to be sworn as provided therein,"[79] "contumaciously and unlawfully refus[ing] to be sworn as a witness before a grand jury, or, when after having been sworn as a witness before a grand jury, [refusing] to answer any legal and proper interrogatory,"[80] and "in violation of a duly served order of protection . . . intentionally or recklessly damag[ing] the property of a person for whose protection such order was issued in an amount exceeding two hundred fifty dollars."[81]

Then, for good measure, the criminal law throws in provisions that punish disobedience of other state officials, beyond judges, police officers, and peace officers, who might issue particular directions, such as subpoenas. Hence, one finds the crimes of criminal contempt of the legislature,[82] and even criminal contempt of a temporary state commission[83] and of the state commission on judicial conduct.[84]

Most interesting for our purposes is the offense of criminal possession of a weapon in the fourth degree, which criminalizes "refus[ing] to yield possession of such rifle or shotgun upon the demand of a police officer" by a "person who has been certified not suitable to possess a rifle or shotgun."[85] As a possession offense that explicitly punishes disobedience of a state official's demand to surrender the object possessed by persons deemed "not suitable to possess" it, this offense is the paradigmatic possession police offense in the guise of an ordinary criminal statute.

The flip side of this disobedience possession offense is an obedience possession defense. A "person voluntarily surrendering" a weapon illegally possessed to the proper police authority thereby joins the select ranks of state officials exempt from criminal possession statutes.[86]

Supplementing offenses that explicitly criminalize disobedience against the state, or rather state officials, are impersonation offenses.[87] These statutes preserve the state's monopoly on oppression not by punishing disobedients, but by exposing impostors. The criminal impersonator attempts to obtain for himself the respect that is due only state officials. He is a disorderly person of the worst kind, an object of police who tries to pass as its subject. He is a personal self-counterfeiter who boldly appropriates the external indicia of insider status, be it in the form of the king's seal or a police officer's uniform. The interesting feature of impersonation offenses is that the impersonation by itself does no damage to the authority of the state. To the contrary, it relies on the very fact that the external indicia of statehood suffice to command obedience from outsiders. Instead, impersonation offenses are offenses against the state because they represent an attempt to circumvent the strict requirements for entry into statehood. The impersonator threatens the very distinction between police and policed, between state and other, by challenging that fundamental distinction itself. The impersonator pretends as though anyone could become a state official worthy of respect and unquestioning obedience, simply by donning a uniform or displaying a badge.

Apart from criminalizing disobedience to state officials at all levels of government, the criminal law also punishes disobedience in more subtle ways that extend far beyond specific disobedience offenses. The law of sentencing, for example, provides for various contumacy premiums. Most obvious and most draconian are the sentencing enhancements for recidivists, which have been a central weapon in the war on crime.[88] These laws permit, and in many case require, the judge to increase the sentence exclusively on the basis of prior convictions. They target those offenders who have revealed themselves as particularly dangerous or particularly disobedient, or both. The period of carceral incapacitation for these "recidivists" is extended, in an increasing number of cases until their death. They have proved themselves impervious to previous threats of punishment and, as undeterrable, must be incapacitated. In most cases, they also have thumbed their noses not merely at the threat of punishment but even at the actual imposition and infliction of punishment. Their repeat offense therefore reflects multiple acts of disobedience against the state and a disregard for its superior power. Recidivists personify contempt of state authority and, for that reason alone, must be put in their place. That place is either prison or, in particularly outrageous cases, the grave, for recidivism is also a symptom of deathworthiness in the American law of capital punishment.[89]

Disobedience is penalized, and obedience rewarded, in other aspects of the sentencing process, as well. As anyone who has ever encountered a police officer—or, for that matter, a DMV official—knows, state officials do not appreciate inconvenience. To state officials, ordinary people represent a potential nuisance by their mere existence. Interactions between members of each group therefore are designed, from the perspective of the former, to abate nuisances. Any additional inconvenience is not appreciated, no matter what form it might take. Least appreciated is any behavior that might be interpreted as a manifestation of disobedience. Sanctions for noncooperation, that is, additional inconvenience, depend on the nature of the interaction and the power of the state official. If we stick with police officers, that sanction may range from formal measures (including further investigation, ranging from frisks to full-fledged searches of the person, objects, and places, or the initiation of proceedings, which may be accompanied by an arrest) to their informal, and far more expedient, analogues (harassment and "police violence," which conveniently compresses the imposition and infliction phases of the criminal process into one act of discipline, as a sort of summary nuisance abatement, including permanent abatement through destruction by the use of "lethal force").

But police officers are not the only state officials in the criminal justice system who do not appreciate recalcitrance. Once a nuisance has been passed on to the prosecutor—which means that the police officer has chosen a formal sanction for disobedience, perhaps as a supplement to informal sanctions imposed and inflicted at the time of the original encounter between state and nuisance—the "suspect" is well advised to display a properly respectful demeanor to prevent his reclassification as a "defendant." Should that reclassification nonetheless have occurred, and a formal charge of one kind or another have been filed, the now-defendant should do everything in his power to minimize any further inconvenience to the prosecutor, and of course to the judge, the next state official whose valuable time might be occupied with the abatement of the defendant-nuisance. Luckily, the modern American criminal process has developed the perfect procedure for this purpose: plea bargaining.

A plea bargain is often nothing more than the exchange of a reduction in punishment for a reduction in prosecutorial and judicial inconvenience. It is a form of personal summary self-abatement. Through an act of submission to state authority, the defendant relieves the state officials in question of the time-consuming task of beating him into submission.

That is not to say, of course, that the superior may not decide to go through with this ceremony of humiliation, nonetheless. It simply means that the inferior is well advised to assume a submissive position—to humiliate himself—in order to maximize his chances of averting the impending attack. This discretion to insist on official humiliation in the face of self-humiliation helps to account for a startling phenomenon in American criminal law, the imposition of the death penalty on defendants who have entered a guilty plea.[90] To enter a guilty plea simply means to throw oneself upon the mercy of the state official in charge, thus acknowledging his superior power.

There is, of course, another model of the plea bargain, which focuses on the fact that it is a *bargain*, rather than that it is a *plea*. And bargaining is said to presume some basic equality among bargainers. As a theoretical matter, this is entirely correct. And, as a participatory model of the imposition of punishment, plea bargaining is attractive.[91] Nonetheless, the reality of American plea bargaining reflects a fundamental inequality of power between defendant and state officials inconsistent with this model, no matter how attractive. That is not to say that plea bargaining must always be more of a plea than a bargain, but merely that it is.

From the perspective of a state official, any resistance to punishment by "defendants" is considered a cumbersome complication of their nuisance abatement, which only aggravates the original nuisance and therefore calls for more radical and permanent abatement. Neither prosecutors nor judges appreciate a defendant who prolongs the abatement proceedings by filing motions, by demanding a trial, perhaps even a trial before a jury, who raises evidentiary objections at trial, who files posttrial motions or even an appeal, not to mention collateral motions, such as a habeas corpus petition.

Defendants who do behave themselves so as to accelerate their own abatement can expect certain benefits, again within the discretion of the relevant state official. A defendant with the proper attitude may receive sentence discounts for "acceptance of responsibility."[92] Or he may receive more lenient treatment in exchange for "substantial assistance to [the] authorities,"[93] much like a dangerous weapon, which can escape complete and permanent incapacitation upon a state official's "certificate that the non-destruction thereof is necessary or proper to serve the ends of justice."[94]

The same pattern continues, in ever more drastic form, as the person is transformed from "suspect" to "defendant" to "convict" to "inmate" and continues even when he becomes "parolee." In prison, guards constantly struggle to extract from inmates the respect owed a state official.[95] Prison guards are particularly eager to separate themselves from the objects of their (and the state's) power because they occupy a particularly low position in the status hierarchy among state officials. Unlike their fellow frontline officials, police officers, prison guards do not enjoy most of the accoutrements of state power that help them gain and, if necessary, enforce respect. Their training is perfunctory, their uniforms unimpressive; they have no patrol cars with special police engines and ever more advanced communications equipment, and, most important, they do not have at their disposal the ever increasing arsenal of the modern police officer, except for its least intimidating and least effective component, the baton.

The most blatant evidence of the state's claim to victimhood in modern American criminal law comes not in the form of punishments for disobedience or rewards for obedience. One finds it where one would least expect it: in the campaign for victims' rights. A federal appellate court determined that the federal government, and in particular the Internal Revenue Service, is a victim of the federal Victim and Witness Protection Act and therefore entitled to crime victim compensation.[96] Likewise, the California Penal Code provides, without the aid of judicial interpretation, that "'victim' shall include the immediate surviving family of the actual victim," as well as "any corporation, business trust, estate, trust, partnership, association, joint venture, *government, governmental subdivision, agency, or instrumentality,* or any other legal or commercial entity when that entity is a direct victim of a crime."[97]

The irony of this move must be savored. Here is the state fighting a campaign on behalf of persons who have been twice victimized, once by the perpetrator of a crime and then by the state itself, whose officials treat the victim like a nuisance, rather than a person. And now that state, which already occupies the positions of both violator and vindicator of victims' rights, classifies itself as the victim for whose benefit it is fighting the war on crime. In the end, then, we have the state violating and vindicating itself.

Small wonder that the war on crime and the campaign for victims' rights have been so tremendously successful. They involve the state and only the state, as offender and as victim.

By including itself among the victims it is protecting from itself, the state does not deny the existence of personal victims altogether. Yet the state is more than just another victim. It is *the* paradigmatic victim of modern criminal law. Apersonal, it is qualitatively different from all other victims, including communal organizations such as corporations and other societal entities. The state is not simply a bigger corporation, a wider community, a broader society. It is an abstraction and, as such, without any connection to persons. It is the pursuit of societal interests itself and, as such, without rights and without interests. Any interference with the state is an interference with the interests it protects. It is selfless in both senses of the word.

From Criminal Administration to the War on Crime

The war on crime represents the most advanced and comprehensive manifestation of this type of apersonal criminal administration, which begins and ends with the state, reducing all persons to objects of hazard police along the way. But modern criminal administration has roots that extend far beyond Richard Nixon's anticrime campaign. At the very height of the civil rights era and the Warren Court, American criminal law already was ripe for the incapacitationist turn of the war on crime.

The beginnings of rehabilitationism during the first quarter of the twentieth century were also the beginnings of the incapacitationism that was to shape American criminal law during the last quarter of the century. By the time the Model Penal Code was completed in 1962, the person already been removed from the heart of criminal law to its periphery.

In the end, the enduring legacy of the Warren Court, in procedural criminal law, and the Model Penal Code, in substantive criminal law, turned out to be the endorsement of threat minimization as a, if not the, central function of the criminal law. And the target of the threats to be minimized was the state, directly and indirectly. The preventive-communitarian-authoritarian model of modern criminal administration was in place long before the war on crime perfected and implemented it on a broad scale.

The Pound-Sayre Model

Pound and Sayre explained that modern criminal law was about social interests, not about individuals.[98] The state was merely the abstract representation of these interests. The state and the interests of society were identical. To protect the state was, therefore, to protect social interests, and to protect social interests was to protect the state.

In modern criminal law, personal victims and the vindication of their rights play at best a supporting role. In fact, one may view the elaborate system of so-called traditional criminal law, with its discoveries of bodies, investigations, arrests, trials, juries, verdicts, victim impact statements, and sentencing hearings, as a convenient cover for the protection of the one apersonal victim that matters in the end: the state. The state thus buys its comprehensive control of society as a whole through the dramatic vindication of the individual rights of some of society's members. In the end, even the protection of individual rights serves the protection of the state's.

In its role as cover, the individual victim appears not as an object of respect, endowed with the dignity of personhood. Whether as the policing of public nuisances (in regulatory offenses) or the unconsidered manifestation of reflexive impulses (in "true crimes"), contemporary punishment respects neither offenders nor victims as persons. The first, administrative, model simply views both victim and offender as expendable. The "victim" is the public (as in "public" nuisances) or perhaps even the state itself (as in pure disobedience offenses). Under the second, traditional model, the victim emerges as consumed by a rage as confused as it is uncontrollable, and the offender as an alien threat to the survival of the herd. Overcome with the grief and sense of powerlessness often associated with victimization, the sobbing victim begs the all-powerful state to apply "a salve to help heal those whose rights and dignity have been violated. . . ."[99] And the state is all too happy to oblige.

In fairness to Sayre, it must be said that he saw not only the promise of a state-based criminal law but he also recognized some of its dangers. He did not fully appreciate the general tendency of modern criminal administration to bend, if not abandon, principles of criminal law. Instead, he focused, somewhat excessively, on the dilution of a single principle, that of mens rea, or criminal intent. By making mens rea the defining characteristic of police offenses, he even can be said to have unwittingly facilitated the radical extension of draconian police offenses that paid homage to mens rea but abandoned other principles, while circumventing mens rea through presumptions. Still, with respect to this particular means of rendering the state's job of nuisance control less inconvenient, Sayre clearly saw the potential for state oppression:

> [T]he modern rapid growth of a large body of offenses punishable without proof of a guilty intent is marked with real danger. Courts are familiarized with the pathway to easy convictions by relaxing the orthodox requirement of a *mens rea*. The danger is that in the case of true crimes where the penalty is severe and the need for ordinary criminal law safeguards is strong, courts following the false analogy of the public welfare offenses

may now and again similarly relax the *mens rea* requirement, particularly in the case of unpopular crimes, as the easiest way to secure desired convictions.[100]

Sayre even captured much of the essence of the modern police regime, which renders it such a formidable machine for the discretionary suppression of state defined nuisances: "convenience in the interest of effective administration depending in part upon the vagueness of its limits."[101]

What's more, Sayre noticed a particular manifestation of this potential for oppression in his own days, which was to play a key role in the blossoming of criminal administration into the war on crime some fifty years later: drug criminal law. As Sayre reminds us, the Supreme Court's cavalier treatment of the mens rea requirement began with a case involving an early federal drug statute, the Narcotic Act of 1914. The defendants in that case, *United States v. Balint*,[102] had been convicted of the tax offense of "unlawfully selling to another a certain amount of a derivative of opium and a certain amount of a derivative of coca leaves, not in pursuance of any written order on a form issued in blank for that purpose by the Commissioner of Internal Revenue."[103] They protested that they weren't charged with knowing that the drugs were "inhibited," so that it wouldn't make a difference if they mistakenly thought otherwise. The trial court agreed and threw out the indictment. In a very short opinion, the Supreme Court unanimously reinstated the indictment on the basis of the following observation:

> [I]n the prohibition or punishment of particular acts, the state may in the maintenance of a public policy provide "that he who shall do them shall do them at his peril and will not be heard to plead in defense good faith or ignorance." Many instances of this are to be found in regulatory measures in the exercise of what is called the police power where the emphasis of the statute is evidently upon achievement of some social betterment rather than the punishment of the crimes. . . .[104]

Sayre's analysis of the *Balint* opinion is appropriately blunt and eerily foretelling: "The decision goes far; it can be justified only on the ground of the extreme popular disapproval of the sale of narcotics."[105] *Balint*, in other words, was not only the beginning of the end of the mens rea requirement, as contemporary accounts of American criminal law would have it: it was a harbinger of the hate-driven war on drugs, which by the end of the century would claim many more casualties among the hallowed principles of criminal law. In fact, the Supreme Court had sent the mens rea requirement packing more than a decade before *Balint*, in *Shevlin-Carpenter Co. v. Minnesota*, a little-known case that involved an offense that would go on to play a distinctly minor role in the development of modern American criminal law: "cutting or assisting to cut timber upon the lands of the state."[106]

In the end, however, Sayre saw only the danger but not its source. To a progressive reformer like Sayre, the solution to the problem of state oppression lay, paradoxically, with the state. The problem was not the state itself but its administration. If only one could place state discretion into the hands of selfless experts, the discretionary state would fulfill the abstract state's potential for good, not evil, and the essential selflessness of the state would manifest itself. If those wielding discretion were good, so was the state. Or, in the words of Justice Frankfurter in an opinion that applied *Balint* some twenty years later: "In such matters the good sense of prosecutors, the wise guidance of trial judges, and the ultimate judgment of juries must be trusted,"[107] in exactly that order of significance, we might add, with a sharp decline from the prosecutor to the jury, since so very few cases ever make it past the prosecutor to any sort of fact finder, never mind a jury.

The police regime of the war on crime, by implementing and developing Sayre's model of a modern administrative system that polices dangers to social interests, rather than punish violators of individual rights, points up Sayre's blind spot, one he shared with Pound and every other social engineer of his time and since: the failure to distinguish state from community, and the resulting failure to perceive the dangers of an authoritarian state that, acting in the name of the community, in fact advances its very own interests. The concept of society (or "the social") is sufficiently ambiguous to refer either to the community or to the state, or to both at the same time. Yet, in the end, it is the state, and not the community, that determines *which* "social interests" deserve its penal protection. It is the state, and not the community, that decides *how* to protect the "social interests" it deems worthy of protection. And it is the state, and not the community, that actually inflicts pain on persons to make these "social interests" stick.

This scenario is troubling only to those who have lost their faith—assuming they ever had it—in the ideal of an apersonal state composed entirely of selfless bureaucratic experts using their discretion in the interests not of any individual (including themselves) but of the community, or "the social." Along with so many of their contemporaries, Sayre and Pound were intoxicated by this ideal. So was an entire generation of American writers on law in general, and criminal law in particular. This trust in the benevolence of the bureaucratic state lies at the heart of the Legal Process School, so many adherents of which cut their teeth during the New Deal and the control economy of World War II. And it forms the foundation of the entire artifice of modern American criminal law, which was constructed by one of the key exponents of this sweeping movement, the great Herbert Wechsler.

The Model Penal Code

The Model Penal Code was a characteristically ambitious attempt to bureaucratize American criminal law in the Legal Process vein. Sponsored by the American Law Institute, a blue ribbon society of concerned jurists, and drafted by Wechsler with the assistance of a group of penological experts drawn from criminal law and other related disciplines such as criminology and psychiatry, the Model Code placed all discretion in the making and application of criminal law in the hands of experts. The very need for the Model Code arose from the inability of amateur legislatures to appreciate the administrative complexities of a truly scientific system of penal treatment. Stuck on atavistic, even barbarian, commonsense notions of punishment according to desert, unreflecting legislators were in desperate need of scientific assistance, which Wechsler and his collaborators were eager to provide.[108]

Once the rules of criminal administration were defined according to the Model Code's expert blueprint, their actual administration had to be controlled.[109] In particular, judicial discretion had to be eliminated as much as possible by a detailed set of interpretative guidelines. While the judge retained discretion in sentencing, that discretion was curtailed by a set of sentencing guidelines based on a fairly elaborate hierarchy of offense grades. These limitations may appear modest from today's standpoint, after decades upon decades of ever more specific constraints on judicial sentencing discretion, culminating in the federal sentencing guidelines.[110] At the time, however, the Model Code's sentencing provisions represented a significant departure from the "law" of sentencing, which then was little more than a set of local customs that varied from courtroom to courtroom and from judge to judge. Moreover, the judge's sentencing decision was subject to review within the first year of penal treatment by the head penological bureaucrat, the commissioner of correction, who could petition the court to resentence the offender if he was "satisfied that the sentence of the Court may have been based upon a misapprehension as to the history, character or physical or mental condition of the offender."[111] Finally, the nature and, most important, the duration of penal treatment lay largely within the discretion of the penological experts in correctional facilities. Under the Model Code scheme, judges merely set the general time frame for "correctional treatment"[112] in the form of indeterminate sentences that might fall, in the case of a first-degree felony, anywhere between one to ten years and one year to life in a "correctional institution."[113]

The problem of criminal codification, to Wechsler and his collaborators, was a problem of criminal administration. As such, it was primarily a staffing problem. The criminal administration was as good as its administrators. And the best administrators were those best versed in the science of criminal administration, penology. The system thus had to be designed to place discretion in the hands of the penologists, at least to the extent of their scientific expertise. Traditional actors retained discretion for two reasons: to maximize the Model Code's chances of adoption in American legislatures by minimizing the appearance of reform and to retain functions that for the moment lay beyond the current state of penology. To illustrate the second point, Wechsler eventually realized that the penologists could not generate a truly scientific insanity test.[114] So, instead of turning the insanity inquiry entirely over to the psychiatrists, he merely revised the traditional common law insanity test but gave psychiatric experts a far greater procedural role in its application. So the Code provided that the court would, as a matter of course, appoint a psychiatrist, who would make detailed findings regarding the defendant's mental condition, that the defendant could have himself examined by a psychiatrist of his own choice, and that the court would hold a pretrial hearing on the insanity question at which the expert or experts would be subject to direct and cross-examination. The experts would take the stand once again at the subsequent trial should the judge permit the defendant to raise the insanity defense on the basis of the pretrial hearing. They might then get to testify a third time at the posttrial civil commitment hearing, should the insanity defense have succeeded at trial, resulting in a verdict of not guilty by reason of insanity. There they would address the question of whether the ex-defendant, having just escaped the custody of the Commissioner of Corrections, should now be entrusted to the care of the Commissioner of Mental Hygiene.[115]

Having recognized the limits of penological science on the insanity question, Wechsler thus had the psychiatrists guide the discretion of the judge and, if necessary, the jury, rather than settle the issue themselves. This arrangement had the additional advantage of outwardly maintaining the status quo, while at the same time strengthening the influence of penological experts in fact.

The significance of shifting discretion on the insanity issue from experts to lay people, in particular jurors, should not be overestimated, for the simple reason that the insanity defense is rarely invoked and, when invoked, is even less likely to make it past a pretrial hearing and before a jury. Still, the role of the jury in the Model Penal Code's bureaucratic scheme deserves some attention. A body of lay judges is an odd fit for a system built on the notion of expert efficiency. Whatever a jury trial may be, it is neither efficient nor particularly scientific. In fact, it would not be an overstatement to say that the jury trial is specifically designed to be cumbersome and unscientific.

What, then, is the jury doing in the Model Penal Code, other than keeping the Code on the good side of the Sixth Amendment? It is *not* the critical voice of the community checking the otherwise boundless power of the state. The jury fulfills two other functions. First, it enables convenient solutions to drafting problems inherent in an attempt to define away discretion in the administration of criminal law. The Model Code drafters repeatedly rely on the law of evidence to solve tricky problems in criminal law, in particular by varying and shifting the burden of proof through affirmative defenses and presumptions.[116] The details of these drafting techniques aren't important here; what matters is that none of them would have been available without the jury. The American law of evidence represents a single sustained attempt to guide the discretion of jurors, who are considered to be unreliable and impressionable fact finders, in contrast to professional judges, whose expert judgments deserve greater respect, though they too are in considerable need of guidance, in the opinion of the Model Code drafters.

Furthermore, and for our purposes more important, the jury plays a direct role in the identification of deviants who are in need of penal treatment in institutions for the correction of the criminally abnormal. Repeatedly, the Model Code drafters stress that the jury should determine whether certain behavior crosses the line between normal and abnormal, between the reasonable and the unreasonable. Especially in borderline cases, it's up to the jury to decide whether the defendant should be marked as deviant, "deserves" the stigma of being labeled a criminal, a felon, a murderer, and so on.[117]

Here one might find the making of a communal corrective of state oppression. Whether the jury actually performs that function, however, depends crucially on the community it is meant to represent. If the jury represents the community of insiders that more or less openly conspires with the state to police outsiders, the jury becomes a terrible instrument of oppression, which contributes to oppression by wrapping it in the mantle of legitimacy. The jury can fulfill its critical function, giving the community a voice in the machinery of state power exercised in its name, only if the community it represents is that of the *object* of state power. In the trial against a black slave defendant, a jury of white slave owners oppresses; a jury of black slaves legitimates.[118]

The Model Penal Code doesn't show much interest in this function of the jury, or in the all-important question of representativeness. Although the Code has a great deal to say about other procedural matters (including, for instance, the elaborate procedures for the participation of experts in insanity cases), that omission by itself is perhaps not significant. Still, by integrating the jury into the comprehensive administrative process of deviance diagnosis, the Model Code in characteristically pragmatic fashion manages to retain a traditional institution of the criminal law, while reinterpreting its function. The fact remains that the jury is fundamentally inconsistent with the Model Code's general bureaucratic approach. The penologist at the heart of the Code's model of criminal administration through the diagnosis and treatment of deviants has about as much need for a lay jury as does a brain surgeon.

At the very least, the Model Penal Code's treatment of the jury did nothing to prevent the jury's subsequent development into that silent instrument of outsider police that it can become if one disregards its function as communal critique of state oppression. The jury of the war on crime represents the insider community of potential and actual victims, bound together through identification with the particular victim's experience. It does not represent the outsider community of offenders. As a result, it merely reinforces the communal hatred captured by the state's accusation, labeling, and eventual disposal of the outside threat to the community of victims. The jury is eager to do its part by aligning itself with the victim in a united front against external evil.

As slave owner juries once sat in judgment of their fellow slave owner, rather than his accused slave, so contemporary American juries more often than not sit in judgment over their fellow victim, rather than his accused victimizer. Now, however, the object of their attention and identification stands to lose nothing from the humiliation and disposal of the ostensible focus of the trial. Unlike the slave owner, whose proprietary interests were at stake in the trial of his human capital, the victim today is seen as *benefiting* from the punishment of "his" offender. Identification and condemnation therefore become indistinguishable: to identify with the victim is to condemn the offender and vice versa. Anything less than an act of communal hatred against the offender would bespeak a failure to identify with the victim. And not to identify with the victim would imply identification with the offender, and therefore exclusion of oneself from the ingroup, thereby revealing oneself as having been deviant to begin with.

The jury in this form facilitates, rather than checks, state oppression. It facilitates state oppression of a particular kind, namely the state-assisted oppression by a societal ingroup with access to state power. Juries have done little to prevent, and much to aid, race-based oppression throughout the United States, and not only because so very few cases are disposed of after a jury trial. Juries simply provide a veneer of legitimacy to state oppression.

Juries can play the same role in direct state oppression, that is, oppression of anyone and anything outside the state understood as the ultimate ingroup. The infamous German *Volksgerichtshof* (People's Court), which handed out scores of death sentences under the Nazis, featured several lay judges, who lacked the formal independence of jurors and therefore provided a thinner veneer of legitimacy. These lay judges made no difference whatsoever to the operation of the Court, apart from whatever little legitimacy they could contribute.[119]

The People's Court lay judges were handpicked by the Nazis for their commitment to stamping out enemies of the state, which Hitler long ago had identified—along with the Nazi party and, of course, himself—as the ultimate manifestation of the German community (the *Volk*) thanks to his claimed ability to identify "its" social interests. These enemies of the state, it bears emphasis, appeared to the naked eye as members of the German community. The *Volksgerichtshof* is most famous for its disposal of actual and suspected participants in the failed assassination attempt on Hitler of July 20, 1944. The defendants, who were humiliated in various ways before the tribunal (for example, by removing the belts from their loose-fitting pants) and then hanged on meat hooks, included high-ranking officers of the German army and public officials, all of whom had acted in pursuit of the well-being of the German *community* by ridding it of the *state* in its personification as Adolf Hitler.

In the total National Socialist state, we therefore find both the identification of community and state and the use of the jury (or, more precisely, lay judges) as representatives of the community to enforce the interests of the state against those of the community. The People's Court manifested the interests of the ultimate state ingroup, Hitler and his associates, against an attack from the community whose interests the state ostensibly protected. The entire community had become the object of police, rather than its subject.

Given the experience of Nazi terror, the result of which Wechsler saw firsthand at Nuremberg, it is surprising that the Pound-Sayre model of state-centered criminal administration survived World War II intact and managed to exert such influence on the Model Penal Code. The jury question here is only symptomatic of a general phenomenon. Wechsler's faith in the benevolent bureaucratic state never wavered. In this fundamental respect, nothing distinguishes Wechsler's 1952 plan for the Model Penal Code[120] from his 1937 blueprint for American criminal law reform ("A Rationale of the Law of Homicide").[121] The 1937 piece itself is a prolonged attempt to work out the implications of the Pound-Sayre model for the doctrine of criminal law in general, and the law of homicide in particular.

Wechsler, in this seminal article, both implemented the bureaucratic model of criminal law and, by expanding it to the heartland of criminal law, illustrated its weakness. Like Sayre, Wechsler's Model Code recognizes the need for strict liability offenses, while limiting this device of prosecutorial convenience to minor offenses. Sayre had gone so far as to *define* his public welfare offenses, which could be sanctioned without proof of intent, as minor offenses. For that reason, he had no room for *serious* strict liability offenses, such as bigamy, statutory rape, adultery, and narcotic offenses.[122] These were, Sayre explained, "wholly unlike public welfare offenses, and although often cited among the cases of the latter, are subject to altogether different considerations,"[123] whatever these considerations might be. (Sayre didn't say.)

Not only that, but also the way the Model Code retains strict liability offenses deserves attention. The Code simply declares that strict liability offenses are not crimes but an altogether different kind of animal, a sui generis category of civil, not criminal, offenses, dubbed "violations."[124]

Moreover, the Code drafters punted on the difficult issue of Sayre's public welfare—and strict liability—offenses by restricting the scope of their project to traditional criminal law. In an appendix, the drafters remark simply that "a State enacting a new Penal Code may insert additional Articles dealing with special topics such as narcotics, alcoholic beverages, gambling and offenses against tax and trade laws."[125]

In this way, the Code could have its cake and eat it, too. It could declare its categorical rejection of strict criminal liability, yet retain strict liability for any offense deemed civil, rather than criminal. And what was a violation? Whatever the legislature declared it to be. Only in the absence of a legislative classification did the Code place any limits on what might be considered a violation and therefore punished without criminal intent: a violation could not be punished by imprisonment, though no limits applied to other punishments, including fines and forfeiture, which the legislature remained free to set at whatever level it pleased.[126] Even these timid limitations were frequently ignored by state legislatures, which picked up the Model Code's general endorsement of strict liability offenses without its limitation on "violations" and defined violations more generously to include offenses threatened with short-term imprisonment.[127]

As we saw earlier, one of the weaknesses in Sayre's conception of public welfare offenses was his obsession with mens rea. He saw strict liability as the essence of modern criminal administration, rather than as a mere symptom. Modern criminal administration is by nature apersonal and state centered. The abandonment of mens rea is merely a symptom of the general irrelevance of personhood and the primacy of convenience in the state's enforcement of its commands. This also means, conversely, that the absence, or even the emphatic rejection, of strict liability does not imply the absence of modern criminal administration. The distinction between "true crimes" and "public welfare offenses" does not survive simply by retaining mens rea for the former.[128]

As Wechsler made clear, modern criminal administration can swallow traditional criminal law, while at the same time proclaiming its strict adherence to the principle of mens rea. He expanded the administration model from the least serious and most modern to the most serious and least modern of offenses, from Sayre's public welfare offense to first-degree murder. With the expansion of offenses came an expansion of sanctions. Where Sayre had to contend only with fines, Wechsler's account of criminal administration covered the entire range of penal measures, all the way to capital punishment.

Sayre sketched a model of modern criminal law as bureaucratic risk management. Wechsler expanded that model to cover the entirety of criminal law, including the societal response to those "true crimes" that Sayre was so eager to leave untouched. In such an apersonal and state-based system of criminal law, the retention of mens rea is of no significance, other than as camouflage. The system of danger control applies equally to a strict liability offense such as the sale of adulterated milk and to a mens rea offense such as premeditated murder. In both cases, the perpetrator appears as a threat to societal interests that requires suppression.

Wechsler's—and therefore the Model Penal Code's—regime of criminal administration is apersonal with respect to both offenders and victims. It treats offenders as nonpersons insofar as it regards them as criminal deviants "disposed to commit crimes" who pose a threat to "individual or public interests." It treats victims as nonpersons insofar as it subordinates the protection of "individual" to that of "public interests" and penalizes interference with the latter without any connection to the former.

Apersonal Offenders. The Model Penal Code did not break new ground in criminal law theory. It merely implemented a long-standing consensus about the objective of penal law: "the prevention of offenses,"[129] where offenses were defined, vaguely, as "conduct that unjustifiably and inexcusably inflicts or threatens substantial harm to individual or public interests."[130] Offenses were to be prevented by extinguishing threats, either through deterrence or, if that failed, through treatment. Treatment, in turn, came in two basic forms: rehabilitative and incapacitative, including the "extreme affliction sanction" of death.[131]

And whatever treatment turned out to be, everyone agreed what it was not and could never be in a rational regime of criminal administration: punishment. Like every other enlightened writer on criminal law since at least the 1930s, the Model Code drafters studiously avoided the term "punishment."[132] Punishment was passé, treatment very much en vogue.[133]

So eager were the Code drafters to extinguish threats, rather than to punish crimes, that their goal was to prevent not only the infliction of harm but also the mere threat of that infliction.[134] Preventing the infliction of harm was too close for comfort. The Code preferred to intervene earlier on, when the threat had not yet appeared, never mind manifested itself in the form of actual harm suffered. *Potential threats* were to be extinguished, before they could blossom into full-fledged threats. The objective of criminal law was to prevent not threats but threats of threats.

If the criminal law, through its criminal code, didn't succeed in extinguishing the threat personified by a particular potential offender, then it was time for penological treatment. In the words of the Code, the time had come "to subject to public control persons whose conduct indicates that they are disposed to commit crimes."[135] That "public control," of course, had nothing to do with the "public," unless the public was taken to be synonymous with the state. State control would take whatever form, and last however long, the "correction" of the offender's particular criminal deviance required. Once that treatment was complete, the offender, now cured of his "disposition to commit crimes," could reenter the community of normals, unless, of course, he turned out to have been incorrigible, in which case some "extreme affliction sanction" or another would be indicated. The corrigible deviants were treated through rehabilitation, the incorrigible ones through incapacitation, but treated they all were, one way or the other.

The Model Penal Code was but the first half of the Model Penal and Correctional Code, as it is properly called.[136] The general and special parts of the Penal Code, dedicated to the general principles of criminal liability and the definition of specific offenses, respectively, guided the penological diagnosis that determined the appropriate correctional treatment. As the Code drafters saw it, "[i]t ought to be the objective of the criminal law to describe the character deficiencies of those subjected to it in accord with the propensities that they . . . manifest."[137] And these character deficiencies, and with them the offender's abnormal disposition to commit crimes, her extraordinary dangerousness, are ironed out according to the scheme laid out in the Code's second half, the Correctional Code, which encompasses parts III and IV of the Penal and Correctional Code, entitled "treatment and correction" and "organization of correction," respectively.

This diagnosis of criminal deviance, with the help of the Penal Code's categories of liability (general part) and offenses (special part), however, not only aided the penologists' prescription of the proper rehabilitative or incapacitative treatment. Before the deviant could be treated, she first had to be identified.

The Code therefore places tremendous emphasis on the detection of abnormally dangerous individuals, those who pose exceptional criminal threats. The criminal law should interfere early and often. There's no reason to wait for the infliction of harm, because the infliction of harm is of no significance, other than as the concrete manifestation of a particular individual's criminal deviance. Other indicia of abnormal dangerousness are far preferable. As a threat radar, the Code consistently errs on the side of early intervention, often long before the threat has transformed itself into harm.

So the Code explicitly criminalizes the creation of danger. It devotes a substantial portion of its special part to defining "offenses involving danger to the person."[138] There we find offenses that do much more than merely "involve danger to the person," including murder, manslaughter, negligent homicide, and rape. The drafters presumably were less worried about the oddness of characterizing a homicide as a type of danger to a person than they were eager to indicate what they considered to be their progressive focus on threats, rather than harm.

This threat-based category made room for a new offense, "recklessly endangering another person,"[139] which codified the general principle of threat neutralization the Code drafters detected behind "antecedent statutes addressed only to ad hoc situations, such as reckless driving or a motor vehicle or reckless use of firearms."[140] Once again, it authorized penal intervention on the basis of potential, and not merely actual, threats. It subjected to state control anyone who "recklessly engages in conduct which places *or may place* another person in danger of death or serious bodily injury."[141]

Another advantage of the new crime of reckless endangerment was that it conveniently supplemented the law of attempt, by authorizing state control of dangerous individuals who lack the proper mens rea— purpose—for an attempt conviction, at least in cases "involving" serious "danger to the person," to wit death or serious bodily injury. In the Code's view of criminal law as threat elimination, "[t]he primary purpose of punishing attempts is to neutralize dangerous individuals."[142] This had draconian consequences. First, the Code expanded the concept of attempt to reach any conduct "strongly corroborative of the actor's criminal purpose."[143] What mattered, in the Code drafters' eyes, was not whether some abstract line separating preparation from attempt had been crossed but whether the offender had revealed that level of dangerousness, that abnormal criminal disposition, that indicated the need for penal treatment.

Second, the Code rejected the impossibility defense. Once again, the focus was on the offender's abnormal dangerousness, not the likelihood—or even the impossibility—of the actual infliction of criminal harm. In other words, the offender's criminal disposition, the threat she poses as a criminal deviant, requires state intervention even if his particular conduct posed no threat to anyone or anything.

Third, it punished attempt much more harshly than before, namely as harshly as its consummation. This must be so because someone who goes through the trouble of attempting a crime is just as dangerous, and suffers from the same general disposition to commit crimes, as the person who succeeds in attaining his criminal goal. "To the extent that sentencing depends upon the antisocial disposition of the actor and the demonstrated need for corrective sanction, there is likely to be little difference in the gravity of the required measures depending on the consummation or the failure of the plan."[144]

Consistent with its treatment—or rather its neutralization—of attemptors as threats, the Model Code did not hesitate to criminalize possession as an inchoate inchoate offense. Possession, like attempt, demanded correctional interference because it indicated that the possessor was "disposed to commit crimes," the assumption being that possession of a particular object wasn't a crime, but its use might be. Still, since the Code sought to prevent crimes, rather than to punish them, the mere threat of a crime could be treated as a crime in and of itself. In the Code, possession is simply another endangerment offense.

In addition to several possession offenses among the Code's special part, part II, which contains the definitions of specific offenses, one finds two crucial and broad sweeping possession offenses in its general part, part I, which contains the general principles of criminal liability that apply to all offenses in the special part: possession of instruments of crime, including firearms and other weapons, and possession of offensive weapons.[145] These two provisions appear, appropriately, in the article on inchoate crimes, which follow the Code's expansive definitions of attempt, solicitation, and conspiracy, each of which criminalizes the propensity to commit some crime or another. The first, and more general, possession provision makes it a crime for anyone to "possess[] any instrument of crime with purpose to employ it criminally," with "instrument of crime" defined loosely as "anything specially made or specially adapted for criminal use" or "anything commonly used for criminal purposes and possessed by the actor under circumstances which do not negative unlawful purpose."[146]

This general possession offense is not so much an offense as a theory of criminal liability, or rather a diagnosis of dangerousness, that no longer has anything to do with punishment for harmful conduct. In the process of making this shift, it stretches the already broad traditional offense of possession of burglar's tools (such as the nineteenth-century English statute that prohibited being "found by Night having in his Possession without lawful Excuse (the Proof of which Excuse shall lie on such Person) any Picklock Key, Crow, Jack, Bit, or other Implement of Housebreaking"[147]) beyond recognizability. It punishes the possession pure and simple, rather than the possession with an intent to commit a particular crime. No such intent need be proved; the possession of "anything *commonly used* for criminal purposes" of some form or another will do. It's punishment not merely for an intent to commit a particular crime, but for an intent to commit *some* crime. In other words, it's punishment for a criminal disposition.

In its search for indicia of dangerousness, the Model Code pays particular attention to one class of objects, weapons. It goes without saying that weapons are included among the instruments of crime, possession of which is criminalized. Weapons are also conveniently defined to include not only firearms but "anything readily capable of lethal use and possessed under circumstances not manifestly appropriate for lawful uses which it may have."[148] Even "firearm" is defined generously to include "a firearm which is not loaded or lacks a clip or other component to render it immediately operable, and components which can readily be assembled into a weapon."[149] What's more, weapons, unlike other instruments of crime, are presumptively possessed "with purpose to employ [them] criminally." And that's not all: even the possession itself is presumed, if the weapon is found in a car.[150] And so mere presence turns into possession turns into possession with intent to use the weapon "criminally." If we put it all together, the Model Code criminalizes being in the presence of "anything readily capable of lethal use." Why? Because that presence alone is a symptom of a "dispos[ition] to commit crimes."

This theory of criminal liability, of course, flies in the face of the Code's very own act requirement. As the Code announces in its general part: "A person is not guilty of an offense unless his liability is based on conduct which includes a voluntary act or the omission to perform an act of which he is physically capable."[151] Even in its most explicit endorsement of incapacitation, the Code insists that one of its "general purposes" is "to subject to public control persons whose *conduct* indicates that they are disposed to commit crimes."[152]

The Code resolves this difficulty with characteristic simplicity: through legislative (or codificatory) fiat. Possession is an act because the Code says it is. Right after the announcement of the categorical act requirement, we learn that "[p]ossession is an act . . . if the possessor knowingly procured or received the thing possessed or was aware of his control thereof for a sufficient period to have been able to terminate his possession."[153] Possession is criminalized as a symptom of criminal deviance. Since only acts may be criminalized, possession is declared an act.

The personhood of the possessor is as irrelevant as the personhood of the criminal deviant. Possession is convenient for the diagnosis of abnormal dangerousness, as opposed to the punishment of persons for wrongful acts, precisely because it is a *state* and, as such, can be experienced by any living creature, persons and nonpersons alike. Animals, in other words, can possess, but they cannot act. Likewise, animals can possess but cannot own; they can behave but cannot act.

The suspension of the act requirement, through the criminalization of either possession or omissions (i.e., failures to act), expands the criminal law beyond the realm of persons. Personhood, then, is no longer a prerequisite for punishment or, rather, treatment. Any living creature can possess; anyone, even anything, can fail to act.

And any living creature, along with a host of inanimate objects and natural phenomena, can pose a threat. In a view of criminal law as singularly concerned with the extermination of potential threats as that underlying the Model Code, the offender is of interest only as a threat personified. As a result, criminal law is radically depersonalized. There is nothing necessarily personal about a threat. Threats can emanate from anything and anybody. And the proper way of dealing with threats is their elimination, without any reference to guilt or other uniquely personal considerations.

This is not to say that remnants of the personal offender can't still be found in the Model Penal Code, at least on the surface. The Code insists on proof of some sort of mens rea for all crimes (as we noted earlier) and provides for various justification and excuse defenses that shield even offenders who act with the required mens rea from criminal liability. But neither the consideration of the offender's mental state nor the availability of defenses implies that the offender is punished as a person. Instead, the Code's mens rea scheme and the grading of offenses on its basis can be seen as classifying offenders by dangerousness. The mental state simply reveals the *level* of criminal disposition, once the general presence of the "dispos[ition] to commit crimes" has been diagnosed. The inquiry into mental states thus allows for a fine-tuning of the general diagnosis of criminal deviance, with an eye toward prescribing the appropriate mode and length of the peno-correctional regimen.

Defenses have a similar function. Causing a threat to relevant interests triggers the penal response. The presence of mens rea indicates a deviant disposition to commit crimes. The levels of mens rea indicate the level and nature of that disposition. The initial diagnosis of deviance based on a finding of mens rea, however, can be adjusted in the exceptional cases where mens rea does not imply deviance. These exceptional cases are captured by the defenses of justification and excuse. For example, according to the Model Penal Code commentaries, the defense of claim or right (where the offender acts under the belief, however mistaken, that the property he stole belonged to him) is needed because "[p]ersons who take only property to which they believe themselves entitled *constitute no significant threat to the property system* and *manifest no character trait worse than ignorance.*"[154]

The availability of defenses doesn't mean that their beneficiaries are persons. They also are not inconsistent with an apersonal regime of hazard control. As we've seen, the New York dog control statute includes a full panoply of justification defenses. What's more, the statute refers to the dog's "conduct," another concept that one might have thought had no application outside the sphere of persons. Here, too, there is a remarkable similarity to the Model Code. Like the Code, the dangerous dog law doesn't focus on conduct for its own sake. Conduct is relevant only as an indication of dangerousness. What matters in the end is whether the dog *is* dangerous, that is, whether it "poses a serious and unjustified imminent threat of harm to one or more persons."[155] That's why the dog is punished not for having done something, namely inflicted harm, but for *being* something, namely dangerous. The only difference between the Code and the dangerous dog law is that the latter doesn't bother with prevention. In the end, both are about the identification and disposal of threats, one personal, the other not.

Apersonal Victims. Having transformed the offender into an apersonal deviant threat, the Model Code also largely depersonalizes the victim. Recall that the Code defines crime as "conduct that unjustifiably and inexcusably inflicts or threatens substantial harm to individual or public interests."[156] The "individual or public interests" protected by offenses defined in the Code include, in that order, "the existence or stability of the state," "the person," "property," "the family," "public administration," and "public order and decency." As we saw earlier, the Code also recognizes the state's authority "to insert additional Articles dealing with special topics such as narcotics, alcoholic beverages, gambling and offenses against tax and trade laws."[157]

In other words, the vast bulk of the Code's criminal law concerns not individual interests but communal interests, ranging from the protection of the "family" (!) to that of the "corporation" or "unincorporated association," then to the "public" and ultimately to the "state." The primacy of public interests, and particularly the interests of the state as such, is easily overlooked, even if the bulk of the Code is dedicated to offenses that threaten communal interests of one kind or another. To conclude that the Code restricts the scope of criminal law to the vindication of personal rights against personal interference is to misunderstand the Code's scope and thereby to mistake the Code for the entirety of criminal law. That misunderstanding, unfortunately, was fostered by the Code drafters themselves. The final version of the Code contains no reference to the "victimless" police offenses. The appendix quoted earlier appeared in the Proposed Official Draft, not in the Final Draft. Similarly, the Final Draft makes no mention of the very first category of offenses, namely those against the existence or stability of the state. Again, only a note in the Proposed Official Draft so much as hints that the Code drafters recognized the existence, never mind the central importance, of this category—and, for that matter, of the state itself:

> This category of offenses, including treason, sedition, espionage and like crimes, was excluded from the scope of the Model Penal Code. These offenses are peculiarly the concern of the federal government. . . . Also, the definition of offenses against the stability of the state is inevitably affected by special political considerations. These factors militated against the use of the Institute's limited resources to attempt to draft "model" provisions in this area. However we provide at this point in the Plan of the Model Penal Code for an Article 200, where definitions of offenses against the existence or stability of the state may be incorporated.[158]

Without this note, the final version of the Code creates the mistaken impression that the first interest to be protected by the criminal law is the paradigmatic individual interest in the existence of the person (in article 210, on criminal homicide). Instead, the firstness of the first interest to be protected belongs to the paradigmatic public interest in the existence *and stability* of the state.

The Model Penal Code does not altogether eliminate the victim as person. If we include the categories of state and police offenses, the second of the seven offense categories, after all, is explicitly dedicated to the protection of "the person." Characteristically, this category deals with offenses "involving danger" to the person and thereby combines the vagueness typical of a police regime ("involving") with its focus on threats, rather than harm ("danger").

The Code defines "person" broadly to include not only "any natural person" but also "a corporation or an unincorporated association."[159] The drafters, however, here appear to have thought of offenders, not victims, and we've already seen that the offender as person had no place in the Code's model of criminal administration through danger control. The Code does not define "victim."

The "person" protected in the category of "offenses involving danger to the person" is the individual, or "natural," person who is the victim of a homicide, an assault, a kidnapping, or a rape. The same could be said for offenses in the next category, "offenses against property," though here the Code turns its attention from the person to an interest, property, which may be either individual or public. It is the interest as such that the Code seeks to protect, not the person holding it. Only one of the offenses against "the property system,"[160] robbery, presumes an individual victim, because it presumes an "offense involving danger to the person," assault: robbery is theft (an offense against property) plus assault (an offense involving danger to the person). The ultimate, or true, victim of a robbery, however, is apersonal, since the core of robbery is theft, and not assault. It is, after all, theft plus assault, and not the other way around. That is why robbery appears among the property offenses, and not among the person offenses. Still, the victim of a property offense *may*, though it need not, be a person. The next offense category, offenses against the family, is the first one explicitly to protect not an individual but a community. Whereas the third offense category protects an interest (property), which may be held by individual or communities, and is in this sense apersonal, the fourth offense category protects not an interest but a community, the family. By definition (or, rather, by categorization), offenses against the family are not offenses against persons, at least not directly. They may be construed as offenses against persons only indirectly, by conceiving of these persons as members of a family. So bigamy, incest, and child neglect obviously (and abortion not so obviously) affect individuals, but they victimize the family, at least according to the Model Code.

The remaining three categories bear an even more remote relation to individual persons. Offense categories five and six concern the "public" (as in "public administration" and "public order and decency"), whereas the seventh, and last, category, that of police offenses, once again protects the state and thereby closes the circle that began with the first category, "offenses against the existence and stability of the state."

In the end, the victim as person plays a subordinated role in the Model Code. It finds itself sandwiched between apersonal victims, beginning (and ending) with the state but also including the family and the public and including an abstract interest, property. The Code begins with the state and ends with the state. Along the way, it touches upon the person, in the second category ("offenses involving danger to the person"), but then immediately proceeds to remove the person by reducing it first to incidental significance (as potential holder of a property interest), then to indirect significance (as member of the family and the public), and eventually to insignificance (as object of state police).

The relative insignificance of personal victims in the Model Code raises the more general question of the significance of so-called traditional, or "true," crimes in modern criminal administration. The Model Code goes a long way toward shifting the core of criminal law from interpersonal crime—persons against persons—to apersonal offense—threats against interests, communities, and, ultimately, the state, a shift first described (and applauded) by Pound and Sayre. This new model of criminal law behind the new model of a criminal code remained unchallenged even during the liberal constitutional challenges against criminal statutes of the 1960s and early 1970s. It found its fullest and most comprehensive implementation in the war on crime of the decades since then.

The War on Crime

In the war on crime, the traditional criminal law, with its central ceremony, the jury trial, is not only pushed into the periphery but also relegated to a mere means to the end of facilitating the enforcement of the new core of criminal law. As a cover for the efficient and silent administration of the bulk of offenses, the entire elaborate system of traditional criminal law serves a function not unlike the mens rea and actus reus principles in the Model Penal Code: its retention, with the requisite exhortations of its crucial significance, serves to hide its irrelevance. In this way, the remnants of traditional criminal law serve to legitimate modern criminal administration. Needless to say, the legitimacy of traditional criminal law itself is beyond question. Theories of punishment are useless not only because punishment is passé but also because there's no need to justify anything.

It's not clear to what extent the war on crime merely spelled out the administrative program of the Model Penal Code or deviated from that program in some significant way. The Model Code, as we saw, obscured its underlying program of criminal administration as state-focused danger control both through the explicit retention of principles of traditional criminal law and through the exclusion of state and police offenses from its scope. Yet all of the weapons of the crime war can be found in the Code, even if they are not apparent to the naked eye. On the surface, we find the heavy use and expansive definition of inchoate offenses, the full arsenal of possession offenses supplemented by presumptions, and, in general, a system of criminal law geared toward the identification and disposal of criminal deviants. Even without the excluded categories of state and police offenses, the Code confines the protection of victims as persons to a minor supporting role.

If one looks closely, one can even make out the ultimate weapon of the crime war: permanent disposal and complete incapacitation through capital punishment. The entire, and extensive, Code section that deals with this "extreme affliction sanction" appears in brackets, expressing the drafters' inability to reach consensus on its legitimacy. Despite its noncommittal brackets, this section provides the blueprint for the revival of capital punishment in the United States.[161] Last but not least, there is the Code's offhand suggestion that legislatures might wish to insert into their criminal codes "additional Articles dealing with special topics such as narcotics, alcoholic beverages, gambling and offenses against tax and trade laws,"[162] a suggestion that legislatures were only too happy to take up in the war on drugs, though surely with an enthusiasm and consequences that the Code drafters didn't anticipate.

In the end, the war on crime took the general system of modern criminal administration as threat elimination sketched by Pound, Sayre, and their contemporaries and belatedly codified by Wechsler and then put it to radically different use. A shift from a presumption of corrigibility to one of incorrigibility produced a concomitant shift in official response from rehabilitation to incapacitation. Eventually, extreme affliction sanctions became the norm, correctional measures the exception. Prisons were transformed from correctional institutions run by penologists into warehouses supervised by inventory managers. Treatment still was the name of the game, but the realities of treatment, as well as its function, had changed in ways unimaginable to the naïvely progressive champions of treatmentism.

In the war on crime, the Model Code's mechanisms for the early detection and diagnosis of correctional needs became a vast net of mass incapacitation. The attemptor was still placed under state control as soon as his abnormal dangerousness had revealed itself, with no regard for traditional worries about the line between preparation and attempt or the impossibility defense. And, having been identified as exceptionally dangerous, she was subjected to the same treatment as the offender who had succeeded in putting her criminal plan into action. Now, however, treatment was no longer designed to cure but instead intended merely to quarantine, and to quarantine for as long as possible, given that her criminal tendencies were presumed to be inherent and permanent.

Possession offenses were thus transformed from opportunities for early correctional intervention into opportunities for lengthy, perhaps permanent, incapacitation. Strict liability crimes flourished, no longer constrained by the Model Code's artificial limitation to "violations" and even extending to serious felonies punished with mandatory life imprisonment without the possibility of parole. In fact, parole was entirely abandoned, rendering supervision and continued diagnosis of inmates unnecessary and maximizing the incapacitative potential of every conviction. Most dramatical, the death penalty, that most extreme of extreme affliction sanctions, which had found only an awkward place in the Model Code, flourished as the most permanent of permanent incapacitation sanctions.

But the Model Code, and the progressive approach to criminal law it represented, was not alone in unwittingly laying the groundwork for the war on crime. As an emergency measure designed to abate a national crisis, the war on crime was not choosy when it came to selecting the tools that helped it accomplish its crime extermination mission. There simply was no time to revamp American criminal law in its entirety. Nor was there any need to do so. The war on crime instead used the principles and practices at its disposal and molded them into tools, turning progressive reforms into draconian incapacitation measures.

The Warren Court suffered the same fate in criminal procedure as the

Model Code did in substantive criminal law. In the war on crime, not only the Model Penal Code but also the Warren Court's Fourth Amendment jurisprudence became a blueprint for policing threats through early incapacitative intervention. Much as the Model Penal Code's greatest influence on substantive criminal law was not its elaborate system of correctional treatment (codified in its parts III and IV, long since forgotten) but its model death penalty statute, so the Warren Court today lives on in millions upon millions of *Terry* stop-and-frisks.

Terry today does not survive as an attempt to bring low-level police intervention within the realm of constitutional scrutiny, however scaled down, but instead stands for the explicit endorsement of police intervention as threat management and, more specifically, and troubling, as management of threats against the state by the state, or, rather, against state officials by those same officials.

Terry turns entirely on the safety of state officials. *Terry* held that a police officer is entitled to "frisk" a suspect he had "stopped" for the purpose of protecting himself. Evidence discovered during such a safety frisk, like Terry's gun, is an unanticipated benefit, not a justification for the frisk. The Supreme Court, after *Terry*, spent a lot of time stressing the exclusively protective justification of the frisk, without recognizing the danger of authorizing state intervention on the basis of threats to an official of the state as perceived by that official. These perceptions were not only unreviewable; in the war on crime, they were also unreviewed. In the crisis of crime that triggered the war on crime, police officers in the trenches had good reason to fear for their safety. What appellate court, comfortably removed from the realities of hand-to-hand combat, would dare challenge the apprehension experienced by an officer in the field who comes face-to-face with the enemy, a criminal suspect?

The result has been that *Terry* today justifies "protective sweeps" of buildings following arrests, car frisks incident to traffic stops, and ever more elaborate connections between ever more innocuous items seized by ever more frightened police officers during protective sweeps and frisks of persons reasonably suspected of criminal conduct. And, with the help of presumption-enhanced possession offenses, modeled on the Model Penal Code, these *Terry* searches and seizures play an important role in the war on crime. *Terry* thus establishes a convenient link between a state official's perception of a person as a threat and the threat's elimination through the person's incapacitation. And that, in a nutshell, is what the war on crime is all about.

PART II

Vindicating Victims' Rights

4

The Legitimate Core of
Victims' Rights

Much of American criminal law was lifted from volume 4 of William Blackstone's *Commentaries on the Laws of England*, published in 1769. Even today Sir William could teach beginning American law students a great deal about "their" criminal law. After two centuries, Blackstone's *Commentaries* remain the most comprehensive and systematic treatment of the American "common law" of crimes.

What's most striking about the continuity between eighteenth-century English and contemporary American criminal law doctrine, however, is not that basic, "time-honored," principles like mens rea and actus reus have changed so little but that the underlying theory of the state has remained virtually unchallenged, as well. So when nineteenth-century American courts and commentators scrutinized the origin and limits of the power of government most closely associated with the power to punish, the so-called police power, they generally were content to quote Blackstone's definition of it.

It is odd that a nineteenth-century treatise on the police power in American law would proceed from a century-old English definition of its subject matter that predated the creation of the modern American state by several years. It is odder still that Blackstone's definition grounded the power to police in the inherent authority of the English king, the one institution that (or, rather, whom) one would expect to have retained no significance whatever after the American Revolution. As we saw, to Blackstone the power to police was simply the king's patriarchal prerogative, as "father" of his people,[1] to provide for "the due regulation and domestic order" of his subjects, conceived of as "members of a well-governed family."[2]

This eighteenth-century Blackstonian definition of police is quoted in every major American treatise on the police power, including the last and most ambitious, published by Ernst Freund in 1904.[3] (In fact, American courts continued to rely on it well into the twentieth century.)[4] For purposes of the police power, from which the state's power to punish was (and *is*) said to derive, absolutely nothing had (or *has*) changed:[5] it belonged to the sovereign on account of its (or his) capacity as *pater patriae*. It made no difference whether the sovereign was the king, the state, or "the people." The power to police was the power of the sovereign qua sovereign, of the father qua father.

To reconstitute itself after the war on crime, American criminal law must find more solid ground than the eighteenth-century speculations about the nature of English royal power by an English jurist who delighted in styling himself "Solicitor General to Her Majesty."[6] Such a modern theory of American criminal law as state governance would take into account some of the more momentous changes that have occurred in American political life since Sir William published his *Commentaries*, including the establishment of a democratic government built on the ideal of equal rights of persons as persons.

Such an account would differ from Blackstone's in several respects. Here are some. Unlike the English king, the American state has no dignity in and of itself. Unlike Blackstone's royal father figure, who "is not only incapable of *doing* wrong, but even of *thinking* wrong,"[7] the American sovereign is not infallible. The criminal law does not serve to ensure obedience to the state so that it may go about its business of defining and protecting social interests. Crimes do not disturb the king's peace and thereby offend him; they interfere with the rights of persons. The essence of crime is not the violation of one's duty of loyalty and obedience to the sovereign but the violation of one person's autonomy by another, equal person.

This book doesn't pretend to lay out a full account of criminal law in the United States as a modern democratic state. It pursues a more modest goal: to begin shifting our perspective away from that of the king (now the state) keeping the peace among the subjects within his (or its) realm to that of the subjects themselves, where "subject" is understood not as the mere object of political power but as its subject. By tracing the implications of a particular concept, the rights of victims as persons, throughout the system of American criminal law, the second part of this book illustrates how the principles and doctrines of American criminal law in general might be reviewed through the eyes of the person.

By taking the perspective of the victim as a person, we are forced to reconsider various doctrines and principles of American criminal law, and eventually the institution of the law of punishment in its entirety. We also see that categorical distinctions between offenders and victims fall away, as we take the more abstract perspective of personhood and recognize the fundamental identity of offenders and victims as persons. Once we reconceptualize the law of offenderhood—"criminal law"—and of victimhood—"victim compensation law"—as different aspects of a law of personhood, the once central distinction between offenders and victims gives way to that between persons and the state. As persons, both offenders and victims must be protected against oppression in a state-centered system of criminal law as apersonal threat control.

The basic idea that underlies the perspective of personhood, and its relevance to an account of law in general, and criminal law in particular, is straightforward. Though this idea would require further elaboration in a full account of American criminal law, and American law generally speaking, the following sketch suffices for our purposes, which are more illustrative than expository.

The significance of the personal perspective reflects what I take to be the fact, or at least the widely shared consensus, that the modern democratic state is grounded in the concept of the person. According to this view of government and law, personhood is understood as the capacity for autonomy, broadly conceived as self-government, which implies, among other things, the ability to act responsibly, a precondition of criminal liability.[8] The legitimacy of the state, and its acts of governance, derives ultimately from this connection to personal autonomy; there is only one legitimate government: self-government. This view of the state, which in American academic writing is often labeled "liberal," is at least as old as the American Revolution,[9] and at least as young as the two most comprehensive and influential political theories of our time, those set out by John Rawls and by Jürgen Habermas.[10]

Under this account, the primary function of the modern state is to manifest and to protect the autonomy of the persons who constitute it. The state discharges this function through affirmative and negative acts of governance. Affirmatively, it sets the background conditions for each person's manifesting her personhood through developing and acting on her capacity for autonomy. Negatively, it prevents and, if necessary, punishes interferences with the manifestation of that capacity by other persons. The criminal law fits into this latter, negative aspect of the state's mission. Criminal law vindicates individual rights, where "individual rights" encompass the various aspects of a person's right to be treated as a person, that is, as endowed with a capacity for autonomy.[11]

For this reason, victims' rights are not antithetical to liberalism, and to a liberal vision of criminal law in particular. On the contrary, they are central to it. Vindicating victims' rights, as personal rights, lies at the very core of a liberal criminal law.[12] It's *illiberal*, state-centered criminal law that has no room for victims' rights. State threat control has no more use for victims' rights than it does for rights of persons generally speaking, as we saw in part I.

For our purposes, the victim's relevant characteristic is not her victimhood but her personhood. To define a person in terms of victimhood is internally inconsistent: essential victimhood is inconsistent with a capacity for autonomy. Recognizing the fundamental significance of personhood also reveals that the victim's perspective, in the final analysis, does not differ from the offender's. Criminal law, as all law, in a modern democratic state is for, by, and of the person. It does not recognize a categorical distinction between victims and offenders, because victim and offender are but temporary and interchangeable labels attached to persons who jointly constitute a phenomenon called "crime" and who are entitled to respect as such.

Given the centrality of the concept of the person and the relative irrelevance of other characteristics, this approach to criminal law rejects not only "victims' rights" as a basic concept. Talk of "offenders' rights" (or even of "suspects' rights" and "defendants' rights") is suspect for the same reason. Rights are aspects of personhood; only persons have them, and have them as persons, not as suspects or defendants. To reduce individual rights to procedural rights (i.e., to rights attached to process participants, such as suspects and defendants), as is so common in American criminal law, is to miss the crucial connection between rights and the function of criminal law in the first place and thereby to overlook the *substantive* significance of rights. To restrict the function of the protection of individual rights to criminal procedure also is to miss the truly foundational significance of the victim, no matter how many rights one assigns to the victim as a process participant: the point of the *entire* criminal law, and not merely its procedural aspect, is to vindicate the victim's right to autonomy.

Any reconception of the victim, then, must begin by acknowledging the insignificance of the victim as such. A victim is essentially a person, and only incidentally a victim. She is a victim because her personhood has been violated in some way. The fundamental distinction is that between person and nonperson, not between offender and victim. "Offender" and "victim," as mere labels attached to persons, are neither essential nor mutually exclusive. As we will see, the same person can, at the same time or at different times, carry both labels.[13]

Claiming rights for victims qua victims, by contrast, is not only incoherent; it is also detrimental to victims. It's literally self-destructive to define oneself, and to be defined by others, as a victim. Tying benefits, or status, to victimhood only provides an incentive to prolong one's victimhood. Most troubling is the tendency to treat victimhood as an essential characteristic of an individual, thus making it not only undesirable but impossible to rid oneself of this badge of passivity, absent some sort of radically intrusive psychological reconditioning, which would violate the personhood of victims as much as it would—and did—violate the personhood of offenders, even if performed in the name of rehabilitation and, therefore, ostensibly in the name of the deviant himself.[14]

This victimological essentialism is not as farfetched as it may sound. Instead, it is merely the flip side of the criminological essentialism characteristic of the incapacitative ideology that underlies the war on crime. Under this view of human nature, "crime" has a dual branding function. It labels the offender as an offender and the victim as a victim. The act of offending reveals the offender's true nature as a source of danger, as a (super)predator. At the same time, the nonact of being offended reveals the victim's true nature, as a target of danger, as a (super?)prey. In the final analysis, the offender and the victim both are stripped of their human nature, their personhood. And thus the victims' demand to be "treated like criminals"[15] is met.

This alienation of both offenders and victims reflects a fundamental fact that is all too often overlooked in public debate about victims' rights but that has long been a mainstay of victimological research: offenders and victims are very much alike. Offenders and victims, as groups, tend to share important socioeconomic characteristics. They are disproportionately young, poor, and black.[16] As Randall Kennedy pointed out, the problem with the war on crime isn't just that it cares little for black offenders but that it cares just as little for black victims.[17]

The remainder of this book explores what it means to treat victims like persons. Ultimately, an account of victims as persons will have to find its place in a comprehensive account of a person-based criminal law, which will assign all participants in the practice of punishment their proper role as persons, including victims and offenders but also state officials at all levels of government, from legislators and judges to prosecutors, police officers, and prison guards, whose personhood is all too often neglected, to the detriment of the criminal process as a whole. As persons, state officials deserve no less, and no more, respect than do the objects of their power. (In fact, demanding respect for offenders and victims as persons at the expense of the personhood of state officials reinforces the distinction between state and society and thereby threatens to cement the very state-centered system of criminal administration one aims to replace.)

No one would disagree that the criminal process should treat victims "with the dignity and respect they deserve,"[18] as the Uniform Victims of Crime Act puts it. The question is *why* this is so. The simple answer is that victims deserve "dignity and respect" not as victims but as persons. "Dignity" is a personal attribute, "respect" an interpersonal attitude, and "desert" an interpersonal claim.

The problem now is that the victim isn't the only person around. The offender, too, is a person and as such has "dignity" and "respect," and "desert" therefor, in equal measure. Put another way, both have the *right* to be treated as persons in the criminal process, as always ("right" being another exclusively personal attribute). The right to be treated as a person is nothing but the right of autonomy, or self-government. It's the vindication of this right that's the state's job, and therefore also the point of the criminal law.

It is this right of autonomy that the offender has violated, or at least has done his best to violate. The law's function is to protect that autonomy from serious interference. The *criminal* law helps the state discharge that function through deterrence and, if necessary, through punishment—that is, through the threat, imposition, and infliction of punishment. In this sense, one might say that the victim has a right to *have* the offender punished, provided that no other measures to vindicate her autonomy, such as the law of compensation, are available.[19] Analogously, the offender can be said to have the right to *be* punished, insofar as treating her as an ahuman source of danger denies her the "dignity and respect" she "deserves" as a person.[20] In the criminal law, the state vindicates both rights, thereby doing its job of manifesting and protecting the dignity of all of its constituents.

The challenge of a person-based system of criminal law thus is to respect and to manifest the personhood of *all* participants in all aspects of the criminal process, including the formulation of rules of criminal liability, the definition of offenses, the criminal process in the narrow sense, and in the actual infliction of punishment. American criminal law generally has focused on one prong of that challenge, the protection of the (putative) *offender's* autonomy. This is understandable, for the criminal process, as a process of determinations or judgments that culminates in a judgment regarding guilt or innocence, provides many opportunities for trampling—or respecting—the autonomy of the accused. At every turn, from investigation to execution, the accused may be coerced through superior power, rather than through principled action. All too easily, and all too often, the criminal process amounts to a process of oppression and exclusion akin to a shaming ritual, or "degradation ceremony," in Harold Garfinkel's phrase.[21]

We concentrate on another prong of the challenge, instead, the manifestation of the (putative) victim's autonomy. But this focus on victims can be no more exclusive than that on defendants. No discussion of victim autonomy can ignore the autonomy of other process participants, not only because victim autonomy may conflict with offender autonomy but more simply because the labels "offender" and "victim" may attach to one and the same person.

When we turn our attention to the role of the victim in the modern criminal process, we shift our focus from the threat disposal system of modern criminal administration to the show trials of traditional criminal law. In this move from reality to pretense, we encounter, among other things, a host of symbolic and toothless provisions that guarantee victims a panoply of rights. This time around, however, we take these symbols, and the commitment to the rights of victims they symbolize, at face value.

We began by revealing the irrelevance of victims (and offenders) in a "war on crime" orchestrated by the state and fought with victimless crimes, including its arsenal of possession crimes. Now we see what a system of criminal law that means what it says when it claims to vindicate victims' rights might look like.

It turns out that taking victims seriously requires a revision of American criminal law, and not always in the way the victims' rights movement might have anticipated. Only interferences with those personal rights the state exists to protect warrant the application of its most awesome power, the power to punish. *Pace* Pound, Sayre, and Wechsler and the entire progressive school of penology, this direct connection to personal rights, rather than its direct connection to the state as *pater patriae*, is the characteristic feature of the criminal law.

To take the victims' rights movement at its word is to adopt its image of the victim. And that image is decidedly personal, at least in ideology, if not in fact, as we see when we take a closer look at the actual beneficiaries of victims' rights legislation. The paradigmatic "victim" in the "victims' rights movement" is a victim of violent *interpersonal* crime.

The question of who qualifies as a victim is no longer only a matter of theoretical conjecture. It has found a definite doctrinal answer (or rather answers) now that certain entitlements, even rights, turn on the classification as "victim." Now that scores of Americans every year seek victimhood to enjoy its benefits, no matter how illusory they may turn out to be, state officials at all levels must generate, apply, and enforce rules that specify the essence of victimhood. What remains to be done is to remove these rules from their particular context, the law of victim compensation, where they continue to go unnoticed by public discourse and scholarly attention, and then to integrate them into a coherent whole, a general account of victimhood, the mirror image of the criminal law's account of offenderhood.

This account of victimhood emerges in three stages. First, in the remainder of chapter 4, we take a look at the various and sundry contexts in which "the victim" appears in American criminal law. Here we pay particular attention to recent reforms prompted by the victims' rights movement of the past twenty years or so. The victim, however, had a role to play in American criminal law long before the victims' rights movement politicized its plight. So, for instance, the victim's conduct has always been considered in assessing, and especially in *mitigating*, criminal liability, as in the case of self-defense. Most significant for our purposes, crime victim compensation statutes began appearing in the mid-1960s, years before the victims issue became a plank in the platform of the war on crime.

Next, we try to capture the image of the victim that drives the victims' rights movement and that underlies the recent wave of victim-based reforms. The prototype of the victims' rights victim is a person against whom another person has committed a serious crime.

This rediscovery of crime as a traumatic interpersonal event represents the most significant contribution of the victims' rights movement to a new view of American criminal law that gives persons their due. It's certainly the contribution to which we devote most of our time. But it's not the only one.

The victims' rights movement also reminds us of two other key facts that a system of criminal law ignores at its peril: the crucial role of interpersonal identification and of emotional responses to the catastrophe of serious crime. Identification with victims and offenders, as persons, is so important because moral judgment, and therefore legitimate punishment, is impossible without it. Neither victims nor offenders may be treated as alien outsiders if punishment is to be distinguished from nuisance control and criminal law from a war on criminals. But, once again, the victims' rights movement takes too narrow a focus and thereby transmogrifies a principle of legitimacy into its direct opposite. While identification is crucial, it's identification with victims and offenders *as persons* that legitimates. The victims' rights movement, by contrast, stands for identification with victims qua victims, coupled with differentiation from offenders qua offenders.

In addition, a system of criminal law that fails to recognize the depth and breadth of punitive emotions unleashed by the experience and observation of victimization condemns itself to chronic instability. The victims' rights movement managed to monopolize emotional responses to crime. Instead, emotional responses in general should be affirmed, not only to crime but also to punishment, not only to victims but also to offenders. Here, too, the demands of the victims' rights movement must be generalized and then applied equally to all persons, victims and offenders alike.

Finally, the victims' rights movement's concept of a victim, suitably generalized, can form the basis of a system of law that takes the rights of victims seriously, more seriously than did the political movement that has taken their name and appropriated their cause. As it turns out, the outlines of such a system already exist. The law of crime victim compensation has for more than thirty years struggled with the question of who counts as a true victim of crime. It has evolved into a law of criminal victimhood that supplements the traditional criminal law, the law of criminal offenderhood. As chapters 5 and 6 show, both systems of law deal with the same general phenomenon: serious interpersonal crime. They represent two parallel legal responses to crime from the perspectives of the two persons who constitute this traumatic event: offender and victim.

The law of punishment regards crime from the offender's perspective, and the law of compensation from the victim's. They are two sides of the same coin. What holds them together is a common experience, crime, and a common subject, the person. They add up to a system of law that gives persons their due, no matter whether they played the part of "offender" or that of "victim" in the event that triggered state intervention, the crime as an assault on the personhood of one person by another. As a whole, they represent the state's attempt to vindicate the autonomy of victim and offender alike.

The Victim in American Criminal Law

Traces of the victim can be found in every aspect of American criminal law, from the general and special part of substantive criminal law to the imposition of penal norms in the criminal process and, eventually, to the actual enforcement of norms upon suspects and convicts. So far, attention has focused almost entirely on the victim's role in the criminal process, narrowly understood as the process of adjudication, such as the victim's right to be informed of hearings, to attend the trial, to be consulted regarding plea bargains, and to submit a victim impact statement at sentencing. This overview is no exception, if only because the victims' rights movement has portrayed itself as a movement for procedural rights, to the extent that it hasn't simply clamored for harsher, faster, and surer punishments. Still, it turns out that the victim crops up in substantive contexts as well, not only in substantive criminal law but also in the law of victim compensation, though in ways that don't necessarily fit into the victims' rights movement's campaign for greater punitiveness.

Substantive Criminal Law

The victim and her interests appear at various places in the general part of American criminal law.[22] To begin with, the victim's characteristics may have jurisdictional significance. American criminal law traditionally has frowned upon the so-called passive personality theory of jurisdiction, which extends criminal jurisdiction to acts committed abroad against any member of a given political community.[23] Still, in recent years this theory has been invoked to bring a number of serious extraterritorial offenses against United States nationals under federal criminal jurisdiction, including homicide, attempt or conspiracy to commit homicide, and other conduct that constitutes serious physical violence.[24]

Once the applicability of a given body of American criminal law is settled, the victim affects the analysis of criminal liability at various levels, as well as the assessment of punishment, in the event criminal liability is found. The law of causation, for instance, may take victim conduct into account if the conduct was so unforeseeable that its effects on the victim can't in fairness be attributed to the defendant. So, when a victim intentionally or at least voluntarily aggravates a minor wound into a fatal one, say by ripping off a bandage, one might hesitate to hold the defendant liable for homicide, rather than for assault.[25]

Victim behavior also determines the availability of a justification or excuse defense. For example, victim consent often amounts to a justification for nominally criminal conduct. Thus, a surgeon is justified in engaging in conduct that would otherwise constitute battery if her patient consents, even if only constructively, to the procedure.[26] This facet of the victim question has recently attracted much attention, as courts have struggled to decide whether a physician who helps a consenting terminally ill patient commit suicide can avail herself of a justification defense.[27]

Perhaps the most prominent example of a victim sensitive justification defense in American criminal law is the defense of self or of property. In either case, it is the conduct of the eventual victim that exculpates the accused, who merely responded to the infliction, threatened or actual, of unlawful harm by the victim. In American practice, cases of domestic abuse in which a woman kills her male partner often come down to the question of who is considered to be the "true" victim, the deceased man or the accused woman suffering from "battered woman syndrome" after years of abuse at the hand of her husband.[28] In cases where self-defense is not available, American criminal law also recognizes a partial excuse defense of provocation, or extreme mental or emotional disturbance, the availability of which likewise turns on the victim's conduct.[29]

In general, excuse defenses tend to reclassify the ostensible offender as a victim. Excuses that derive from temporary loss of self-control caused by another person (such as duress, military orders, extreme emotional disturbance, or imperfect self-defense) portray the ostensible offender as the actual victim, be it of the ostensible victim (as in extreme emotional disturbance or imperfect self-defense) or of another person (as in duress or military orders). Justification defenses do not. The paradigmatic justified actor instead chooses, responsibly and freely, the right course of action. A claim of victimization thus undermines a justification but bolsters an excuse.

The victim also impacts the law of punishment upon conviction, that is, the law of sentencing.[30] For example, the mandatory sentencing guidelines for federal courts provide that the sentence be increased in noncapital cases if the victim displayed certain characteristics known to the offender, including race, color, religion, national origin, ethnicity, gender, disability, sexual orientation, unusual vulnerability, or government service.[31] Note, also, that victim *mis*conduct at the time of the act, particularly in the form of aggression directed at the eventual offender, may *mitigate* the offender's punishment, even if defenses such as self-defense or provocation aren't available.[32]

The bulk of the special part of American criminal law traditionally has concerned itself with protecting the interests of personal victims in their life (e.g., homicide), liberty (e.g., unlawful imprisonment), and property (e.g., theft). As we saw in the previous chapter, however, so-called victimless crimes long ago began to challenge traditional personal crimes for dominance both in the books and in action. The victim behind these victimless crimes is the state, directly (as in crimes "against the existence or stability of the state") or indirectly (as in crimes against state-defined communities and institutions like "the public," "society," "the community," or "the family").

Many traditional offenses not classified as "victimless" generally have been purged of references to particular victim characteristics. So rape has been widely redefined to do away with the distinction between rape and (nonpunishable) marital rape, that is, rape of a victim who happens to be one's spouse. Similarly, many sex offenses have been rendered gender neutral, thus also criminalizing homosexual and female-male rape. Some sex offenses, however, continue to differentiate among victims on the basis of their age, notably "statutory" rape, which also tends to retain the traditional limitation to male perpetrators and female victims.

Statutory rape is not alone in continuing to differentiate among types of victim. One distinction between noncapital and capital murder, for instance, turns on the victim's status as a state official, such as a "police officer," a "uniformed court officer, parole officer, probation officer, or employee of the division for youth," an "employee of a state correctional institution or a local correctional facility," or a "judge."[33] As we saw in the previous chapter, modern criminal law is shot through with statutes that impose a punitive premium on acts committed against state victims, and even the state itself.[34] These statutes create either new crimes or aggravated versions of existing ones.

So-called hate crimes, which recently began to appear in American penal codes, operate in much the same way, except that they provide enhanced protection for a different type of victim.[35] For example, in 1982, two aggravated harassment offenses were added to the New York Penal Law, both of which turn on the victim's "race, color, religion or national origin."[36] Similarly, the Illinois Criminal Code contains an offense entitled "hate crime," making it a felony

> by reason of the actual or perceived race, color, creed, religion, ancestry, gender, sexual orientation, physical or mental disability, or national origin of another individual or group of individuals, [to] commit assault, battery, aggravated assault, misdemeanor theft, criminal trespass to residence, misdemeanor criminal damage to property, criminal trespass to vehicle, criminal trespass to real property, mob action or disorderly conduct . . . , or harassment by telephone . . . against a victim who is: (i) the other individual; (ii) a member of the group of individuals; (iii) a person who has an association with, is married to, or has a friendship with the other individual or a member of the group of individuals; or (iv) a relative (by blood or marriage) of a person described in clause (i), (ii), or (iii).[37]

Whenever criminal liability—or at least the particular nature of the criminal liability—turns on the victim's characteristics, one might expect that it would matter, first, that the victim in fact possessed these characteristics and, second, that the perpetrator knew she did. That's not necessarily so, however. An Illinois court recently held that its state's hate crime statute (just quoted) applies even in cases where neither of these conditions is met, on the ground that the primary victim of hate crimes is "the community," rather than "individual persons."[38]

Criminal Procedure

Apart from their significance in substantive criminal law, victims also play important roles throughout the criminal process, at least on paper.[39] To begin with, the victim in most cases determines whether the criminal process is set in motion at all. For example, even if marital rape is criminalized, women may in fact immunize their husbands from criminal liability by failing to report instances of rape in their marriages. Even after a possibly criminal act has come to the attention of the state without a victim complaint, the victim can influence the process in various ways, such as by deciding whether to pursue the case or, later on, by deciding whether to testify. Occasionally, recent reforms have *limited* the victim's influence on the criminal process to protect her interests in the long run. For example, several jurisdictions in the United States have enacted mandatory arrest laws in domestic violence cases that remove the victim's discretion whether to press charges.[40]

164 | The Legitimate Core of Victims' Rights

Rules regarding the initiation of prosecution differ widely among American jurisdictions and among felonies and misdemeanors within any given jurisdiction. In general, a complaint or an information suffices to initiate a misdemeanor prosecution, whereas felony prosecutions require an additional charging document, the indictment, which is issued after a preliminary hearing before a magistrate or a grand jury. Some states permit any person, including the victim, to file a complaint directly with the magistrate, who determines whether probable cause exists. Under the law of other states, as well as federal law, the complaint is subjected to a preliminary review by the prosecutor before it is submitted to the magistrate. In some jurisdictions, prosecutors are required to consult the victim before making a charging decision, at least in serious cases.[41]

In general, however, the prosecutor enjoys virtually unlimited discretion on whether and, if so, how to prosecute. Judicial interference with that discretion is thought to run afoul of the separation of powers. For example, the writ of mandamus generally cannot be used to compel a prosecutor to exercise her discretion one way or the other, even in the face of an apparently mandatory statute providing that "[t]he district attorney *shall* institute proceedings before magistrates for the arrest of persons charged with or reasonably suspected of public offenses when he has information that such offenses have been committed. . . ."[42]

At least in theory, if not in practice, victims retain several avenues by which to challenge a prosecutor's decision not to prosecute. Victims may challenge that decision on constitutional grounds, including the right to equal protection,[43] and on the basis of a federal statute "authoriz[ing] and requir[ing]" the prosecution of certain federal civil rights laws.[44] The prosecutor also remains subject to general provisions that criminalize malfeasance or nonfeasance in office. These provisions, however, are virtually never enforced. At any rate, they do not cover noncorrupt, discretionary judgments.

A prosecutor, however, can exercise her discretion only if she is in office. It should therefore not be forgotten that most American prosecutors' offices are run by elected officials. As a result, the charging decisions, policies, or trends of a particular prosecutor's office are subject to electoral review. For example, prosecutors who fail to pursue drunk driving cases with sufficient vigor may face a tough challenge from organized victims groups like Mothers Against Drunk Driving (MADD).

Should the case go forward, the victim continues to shape the process in various ways both before and during the trial. Many states assign victims the right to be notified of the defendant's release on bail, even to be present and to testify at the bail hearing.[45] The victim also often plays a crucial role at the investigatory stage. Some forms of victim participation (e.g., financing the investigation) may be improper because they create a conflict of interest in the public prosecutor regarding the interests of the victim and the public, which, at least according to a recent California decision, includes also "the defendant and his family and those who care about him,"[46] however difficult that is to believe, given the martial realities of prosecutorial practice in a war on crime.

American law also places limits on the appointment of private persons, including victims' attorneys, as special prosecutors. So a defendant's due process rights were held to have been violated when an attorney for the victim was appointed to conduct criminal contempt proceedings to enforce a court order that prohibited the defendant from infringing the victim's trademark.[47] In considering whether to permit private prosecution of a case, courts generally consider the severity of the offense and the public prosecutor's consent. Especially in jurisdictions with limited prosecutorial resources, victims may be permitted to privately prosecute minor everyday offenses, such as assault and battery.[48]

Currently, victims are not entitled to legal representation at state expense. In effect, the representation of the victim's interests is entrusted to every participant in the criminal process, except the defendant and her attorney. The prosecutor is required to represent the interests of the entire community (or "district"), which in theory includes not only the defendant (as we just saw) but also, and more obviously, the victim. The prosecutor's identification with the victim reveals itself clearly in the victim's presence at the prosecution's counsel table during some trials. (Needless to say, one would not expect to see the *defendant* sitting next to the prosecutor, no matter how much the prosecutor might be required to have his interests at heart, as a fellow member of "the public.") The judge similarly is sworn to consider the interests of justice, which generally are interpreted to include the victim's interests as well (and, once again, the defendant's). And judges, of course, in many jurisdictions are subject to the same electoral control, and therefore the political power of organized victims' groups, as are prosecutors and legislators (and even chief law enforcement officials, such as county sheriffs). Only the offices of those who oversee the eventual *infliction* of punishment have never been elective. The heads of bureaus of prisons and correctional services, as well as the directors of particular penal institutions (wardens), have always been administrators and appointed bureaucrats.

At trial, the jury has emerged as another important representative of the victim's interests. Unlike in the case of the legislative aspect of criminal law,[49] victims may not participate directly in its adjudicatory aspect. So victims may not serve as jurors or judges in their own case, though their victim status does not automatically bar their participation as jurors in other cases, provided their impartiality remains unaffected.[50]

A jury of potential victims, however, may threaten the legitimacy of its judgment. Insofar as the community is a community of potential (and actual) victims, rather than of potential (and actual) offenders, its representatives are more likely to view themselves as representatives of the victim than of the offender. To the extent that the jurors' identification with the victim comes at the expense of their identification with the defendant, the jury can no longer contribute to the legitimation of the criminal process. The jury, after all, was designed not to represent the community in general, never mind the victim, but the *defendant's* community. The defendant, not the victim, has a constitutional right to trial by a jury of her peers.[51] Yet at least one state now grants the *victim* the constitutional right to a trial before an offender-free jury "selected from registered voters and composed of persons who have not been convicted of a felony or served a felony sentence within the last 15 years."[52]

Even if victims generally may not directly participate in the prosecution or adjudication of their case, any private person, including the victim, may assist the public prosecutor's investigation by providing the prosecution with evidence, even if that evidence was obtained illegally.[53] Similarly, private persons, including victims, are authorized to perform warrantless "citizen's arrests" of persons they reasonably suspect of having committed a felony or a misdemeanor that constitutes a breach of the peace in their presence, as well as to question suspects, as long as they promptly surrender the suspect to a magistrate or law enforcement official.

Once the prosecution has been initiated, the victim can influence the disposition of the case in various ways. It is clear that the victim has no authority to dismiss charges on her own account.[54] At the same time, the prosecutor in some states may not dismiss charges without having "consulted" the victim, which is not to say that the victim actually gets to infringe on the prosecutor's traditional and well-entrenched discretion to manage his caseload as he sees fit.[55] In general, the prosecutor's dismissal is subject to judicial review in light of the "public interest," which once again presumably includes the victim's—and the defendant's—interest.[56] Many states also provide for judicial dismissal, even in the face of prosecutorial objection, "in the interests of justice."[57] Unlike prosecutors, judges are generally not required to consult the victim regarding a contemplated dismissal.

Dismissals based on an alternative, informal arrangement between the offender and the victim assign the victim a central role. For example, cases that involve certain trivial offenses can be disposed of by "civil compromise" between victim and offender. Upon judicial, and in some states also prosecutorial, approval of the compromise, the criminal case is dismissed. Victim-offender mediation similarly results in dismissal, or even a decision not to initiate a criminal prosecution in the first place.

In fact, the alternative disposition of facially criminal cases occurs rarely and unsystematically, even in minor cases. In the punitive climate of the past decades, so-called restorative justice programs have operated quietly on a small scale, even if the results have often been encouraging. They generally have not attracted much attention among policymakers beyond the local level or even among commentators, with the exception of the occasional article sounding a cautionary note.[58] Most important, they have not been embraced by the victims' rights movement, whose attention has concentrated on converting defendants' rights into victims' rights in the formal criminal justice process and, in what is generally considered to be a related objective, increasing criminal punishment, including the more frequent use of the death penalty.

The vast majority of criminal cases in the United States are disposed of by plea agreements. The victims' rights movement has called both for the outright abolition of plea bargains, at least in serious cases, and for the victims' participation in whatever plea bargaining persists. The first strategy, of prohibition, has borne little fruit.[59] Many states, however, provide for, and occasionally even mandate, some form of victim participation at various stages in the plea bargaining process, including the right to be consulted by the prosecution and to address the court prior to its ruling on the acceptability of the plea agreement.[60] It has even been proposed that victims join the plea bargaining process as a party that must consent to any agreement.[61]

Nonetheless, in law and in fact, prosecutors as a general rule do not, and may not, delegate the ultimate decision regarding a plea agreement to the victim or, in homicide cases, to her relatives.[62] The victim's right to participate in plea bargaining has been as difficult to enforce as any of the other procedural rights that victims recently have been accorded with considerable fanfare. At worst, public officials who disregard victims' procedural rights may run afoul of ethical rules.[63] In general, however, these rights are as unenforceable as they are unenforced.

The victim's influence on the criminal process does not end when the investigatory phase ends and adjudication begins. Several states now grant victims the right to have their interests considered in decisions regarding joinder and venue and the right to a speedy trial, as well as the right of access to the prosecutor's file (though not to the defendant's).[64] Many jurisdictions also limit the defendant's right to discovery from the victim in various forms, including interviews and psychological and physical examinations, at least without the presence of a support person.[65]

Once the trial begins, the victim may provide crucial, though not always reliable, eyewitness testimony. In addition, victims have the right to attend the trial and even, in some jurisdictions, to join the prosecutor at counsel table.[66] Many states also permit a "victim's advocate" to accompany the victim to the trial.[67] In addition to allowing the victim to proceed as a private prosecutor who acts in the public prosecutor's stead (such as in the rare trivial case, as discussed earlier), some states also permit the participation of a parallel private prosecutor who, compensated by the victim, assists the public prosecutor at trial.[68] With the public prosecutor's consent, the parallel private prosecutor may examine witnesses, introduce evidence, and make opening statements and closing arguments.[69] It has even been suggested that the victim herself be permitted to participate at trial as a "co-prosecutor," perhaps by examining witnesses or by delivering a statement even if she could not testify as a witness.[70]

Victims' interests also shape the law of evidence. Many constitutional victims' rights amendments require the admission of all relevant evidence, presumably because excluding relevant incriminatory evidence would harm victims' interests by barring—or at least hindering—conviction of "their" offender. These constitutional amendments, however, have not had much of an effect on evidentiary rulings in actual cases. It has also been argued that they violate, or at least eviscerate, constitutional rights of the defendant that, like the Fourth Amendment's protection against unreasonable searches and seizures and the Fifth Amendment's privilege against self-incrimination, become toothless without the exclusionary rule, which throws out illegally obtained evidence, no matter how relevant or incriminatory.

At the same time, other victim-based reforms of the law of evidence *prevent* the admission of relevant evidence, provided that its admission would benefit the defendant. For example, rape shield laws limit the admission of potentially relevant evidence regarding rape victims' prior sexual conduct.

The victim's influence extends to the very end of the trial and beyond. George Fletcher has recently proposed that the verdict in criminal cases be reformed to avoid the perception that an acquittal necessarily reflects disrespect for the victim.[71] According to Fletcher, criminal verdicts should be divided in two. The first part would address the question whether, on the basis of the facts established at trial, the accused violated the penal provision in question (and therefore the victim's right safeguarded by that provision). The second part would determine whether the accused nonetheless should be acquitted because her conduct was either justified or excused.

Once guilt has been established, victims can affect the assessment of punishment in various ways. Although victim testimony may play an important role at the sentencing phase of any criminal case, it has attracted the most attention in capital cases. The U.S. Supreme Court now permits the use of so-called victim impact statements that detail the victim's personal characteristics, as well as the harm suffered by the victim's family, in a capital trial's second phase, during which the sentencer, most often a jury, chooses between life imprisonment and death.[72] In theory, victims still are precluded from recommending a specific sentence at the sentencing hearing in capital cases. In fact, a murder victim's (or, rather, her surviving relative's) opinion about the proper sentence in a capital case tends to come through loud and clear.[73]

By contrast, in noncapital cases, some trial judges have been remarkably solicitous of victims' (or their relatives') specific recommendations regarding punishment, particularly in tailoring "creative" sentences to a specific offender and her act. For example, a Colorado judge recently followed the request made by the relative of a homicide victim at the sentencing hearing "that pictures of the victims and videos of the crime be sent with the defendant to prison in order to remind him of the impact of his crimes."[74] Similarly, an Arkansas judge took up the suggestion by another homicide victim's parents to have the defendant, "[o]n the 19th of each month for the next seven years, . . . mail $1 to an account set up in [the victim's] memory."[75]

The right to make victim impact statements was one of several victims' rights that featured prominently in the capital trial of Timothy McVeigh, the man convicted of and executed for the 1995 bombing of the Alfred Murrah federal building in Oklahoma City. In fact, the victims' right to testify at sentencing initially collided with another right, the right to attend the public trial; the trial judge barred victims who planned to give victim impact statements from the courtroom during the guilt phase of the trial. It took an act of Congress to resolve this conflict by removing the statutory obstacle to the victims' attendance at the trial so that the victims could exercise both rights.[76]

Not only the assessment of punishment but also the punishment itself takes victims into account. In addition to sporadic opportunities for informal victim restitution provided by more or less ambitious mediation programs throughout the country, several American jurisdictions now provide for formal restitution as part of the court-imposed sentence.[77] As the National Victim Center's Victims' Rights Sourcebook explains, "[t]oday not only do victims themselves qualify for restitution, but, in some states, family members, victims' estates, private entities, victim service agencies, and private organizations who provide assistance to victims can seek restitution as well."[78] Restitutable losses, the Sourcebook continues, may include "psychological treatment, sexual assault exams, HIV testing, occupational/rehabilitative therapy, lost profits, moving and meal expenses, case-related travel expenses, and burial expenses."

Unlike restitution, victim compensation is paid by the state, not by the offender.[79] And it's not part of the official criminal process. In particular, it has nothing to do with the imposition of punishment. Whereas restitution is imposed by the court along with other penalties following an adjudication of criminal guilt, compensation is dispensed by separate agencies, boards, or commissions (and only occasionally courts) formed to process compensation claims submitted by purported victims under victim compensation statutes.

The first American compensation scheme was set up in California in 1965, a good three years before President Nixon launched the war on crime in earnest and seventeen years before the punitive incarnation of victims' rights first made national headlines with the passage of California's Proposition 8, the first "Victims' Bill of Rights."[80] Since the 1960s, a fairly complex law of victim compensation has developed, consisting of formal and informal rules buried in statutes and administrative regulations and guidelines. And it's this body of victim law that we study carefully here as the most comprehensive effort to formulate a legal response to victimization directly, rather than indirectly via the offender-focused criminal process designed to determine the defendant's guilt or innocence, and to mete out the punishment to the convicted offender.

Victims' rights may even have a place in the appellate process. In a remarkable opinion, an Illinois court recently held that the 1992 Victims' Rights Amendment to the Illinois Constitution required appellate courts to end their long-standing practice of vacating a conviction if the defendant dies while that conviction is on appeal.[81] The court explained that this practice

> emanate[d] from the view that criminal prosecutions should punish the guilty and protect society from any future criminal misdeeds of the defendant. Once the defendant has died, these objectives are no longer possible. This traditional view began to change nationally, however, in the late 1970's and early 1980's with the recognition that crime victims and witnesses also have important, personal interests at stake in criminal proceedings.[82]

This dramatic paradigm shift from offenders to victims required a fundamental reassessment of all aspects of the criminal process, including the appellate stage, in light of its potential impact on victims:

> Abating the proceedings ab initio, after trial, conviction and judgment, creates an unacceptable and ultimately painful legal fiction for the surviving victims which implies that the defendants have somehow been exonerated. . . . [T]o wipe out the convictions of [the] defendants . . . on [a] legal technicality . . . would serve only to increase the misery of victims who have endured enough suffering. In our view, *the law should serve as a salve to help heal those whose rights and dignity have been violated*, not as a source of additional emotional turmoil. To this end, we hold that the victims of violent crime are entitled to retain whatever closure that may have been brought about by the finality of a criminal conviction.[83]

A concurring opinion added that vacating the convictions of the deceased appellants would not only pain their (putative) victims but also give the (putative) offenders the last laugh, especially in the case of appellants who had committed suicide. They, after all, had "deprived themselves of [the] right [to appeal] by their own hand."[84] Having "waived their right to appeal as well as their right to life," these (dead) appellants "should not be rewarded by vacating their convictions."[85]

Punishment

So far, we have touched on ways in which the victim shapes the definition and imposition of criminal norms in substantive and procedural criminal law, respectively. Victims, however, can also impact the third and final stage of the penal process, when the punishment threatened in the codes and imposed in the courts is actually inflicted on the offender.

In so-called victim-offender confrontation sessions, victims have the opportunity to confront offenders with the painful consequences of their criminal acts and perhaps to make sense of their own suffering. In thus shaming offenders, victims also contribute to offenders' punishment in the short term and, perhaps, to their rehabilitation and reintegration in the long term. The sessions may either be formally incorporated into the sentence, such as in drunk driving cases, or be arranged informally as part of a victims' assistance program, with no impact on the offenders' punishment apart from whatever consideration prison officials or parole boards might give to their participation.

In general, victim participation in the actual infliction of punishment remains limited. Victims are no longer allowed to spit on, slap, or insult offenders, practices that once constituted an important part of infamous public punishments, such as the pillory. Even the more modest shaming sessions just mentioned occur in private rather than in the market square. More public are the victim impact statements delivered in open court at sentencing hearings, which have punitive significance insofar as the process is always also part of the punishment.

In informal mediation settings, however, victims may find themselves monitoring offenders' adherence to the conditions of their punishment, particularly if the penalty requires the performance of certain acts designed to benefit the victim, whether in the form of financial restitution, public or private apologies, or personal services (such as the rebuilding of a damaged garage or the repainting of a defaced wall). In a well-known recent case in Washington State, the victim actually determined the length of an otherwise indeterminate punishment. In this case, the court suspended a prison sentence pending the banishment by a tribal court of two Native American offenders to separate corners of an uninhabited Alaskan island for twelve to eighteen months.[86] According to one of the tribal judges who occasionally visited the exiles to monitor their contrition, "[n]othing is over until the victim feels like he is fully compensated for his loss and says so."[87] Occasionally, the victim even becomes literally part of the punishment itself, as in a 1995 Ohio case where the trial judge sentenced a sexual abuser to marry his victim.[88]

Victims also are not permitted to observe offenders' punishment in its most common forms, imprisonment or supervised release. Nor have they been given a say in the conditions of offenders' imprisonment (yet).[89] So far, matters such as an offender's placement in a particular facility and the availability of amenities and services there have been left to the discretion of prison officials, with no obligation to consult the victim. In the case of capital punishment, victims likewise have no influence on the time or manner of execution, although victims' interests have been invoked in support of efforts to accelerate the disposition of death penalty cases. Capital punishment is unique, however, in that victims (or, rather, their surviving relatives, since the death penalty is limited to homicide, in practice if not on paper)[90] may observe its infliction. Most recently, hundreds of victims, and their relatives, of the Oklahoma City bombing were allowed to witness the infliction of the death sentence on Timothy McVeigh, either in person or on closed-circuit television, "to ease their grief over the bombing."[91] (Similar arrangements had been made for McVeigh's trial but were rejected for the appeal.[92])

Finally, victims can have a say in deciding when the infliction of punishment upon their offender is to come to an end, or at least when one type of sanction is to be transformed into another, say from carceral to noncarceral supervision. Victims in many jurisdictions have the right to be heard on the prisoner's eligibility for parole and, in some cases, even the propriety of an executive pardon.[93]

Beyond Symbols

This brief overview suggests that the American victims' rights movement has been remarkably successful. Today, constitutions, statutes, and court opinions loudly proclaim the victim's right to have a voice in all aspects of American criminal law. The question remains, however, whether the victim's place in American criminal law is in fact secure. In particular, it is yet to be seen whether the victim will retain its current significance after the war on crime has run its course, given that the victims' rights movement is so closely associated with this campaign of criminal mass incapacitation.

To achieve legal credibility, as opposed to political salience, the issue of victims' rights must be disentangled from the war on crime. This means, among other things, that the interests of victims should be investigated and protected, *even if* they do not result in more punishment for more offenders more quickly. The movement for victims' rights is entirely separate from the movement against offenders. Our overview already has identified several instances in which considering the victim results in less, rather than more, punishment, as in the case of the consent defense or in victim-offender mediation. In one case, giving victims their due, quite literally, has no effect on punishment whatsoever: the law of victim compensation dispenses *victim* compensation even in the absence of *offender* punishment.

Without a considered account of the experience and significance of victimhood in and of itself, independent of its implications for the treatment of offenders, the achievements of the victims' rights movement may survive at best as symbols, which may in the end constrain the victim's role, rather than cement it. Once symbolic protections are in place, any victim-oriented reform proposal must establish the need for further measures, no matter how toothless previous measures might have been. And putting teeth in existing protections may prove trickier than establishing the protections in the first place. From the very beginning of the modern victims' rights movement, victim-oriented reforms have failed to transform symbolic "victims' bills of rights" into penal practice. As we saw earlier, neither the constitutional prohibition of plea bargaining nor the constitutional guarantee of "truth-in-evidence" contained in California's Proposition 8 in 1982 had their expected radical impact on the way California prosecutors dispose of their cases or on the way California judges control the evidence in their courtrooms.

It is no surprise that the history of a thoroughly political movement such as the victims' rights movement has been the history of constitutional amendments. Constitutional amendments, of course, are powerful symbols as they solemnly etch reforms, and particularly rights, into the foundational documents of American political communities. Constitutional guarantees, however, are also notoriously difficult to enforce, whether they are claimed by victims or by defendants.

For the victim to assume a place in American criminal law in the long term, the victims' rights movement must move beyond a political reaction to the perceived expansion of defendants' constitutional rights in the 1960s. Rather than fight symbolic constitutional protections with symbolic constitutional protections, the victims' rights movement must integrate itself into a comprehensive reform of American criminal law in theory and fact that assigns all persons, victims and offenders alike, their legitimate place.

To contribute to this reform is the goal of this book, by developing an account of victims' rights free from the punitive frenzy of the war on crime, without rejecting the cause of victims' rights through guilt by association. We begin by isolating the concept of the victim at the core of the victims' rights movement.

The Victim in Victims' Rights

From the start, the victims whose cause the modern victims' rights movement wrote on its banners have been victims of interpersonal crime, and of interpersonal *violent* crime at that. They are, in other words, the victims of traditional criminal law. In the righteous, and oft-quoted, words of the 1982 Final Report of the President's Task Force on Victims of Crime, a central document in the evolution of the victims' rights movement: "*Violent* crime honors no sanctuary. It strikes when least expected, often when the victim is doing the most commonplace things."[94] And it's "[v]ictims *who . . . survive their attack*" who find themselves "treated as appendages of a system appallingly out of balance," one that "serve[s] lawyers and defendants, treating victims with institutionalized disinterest."[95] That same year, Congress passed the first federal victims' rights statute, the Victim and Witness Protection Act. In the congressional findings and declarations of purpose that accompany it, we read that "[a]ll too often the victim of a *serious crime* is forced to suffer physical, psychological, or financial hardship first as a result of the criminal act and then as a result of contact with a criminal justice system unresponsive to the real needs of such victim."[96] Two decades later, the proposed federal victims' bill of rights remains limited to "victim[s] of a crime of violence."[97]

It goes without saying, but warrants saying nonetheless, that whenever politicians find it expedient to declare their support for "victims' rights," they don't invoke narratives of victimization at the hands of embezzlers, insider traders, drug possessors, money forgers, river polluters, or computer hackers. Instead, they speak of the victims of serious violent crime. When Al Gore announced his support for a federal victims' bill of rights during his 2000 president campaign, prominently featured among the "more than a dozen victims, relatives of victims and law enforcement officers, who told [him] their stories today" was a woman who had been "kidnapped, held captive for five days without water or food and raped repeatedly by three men."[98]

Expressions of support for the cause of "victims' rights" invariably begin with images of violent interpersonal crime. A recent law review article, written in support of victims' bills of rights, set the stage by reminding its readers that "[s]tatistically, eight of every ten Americans will be victims of *violent* crime at least once in their lives," followed by a series of snapshots of violent criminalization drawn from newspaper reports:

> A 7-Eleven clerk shot in the face after two robbers took $18.87 from him and were leaving the store. The senseless shooting left the clerk in serious condition after the "bullet barely missed his spinal cord and an artery in his neck."
>
> A five-year-old girl kidnapped while taking out the garbage. Later she is stripped, bound, gagged with tape, and then stuffed into a cardboard box.
>
> A Salt Lake City man shot to death by a teenager. The teenager wanted to use the pay phone that the man was using.[99]

The image of victims in the victims' rights movement is that of helpless individuals who are "either ignored by the criminal justice system or simply used as tools to identify and punish offenders."[100] They are "family members [who] speak about the pain they feel when they are excluded from the courtroom as the fate of their child's killer is decided, the dismissive tone from prosecutors when they are asked for an update on the case, and the disregard from the parole board when it is asked about the status of an impending release."[101]

These victims are sympathetic in the true sense of the word. Their suffering speaks to us precisely because they are like us. We have no difficulty imagining ourselves as the victim of a violent crime. Perhaps we even have experienced victimization firsthand, even if not in the extreme form of a violent crime, but in a milder version—perhaps our car radio has been stolen, or our house broken into. Extrapolating from minor victimizations to major ones takes little effort and even less imagination, thanks to the constant visual display of violent victimization in the media. And, having placed ourselves in the victim's shoes, we quickly come to feel her pain as ours, aided by the myriad victim narratives that crowd American public discourse.

The victims' rights movement works because it invokes a particular three-part image of the victim: the victims in victims' rights are *personal*, they are victims of *serious* interpersonal crimes, and they are *helpless*. We address each aspect in turn.

As personal, victims are literally identifiable. As definite targets for our identification, they can function as communal icons into whom we can imaginatively pour our selves. As personal targets, they allow us to iden-tify with them as persons.

The image of the victim held up by the victims' rights movement is personal in another sense. It depicts one person being victimized by *an-other person*. The personal nature of the offender is important; victims of natural disasters, or even of state oppression, can be just as personal (and personable) as the victims in victims' rights. Their plight, however, is ir-relevant to the victims' rights movement.

The victim of a hate crime epitomizes the victim image of the victims' rights movement: as an identifiable person victimized by another person for the purpose of subjugation. Or so one would think. In fact, however, the hate crime issue has occupied at best a minor role in the catalogue of demands associated with the victims' rights movement. The victims' rights movement was slow to embrace the cause of hate crime victims.[102] Why? Because the participants in the victims' rights revolution did not identify with the victims of hate crimes, and for the same reason that hate crimes were committed in the first place: race.

The difference between hate crimes and other crimes from the per-spective of victims' rights is clear. The paradigmatic victim of a hate crime is black. The paradigmatic victim of the victims' rights movement is white. The paradigmatic *offender* of the victims' rights movement is black. As a component of the war on crime, the pursuit of victims' rights carries strong racial connotations, which tend to remain submerged but occasionally and disturbingly bubble to the surface, as in the now infa-mous Willie Horton episode in George H. W. Bush's 1988 presidential campaign.[103]

Moreover, the victims' rights movement is dominated by whites at all levels, and most certainly at the levels of power, both outside and inside government.[104] These fighters for victims' rights either have been, or imagine themselves to be, victims of crime or, in the paradigmatic cases of homicide, are related to someone who has been a victim of crime. That crime never is a hate crime.

This was not always so. Early on, the crime of rape, understood as a crime motivated by hatred of women, not by some amorphous "*gender animus*"[105] but by misogyny, played a central role in the emergence of a victim's perspective in criminal law.[106] No matter how important, even revolutionary, they were in their time, the early contributions of the women's rights movement retain no influence on the victims' rights movement as it exists today. Instead, the pursuit of the rights of women victims of misogynistic crime has been integrated into the war on crime, along with the cause of victims' rights generally.

Take, for instance, the 1997 case of Rita Gluzman. No doubt much to her surprise, Ms. Gluzman found herself convicted of "interstate domestic violence" under the federal Violence Against Women Act for murdering her husband.[107] Not surprisingly, Ms. Gluzman objected that hers wasn't a case of misogynistic violence against women, nor of nonmisogynistic violence against women, nor for that matter of any kind of violence against women, but was that of a woman who was accused of having killed a man (with the assistance of a male cousin). The court was unimpressed, pointing out that "[t]he statute is decidedly gender neutral" and that, while "[t]he legislative history recognize[d] that women are the 'most likely target' of gender-based violence," it did "not exclude men as potential victims."[108] The Violence Against Women Act, it turned out, was directed not against misogynistic crime at all but against "gender-motivated" crime.

It was this facial neutrality that qualified the Violence Against Women Act as a crime-fighting tool with the flexibility needed in today's comprehensive war on crime. It could be employed against anyone, even against the very women it was ostensibly designed to protect. Ms. Gluzman was the first person, man or woman, to be convicted of homicide under the statute. She is serving a sentence of life imprisonment without the possibility of parole.[109]

The flexibility of facial neutrality, however, was not the only feature that distinguished the offense of "interstate domestic violence." As a federal statute, it could be used not just against anyone, but also anywhere. As we saw in our discussion of the seamless web of possession police, nothing short of complete and seamless cooperation among the various law enforcement agencies will suffice if the American war on crime is to attain its goal of crime extermination. And the Gluzman case shows just what interjurisdictional cooperation can achieve if the enforcement officials only put their mind to it, as they are doing on an ever increasing scale, from the cooperation of federal and state officials in drug cases to Project Exile, the nationwide local-federal collaboration aimed at incapacitating felons in possession of a firearm.[110]

The Gluzman case landed in federal court, rather than in state court, where it belonged, because the federal law of evidence was more favorable to the prosecutor than was New Jersey's. (The federal prosecutor, unlike his state colleague, could use uncorroborated testimony of an accomplice—her male cousin—against Ms. Gluzman.)[111] It illustrates the potential benefits of coordinated federal-state crime extinction efforts, rather than the vindication of victims' rights in general, or of the rights of victims of hate crimes in particular.

The federal Violence Against Women Act thus exemplifies the state's use of the victims' rights agenda to further its systematic campaign against crime and, as we saw in the previous chapter, potentially against any source of inconvenience, including the victims in whose name the campaign is conducted. In the Gluzman case, a law passed for the protection of women victims of domestic violence was used to maximally incapacitate a woman. We find further evidence of this misappropriation strategy when we take a closer look at the definition of victim in legislation that manages to protect state interests under the guise of the fight for victims' rights.[112]

But, for now, let us remain for a moment on the subject of the image of the victim that powers the victims' rights movement. Let us try to appreciate the power of this image before analyzing its abuse. For, to understand its abuse, we must understand its attraction.

The icon of the victims' rights movement, and of the community of actual and potential victims, is not only a person victimized by another. She is also the victim of a *serious* crime. To enable the desired sympathetic response, the victim must be a person. To trigger the desired sympathetic response at the desired intensity, the victim must be the victim of a serious crime. In general, the intensity of the response is proportional to the perceived identity between observer and victim and the perceived degree of victimization.

This principle leads the victims' rights movement to put homicide front and center. Complications result. Homicide is both the most serious and the most victimless of crimes. Its impact on the victim is so catastrophic that it leaves no victim behind.

This peculiarity of the crime of homicide is mirrored in the tort of wrongful death. Until the mid-nineteenth century, there simply was no tort analogue to the crime of homicide. The tort, it was said, had died with the victim.[113] Wrongful death actions entered Anglo-American tort law only in 1846, through a statute known as Lord Campbell's Act, which eventually was copied more or less closely by every American jurisdiction.[114] Wrongful death is anomalous in that, unlike other torts, it does not compensate the tort victim for an injury. The person who sustained the injury, death, is no longer around to receive the compensation. Her death is the only relevant fact, her experience of that fact irrelevant. What matters is not the pain of dying but merely the effect the victim's death had on someone else.[115] And only a particular effect on the surviving, indirect victims is relevant, namely the loss of future financial support. In a wrongful death action, the victim's "pain and suffering" are as irrelevant as her survivors'.

Homicide clearly occupies the center of the crime universe invoked by the victims' rights movement, around which all other crimes revolve. Beyond homicide, one finds a smattering of other violent crimes. Property crimes play a minor role; if we go by victims' rights legislation, their significance appears to lie less in the trauma of the first victimization than in the inconvenience of the second, experienced at the hands of state officials who, as we just saw, repeat or at least prolong the victimization by holding on to stolen property "for long periods of time . . . , until the trial and sometimes appeals are over," "many times" even allowing the property to be "damaged or lost, which is particularly stressful for the elderly or poor."[116]

The victim of the victims' rights movement, then, is identifiably personal, rather than abstractly communal. It also is the victim of a serious, preferably violent, crime. And, finally, the victim is *helpless*. The victims in the two Supreme Court cases on victim impact evidence in capital cases were an elderly couple and a mother with two little children.[117]

Nothing excites the communal punitive reflex of all potential victims (that's all of us) more than the murder of a child. No victim is more helpless than a homicide victim, except for a homicide victim who is also a child and even more so, a girl. One of the most haunting images associated with the victims' rights movement is that of twelve-year-old Polly Klaas, who was abducted and murdered in 1993. Here is her father's account of "The Polly Klaas Story," as featured on the Web site of the Klaas Foundation for Kids:[118]

> During a slumber party in October of 1993, 12 year old Polly Hannah Klaas was abducted at knife-point from her Petaluma, California home. Thousands of residents from the surrounding community immediately responded with the largest manhunt in American history. Hundreds of selfless volunteers abandoned normal daily routines for 65 days. They answered countrywide calls, read thousands of letters and searched for Polly. A mass distribution of 2 billion images of Polly was sent worldwide. She had soon become a symbol of love and lost innocence.
>
> The world froze one cold evening in December when the media reported that Polly, "America's Child," the beautiful girl with the warm

brown eyes shown smiling in home videos for millions of TV viewers, was not found alive. The country was outraged. The public cried out for change in legislation and pro-action in crime prevention.

Then there is seven-year-old Megan Kanka, raped and murdered three years later. Among the most visible statutory reforms pushed through by the victims' rights movement is "Megan's Law," which requires that sex offenders register with the police after their release from prison and that "the community" be notified of their whereabouts. The press release that accompanied the ceremonial signing of the New York version of Megan's Law by then newly elected Governor George Pataki captures a ritual repeated throughout the country, whenever and wherever victims' rights legislation is signed into law.

> Governor Pataki was joined by Maureen Kanka, mother of 7-year-old Megan Kanka, who was abducted, sexually assaulted and murdered in July 1994; Pastor Robert Wood, father of 12-year-old Sara Anne Wood, who was abducted in Frankfort, New York in August 1993 and whose body has never been found; and Marc Klaas, father of 12-year-old Polly Klaas, who was abducted from her home in Petaluma, California and murdered in October 1993.[119]

In addition to the representative victims, the ceremony also featured the obligatory state officials. In addition to the governor, one could find "Attorney General Dennis C. Vacco, Senator Dean G. Skelos, Assemblyman Daniel L. Feldman, Senate Majority Leader Joseph L. Bruno and members of the Senate and Assembly." Pataki explained, somewhat prosaically, that Megan's Law would "provid[e] parents, communities and law enforcement with a powerful new tool that will help protect children from convicted sex offenders." The other officials echoed Pataki's sentiments:

> "Experts document that a pedophile's predatory behavior does not decrease over time," said Senator Skelos, the Senate sponsor of the legislation. "Our version of 'Megan's Law' will not only empower parents with the knowledge needed to protect their children, it will also give women a valuable tool in safeguarding themselves from the violent sexual predators in our community."
>
> "New York's 'Megan's Law' gives parents the information they need to protect their children and gives law enforcement an important tool to help prevent abuse," said Attorney General Vacco. "My office is prepared to defend the legality of this new law in order to protect the rights of our citizens to be safe from those who would prey upon children or otherwise use them for their own fiendish purposes."

"Law enforcement has information that when made available to the public will save lives and prevent further victimization," said Assemblyman Feldman, the Assembly sponsor. "With this new law, the people of New York will know what the State of New York already knows. Our 'Megan's Law,' built on the experience of other states, guarantees as far as possible our success against Constitutional challenge and irresponsible attempts to abuse the information that it will provide."[120]

In an act laden with symbolism, one gesture—also oft repeated— stood out as particularly dramatic: "Governor Pataki used three pens to affix his signature to the law. For their tireless efforts on behalf of sex offender community notification, the Governor presented one pen each to Mrs. Kanka, Pastor Wood, and Mr. Klaas."[121]

A few years later, Pataki signed "Jenna's Law" which, among other things, effectively eliminated parole for "violent felony offenders." That piece of victims' rights legislation was named after Jenna Grieshaber, who, to quote from the accompanying press release, was "a nursing student at Russell Sage College who lived in Albany when she was murdered on November 6, 1997, *allegedly* by a violent felon out on parole."[122]

In the now familiar ritual, the surviving relatives of the victim joined Governor Pataki at the signing. Also present were "the family of slain New York City Police Officer Anthony Mosomillo, who was killed by a parolee on May 26, 1998."[123]

And there was also the requisite lineup of state officials, all of whom voiced their unequivocal support for Jenna's Law. Compared to the Megan's Law signing three years earlier, there were more officials, and their remarks more colorful. The governor commended the Grieshabers for their "tireless efforts" and identified the law as "another important milestone in New York's historic success in fighting violent crime": "We passed the death penalty, ended work release for violent felons, and ended parole and increased sentences for repeat violent felons." And the attorney general spoke of "the crusade waged by Bruce and Janice Grieshaber, who have distinguished themselves as profiles in perseverance for their efforts to make our streets a safer place for our families."

From there, the procession of officials continued all the way down to the chairman of the state parole board:

Senate Majority Leader Joseph L. Bruno said, "As a result of the Governor's leadership and the courage and perseverance of Bruce and Janice

Grieshaber, we now have a law in place that will keep more violent criminals behind bars and off our streets.

This builds on our previous criminal justice reforms that have caused crime to drop significantly throughout the state."

Senator John DeFrancisco said, "Keeping violent felons behind bars where they belong is in the best interest of public safety.

Jenna's Law sends a clear message that violence against honest, hard working citizens will not be tolerated. I would like to thank my constituents the Grieshabers for their determination to turn their personal tragedy into something positive by working with us to help end parole for violent felons."

Senator Dale Volker, Senate sponsor of Jenna's Law, said, "As a long-standing opponent of parole for first-time violent felons, I am pleased to see the Governor sign this bill into law. Jenna's Law is an aggressive sensible approach to protecting New Yorkers from dangerous criminals and ensuring that, when they are eventually released, that they are closely monitored to make certain that public safety is not compromised."

Assembly Republican Leader John Faso said, "Jenna's law will protect our citizens, protect our cops, and save lives. It is a fitting tribute to Jenna and her parents, Bruce and Janice Grieshaber, who reminded all New Yorkers what democracy is all about."

Assemblyman Hal Brown said, "I am delighted that the Speaker of the State Assembly finally did the right thing and allowed a vote on this important measure. All New Yorkers owe a tremendous debt of thanks to the Grieshaber family for their tireless efforts to get this job done."

"Jenna's Law is going to sharply reduce the number of New Yorkers who suffer at the hands of violent criminals," State Director of Criminal Justice Katherine N. Lapp said. "There is nothing that Governor Pataki takes more seriously than his obligation to protect the people of New York State from violent criminals."

"This law serves as a testament to the Governor's commitment to the safety of all New Yorkers as well as a tribute to the memory of Jenna Grieshaber," William J. Fitzpatrick, President of the New York State District Attorney's Association said.

"Jenna's parents, with their tenacity and dedication, have performed a political miracle and their daughter's legacy will one day be that future laws will be passed based on the needs of the people, not in memory of murdered children."

"We know that much needs to be done, and as President of the NYS District Attorneys' Association, I look forward to working with the Governor and the Grieshabers on the important issues of Sexual Assault Reform,

Juvenile Justice and alternatives to prison for non-violent offenders," DA Fitzpatrick said.

Parole Board Chairman Brion Travis said, "Jenna's Law will enhance community safety by providing for lengthy periods of post-release supervision by highly trained parole officers. It is a common sense approach that, thanks to the determined efforts of Governor Pataki and the Grieshabers, will result in even further reductions in serious crimes throughout the state."[124]

Continuing the trend of naming victims' rights laws after female homicide victims, New York recently enacted "Kendra's Law." Kendra's Law provides for "involuntary outpatient treatment" of "potentially dangerous" mentally ill persons who fail to take their medication. (There's also an "Elisa's Law," a "Kieran's Law," and a "Jeremy and Julia's Law.") According to the governor's press release, Kendra's Law was "named in memory of Kendra Webdale. In January 1999, the thirty-two-year-old Buffalo native was killed after being pushed into the path of a New York City subway train by a mentally ill person who had a history of non-compliance with treatment. She was an aspiring screenwriter who dreamed of writing a movie screenplay."[125] (Presumably because this mental health measure packed much less punitive punch, the only state official, other than Pataki, who showed up at the signing was the state mental health commissioner; no victim relatives were there.)

A murdered girl is perceived as helpless three times over. According to the still dominant construction of childhood and gender in American society, a murdered girl, both child and female, already was doubly helpless before the crime. As a result of her murder, she remains helpless thereafter. Much of the cruelty of a child homicide lies in its permanent cementation of the victim's helplessness. The murdered child will never have the chance to shed her helplessness by maturing into a fully autonomous adult.

The helplessness of the victim is important for an understanding of the victims' rights movement because it is this helplessness that calls for state action, for help. Without our help—and "our" here means "the state's"—the victim will remain mired in her victimization. Without us, she will not be able to reassert herself as something other than the object of the offender's crime. So we leap to the victim's aid, consumed by sympathy and moved by pity, to help her recover what the offender took away: her personhood.

The image of the victim that drives the victims' rights movement is as powerful as it is internally inconsistent. To trigger the strongest sympathetic response, the paradigmatic victim of the victims' rights movement is nonexistent—she has not survived the crime. She has become the victim of her own victimization. Moreover, the paradigmatic victim is a person, and thus a target of interpersonal identification, yet at the same time she is entirely deprived of personhood, to trigger action rather than mere sympathy. The emotional and motivational impact of the victims' rights movement comes at the price of conceptual confusion.

That confusion has remained hidden for two reasons. First, the place of the absent homicide victim has been assumed by her very present relatives. Instead of Polly Klaas, we heard from her father, Marc Klaas; instead of Megan Kanka, from her parents, Maureen and Richard Kanka. Since homicide was the prototypical crime, murderers the prototypical offenders, and homicide victims the prototypical victims, the dominant victim voices in the victims' rights movement were not those of the victims themselves but those of their surviving relatives. These "victims by proxy," as Brent Staples, himself an indirect murder victim, points out, "now hold regular press conferences, as did Ronald Goldman's father almost every day at the O. J. Simpson trial," and are "gradually becoming a permanent victim class."[126]

As a result, the victims' rights movement looked more like the relatives of victims' rights movement. Homicide "co-victims" like Marc Klaas and the Kankas, for example, were lifted out of obscurity to national prominence.[127] They created foundations, appeared on television, gave lectures, attended conferences, lobbied for victims' rights legislation, and met with political figures eager to show their concern for victims. From the materials related to the conference "The Serial/Sexual Predator," held at Michigan State University in 1998, which featured Marc Klaas and Maureen Kanka as speakers, we get a good sense of the victims' rights credentials of both:

> Maureen Kanka—became a national child advocate after the brutal rape and murder of her seven-year-old daughter Megan at the hands of a twice-convicted pedophile. As a result of Megan's death, Maureen and Richard Kanka established the Megan Nicole Kanka Foundation. They worked with the State of New Jersey for passage of Megan's Law, which notifies community residents when dangerous pedophiles move into their neighborhoods. Mrs. Kanka has worked with many state agencies and policymakers. By

creating much-needed awareness, she has enabled several states to pass their own versions of Megan's Law. The Kankas were also instrumental in getting Megan's Law signed into federal law by President Clinton on May 17, 1996.[128]

According to the same conference materials, Marc Klaas's nationwide efforts on behalf of victims have been extensive as well:

> Marc Klaas—is the father of murder victim Polly Klaas. Upon the discovery of his daughter's body, Klaas gave up a lucrative business as a Hertz franchise owner to concentrate his efforts on stopping crimes against children and ending child abuse. He has emerged as a national leader in his efforts to achieve proactive approaches to protect and educate America's at-risk children, their families, policymakers, and concerned citizens. He has been instrumental in the passage of five California State anti-crime bills. All of his legislation is designed to increase the protection of children.[129]

A more detailed account of the origin and extent of Klaas's activities as victims' rights and "anti-crime" activist appears on the Web site of the Klaas Foundation, which he founded. So we learn from "The Polly Klaas Story" that her father

> immediately dove into a campaign to put children higher on the national priority list. With no prior media, political or public speaking experience, he immediately became savvy in affecting proactive legislation, and sought to advocate children's issues and speak out on crime prevention.
> Within a year the Klaas Foundation for Children was formed.[130]

Since then,

> Marc Klaas has been instrumental in the passage of several state and federal anti-crime bills. All of this legislation is designed to increase the protection of children. At the Federal Crime Bill signing, President Clinton dedicated the Crime Bill to Polly Klaas and two other crime victims. Mr. Klaas has met several times with President Clinton and U.S. Attorney General Janet Reno.[131]

The site, under the heading of "KlaasKids Foundation Accomplishments," then goes on to list Marc Klaas's extensive victims' rights c.v.:

- Legislative Testimony (15 entries, as of Oct. 18, 2000),
- Publications (18),
- Keynote Speaker—Conferences (24),
- Keynote Addresses (33),
- TV Specials (10),

- Child Safety Town Hall Meetings (11), and
- TV Shows (59), including an appearance on the Oprah Winfrey Show

Other surviving relatives of homicide victims have not been content to lobby for victims' rights and anticrime legislation. They have become legislators themselves. Brooks Douglass, an Oklahoma state senator who as a teenager watched his parents being murdered, fought for the right of indirect murder victims to attend the execution of the person sentenced to death for the murder. He succeeded and watched his parents' murderer die by lethal injection.[132] After the execution, Douglass "spent a lot of time . . . working with crime victims and doing television shows on the rights of victims."[133] A year later, he was "negotiating with a company that wants to film a movie about the murders and his life since then."[134]

Then there is the former Texas chiropractor who attained some national notoriety for invoking her status as an indirect, or "derivative,"[135] victim to stand up for her right to carry concealed guns. Suzanna Gratia Hupp has fought for the repeal of restrictions on concealed weapons ever since her parents were among twenty-three people killed by a deranged gunman in a cafeteria in Killeen, Texas. Why? Because she feels that she could have prevented the murder had she only had her gun that day. She, too, has succeeded, and in more ways than one. The concealed handgun law was passed. What's more, she "rode her campaign to a seat in the Texas state legislature."[136] And she is riding it still. Most recently, she could be seen on national television recounting, once more, her story as the keynote speaker of the Second Amendment Sisters counterrally to the Million Mom March, the demonstration for tighter gun control held in Washington, D.C., in May 2000.[137]

With so many articulate indirect victims pushing so loud and hard for "victims'" rights, the interests of the silenced homicide victims themselves can recede into the background. In all the attention showered on homicide "survivors," it's all too easy to forget the true victim of a homicide, the undeniable and unalterable fact recently captured by one father who had lost his twenty-three-year-old daughter: "I wasn't the victim; she was."[138] It is, tragically, impossible by definition to push for the rights of homicide victims. The only rights at stake are those of the "survivors."

The Douglass and Hupp cases illustrate this point. The immediate beneficiary of Brooks Douglass's victims' rights campaign was Brooks Douglass. He and his sister were the first to exercise the victims' right he had succeeded in establishing. Hupp invoked the rights of absent murder victims, her parents, to claim a secondary right of their relative, herself, the existence of which at the time of the murder she claims would have prevented the victimization in the first place. The secondary right claimed by the indirect victim therefore connects not to the murder victims' rights but at best to the rights of all *potential* murder victims who would be protected from actual victimization by the recognition of the secondary right.

A murder victim could benefit from the right to carry a concealed weapon about as much as from the right to attend the execution of her murderer. Once again, the victim's relative is claiming a right not for the victim but for herself. The victim's role is reduced to that of a facilitator. The victim's rights are invoked to claim rights for another.

This duality of the victim as end and means, as beneficiary and facilitator, as subject and object, lies at the heart of the victims' rights movement. The conflict between these two faces of victimhood emerges most clearly in the tension inherent in an image of the victim that is both endowed with personhood and crippled by victimization. The victim's personhood is important because it allows us to identify with her. We can identity with the plight of a person, not with that of an interest, a community, or even an institution. But with personhood come assumptions about the victim's capacity for autonomy. To recognize the victim as a person is to see her not only as like us but also as endowed with the capacity to govern herself.

The image of the victim as subject, however, stands in stark contrast with that of the victim as so consumed by suffering and hatred for her victimizer that she is incapable of freeing herself from the offender's control and thereby recovering her personhood without state intervention. But it's this helplessness that transforms victims' rights from a sociological theory into a political movement. To quote, once again, from the 1982 Task Force on Victims of Crime, state action is required because "the system has deprived the innocent, the honest, and the *helpless* of its protection."[139] Without the helpless victim, the "needy person" in Kentucky's victim compensation statute,[140] there's no need for help.

The helpless victim is precisely the sort of victim that plays into the hands of those state officials who are eager to misappropriate the cause of victims' rights to serve their own ends, in particular to cement their power and the power of the state they serve and represent. A helpless and absent victim is a manipulable victim. The acute misery of victimization makes the victim vulnerable to the influence of state officials who present themselves as sympathetic enforcers of her interests. In fact, the state official may well help the victim distill these interests out of the chaotic onslaught of emotions brought on by the experience of victimization. A victim may well appreciate how the prosecutor's advice simplifies her conflicted emotions into a single aim: to exterminate the offender. The victim thus can become a powerful tool in the prosecutor's arsenal as he wages war against crime and criminals, a war all too often fought for the greater glory of the prosecutor, rather than for the sake of the victim's rights as a person.

On a broader scale, the helpless victim is precisely the sort of image that fits into a state-centered system of criminal administration. Generally speaking, victims are an inconvenience to the state. They demand attention and compromise the efficiency of the criminal disposal process. Helpless victims, by contrast, pose no such challenge. They are eager for state assistance and easily manipulable. As a result, they constitute a valuable source of legitimacy for the state's pursuit of its self-aggrandizement.

To fully appreciate the significance of the fact that the paradigmatic victim of the victims' rights movement in the United States is a child murder victim, let's take a look outside our borders. In Germany, the leading voice on the rights of crime victims belongs not to the father of a slain girl but to a direct adult victim of a serious but nonfatal crime. It is astonishing to see what difference an articulate victim can make, a victim whose personhood is not in doubt and who nonetheless struggles to reconcile that personhood with his experience of victimization by considering, as a victim and as a person, what the rights of a victim might be, and how they could be vindicated in the criminal law.

In 1996, Jan Phillip Reemtsma was kidnapped and kept in a basement room for almost five weeks.[141] *In the Cellar*, his account of these weeks of captivity, became a best-seller in Germany.[142] More recently, Reemtsma has begun to think publicly about the right of victims to have their offender punished.[143] Instead of proposing specific reforms, or even a comprehensive victims' rights agenda complete with grass-roots organizations, letter-writing campaigns, lobbyists, and "victims' rights" rankings of lawmakers, Reemtsma has called for greater recognition of victims, and particularly their retributive emotions, in the criminal process. In particular, he has reflected on the powerful "sense of justice" triggered by the identification with, and "emotional proximity" to, victims of crime.[144] Stressing the importance of identification not only with the offender but also with the victim, Reemtsma points out that a victim who has sustained the trauma of criminal victimization, and not only the offender, requires reintegration into the community.[145] In the end, Reemtsma derives a "victim's right to have the offender punished . . . from the duty of the state to limit the social harm caused by a serious crime."[146] These are suggestive remarks. What matters here, however, is not so much the substance of Reemtsma's public, and much debated, ruminations on victims' rights but the fact of their existence.

By contrast, the victims' rights movement in the United States once again, and once again not surprisingly, hides the tension between the personal and the helpless victim, instead of trying to address and perhaps even to resolve it. The victims' rights movement relies on victim narratives that emphasize the agony of victimization. It prefers cries for help to confident explorations of the meaning of personal victimhood and of victims' rights, whether or not their vindication requires state intervention on the victim's behalf. (For this reason, narratives of adult female rape victims that, like Reemtsma's, preserve the victim's personhood in an attempt to come to grips with the meaning of victimization have been marginalized in today's victims' rights movement.)[147] The idea of victim self-help does not fit into a movement built on the inability of victims to help themselves, no matter how obviously useful, even necessary, the victim's contribution to the recovery of her autonomy as a person might be.[148] Reemtsma's careful analysis of victims' rights illustrates that victims' participation is helpful not only in the attempt to reconcile victimhood with personhood in particular cases, perhaps even through counseling, but also in the development of a concept of victims' rights in general.

As a *political* movement, the victims' rights movement today is shaped by political considerations of expediency, rather than by theoretical concerns about consistency. The victims' rights movement will come to the aid of victims, whether they want or need help or not. Part of what it means to be a victim is not to know when one needs help. The tension between victim as subject and object, as active and passive, is covered up in two complementary ways: by replacing shared personhood with another point of identification between observer and victim, such as race, and by shifting the focus from the victim to the victim's spokesperson. The second move is made possible by the sub rosa replacement of direct victims with indirect victims, and in particular outspoken relatives, as we just saw. Here, once again, the parents, often the fathers, of child victims assume paradigmatic significance. As the personification of subjecthood, the image of the parent demanding swift legislative "anticrime" action on behalf of his slain daughter, other potential slain daughters, their parents, and, in fact, all actual and potential crime victims generally or standing behind the president as he signs yet another tough-on-crime bill thus displaces the image of the helpless child victim who remains as silent as ever.

It's important to see that even these adult victims by proxy, these personifications of subjecthood, these prototypes of self-governance, have a purely political significance. Their rights, for their own sake, are as irrelevant as the rights of the victims they represent. Derivative homicide victims are of political interest only to the extent they can make a contribution to the war on crime, of which the victims' rights movement is but one part. The victims' rights movement has no use for derivative victims who do not fit the politically useful stereotype of the hate-filled victim relatives, who seethe with "bloodlust and revenge" and "leave the courtroom with high fives and fists in the air, as though sentencing someone to death were no more serious than a football game."[149] An indirect homicide victim who, like Brent Staples, refuses to "see [him]self as a 'victim'" and to "dwell in a place where there is only pain" and who views bereavement as "a period of reflection," rather than "a raucous and public blood sport,"[150] threatens to interfere with, rather than to aid, the crime war effort and is therefore ignored.

Perhaps nothing illustrates the irrelevance of victims for their own sake more poignantly than the suppression of *mitigating* victim evidence in capital cases, regardless of whether it stems from a derivative victim or even, and most remarkably, from the victim herself. Surviving relatives are prevented from expressing their opposition to capital punishment in general, or to the imposition of capital punishment in the particular case.[151] One might think that this evidence is considered inappropriate because it doesn't, or, perhaps, cannot possibly, reflect the direct victim's interests. Why, after all, should antideath penalty advocates who happened to have a loved one murdered be permitted to push their political agenda at the expense of their silenced relative?

But that can't be it. The mitigating voice of the direct victim, after all, is silenced, as well. Evidence of the direct victim's opposition to capital punishment in general is categorically excluded.[152] (Evidence of a homicide victim's opposition to capital punishment *in the particular case* is hard to come by, for obvious reasons.)

Courts throughout the nation agree that mitigating victim impact evidence, whether from derivative or from direct victims, must be kept out of capital sentencing hearings at all costs. This evidence, they announce categorically, is "unrelated to the defendant's culpability—it has nothing to do with the defendant's character or record or the circumstances of the crime—and thus is irrelevant to sentencing."[153] It's merely "opinion" evidence. It relieves the sentencers of their job entirely, rather than providing assistance.

Unfortunately, courts have not been nearly as categorical in their condemnation of *aggravating* "opinion" evidence. Where they have not admitted opinion evidence outright,[154] courts have bent over backward to interpret aggravating victim impact evidence as anything but an opinion regarding the "victim's" preferred sentence.[155] Testimony by an indirect homicide victim that details the direct victim's excruciating suffering during and after the homicide, as well as her own, and is presented by the prosecutor in support of her call for capital punishment can leave no doubt in the sentencer's mind regarding the witness's opinion about the appropriate sentence. (That's why prosecutors use victim impact evidence: sentencers are more likely to impose the death penalty if they feel that they can help salve the derivative victim's wounds by satisfying her understandable desire for vengeance.) Courts fail to see "opinion" evidence even in cases where surviving relatives use their victim impact evidence to refer to the defendant as a "piece of trash,"[156] or ask the sentencing jury to "show no mercy,"[157] and to "[r]enew our faith in the criminal justice system and bring a phase of closure to this ongoing nightmare that fills our lives."[158]

Celebrated as a success of the victims' rights movement, the introduction of victim impact evidence in capital cases in fact is a success of the war on crime.[159] Victim impact evidence is used to further the war on crime's goal of maximum incapacitation of dangerous elements, rather than to manifest the rights of direct, or indirect, crime victims and, least of all, to "giv[e] a 'voice' to those silenced by their killers."[160]

But even derivative victims who are willing to play their political part see their salience wane with the memory of the victim from whose victimization they derive their status. After a slew of appearances on national television and "several" meetings with "President Clinton and U.S. Attorney General Janet Reno," it has grown quiet around Marc Klaas in recent years, judging by the c.v. on his foundation's Web site.[161] To maintain its fever pitch of hatred, the war on crime needs ever more, and ever more sympathetic, victims.

So much for the use of derivative victims by the victims' rights movement. Another way of softening the tension between the victim as self-governing person and as helpless plaything of overpowering emotions triggered by the offender is to invite identification with the victim not as a person but on some other basis. The political function of the victim's image as a person is, after all, not so much to portray her as endowed with certain rights—namely victims' rights—but to lay the foundation for the sympathetic response that, aided by the perception of helplessness, will blossom into the call for political action, however symbolic. What triggers this original identification is, politically speaking, of secondary importance. What matters is that the connection is made, not what makes it.

The most common, and the most troubling, of these points of contact between observer and victim is membership in the same race.[162] Shared race, however, is as irrelevant to the moral judgment that underlies every assessment of criminal liability as all other points of identification, except for one: personhood. The relevant unit of moral judgment is the person. It's as persons that we judge, and it's as persons that we are judged. And, in the criminal law, it's as persons that we are ultimately punished. Racial characteristics, however, are irrelevant to personhood. To be a member of one race or another has as little effect on one's status as a person as where one happens to be born or where one happens to live (or have lived) at a particular moment in time, what language one speaks, how tall one is, or what clothes one wears. This reduction of all characteristics except personhood to moral irrelevance is the hallmark of the modern conception of morality, and it is therefore also the hallmark of modern law, which recognizes that conception as its foundation and the source of its limits.

To the extent that it fails to clarify the distinction between permissible and impermissible bases for identification with the victim, the victims' rights movement pays too heavy a price for its political punch. The implicit identification of white observers and white victims—or, rather, of potential and actual white victims—that drives the victims' rights movement undermines its legitimate basis. Victims deserve rights because persons deserve rights. Any attempt to ground the pursuit of victims' rights on a concept other than that of the person therefore is self-defeating.

The tension between the victim as victim and the victim as person underlies any attempt to develop a theory of victims' rights. The problem with the victims' rights movement is not that it is faced with this tension but that it doesn't face it and, by denying the tension, does nothing to resolve and much to aggravate it. The central danger of victims' rights is that the attempt to help the victim overcome her victimization might backfire: the effort to end victimhood may end up affirming it. The well-meaning attempt to recover the victim's capacity for autonomy may interfere with that capacity and may even damage or destroy it. This phenomenon is familiar not only from the counseling of battered women but also from psychotherapy.[163] The therapist, by trying to help the patient control her urge to act out and, more generally, to recover her psychological autonomy, that is, self-control, may end up replacing one heteronomy with another, his own. The victim counselor likewise may end up merely replacing the offender as the controlling agent in the victim's life, rather than eliminating control by another person altogether.

This danger of victimizing victims in the name of victims' rights must be avoided, or at least minimized, at all costs. To this end, everything must be done to recognize victims as persons first and victims second. Victims do not need our help or our pity. The victim, as a person, is entitled to the rights enjoyed by every person. It is important to view the victim not in her particularity but in her basic quality as a person, a quality that we all share and that we recognize as the foundation of modern law, to which respect is due by all, including the state. By broadening the focus from the plight of the particular victim and by treating her as the person she was, is, and will remain, we both come to recognize ourselves in her as a fellow person and encourage her to live up to her promise as a person.

In other words, we should treat the victim exactly as we should treat the offender, that is, as a person capable of autonomy. That way, we fulfill the criminal law's promise of vindicating the autonomy of all participants in the criminal process.

In a criminal process designed to vindicate autonomy, an essentially helpless victim has no place. This aspect of the victim image, which underlies the victims' rights movement, therefore must be taken with a grain of salt. As a political device to trigger state intervention, it can be discarded without affecting the basic concept of the victim at the heart of the victims' rights movement. For the development of a law of victimhood, the two remaining characteristics, personhood and seriousness of the crime, suffice.

Still, to fight victimological essentialism at every turn is not to deny the relevance of the victim's need for a state response to the serious crime perpetrated upon her by the offender. Similarly, welfare isn't illegitimate simply because it is limited to the poor. It's illegitimate only if it presumes that its recipients are essentially, rather than incidentally, in need of state assistance and, therefore, by their nature incapable of autonomy.

A state response to crime is required if, *and only if,* the victim requires it. A victim whose sense of autonomy is not affected by the experience of crime, who laughs off the offender's clumsy attempt to treat her as a non-person, is in no need of state assistance in the form of a legal response, in the form of either punishment or compensation.

As long as one keeps in mind that victims are not by their nature helpless, the requirement that they *in fact* require the state's assistance provides an important, and necessary, limitation on state interference. Unless there is harm to a person's autonomy, there's no need to fix it. Moreover, if the victim is perfectly willing and able to reassert his autonomy in the face of crime, there's no need for *the state* to do it for him.

Determining whether a victim requires state assistance to regain her sense of autonomy is, of course, difficult. Victim compensation law leaves this decision up to the victim. No victim is compensated without having filed a compensation claim. Once a compensation claim has been filed and the victim has been identified as a "needy person," the compensation commission then reviews the assertion of neediness, along with every other component of the compensation claim. Some statutes make this point as explicit as the Kentucky statute quoted earlier. Others more obliquely condition compensation on a finding that "unless the claimant's award is approved he will suffer financial difficulty."[164]

In compensation law, the initial neediness determination is made by the victim herself. Merely the financial component of the neediness issue is then reconsidered by the compensation commission. But what matters is not the financial difficulty caused by crime but its effect on the victim's autonomy.

The victim is not always the best judge of her need for state intervention through law. Her experience of victimization may lead her to overestimate, or to underestimate, the harm caused by the crime. Victims often have difficulty making life decisions in general. After all, it's precisely their ability to manage their own affairs, their autonomy, that was threatened, and perhaps compromised, in their victimization.

Even worse, the offender's oppression may continue even after the specifically criminal oppression. Perpetrators of domestic violence may exert their continued power over the victim to prevent her from turning to "the law" for help. It's to diffuse this very real danger that mandatory arrest laws have been implemented in cases of suspected domestic violence.

Current *criminal* law generally assigns the neediness determination not to the victim but to the state, specifically to the prosecutor. So a prosecutor can pursue the offender's punishment—though not the victim's compensation—even against the victim's protestations that no state interference is required. On the flip side, the prosecutor also always retains the option of *not* setting the machinery of criminal law in motion should he decide that no reaffirmation of the victim's autonomy is needed, for whatever reason, be it because no crime occurred or because the harm was "de minimis." The prosecutor's neediness determination then may, in turn, be subject to review by another state official, the judge.[165]

One might think that, in the criminal law, the state enjoys ultimate discretion on the question of whether a victim is or isn't in need of vindication because leaving that decision up to the victim herself would be impossible. That's not so, however. The state gets to decide this crucial question—and therefore determines the limits of its own power—because crime is said to constitute an attack upon the state. Since it's the state's interests that are at stake, it should be up to the state to decide whether these interests need reasserting. As the ultimate victim, the state determines whether it has been victimized sufficiently to warrant the state's intervention on its own behalf.

As we've seen, however, this view of crime is woefully out of sync with the fundamental principles that undergird the modern state, which, unlike the king, has no dignity to defend and no interests other than protecting the interests or, rather, the rights of its constituents. Under the proper view of criminal law, which recognizes only one victim, the person, the statist argument that the state, as the true victim of crime, gets to monopolize the neediness decision leads to the opposite result. Since it's the victim as a person whose rights are at stake in crime and not the state's, it's she, and not the state, who determines whether these rights require vindication through law.

To say that the victim's decision about whether the law of punishment or compensation should come into play doesn't mean that this decision can't be reviewed, any more than to let a defendant enter a guilty plea means that all guilty pleas must be accepted without further inquiry. (Never mind that this tends to be the case in fact.)[166] Just as in every other case where persons get to make choices that may adversely affect them, the voluntariness of that choice must be scrutinized. This is notoriously difficult, but no one has yet called for the abandonment of consensual searches because the voluntariness of consent can't be assessed. The difficulty of making the determination is no excuse for not making it, especially since it's crucial to keep state responses to crime, in whatever form, tied to the state's foremost function: the manifestation of the rights of the persons who constitute it.

So much for the third, and last, component of the victims' rights movement's concept of a victim: helplessness. It must be discarded if it reflects an essentialist victiminology that regards all victims as eternally victimized. Properly understood as an incidental quality that the victim may need state intervention to overcome, however, neediness—rather than utter helplessness—does deserve a place in a victim-sensitive legal response to crime. That place is at the outset of the legal process, at the point when it must be decided whether the process needs to be set in motion in the first place.

In sum, for purposes of our parallel inquiry into the substance of the law of victimhood and the law of offenderhood, we can distill the following preliminary concept of the victim from the rhetoric of the victims' rights movement:

> a victim is a person against whom another person has committed a serious crime.

This concept of the victim as person, and of crime as interpersonal, is the first, and most important, contribution the victims' rights movement can make to a personal, rather than a statal, law of crime. As we will see, the law of victimhood can be read as a detailed analysis of this notion, resulting in rules guiding the determination of victimhood in particular cases.

An analysis of the law of victimhood as one aspect of the law of personhood, however, requires more than a complementary reading of compensation law and criminal law. To put our doctrinal analysis of victimhood in context, we must explain why victimhood *matters*. The answer lies in the victims' rights movement's other contribution to a reconstruction of a personal criminal law: the significance of empathy through identification.

The Victim in All of Us

To conceive of a law of victimhood based on the victim as person, one needs more than a concept of the victim and of the person. One needs an account of how the victimization of a given person achieves communal significance. In other words, one needs to understand how victimhood can be transferred from person to person, how one person's experience of victimhood can be accessed by another—in short, why one person's suffering at the hands of another should matter to anyone other than herself. Otherwise, one may have an account of personal victimhood, but one does not have an account of the *law* of personal victimhood, since without intersubjectivity no experience, no matter how painful, can attain moral or legal significance.

The question of legal relevance does not arise if the state (or some other apersonal entity) is the true victim of crime. In that case, there is no victimhood to be transferred. The state is the victim and takes appropriate action to respond to the criminal assault against its dignity. There's no need for intersubjectivity, for vicarious experience of suffering. For one thing, there is no suffering to be transferred: an abstract concept does not suffer. Moreover, there is no need for any particular *person* to reexperience (or coexperience) the victim's suffering for the simple reason that personal victimhood is irrelevant, or at least not required, for purposes of legal interference, say, in the form of punishment. No, the victimization of the state *is* the legally relevant fact. The determination of when that victimization has taken place and what is to be done about it is left to experts, the state officials, who define the norms, apply them, and enforce them.

Once the victim in criminal law is narrowly defined, as in the victims' rights movement, to include only the victim as person, things get more complicated. Now one must address the question of how the experience of personal victimhood can become relevant to persons other than the victim herself. This question is important for an understanding of victims' rights, as the paradigmatic role of homicide victims in the victims' rights movement makes clear.

A look at the phenomenology of the victims' rights movement suggests an answer. The experience of one person is accessible and therefore relevant to others only through the process of *identification*. This process deserves much greater attention than it has so far received, for it is through identification generally that we render moral and legal judgments about persons and can act and decide on their behalf.

The victims' rights movement's intuitive appeal relies on implicit identification between the general public and victims. And specific procedural reforms in the name of rights of victims, particularly in the area of capital punishment, likewise are aimed at strengthening the identification between victim and others, in this case the sentencing jury.

To recognize the significance of identification in the victims' rights movement is, of course, not to endorse it. Identification is necessary for representation, for taking the place of another in vicarious decision making. To say this much, however, is not to say much at all. Two crucial questions remain. First, there is the nature, or origin, of the identification. This determines whether the identification has moral or legal significance. Certain characteristics are morally and legally insignificant. The list is familiar from constitutional law and the statutory law of discrimination: race, gender, sexual orientation, ethnicity, national origin, and so on. These characteristics are incidental from the perspective of morality and law. Assuming jurisdiction, legal judgment concerns itself with only one characteristic: personhood, or the capacity for autonomy. Without this essential characteristic, the object of identification is not a moral or legal subject.

Once identification has been tied to personhood in this way, it becomes clear that the failure to identify oneself with the victim amounts to a disrespect her personhood. The fundamental right of the victim is to be respected as a person, and to ignore her suffering, to judge her unworthy of identification, violates that right. This is one way of capturing the legitimate core of the victims' rights movement. And this is why Randall Kennedy was right to criticize the Supreme Court for ignoring the discriminatory import of the disproportionate decision by Georgia prosecutors *not* to seek the death penalty in homicides with black *victims*. In *McCleskey v. Kemp*, the Court instead had considered (and rejected) only the possibility of discrimination in the invocation of the death penalty in homicides with black *offenders*.[167] Victims are entitled to respect as persons, too, as Kennedy demonstrates by analyzing prosecutorial discretion from both the offender's and the victim's standpoints.

The entire system of public criminal law depends on a process of identification between victim and state officials. The response to violations of personal rights is transferred from one person (the victim) to others (state officials). These state officials now have the right to punish. (As an apersonal entity, the state itself has no rights, strictly speaking.) The victim, as a person, retains only the right to *have* punished and the offender, as a person, the right to *be* punished, rather than to be disposed of like an apersonal risk carrier.[168] The threat, as well as the execution, of that punishment depends on the ability and the willingness of the relevant state official, from the legislator to the police officer to the prosecutor to the judge to the juror and even to the prison guard, to identify with the victim. If an entire class of victims falls beyond the identificatory range of legislators, for example, interference with their personal rights will not even be *threatened* with punishment. And even legislative norms that protect the rights of certain persons will not be *enforced* without the requisite identification between state officials in the executive and judiciary and these legislatively protected persons.

Identification thus is the prerequisite for vindication of the victim's rights (in particular, the right to have punished). This much we can learn from the victims' rights movement.

But, and here we once again expand the victims' rights movement into a movement for persons' rights, identification is also the prerequisite for vindication of the *offender's* rights through punishment (in particular, the right to be punished). Punishment, in this context, is understood broadly to encompass the entire criminal process, ranging from the threat to the imposition and, eventually, the infliction of punishment, or, in the words of the New York Penal Law, "the accusation, prosecution, conviction and punishment of offenders."[169] In all of these aspects of the criminal legal process, a person must be treated as such, that is, with the requisite respect for her autonomy, no matter what label she might bear depending on where she might find herself in that process. The person is the common thread that connects the various stages within the criminal process, as well as the criminal process itself to the outside world.

Everyone will agree that at the beginning of the criminal process stands the person. The central challenge of a legitimate criminal process is to ensure that the person also stands at its end. The threat of punishment in a criminal statute is addressed to *all persons* within the area of the statute's application. To put it procedurally, the criminal law applies to all persons within the jurisdiction of a particular court charged with applying it, that is, to all justiciable persons. All justiciable persons in this sense are potential offenders. (Here, incidentally, lies an important distinction between moral and legal persons, and morality and law. Moral norms are addressed to all persons as such. Legal ones are addressed only to justiciable persons.) The justiciable person then becomes the "suspect," who turns into the "accused" and, of course, the "defendant" and then the "convict" and eventually the "inmate," "prisoner," or "client," or perhaps the "patient," not to mention the "probationer," the "parolee," or the "ex-con" and, at the very end of the line, the "condemned," who eventually becomes simply "the body of an inmate upon whom a sentence of death has been carried out."[170]

The victims' rights movement defines itself in contradistinction and in response to a perceived offenders' (or defendants' or criminals') rights movement, vaguely associated with the Warren Court. Paradoxically, the very effort to define victims' rights against offenders' rights merely reaffirms the offender's dominance over the victim. The pursuit of victims' rights flips the pursuit of offenders' rights upside down but retains its mold. Even in her elimination from our hearts and minds, the offender thus controls the victim's identity as the nonoffender. The less we focus on the victim, the less we respect her. Yet, the more we focus on the victim *for the sake of* disrespecting the offender, the less we respect her as her own person, not to mention that we disrespect the offender at the same time.

The only way out of this dilemma is to discard the conventional concepts of victim and offender and to reconstruct them in terms of the one concept that matters in a modern democratic state: the person. The objective of the criminal process, broadly understood, is to vindicate the rights of persons, not to oversee or (re)enact the struggle of victim and offender. The current, so-called adversarial process of winner-takes-all reduces the protection of defendants' and victims' rights to a zero-sum game. The paradigmatic trial of this process is a series of conflicts between defendant and victim. Either the defendant wins, by having incriminating evidence excluded, or the victim does, by having it admitted. Either the defendant wins, outright by acquittal or by default through a hung jury, or the victim wins, by conviction. Finally, either the defendant wins, by escaping with his life, or the victim does, by having the defendant sentenced to death. And the debate about defendants' and victims' rights follows the same pattern. Whatever rights the defendant gains must be taken away from the victim, and vice versa. More broadly, whatever suffering is inflicted on the defendant transforms itself into the victim's joy. So victims' rights are protected by curtailing defendants' rights, by admitting otherwise excludable incriminating evidence, by increasing prison sentences, and by expanding the use of capital punishment.

As we saw in the previous chapter, there is only one winner in this game: the state. By pitting "defendant" against "victim" in the paradigmatic trial by combat, the state creates the false impression that one of the two will emerge as the winner, the other as the loser. But this is not so. Both defendants and victims lose in a game that is played by the state for the purpose of hiding its awesome power over defendants and victims alike. By stressing the role of the victim in the criminal trial, the state merely hides behind the sympathetic figure of the victim. It is, of course, the state, and not the victim, who takes up arms against the defendant. It is the state prosecutor who becomes intoxicated with his own power and uses every weapon at his disposal to annihilate the defendant and his proxy, the defense attorney. The wishes of the victim are relevant only insofar as they confirm the prosecutor's judgment. The victim who expresses a desire for leniency in a case where the prosecutor stands in the full heat of battle is as irrelevant as the victim who calls for harshness in a case where the prosecutor has, for one reason or another, decided to dispose of the matter quickly and quietly so that he can stand ready to fight the battle in another case on another day.

It doesn't help matters that the paradigmatic trial by battle is also imaginary. Most prosecutors spend most, if not all, of their time processing more or less unconditional surrenders. Like a chess master, they play several games against a group of vastly inferior opponents at a time. The full extent of their righteous ire is reserved for those opponents who dare to interfere with the quick disposal of their pathetic attacks against the grandmaster. These few obstreperous ones must be stamped out and put in their place. Rather than admit that the authority of the prosecutor, and therefore the state, is at stake, it is far more convenient to invoke the rights of the victim, who all too often is all too willing to play the part of the discombobulated heap of helplessness in need of state protection from the forces of evil.

And so both defendant and victim become mere tools in the enforcement of superior state authority. The only difference between defendants and victims in this respect is that the victim *thinks* she's the winner. In fact, both are losers.

To break this state dominance, defendants and victims must transform themselves from objects of state control into subjects. And to transform them into subjects is to recognize them as persons. Defendants and victims can be tools of state oppression; persons cannot.

Person is the relevant lowest common denominator, or point of identification, for judge, offender, and victim. Although the concept of citizen captures the political aspect of law, including criminal law, it is not sufficiently broad. The criminal law norms of a particular political community do not protect only the citizen-member against interference, nor do they concern themselves only with offenses committed by citizens. Moreover, the rights that the criminal law vindicates are not rights of citizenship but rights of personhood. An assault, for example, interferes with the right to self-determination enjoyed by every person, rather than merely by all citizens. This is not to deny that the right of autonomy has other components, or subsidiary rights, the exercise of which may be limited to citizens. Interference with the right to vote, for instance, may be punished. That a given political community punishes interference with that right only if the victim is a citizen, however, is a matter not of principle but of political fact. The right to vote is a personal right; the right to vote in a particular election is a citizen right, that is, the right of a member of the particular political community in question.

After all this talk about the need to avoid differentiation among judges, offenders, and victims, it's important to remind ourselves that significant distinctions remain. The point is simply that these distinctions aren't what matters at the end of the day. Personhood is the *essential* property shared by all process participants. It is the function of the criminal process to highlight their continued identity, despite outward appearances and labels to the contrary. As persons, all three share the capacity for autonomy. This capacity must be preserved throughout.

The personhood of the judge remains unaffected throughout the process, except vicariously through identification with victim and offender. By contrast, the victim directly experiences an assault on her autonomy at the hands of the offender. The offender manifests his autonomy at the expense of the victim's. In his criminal act, he removes the victim's self from the position of control and replaces it with his. In some cases, this act of interpersonal violence results in the permanent destruction of the victim's capacity for autonomy, through death or catastrophic brain injury. In others, it affects the victim's ability to exercise that capacity to a greater or lesser degree.

To illustrate the immediate experience of criminal subjugation, as well as its lingering effect on the victim's sense of autonomy, consider the following particularly articulate account by a New York City mugging victim:

> She was walking by the East River on an early summer evening when an arm curled around her neck and pulled her back into the dark. She fought and kicked and tried to scream, but the arm cut off her breath. Losing consciousness, she thought she was going to die.
>
> "I was terrified, I was so terrified," Shelby Evans Schrader said yesterday morning as she testified in State Supreme Court in Manhattan about her

encounter with a man prosecutors say is John J. Royster. . . . She stopped and glanced down at her hands. "Excuse me," she said. "It comes back. This makes all of it come back. . . ."

In recounting the June 5, 1996, attack, Ms. Evans Schrader, a writer, said that the night before, she had just finished a novel. The next day was her birthday, and she started a brisk walk in the early evening. Before she left, she tucked $15 in her pocket and kissed her husband.

She remembers little of the attack and never saw her assailant's face.

"The next thing I remember was lying flat on my back on the asphalt and my nails were full of grit," she said. "I lay there for a minute trying to find out what happened."

Her nose had been smashed flat and her head was battered. Ms. Evans Schrader spent the next five hours undergoing plastic surgery with only local anesthesia because the surgeons were worried about brain damage.

At the hospital, she was given a private room. "There was a mirror in the bathroom and I saw myself," Ms. Evans Schrader testified. "I looked at myself in the mirror and I screamed. I will never forget that, the sense of a stranger in the mirror."

. . . Ms. Evans Schrader described how the attack changed her, ruining her sense of balance and leaving her feeling vulnerable and afraid. "My life is changed, like there is a cage around me," she said. "I fear a stranger behind me."[171]

The criminal process aims to reassert the victim's autonomy without denying the offender's. To avoid the official reenactment of the offender's oppression of the victim, the judge must switch perspectives to identify not only with the victim but also with the offender. Punishment thus differs from crime in that it manifests the autonomy of all persons, rather than merely the autonomy of one at the expense of another's.

Strictly speaking, the criminal process doesn't restore the victim's autonomy; it *vindicates* it. Restoring the victim's autonomy would imply that the offender had succeeded in damaging it. This would concede too much. The offender's oppression of the victim in the act of crime, by supplanting the victim's autonomy with his own, can never be more than an attempt to interfere with the victim's autonomy. The victim's *capacity* for autonomy, and therefore her personhood, instead remains intact throughout and despite the crime. It is up to the law of criminal procedure to ensure that her personhood survives the process of punishment, as well.

Even in cases where the offender managed not only to interfere with the victim's ability to exercise her capacity for autonomy but to destroy that capacity altogether (as in homicide and certain severe assaults), the victim's autonomy is vindicated, vicariously, by her representatives, as well as by the state itself acting on behalf of the victim, rather than merely in the interest of enforcing its commands. Nothing less is required to rebuff the offender's usurpation of another's right of personhood, which the state exists to protect. Only then is the offender's attack exposed as temporary and futile, by demonstrating that the target of his assault, the victim's personhood, remained intact.

Still, vindicating the victim's personhood in cases where that personhood has been destroyed is difficult, at least compared to the bulk of cases in which the physical preconditions of personhood have survived the crime. And here one must further differentiate among homicide and other offenses that end not the victim's existence altogether but only certain vital capacities. In the latter case, other persons can represent the victim, can exercise her rights vicariously as she would have. In the former, the rights of the victim vanish with the victim. Surviving relatives of homicide victims claim rights not vicariously but directly as indirect victims. They are acting not for the victim but as victims. Rather than *represent* primary victims, they *are* secondary victims.

The case for victims' rights, therefore, is both strongest and weakest in homicide cases. It is strongest because homicide is the most serious offense, the only offense that destroys the very essence of personhood, the capacity for autonomy. It is weakest for the same reason. It destroys the victim and therefore leaves no person behind whose rights can be vindicated. Homicide, therefore, is both the paradigmatic person offense and the paradigmatic state offense. The crime is entirely personal, its punishment entirely statal.

Speaking of victims' rights in a homicide case is therefore something altogether different from speaking of victims' rights in any other case. The relatives of a homicide victim are not the victims of a homicide. A homicide prosecution is about the offender and the state, period. The state pursues the case in order to vindicate the rights of the victim in the only way possible, namely indirectly by demonstrating to the offender and the public that it will not stand for the offender's attempt to interfere with the victim's personhood, or, as the Restatement of Torts puts it, the victim's "interests of personality."[172]

Relatives of homicide victims, therefore, must be distinguished from relatives of surviving victims whose ability to exercise their capacity for autonomy has been compromised, rather than destroyed, by the offender's criminal act. The latter act for the victim, rather than claiming victimhood for themselves. And only they are enforcing victims' rights.

This distinction is as crucial as it is generally ignored. As a result, the interests of the relatives of homicide victims again and again have been confused with victims' rights. For example, the Supreme Court's about-face on the question of victim impact statements in capital sentencing proceedings is generally (mis)understood as an early triumph of the victims' rights movement. The testimony of relatives of the homicide victim (or of anyone else somehow connected with the victim)[173] may be relevant to all sorts of issues; the one person it has, and can have, nothing to do with is the victim and therefore her rights.

Simply put, victim impact evidence in capital cases is not about victims. It is about something else entirely, namely the venting of powerful emotions that do not have an outlet in the traditional criminal process that reduces victims *and their relatives* to mere witnesses, who expose themselves to the acid test of cross-examination. In this sense, but only in this sense, the distinction between victim and relative becomes irrelevant as both direct and indirect victim receive the same marginalizing treatment.

The pursuit of victim impact testimony in capital cases as a platform for the validation of emotions, rather than the vindication of rights, in the name of victims' rights illustrates a general trend toward expanding the victims' rights agenda far beyond its core, namely the rights of victims of interpersonal crime. Not only the rights of relatives of victims are pursued in the name of victims; so is every other policy that is seen as expressive of the hatred of offenders validated in the institution of victim impact evidence.

Still, simply because these vengeful emotions have nothing to do with victims' rights doesn't mean that they should be ignored. To the contrary, it is another lasting contribution of the victims' rights movement to have exposed the instability of a system of punishment that fails to recognize the depth and breadth of punitive emotions unleashed by the experience of direct and indirect victimization.

Here, too, the demands of the victims' rights movement must be generalized and then applied equally to all persons. To return to our example, capital sentencing juries must be permitted and encouraged to emotionally identify not only with the victim and her surviving family members (as they are now) but also with the perpetrator of the tragic offense and her relatives, if any (as they are not).[174]

The significance of emotional responses is closely related to the significance of identification. Identifications both enable and block certain emotional responses, much as they enable and block certain types of judgment, as we saw earlier. For instance, the unmitigated hatred that characterizes many victim impact statements—in the press, on the stand, or in written statements—is inconsistent with the recognition of a fundamental identity between victim and offender. This emotional response has nothing to do with moral judgment. It also has nothing to do with victim autonomy, as it resembles "acting out," in the psychotherapeutic sense, rather than the processing of the crisis of victimization.[175] It perpetuates victimization, rather than overcoming it. Instead of validating acting out as an instance of unreflected self-protective impulses, the criminal process should vindicate the victim's autonomy, the ability to take charge of oneself and therefore also of one's emotional responses. These are by definition responses to the offender, who thereby retains the very domination manifested in his crime that the criminal process is charged with breaking and turning into a manifestation of the victim's autonomy, as well as the offender's.

To confuse the vindication of victims' rights with the validation of relatives' hatred may even have a detrimental effect on the rights of the victim. Not only the relatives' autonomy suffers in a criminal process that gives their uncontrolled hatred a formal forum. So does the victim's. Even if it were not self-contradictory and therefore unlikely to succeed, the attempt to use relatives' victim impact testimony as a treatment for the relatives' psychosis—which may or may not stem from the experience of indirect victimization—threatens to shift the focus of the criminal process from the homicide victim to the survivors. What's at stake, however, is not the relatives' suffering, no matter how extensive, but the destruction of the person of the victim, and therefore also her personhood. The essence of homicide, and the reason why it is punished with such severity, is not its effect on the well-being, psychological or financial, of relatives, friends, or "the public" but the extinction of precisely that capacity for whose protection the state, and therefore the criminal law, exists. This fact remains the same whether the homicide victim had ten, five, or no friends, was good, bad, or somewhere in between.

That victim impact evidence should enter American criminal law precisely in that class of cases where it has nothing to do with victims' rights, namely in capital cases, is surprising, at least until it becomes clear that capital punishment itself has little to do with victims' rights. The capital sentencing process, after all, is designed to identify those offenders who demand destruction, rather than mere punishment, as the incarnation of evil or of dangerous deviance. The capital sentencing process continues in dramatically compressed and individualized form the old search for the essence of the evil mind.

Capital punishment does not, as it once did, apply to anyone who extinguishes another person, and therefore her personhood. It incapacitates those who have revealed themselves as beyond the pale of the moral community and, therefore, also beyond the pale of moral judgment. The testimony of victim relatives at capital sentencing therefore concerns not the rights of the victim; instead, it confirms the preliminary diagnosis of the state prosecutor that the offender has forfeited all rights of personhood, assuming we give the offender the benefit of the doubt and grant him personhood before the offense. By the time of the capital sentencing hearing, the offender already has been convicted of, or at least pled guilty to, an intentional homicide. The only question at capital sentencing is, therefore, not whether the offender is evil, but inherently so, or not only dangerous, but incurably so.

The capital sentencing hearing, in other words, is about everything but the actual victim. It is about the offender first and about his potential future victims second. It is about the offender insofar as the death sentence can rest on the finding that the offender manifests evil in its pure form. It is about potential victims insofar as the death sentence can rest on the finding that he suffers from an incorrigible criminal disposition. The relatives of the actual victim act as spokespersons for the offender's future potential victims. The jury, in turn, functions as a sort of focus group whose response to the offender—or, rather, to his portrayal at the sentencing hearing—gives one a rough sense of the response of the wider group of potential victims. By using the jury/focus group, the state saves time and money. At the same time, the vast majority of members of that enormous class of potential victims (who of us wouldn't see himself as a member?) is spared the agony and inconvenience of being confronted with the often gruesome details of a homicide, amplified by the emotional testimony of the victim's relatives and friends.

That the validation of the hatred felt by the relatives of homicide victims has nothing to do with the *victim*, and specifically her autonomy, isn't the only reason that this validation does not have a place in the criminal process. It also flies in the face of the *offender's* autonomy, without doing anything to vindicate the victim's.

In fact, the prosecutor's use of relatives' testimony to establish the offender's double deviance—her "exceptional depravity"[176]—is not only inconsistent with the offender's personhood but is aimed directly at labeling her as a nonperson and, therefore, as fundamentally different and beyond the realm of identification. Rather than as a person endowed with the capacity for autonomy, the prosecutor portrays the offender as a nonperson driven by her inherent criminal nature. As an amoral source of danger, the offender must be exterminated, rather than merely punished. In the end, the use of this testimony is as illegitimate as the strategy it is meant to support. And so patently illegitimate is the strategy and so pernicious its effect that no gain in the vindication of the victim's autonomy could legitimate it, no matter how substantial that gain may be—and in this case, there is none whatever.

5

Vindicating Victims

The legitimate core of the victims' rights movement boils down to this. First, crime is the serious interference with one person's autonomy (the "victim") by another (the "offender"). The state's response to crime must be designed to reaffirm the autonomy of the former without denying the autonomy of the latter. Second, this vindication of the victim's rights, and in particular her right to autonomy as a person, presumes identification with both victim and offender as persons. Third, the state's legal response to crime must acknowledge the significance of emotional responses to the trauma of crime that are a necessary concomitant of this interpersonal identification. Otherwise, law gives way to the gratification of communal desires to eliminate "offenders" as alien threats.

It's time to fill in this general account of a victim-sensitive state response to crime. In particular, it's time to ground the paradigmatic victim in actual legal definitions of the victim, in the new law of victimhood and in the old law of offenderhood. We see that the law of victimhood generally reflects the personal victim concept that powers the victims' rights movement. But we also come upon certain instances where the state has expanded the victim concept to include communal entities, institutions, and, most disturbingly, even itself. Not surprisingly, the law of offenderhood (the traditional criminal law) generally pays little, if any, attention to the question of how to define victimhood. Without an explicit definition of victimhood generally speaking, we have to assemble an implicit definition based on the various concepts of victims (and "persons") that underlie particular principles of criminal liability as well as offense definitions.

In our search for the victim in law, we generally follow the following procedure. We begin with the law of victimhood. In particular, using the victim definition of the victims' rights movement as our guide, we try to assemble a coherent jurisprudence of victimhood by assembling the often inconsistent definitions of victimhood found in various crime victim laws, as summarized in our overview in the preceding chapter. In this way, we can slowly but surely piece together a general law of victimhood, consolidating the myriad crime victim provisions that have sprung up in all corners of the American legal landscape.

We then switch perspectives, from the victim to the offender and from the law of victimhood to the law of offenderhood, and run the explicit and implicit definitions of victimhood populating American *criminal* law through the sieve of the personal victim image that underlies the victims' rights movement. As a result, much of what we know as criminal law falls by the wayside, as do some laws of more recent vintage that attempt to stretch the victim concept beyond recognition and, more important, beyond the definite contours of the powerful concept that motivated the victims' rights movement and that alone can guarantee the vindication of victims' rights in the future, after the frenzy of the war on crime has subsided and the rights of victims find a place in a criminal law of persons.

At the end, we will combine the two perspectives and collapse the distinction between victim- and offender-based law. When all is said and done, we are left with an account of the law of crime as the violation of one person's autonomy by another that gives both persons involved, offender and victim, their due, with the law of crime falling into two prongs, the law of (offender) punishment and the law of (victim) compensation.

Varieties of Victimhood

The most elaborate treatment of the question of criminal victimhood appears in the law of victim compensation, as it has developed over the past thirty-odd years. Definitions of the victim also appear in other legal contexts. The more benefits and rights were bestowed upon victims, the more important became the question of who qualified for these benefits and rights. The entire project of defining the victim, in general and in different contexts, thus is a fairly recent phenomenon. Traditional criminal law did not concern itself with this question (except perhaps, indirectly, in the law of jurisdiction). Even the law of victimhood was slow to address it. As recently as 1982, Congress could pass a Victim and Witness Protection Act that neither defined "victim" nor distinguished between victims and witnesses in principle.[1]

By contrast, victim compensation statutes raised the question of victimhood from their inception, long before victims' rights became a national political battle cry. After all, something real was at stake here from the very beginning; here the ascription of victimhood resulted in a palpable benefit, namely a compensation award, and, what's more, a compensation award paid by the state. (Offenders contribute only indirectly to victim compensation, though not to the compensation of "their" victim; victim compensation programs often are funded in part through a variety of fees imposed upon convicted persons and prison inmates.)[2]

Victim compensation schemes thus convey an actual, measurable benefit, unlike the mass of victims' rights legislation, which relentlessly extols the inalienable rights of victims without working any real change in the operation of the criminal process. The paradigmatic illustration of the bulk of high-minded but toothless state "action" is, of course, the victims' bill of rights. A victims' bill of rights communicates the legislature's concern about a problem without doing anything to address it and symbolizes the fundamental nature of a right without doing anything about enforcing it. Just in case a victim misinterprets this symbolic handwaving as granting her an enforceable right or perhaps even entitling her to compensation in the event of its violation, today's virulently "pro-victim" and "anticrime" lawmakers have found it prudent to supplement their grandiose pronouncements of principle with small print of the following nature (taken from a version of the proposed federal victims' bill of rights):

> Nothing in this article shall give rise to or authorize the creation of a claim for damages against the United States, a State, a political subdivision, or a public officer or employee.[3]

Consider also this note, found in a "miscellaneous" section tucked away at the very end of the Fair Treatment Standards for Crime Victims, codified in the New York Executive Law:

> Nothing in this article shall be construed as creating a cause of action for damages or injunctive relief against the state or any of its political subdivisions or officers or any agency thereof.[4]

In fact, even the sobering small print on the back of today's grand declarations of victims' rights now fulfill the victims' wish of being treated like criminals. Not only do they now enjoy the rights long enjoyed by criminal defendants; their rights are as useless to them as they are to defendants. To quote once again from the proposed federal victims' bill of rights,

> [n]othing in this article shall provide grounds to stay or continue any trial, reopen any proceeding or invalidate any ruling, except with respect to conditional release or restitution or to provide rights guaranteed by this article in future proceedings, without staying or continuing a trial.[5]

But it's the 1997 Victims' Rights Constitutional Amendment Implementation Act that captures its own toothlessness, for victims and offenders alike, most clearly and poignantly:

> This section does not create a cause of action or defense in favor of any person arising out of the failure to accord to a victim a right provided in subsection (a), and nothing in this section
> (A) provides grounds for the victim to overturn a charging decision, a conviction, or a sentence; to obtain a stay of trial; or to compel a new trial; or
> (B) provides grounds for the accused or convicted offender to obtain any form of relief.[6]

Oddly enough, symbolic victims' rights legislation thus brings victims and offenders together again. Victims and offenders find themselves on the outside looking in, reduced to potential sources of inconvenience who might interfere with state officials' discharge of their duties.

Victim compensation statutes are different. Not only do they translate into money; they translate into money *from the state*. Small wonder, then, that the state has tended to be considerably more circumspect when it comes to determining who's enough of a "victim" to qualify for compensation, as opposed to receiving restitution from the offender, submitting a victim impact statement at the offender's sentencing hearing, or enjoying other victims' rights, to the point that the state itself appears among the "victims" entitled to restitution.

For instance, courts have tended to take a broad view of victimhood when faced with the question of which necessarily indirect victim may give "victim" impact evidence at capital sentencing hearings. As Wayne Logan reports after a careful survey of the law in various states, "family, friends, neighbors, and even co-workers all regularly provide impact evidence."[7] Even in states where the statutory definition of "victim" for purposes of victim impact statements is limited to surviving family members, courts have shown their support of the victims' rights movement by stretching the concept beyond the breaking point, collapsing the distinction between the personal victim of a homicide and the entire community of honest citizens. So large was the group of potential victim impact evidence, so expansive the circle of sympathy surrounding the murder victim, that the Virginia Supreme Court abandoned any attempt at an affirmative definition of who counts as the victim impact victim. Instead, it declared that anyone was a potential victim impact victim as long as she was not "so far removed from the victims as to have nothing of value to impart to the court about the impact of these crimes."[8]

In other words, the only reason that the entire community of upstanding men and women of Virginia wouldn't be permitted to testify as victim impact victims in every capital sentencing hearing in that state is that, after a while, their testimony might become somewhat duplicative, and *not* that each and every one of them wouldn't qualify for victim impact victimhood. It's thus a basic principle of the law of evidence—itself based on the need to move things along at trial and not to confuse the jury—that stands between a mass procession of victim impact witnesses at every murder trial, not any limitation on the concept of the victim.[9]

The Virginia Supreme Court might have given a surprisingly flexible reading to Virginia's apparently narrow and unambiguous definition of the victim impact victim as "a spouse, parent or legal guardian of such a person who . . . was the victim of a homicide."[10] But it thereby simply made the implicit explicit. As we noted earlier, if there is one thing we know about victim impact evidence, it is that it isn't, and can't be, about the victim of a homicide. Instead, it's about everyone else. And that's precisely what the Virginia Supreme Court said.

By throwing the doors of the victim concept, and of the courtroom, wide open to anyone who might have been affected by the victim's death, the Virginia court brought out the analogy between the ceremony of victim impact evidence and that of the funeral service. Certainly, every good citizen of Virginia has the right to express his deep sorrow about the death of a beloved friend, relative, teammate, coworker, and anyone else who touched his or her life in any way. In fact, there's no need to limit the group of victim impact victims to Virginians. Aren't we all affected by human suffering, no matter where we might be? Drawing on the analogy between victim impact testimony and eulogies, would we not at least want to include anyone who might have wanted to say a few words at the funeral service? If the president of the United States should be assassinated, for example, would we not expect to hear from every member of the international diplomatic corps?

To deny anyone the right to give victim impact evidence is to deny him the right to read a eulogy at the victim's funeral. It amounts to denying the intensity or, literally, the relevance of his suffering. This insult becomes that much more pointed if one gets into the business of selecting among those more or less entitled to "testify." To allow one person but not another to testify, in the general sense, at a victim impact ceremony or a funeral service is to tell the excluded one that his suffering is *less*, or at least less relevant, than the other's. Victim impact evidence is, strictly speaking, never duplicative. Anything else would fly in the face of the particularity of human experience. No one suffers the same way as anyone else, no matter what the law of evidence might say.

A capital sentencing hearing, however, is no funeral, and victim impact evidence no eulogy. The relative social, perhaps the religious, standing of a man may be reflected by how many people attend his funeral, how grief stricken they are, and how eloquently they express that grief. Before the law, the life of every person has identical worth, and its destruction by another person inflicts identical harm. Victim impact evidence thus not only improperly (and impossibly) differentiates among the sufferings of *indirect* victims but also among the worth of the lives of *direct* victims.

Still, at least victim impact victims are persons and therefore aren't completely detached from the image of the personal victim of interpersonal crime that's behind the victims' rights movement. The same cannot be said for other victim laws, including many restitution statutes, victims' bills of rights, and even some compensation provisions. The victim in a fairly typical compensation scheme includes "a person who suffers personal physical injury as a direct result of a crime."[11] As we'll see, many compensation statutes limit victimhood to victims of "violent crime"[12] or those who suffer "serious personal injury or death."[13] By contrast, the victim in a relatively narrow restitution scheme includes not only "the victim of the offense" but also "the representative of a crime victim . . . , a good samaritan . . . and the crime victims' board or other governmental agency that has received an application for or has provided financial assistance or compensation to the victim."[14] In a more typical, and broader, restitution statute, the crime victim also includes "any corporation, business trust, estate, trust, partnership, association, joint venture, government, governmental subdivision, agency, or instrumentality, or any other legal or commercial entity when that entity is a direct victim of a crime"[15] or, simply, "any *entity* which has suffered property damage or property loss as a direct result of the crime. . . ."[16] (Remember that restitution is paid by the offender, not the state.)

Hidden in these sweeping definitions of victimhood are two dramatic expansions of the victim concept, far beyond the heart and soul of the victims' rights movement. First, victims are no longer limited to persons. Second, apersonal victims now include the state.

Victimhood is extended to communal entities and, more generally, to "any legal or commercial entity." We saw that the circle of victim impact victims has been expanded from person to person. Persons were entitled to testify at capital sentencing hearings to detail their very personal suffering caused by the victim's death, or, rather, by her murder. The impact in victim impact evidence therefore remained personal—in fact, it was its personal nature that required its expression in the victim impact ceremony.

By contrast, victim laws that, like the restitution provisions quoted earlier, expand the victim concept to encompass apersonal entities cannot do without "representatives," that is, without persons who speak not for other persons but for apersonal entities, legal, commercial, institutional, or communal. How else could an apersonal "entity" claim restitution or otherwise enforce *its* "victims'" rights? Completely confused is the 1997 Victims' Rights Constitutional Amendment Implementation Act, which we've already encountered, when it extends victimhood to any "person . . . that [!] has suffered direct physical, emotional, or pecuniary harm as a result of the commission of a crime, including . . . in the case of a victim that is an institutional entity, or an authorized *representative* of the entity."[17]

One would never find the representative of an apersonal victim at a capital sentencing hearing. Apersonal victims are by definition incapable of suffering physical or emotional harm. Assuming it makes any sense at all to speak of, say, an institution as "suffering" anything, the only harm it might suffer is pecuniary. (That's why corporations are, and can be, punished by fines only, even in American criminal law, occasional talk of the "death penalty" for corporations notwithstanding.) Pecuniary harm, however, by itself is irrelevant. From the perspective of the law of crime, the only harm that matters (physical, psychological, whatever) is harm to the victim as a person. So even if an apersonal entity can "sustain" harm of any kind, that harm could never be criminal harm.

For that reason, apersonal victims have no place in the victims' rights movement or in a system of law constructed from the victim's point of view. Apersonal victims are not victims whose rights can be violated by crime or vindicated by law. Insofar as rights are attached to persons, and to persons only, apersonal entities such as corporations or institutions are as incapable of bearing rights as are animals or any other entity without personhood. Apersonal "legal or commercial entities" have no autonomy that the criminal process could reaffirm after their having been made the object of a crime, or rather of the person committing the crime.

No statutory sleight of hand can gloss over the fundamental distinction between persons and entities. The victims' rights victim is a person against whom another person has committed a serious crime. Neither the English language nor the concept of victims' rights can accommodate the hopelessly conflicted construct of a victim that is "a person or entity, who [!] suffers economic loss or injury as the result of the defendant's criminal conduct."[18] To define victim as "any natural person or his personal representative or any firm, partnership, association, public or private corporation, or governmental entity *suffering* damages caused by an offender's unlawful act" may be (slightly) less offensive, grammatically speaking, but can do nothing to hide the fundamental conceptual confusion of personal and apersonal victims.[19]

Apersonal victims are not the sort of victim that the victims' rights movement emerged to protect, nor are they the sort of victim that the state was formed to protect in the first place. In our reading, the victims' rights movement, after all, is nothing more than the attempt to reduce criminal law to its original, and most powerful, core: the vindication of personal rights against personal attack. The victim of the victims' rights movement is none other than the person whose autonomy the state is charged with protecting. The state could retain, and in fact extend, the monopoly of violence, despite the critique of its legitimacy during the Enlightenment, only by restricting the scope of its authority to the protection of certain core rights of the very individuals who mounted that critique. While the criminal law soon and at an ever increasing rate took up the protection of amorphous interests of amorphous entities, that expansion of its punitive authority was possible only because the original critique of the state's legitimacy had subsided and eventually disappeared, as the original critics became integrated into the state they had once regarded as their oppressor.

Paradoxically, the victims' rights movement reconnects us with the spirit of the Enlightenment by reminding us of what the state's punitive power is—and must be—all about, the protection of the person against serious interference with her right to govern herself. Only in these extreme cases, where the integrity and existence of the state's very foundation is at stake, may the state reach for the ultimate sanction, punishment.

Only the vindication of the victim's right as a person, that is, her autonomy, can justify the vindication of the offender's right as a person in the form of punishment.

Apersonal entities thus simply have nothing to do with the criminal law. They have no autonomy to lose and therefore no autonomy in need of state reaffirmation. They have no fundamental right of autonomy and therefore also no right to have anyone (or anything) punished.

As rightless entities, they also have no right to *be* punished. It's in this context that the status of apersonal entities in the criminal law traditionally has been discussed. The question has been whether—or, rather, how—nonpersons can be punished. Can a nonperson be an offender? Our question instead is whether someone else can be punished for having committed a crime *against* these apersonal entities: can a nonperson be a victim?

The answer to both questions is no. Crime is the assault by one person upon the autonomy of another. It is not simply the interference with the autonomy of a person, no matter by whom or what. Thus, the state's use, in the nineteenth century, of the criminal law to punish organizations of laborers, labeled "conspiracies," was twice illegitimate.[20] First, it vindicated the interests of nonpersonal business entities. Nonpersons, however, are not *victims*, criminally speaking. Second, even if the unions, as opposed to individual members, inflicted harm on real persons (strikebreakers, say), either through violence or intimidation, in the course of a labor dispute, they could not be punished as such. Nonpersons, after all, also are not *offenders*, criminally speaking.

The example of the criminal liability of unions as an apersonal entity is instructive. The general tendency in the United States is to view criticism of the expansion of punishment beyond personal offenders as a thinly veiled attempt to shield giant corporations from criminal liability. This perception may have some empirical basis. As a matter of principle, however, it is dangerously confused.

Much as the victims' rights movement is powered by an image of the helpless victim of violent crime, so calls for the punishment, in fact the ever *harsher* punishment, of "corporate crime" feed off an image of the crooked "white-collar criminal" who pursues profit by any means necessary. In the rush to punish, distinctions between persons and institutions evaporate, as individuals are held liable for the corporation, and vice versa. Fancy doctrinal distinctions, such as the one between strict and vicarious liability or liability without intent and guilt by association, suffer the same fate; in addition, the imposition of strict or vicarious liability, jointly and severally, represents a remarkable departure from the vaunted principles of the Anglo-American common law of crimes.[21]

That minor businesses and small-time entrepreneurs, not giant corporations and their CEOs, tend to end up as the targets of white-collar crime prosecutions makes no difference to hysterical calls for vengeance against corporations and those "involved with" them as amorphous sources of dangers to innocent victims incapable of protecting themselves against mislabeled cold medicine. The fundamental error of this approach is that it accepts, rather than attacks, the fundamental premise of the war on crime: that offenders are evil aliens and that punishment serves to express our hatred for these despicable creatures, as apersonal threats to "our" convenience. To call for the punishment of corporations as such, without regard to their (non)personhood, is merely to expand the war on crime against yet another apersonal threat.

In this context, it's worth reminding ourselves that the illegitimacy of the war on crime derives not only from the fact that it has, as an empirical fact, been fought against blacks and the poor (as opposed to rich white corporate executives). The problem lies deeper. The very idea of a war on crime as the manifestation of hatred for others flies in the face of the foundational idea of the modern state: the idea of equality based on shared personhood. The war on crime presupposes difference, not equality, and denies personhood, rather than vindicating it.

Moreover, the call for corporate criminal liability makes no sense even on its own terms. The recognition of corporate crime, that is, crimes by corporations as such, has nothing to do with the punishment of individuals who commit crimes in their corporate jobs. Corporate criminals are possible without criminal corporations. That is not to say, of course, that criminal corporations aren't easier to come by than corporate criminals, or that they don't tend to have deeper pockets. Moreover, it is undoubtedly easier to punish corporate criminals once the corporation to which they belong has been criminalized. Once the taint of criminality attaches to the corporation as a whole, it is upon the corporate officer to cleanse herself of the taint.

Either way, the convenience of directly criminalizing corporations and other apersonal entities cannot be denied. It's clearly more convenient for the prosecutor if he can deal with a lifeless being, such as a corporation or a union. There will be no tricky questions of mens rea (how is a corporation supposed to have an evil mind, or a mind of any kind?), no questions of actus reus (what does it mean for a nonperson to "act"?), no defenses (self-defense? mistake of law? insanity? infancy? what about intoxication?). In terms of the prosecutor's convenience, entities of this kind share many of the advantages of similarly person- and defenseless objects of state control. And, once the entity's criminal taint has been found, it's simply a matter of establishing some connection between the entity and the ultimate target, the person. Establishing that connection is much easier than establishing the person's guilt directly. Since the entity has been revealed to be criminal, there is no need to inquire into the criminality of the person connected to it.

To illustrate, criminality is transferred from a corporate entity onto any person who "stands in . . . a responsible relation" to whatever activity or inactivity on the part of the corporation established its criminality.[22] Given that "responsible relation," the person is liable, period, without further inquiry into mens rea, actus reus, or defenses of any kind. The only "defense" available to a person identified as a "responsible corporate officer" is to establish his powerlessness to avoid or correct the corporation's "violation" of some criminal statute or other.[23] Proving this defense, however, amounts to nothing less than proving that whatever connection existed between the person and the criminal corporation on paper (literally, on the organization chart) existed on paper alone. In other words, this "defense" is no defense at all but merely allows the targeted person to rebut the presumption of criminality by denying the connection between her and the corporation, the source of the presumption. It has nothing to do with her guilt.

What's more, a look at recent restitution statutes reveals, remarkably, that the state now appears among the victims whose rights deserve protection, by the state. Granting apersonal entities victimhood is bad; granting it to the state is worse still. In Minnesota, for instance, the legislature determined that "victim" for purposes of restitution meant not only "a natural person who incurs loss or harm as a result of a crime" but also "a government entity that incurs loss or harm as a result of a crime."[24] Some states even go so far as to define a restitution victim as a government entity first and a natural person second. According to the Maine legislature, victim means "a government entity that suffers economic loss or a person who suffers personal injury, death or economic loss."[25] In Nevada, a restitution victim includes "(a) A person, including a governmental entity, against whom [!] a crime has been committed" and "(b) A person who has been injured or killed as a direct result of the commission of a crime."[26]

Having overcome initial resistance in some federal courts, the federal government today can count itself among the "victims" entitled to restitution under its very own Victim and Witness Protection Act.[27] It matters not that this victims' rights law was passed in 1982, as we noted earlier, to address the "physical, psychological, or financial hardship" suffered by "the victim of a serious crime."[28] Apparently unable to shed their uneasiness at the sight of the state receiving restitution in the name of victims' rights, some courts still deny the federal government restitutional victimhood in the case of offenses, such as the possession of drugs[29] and of false identification documents,[30] that "do not directly harm the government."[31] All that needs to be done is to recognize the full scope of this rationale. Nothing "directly harm[s] the government," as an apersonal entity; therefore, the government cannot qualify for victimhood, period, no matter how much it would like to recover the costs of waging a war on victimless crime, such as the often considerable sums undercover agents pay to buy drugs.[32]

At first sight, the inclusion—even the primacy—of the state (or, more precisely, "any . . . government, governmental subdivision, agency, or instrumentality"[33]) among victims entitled to *restitution* from the offender seems innocuous enough. The state couldn't very well entitle itself to compensation from a crime victim compensation board, that is, ultimately, from itself. But what's noteworthy, even startling, about the appearance of the state among restitution victims is not that it entitles itself to restitution but that it classifies itself as a crime victim *at all*.

From the perspective of the victims' rights movement, the state cannot be a victim. As a radically and consciously apersonal entity, the state is precluded from victimhood for the same reasons that apply to all apersonal entities and that we needn't repeat here. Classifying the state as a victim, however, does more than dilute the personal foundation of the criminal law. It stands the concept of victim on its head. The state is not only the protector of the rights of persons, victimized or not; it also represents at the same time the greatest threat to these rights. Equipped by its constituents with the monopoly of violence, the state has a potential for oppression that far exceeds that of any other entity or person. The great gamble of the modern state is the transfer of punitive power from the person to the state in the hope that the state will employ that power not to destroy the autonomy of the person but to protect it against other persons, including even state officials.

The line between punishing to vindicate the rights of persons and policing to trample them is as fine as it is easily crossed, and it therefore must be inspected with the utmost vigilance. To recognize the state as a victim creates a system of criminal law in which the vindication of personal rights has no place. Whatever punitive power the state wields in such a system it wields for its own sake, rather than as the representative of its constituents. And it is against these constituents that it exercises that power, thus turning the constituents' delegated power against themselves.

If we want to capture the spirit of the victims' rights movement and, therefore, also that of the origins of modern criminal law, we must reject any attempt on the part of the state to dilute the concept of the victim as person and certainly to turn the protection *of* the victim into the state's protection *from* the victim. The most obvious and direct way to strengthen the personal foundation of the victims' rights movement and of a criminal law after the war on crime is to insist on a definition of the victim as person.

Only the victim was the *object* of the criminal act of another or, in terms of the definition we distilled from the victims' rights movement, the person *against* whom the crime was committed. And only the object of the criminal act has a right to have her subjecthood reaffirmed by the criminal process, broadly defined. Hence, only she is entitled to victims' rights in the criminal process.

Others may also have suffered as a result of the crime without having been its object. They are not victims of crime and thus have no right to have their autonomy reaffirmed through the criminal process; they have no right to have the offender punished. That's not to say that the state may not decide to minimize their suffering, much as it may decide to compensate flood victims or workers injured on the job for their losses. But crime victims they're not.

This crucial distinction between criminal victimhood and other forms of victimization may be lost in definitions of the victim as a person who (or an entity that) "sustains,"[34] "incurs,"[35] or "suffers"[36] some sort of damage. Anyone and, more important, anything can "sustain" or "incur," perhaps even "suffer," harm, damage, or even loss. Only persons can be victims against *whom* a crime can be committed in the first place, the Nevada victim compensation statute quoted earlier, that recognizes a governmental entity "against whom" a crime was committed, notwithstanding.[37] And only the direct victim of the crime can be the person *against* whom the crime was committed. Definitions of the victim as someone who has been "injured"[38] by some sort of act retain the first distinction, between personal and nonpersonal victims, insofar as only the former can be said to be "injured."

Other statutes better capture the essence of criminal victimhood. Most common are statutes that define the victim as a person "against whom"[39] a crime was committed, among them the Uniform Victims of Crime Act. Others define the victim as the "target"[40] or the "object"[41] of a criminal act. At least one statute defines victim as a person who has been "subjected to"[42] a crime. All of these definitions get at the nature of crime and, therefore, the nature of criminal victimhood. In crime, the offender treats the victim as an *object* and thereby *subjects* her to treatment inconsistent with her status as a self-governing subject. By treating her as an object, the offender denies any relevant distinction between herself as subject and the victim as subject. The act of subjugation is also an act of bringing the victim, as an object, within the subject of the offender. In the end, crime leaves only one subject, the offender; the other subject, the victim, has been subjected to objectification.

Bland definitions of the victim as someone, or something, who, or which, has incurred damage or loss, however, not only make room for the inclusion of apersonal and peripheral personal "victims." They also abstract from the person of the offender. There is an important difference between victimization through an occurrence, or even an act, and through a person, or an actor. Criminal victimization is personal victimization of one person by another.

It is preferable that statutes make explicit the personal nature of criminal victimization. It is, after all, not the offense that victimizes but the offender who victimizes. That's why the offender, not the offense, is suffering punishment, and that's why an offense-based criminal law is a logical impossibility—without an offender, criminal law cannot be criminal.

Statutes of this kind are few and far between. They tend to deal with restitution or other matters of criminal law, such as sentencing or parole. This makes sense, since it is more difficult to deny the significance of offenders in a system of law that is offender based, as opposed to the victim-based law of compensation. It's hard to think about punishment without thinking about the person being punished. Here, one is more likely to forget about the victim. The exact opposite is true of victim compensation statutes, which tend to abstract from the offender.

If she appears at all in the new law of victimhood, the offender tends to appear in her procedural, and preliminary, capacity of "defendant,"[43] as in the Wyoming restitution statute, which defines victim as a "person who has suffered pecuniary damage as a result of a *defendant's* criminal activities."[44] Occasionally, the offender appears as just that, an "offender."[45] Other statutes make the personal nature of the offender more explicit. Rhode Island defines a compensation victim as "a person who is injured or killed by any act of a *person or persons.*"[46] In Mississippi's criminal code, we find a victim crisply defined as a "person who was the object of *another's* criminal trespass."[47]

South Carolina's compensation statute contains an interestingly ambiguous definition of the victim as "a person who suffers direct or threatened physical, emotional, or financial harm as the result of an act by *someone else*, which is a crime."[48] It's not clear whether this definition is meant to reflect the personal nature of the offender (someone) or to exclude offenders from the scope of victim compensation (someone *else*). For purposes of the current discussion, let's focus on the identification of the offender as someone, rather than some*thing.*

The exclusion of offenders from compensation as victims, no matter how severely they may have suffered, is an important question, which we address in greater detail later on.[49] At this point, it's enough to point out that definitions of victimhood that make no mention of the person doing the victimizing and instead identify some occurrence as the victimizing cause extend victim status to that very person. Many an offender turns out to be a "person who suffers personal injury, death or economic loss as a result of a crime,"[50] as the Maine restitution statute puts it. According to this definition, any robber who shoots himself in the foot or breaks a leg during his escape would qualify for restitution from himself. What's more, so would every single offender, since the effect, perhaps the point, of punishment, and of the criminal process as a whole, is to inflict "personal injury, death or economic loss" on the offender. And not only offenders but anyone suspected or accused of or arrested for any crime, regardless of whether criminal proceedings are even initiated or how they are resolved (through dismissal, acquittal, or conviction), would qualify as a "person who sustains physical, *emotional or financial injury* or death as a result of the commission or attempted commission of a crime or act of delinquency."[51]

This problem of granting offenders facial victimhood is only exacerbated by statutes that define a victim not as a personal object of the crime but as someone or something that has "sustained," "incurred," or "suffered" harm. That someone or something certainly includes the offender. By contrast, if a victim is defined as a person "against whom" a crime has been committed, the offender does not qualify for victimhood, even if the "crime" is identified as the victimizer, rather than the person who commits it.

The point here is not simply that it makes no sense to have offenders receive restitution from themselves, to have offenders give victim impact testimony against themselves, and so on. The problem isn't even so much that the state has no interest in compensating anyone who might in one way or another have been negatively affected by crime and the criminal process, expanding the victim compensation model into a general insurance scheme for crime-related damage, perhaps as part of a comprehensive national disaster insurance.

The real problem is that offenders are the last people who are meant to receive victims benefits. As weapons in the war on crime fought on behalf of victims, victims' rights statutes turn on a radical and fundamental distinction between offenders and victims. Offenders are not victims, by definition. To grant offenders victims' rights would amount to giving aid and comfort to the enemy in the crime war; it would amount to nothing less than treason.

In the current climate, the distinction between, and the utter incompatibility of, offender status and victimhood is so crucial that it must be drawn at the most fundamental level. Offenders are not, and cannot be, victims. Once a person harmed by crime is identified as an offender, he becomes ineligible for victim compensation, without any need to inquire into the particular facts of the case.

It is the very same desire to keep offenders out of the law of victimhood that accounts for their absence from definitions of victimhood. The refusal to mention the offender reflects the intensity of the desire to construct a victim-based system of compensation, in conscious contrast to the offender-based traditional system of punishment. So hated is the offender that even to mention his name is forbidden. Thus demonized, the offender hovers behind the suffering of victims but remains unidentified.

Victims are entitled to compensation not because they have been victimized by an offender but because they happened to have suffered a loss because of some crime. That loss is to be compensated by the state. Victim compensation therefore involves victims and the state, and no one else, least of all the offender. Perhaps the offender will be arrested, prosecuted, convicted, and punished. And perhaps not. None of this matters when it comes to compensating the victim for her crime-caused damage.[52]

The price for this excision of the offender from victim law is high. Without the offender, the question of victims' rights loses its urgency. It's one thing to suffer a loss. It's quite another thing to be victimized by another person through crime. When the law gets rid of the offender, the victim gets all the attention. But, at the same time, the reason for paying attention to the victim has disappeared. We care about the victim, and we demand her compensation, and the offender's punishment, because she is a victim of crime. Her subjugation by another person is essential to her personal and to our vicarious experience of criminal victimhood. Moreover, as we just saw, refusing to acknowledge the offender's role can have the unintended, and self-defeating, effect of collapsing the distinction between offender and victim.

The distinction between criminal victimhood and other types of victimhood raises the question of how one should handle cases at the borderline between the two. Who, for instance, counts as the *victim* of a crime of negligence, that is, a crime committed unintentionally, without any awareness of the fact or even the risk of inflicting the proscribed harm?

American compensation statutes generally do not, on their face, distinguish between intentional and nonintentional crimes.[53] Still, it often turns out that they do in fact, at least in compensation statutes that concern themselves only with serious or violent crimes. These crimes, in turn, tend to be intentional ones, most obviously murder, rape, and assault.

The distinction between intentional and other crimes comes out not where one might expect it (and where it belongs), namely in the definition of whatever conduct (crime or criminally injurious conduct or whatever) gives rise to a victim compensation but in the context of a subsidiary issue: the compensability of traffic offenses. As we see later on, traffic offenses, including drunk driving, are problematic from the point of view of victim compensation because they are not result offenses, that is, they don't require that the perpetrator cause any harm whatsoever. They are prototypical conduct offenses, which require merely the doing of something (in this case, driving) under certain circumstances (say, being drunk), without more.

Traffic offenses, however, are also problematic because they tend to be strict liability offenses. This means that they don't require any sort of intention, or even awareness, on the part of the person committing them. I'm "speeding" even if I don't know I'm speeding; and I'm "driving while intoxicated" even if I don't know it. Traffic offenses, in other words, are also prototypical *nonintentional* offenses.

Many compensation schemes specifically exclude traffic offenses or "conduct arising out of the ownership, maintenance, or use of a motor vehicle," to quote from the Ohio statute. But, at the same time, they provide an intentionality exception to this exception in cases where "[t]he person engaging in the conduct *intended* to cause personal injury or death."[54]

In other words, it's the intentional nature of the conduct (combined with a particular kind of harm) that elevates a traffic offense to the level of a crime and therefore qualifies persons who suffer as a result for compensation as victims of *crime*, as opposed to victims of a car accident. What, precisely, is meant by "intentional" (or "intended") in this context is, of course, another question altogether, and one that has occupied the criminal law for quite some time. In fact, when courts do tackle this question in compensation law, they take approaches and draw distinctions that are familiar to any student of criminal law. For example, a Minnesota court considered "involuntary manslaughter" an intentional act, even though this particular variety of homicide requires only recklessness (i.e., accepting a substantial risk that death will result), rather than purpose (i.e., having the conscious object of causing death) or knowledge (i.e., being virtually certain that death will result).[55] In an earlier opinion, a Pennsylvania court insisted, by contrast, that "intent" in its state's motor vehicle exception be limited to so-called specific intent, rather than "general intent," with specific intent being defined as purpose or knowledge but not recklessness.[56] Drawing on definitions of intention found in a criminal law treatise and in the Second Restatement of Torts, the court explained:

> [A] motor-vehicle injury could be "intentionally inflicted" only if the act resulting in injury was committed (1) with the purpose of causing the injury or death of another or (2) with knowledge that the injury or death of another would be an inevitable consequence. The first situation might be illustrated if a person uses a car as a weapon with the design of killing or injuring another, such as by running down a rival or an enemy. The second situation might be illustrated if a person uses a car in a manner which he or she knows will inevitably result in death or injury to another (even though no particular harm is desired), such as driving purposefully into a crowd of people who are blocking his or her passage.[57]

What's important here, however, is not that these courts disagreed about the scope of intention but that in both cases intention was required

to bring certain conduct—in this case conduct amounting to a traffic offense—within the scope of *crime* victim compensation. Moreover, both
courts agreed that, however intention might be defined, it didn't include
negligence. Perhaps recklessness, the acceptance of a substantial risk of
harm, might be considered intention, perhaps not. But negligence, as the
failure to perceive a risk of any kind, could never amount to intention
and could never transform a traffic accident, no matter how severe the
harm it might have inflicted, into a crime for purposes of compensation.

This is not to say that it's impossible to imagine a crime victim without
considering the mental state of the person who made her suffer. For instance, one might define the victim, formally and simply, as the person
who brings the offender's behavior within the realm of criminal law, that
is, within the definition of a criminal statute. The victim of the crime of
negligent homicide, say, would be the second "person" in the definition of
the offense, the offender being the first: "A person is guilty of criminally
negligent homicide when, with criminal negligence, he causes the death
of another person."[58] And, in fact, negligent homicide does appear among
lists of compensable offenses.[59]

The victim of a negligent homicide, however, cannot be considered the
object or *target* of the offender's act, the person "against whom" the crime
was committed. Negligent crimes are not crimes in the true sense of the
word. Even proponents of negligent crimes don't deny that they are
crimes in a *different* sense from intentional ones. This difference emerges
clearly when we take the victim's perspective. A person harmed as a result
of a negligent crime is not victimized, or at least is victimized in a fundamentally different sense from the victim of an intentional crime.

Negligent and intentional crimes share several features. So negligent
crimes may end up severely compromising a person's autonomy, even to
the point of destroying her autonomy altogether (as in the case of negligent homicide). They also are committed by a person, rather than a dog,
or a tree and thereby satisfy another aspect of the definition of crime as
the assault by one person upon the autonomy of another.

But negligent crimes differ from intentional ones in that they do not
represent an attempt by one person to subjugate another. They may interfere with a person's autonomy, but not for the greater glory of another.
The victim of a negligent crime does not experience herself as being sub-
jugated by another person. She suffers harm, even serious harm, to her
ability to exercise her capacity for autonomy but not the indignity of having been treated as the means to another person's self-aggrandizement,

taken in its strict sense, that is, as the expansion of the offender's self to engulf the victim as a mere appendage.

It is this personal assault on her personhood that entitles the crime victim to victims' rights, in particular the right to have the offender punished. The offender's punishment is nothing but the dramatic reaffirmation of the victim's autonomy after the offender's criminal attempt to deny that autonomy for the sake of her own. And a crucial aspect of that reaffirmation is putting the offender in her place, among the community of persons, alongside the victim. The victim's personhood therefore is reaffirmed by exposing the offender's attempt to deny it as unsuccessful and, in fact, futile. Punishment communicates to the offender, the victim, and the onlooker that the offender has not succeeded, and could never have succeeded, in reducing the victim to a nonperson. The offender at best can *treat* the victim as a nonperson; she cannot transform him into one.

This process of autonomy affirmation does not, and cannot, take place in negligent crimes. Since negligent crimes are not crimes in this sense, their victims are not victims of crime. There are "objects" of negligent crimes, as there are "objects" of torts, only in the general, formal sense of object as that person who suffers the harm described in the definition of the negligent crime or tort. Only in this formal sense can one define victim as "the person who is the object of a crime *or tort*,"[60] provided one keeps in mind the fundamental, substantive distinction between victims of crime and victims of tort (or negligent crime).

Taking the victim's perspective thus allows us to elucidate the distinction between criminal and civil law. In fact, we might go so far as to say that, from the victim's perspective, the punishment of negligent crimes is not only illegitimate but impossible, for the simple reason that the very concept of negligent crime is self-contradictory. What distinguishes crime victims from all other victims is that they suffer an assault on their personhood at the hands of another person. This assault is absent in the case of negligent crime, which by definition precludes any awareness on the part of the perpetrator, never mind an intention of any kind, not to mention an intention directed at a particular victim, and certainly not a specific intention to deny the victim her right as a person to govern herself.

The punishment of negligent crimes threatens to violate, rather than vindicate, victims' rights insofar as it obscures the central function of the criminal process: the reaffirmation of the victim's autonomy as a person. As we have seen, the criminal process does far more for the victim than merely compensate her for the damage she has suffered. The offender's punishment itself manifests the victim's autonomy, her basic right, by vindicating her right to have the offender punished while, at the same time, treating the offender as a person by vindicating *her* right to be punished. This ritual of equal treatment of victim and offender as persons does not occur in the punishment for negligent crime.

The criminal punishment of negligent crimes thus has an effect similar to that of the criminal punishment of victimless crimes, which we discussed in the first part of this book. Victimless crimes, from the victim's perspective, are an obvious oxymoron. In a victim-based system of criminal law, they can have no place. The more crimes of negligence, crimes of strict liability (which don't even require negligence), and victimless crimes are handled by the criminal process, the more true crimes will be pushed to the periphery of criminal law. Eventually, the point of criminal law will be forgotten, and the victim will find herself on the outside looking in.

In a criminal process dominated by offenses without offenders and without victims, the distinction between criminal and civil liability, between punishment and compensation, disappears. No one remembers that the point of the criminal process is to reaffirm personhood, of victims as well as of offenders. In the end, the criminal process is neither about punishment nor about victims, and least of all about victims' rights. This, of course, is precisely what has happened.

To punish negligent crimes is one thing; to compensate for harm negligently inflicted is another. There is, of course, nothing wrong with the state compensating victims of crimes of negligence or even strict liability, along with anyone else who might have been harmed by the crime. But the fact that the harm was caused by a *crime* is entirely irrelevant. The only thing that matters is the fact of harm, not the criminality of its cause. Compensation schemes of this sort operate as state insurance schemes that supplement the existing tort remedies.

These compensation schemes are unobjectionable, provided they are not mistaken for having anything to do with crime or punishment or with the offender. Otherwise, victim compensation schemes that go beyond the victim strictly speaking, that is, the person against whom the crime was committed, run the risk of diluting the personal basis of criminal law. Once again, crime victims differ fundamentally from all other victims in that they have been victimized by another person. The tragedy of criminal victimization differs from the tragedy of noncriminal victimization in that it affects the core of the victim's personhood, rather than merely the external conditions for its enjoyment. Only crime may require more than compensation; only crime may require punishment.

Still, even in the face of this important caveat, the law of victim compensation remains the best source for treatments of the question of victimhood in contemporary law. That the law of *victim* compensation is not a helpful source for exploration of *offenderhood* should come as no surprise. We cannot expect to find a complete law of crime buried in victim compensation statutes. But we *can* find the outlines of one half of such a system, the victim-based half. The system will not be complete until after we have considered the other, offender-based half, which has been developed with much greater care in traditional criminal law.

Victim Compensation Victims

A close look at victim compensation statutes promises two results. First, and most immediate, the law of victim compensation has significance in and of itself. It represents a process for the disposition of *victimful* crime, that is, crime properly speaking, that operates parallel to the system of punishment. It provides an important *supplement* to the criminal and tort processes for persons who have suffered damage as a result of a crime. It also provides an *alternative* to the criminal process for direct victims in cases where criminal punishment is not necessary, or impossible (perhaps because the offender couldn't be identified, apprehended, prosecuted, convicted, or punished.)

Second, we find there the beginning of a law of crime that is based on victims and offenders alike. True, the law of victim compensation is a general law of victimhood that often fails to distinguish between criminal and civil victimhood with sufficient clarity. Simply describing existing victim compensation statutes, therefore, isn't enough. To derive a law of *criminal* victimhood from the law of victim compensation, we need also to strip it of its civil elements, using the victims' rights movement's concept of criminal victimhood as our guide.

But what is the law of victimhood that we find in victim compensation statutes? The law of victim compensation, in general, addresses two questions: is the applicant eligible for victim compensation, and, if so, to how much compensation is she entitled? So far, we have focused on the initial inquiry, into eligibility. It is here that we find general definitions of victimhood. As we saw earlier, victims, however, are not the only ones entitled to "victim compensation." Eligibility often extends to other persons, as well. For instance, the New York compensation statute, in section 621(5) of the New York Executive Law, defines "victim" as :

(a) a person who suffers personal physical injury as a direct result of a crime;

(b) a person who is the victim of either the crime of (1) unlawful imprisonment in the first degree . . . , (2) kidnapping in the second degree . . . , or (3) kidnapping in the first degree . . . ; or a person who has had a frivolous lawsuit filed against them.[61]

Eligible for victim compensation, however, are the following persons, as provided in section 624:

(a) a victim of a crime;

(b) a surviving spouse, grandparent, parent, stepparent, child or stepchild of a victim of a crime who died as a direct result of such crime;

(c) any other person dependent for his principal support upon a victim of a crime who died as a direct result of such crime;

(d) any person who has paid for or incurred the burial expenses of a victim who died as a direct result of such crime, except such person shall not be eligible to receive an award for other than burial expenses unless otherwise eligible under paragraph (a), (b) or (c) of this subdivision;

(e) an elderly victim of a crime;

(f) a disabled victim of a crime;

(g) a child victim of a crime;

(h) a parent, stepparent, grandparent, guardian, brother, sister, stepbrother or stepsister of a child victim of a crime;

(i) a surviving spouse of a crime victim who died from causes not directly related to the crime when such victim died prior to filing a claim with the board or subsequent to filing a claim but prior to the rendering of a decision by the board. Such award shall be limited to out-of-pocket loss incurred as a direct result of the crime; and

(j) a spouse, child or stepchild of a victim of a crime who has sustained personal physical injury as a direct result of a crime.[62]

This list of eligible persons includes a mix of direct victims, representatives of direct victims, and indirect victims that is typical of compensation statutes, which generally pay little attention to the distinction between criminal and other victims. The persons listed in subsections (a), (e), (f), and (g) are direct victims of the crime and therefore are entitled to criminal victimhood. Those in (c), (d), (h), and (j) are not direct victims of the crime and, as such, do not qualify for criminal victimhood, though they may well qualify for compensation as persons who suffered damage as a result of the crime. It's not clear whether persons under (b) and (i) act as representatives of the dead victim or on their own behalf. In either case, they are not entitled to criminal victims' rights, since those rights are extinguished with the victim's death.

The point of eligibility lists of this kind is to define the scope of "derivative" victimhood: who, other than the "victim" (or "direct victim"), is eligible for victim compensation?[63] Since criminal victimhood concerns itself only with the victim himself (and, if necessary, his representatives), these lists are not particularly useful for our project of extracting a law of criminal victimhood. The definition of victim, in section 621, is not only logically prior but also more promising.

We already have spent some time on the general definition of victim in compensation statutes. We therefore won't discuss the definition found in this particular statute in any detail. Still, it's worth noting that it includes not only persons who suffer "personal physical injury as a direct result of a crime" but also victims of various crimes that involve interference with their freedom of movement, namely unlawful imprisonment and kidnapping, as well as persons who have "had a frivolous lawsuit filed against them."[64]

The reason for including unlawful imprisonment and kidnapping seems clear enough. Although these crimes do not inflict, or do not necessarily inflict, "personal physical injury" on the victim, they nonetheless reflect the offender's attempt to subjugate the victim.[65] It is less clear why other crimes of similar import are *not* included. One would expect, for instance, to see included various kinds of interference with sexual autonomy, which needn't result in "physical injury." These omissions are all the more surprising given the inclusion of defendants in "frivolous lawsuits," even if a frivolous lawsuit is restrictively defined as "a lawsuit brought by the individual who committed a crime against the victim of the crime, found to be frivolous, meritless and commenced *to harass, intimidate or menace the victim. . . .*"[66]

The kernel of a general account of victimhood lies not in any haphazard list of compensable offenses but in the general definition of victimhood that precedes and underlies it: a victim is "a person who suffers personal physical injury as a direct result of a crime." To receive compensation, mere victimhood is not enough. Not victims but *innocent* victims trigger the legislature's empathy. In the words of President Reagan's 1982 Task Force on Victims of Crime: "[T]he *innocent* victims of crime have been overlooked . . . their pleas for justice have gone unheeded, and their wounds—personal, emotional, and financial—have gone unattended."[67] With innocent victimhood comes eligibility for compensation, as the "declaration of policy and legislative intent" at the very beginning of New York's victim compensation statute makes crystal clear:

> The legislature recognizes that many *innocent* persons suffer personal physical injury or death as a result of criminal acts. Such persons or their dependents may thereby suffer disability, incur financial hardships, or become dependent upon public assistance. The legislature finds and determines that there is a need for government financial assistance for such victims of crime. Accordingly, it is the legislature's intent that aid, care and support be provided by the state, as a matter of grace, for such victims of crime.[68]

Combining the definition of "victim" and the declaration of legislative intent, we end up with the following test of compensability: to qualify for victim compensation in other words, a claimant must be:

(i) "a person who suffers personal physical injury as a direct result of a crime" and
(ii) "innocent."

The Analysis of Compensability

A compensable victim is, in short, *an innocent person who suffers personal physical injury as a direct result of a crime.*[69]

Starting with these two basic building blocks, and with the help of victims legislation from throughout the country, we can construct the outline of a general law of compensability. The analysis of compensability falls into two stages:

(1) At the first stage, the victim's general, eligibility for compensation is determined. To be facially eligible for compensation in the abstract, a "claimant" must establish

   (a) that she falls within the scope of the relevant compensation statute ("jurisdiction") and

   (b) that she is capable of being a victim ("an innocent *person* who suffers personal physical injury as a direct result of a crime").

Assuming she is eligible in the abstract, she must establish that she is eligible in particular, by showing

(c) that she was in fact the victim of a crime ("an innocent person *who suffers personal physical injury as a direct result of a crime*") and

(d) that she was in fact not responsible for that crime ("an *innocent* person who suffers personal physical injury as a direct result of a crime").

If she succeeds on all four counts, and she bears the burden of proof on all of them,[70] she is compensable.

(2) The inquiry then proceeds to the second stage, where the amount of compensation is determined. That amount will depend on various factors, including

(a) her responsibility for the crime, if any,

(b) the actual harm suffered, and

(c) her neediness.

This analytic scheme of compensability bears a striking resemblance to the analytic scheme of punishability familiar from traditional criminal law. As we consider its various elements in greater detail, we find that the victim-based system of compensation parallels the traditional, offender-based system of punishment, so much so that one appears as the mirror image of the other.

Both inquiries address the same issues, but from different—opposite, yet complementary—viewpoints of the victim and the offender and therefore in fundamentally different, yet interrelated, ways. The victim seeks to attain victimhood as the offender seeks to avoid offenderhood, and the success of each depends on the failure of the other. Given a general presumption in favor of equal personhood and against differentiation among persons, the burden of proof properly rests on those who wish to establish the extraordinary status or attach the temporary label (the victim in one case, the state in the other).

Since the analysis of compensability thus complements the analysis of punishability, we can use either to reconsider the other. Since they struggle with the same central issue, the nature of crime and the law's response to it, from complementary viewpoints, we may be able to identify, and perhaps even to fill, gaps in one with the help of the other. More important, by continuously switching our point of view from the victim's to the offender's, and from compensability to punishability, we may end up with an account of criminal law that centers on the nature of crime as a matter between two persons, temporarily labeled victim and offender. In this way, we may be able to unify the theories of compensability and punishability and the laws of compensation and of punishment.

Any comparison between the analytic frameworks of victim compensation and of criminal liability is, of course, unfair. The analysis of criminal liability has emerged over centuries; the analysis of victim compensation is a recent development. As a result, even to speak of a *law* of victim compensation at all is a stretch. The primary sources—statutes, regulations, cases, rulings, and attorney generals' opinions—are too sparse to assemble themselves comfortably into a unified doctrinal picture. Many gaps remain, and even more inconsistencies, not only among but also within jurisdictions.

So, when thinking about different levels and prongs of compensation analysis, it's important to keep in mind that these conceptual distinctions are often honored in their conflation, which remains true of the analysis of punishability as well, even after centuries of refinement. It's often not clear where eligibility ends and the award question begins. For example, the question of innocence is both a categorical matter and a gradual one. As a categorical matter, it deprives certain claimants of compensability altogether—those who qualify as "coparticipants." As a gradual matter, it can reduce the compensation awarded to compensable victims, even to the point of a complete denial of compensation—the "100 percent contribution" of some compensation schemes.

Even as a categorical question, innocence is difficult to pin down. Is a non-innocent victim a victim? Some statutes restrict the status of victimhood to "innocent" (or non-"accountable") "claimants," while others define victim more broadly and then take account separately of the victim's non-innocence ("responsibility," "accountability," "contribution," or "participation," but never "guilt," which is reserved for offenders), perhaps as late as the compensation stage, reducing the award in proportion to the level of the victim's non-innocence.

The New York compensation statute exemplifies the second approach. As we saw, it defines victim as "a person who suffers personal physical injury as a direct result of a crime." It then limits compensability to "innocent victims": "A person who is criminally responsible for the crime upon which a claim is based or an accomplice of such person shall not be eligible to receive an award with respect to such claim."[71] Other schemes simply declare that "'[v]ictim shall not include any participant in the defendant's criminal activities."[72]

Compensability and Punishability

The connection between offender punishment and victim compensation becomes clear as soon as we regard the established analysis of criminal liability as a system for the assignment of offenderhood, rather than as a system for the classification of certain behavior as criminal. Once we go behind the external doctrinal layer, which ostensibly concerns itself exclusively with criminal offenses rather than offenders, we find a two-pronged analytic scheme. The first question under this offender- (rather than offense-) based scheme is whether the offender qualifies for offenderhood. If she does, then we move on to the second question: how much punishment does she deserve in proportion to her degree of offenderhood?

The test of offenderhood that determines eligibility for punishment is the mirror image of the test of victimhood we just encountered. A victim is "a person who *suffers* personal physical injury as a direct result of a crime." An offender is "a person who *inflicts* personal physical injury as a direct result of a crime." Or, take the definition of the victim that we found at the core of the victims' rights movement: "a person against whom another person has committed a serious crime."[73] The offender then is defined as "a person who commits a serious crime against another person."

The victim is the passive complement to the active offender. The offender commits against the victim. The victim is committed against by the offender. The victim's passivity is the flip side of the offender's activity. It is in this sense, and in this sense only, that the definitions of victim and offender differ. In all other respects, they cover the same ground.

And even on this one point of divergence, offender and victim remain intimately connected. It's not as though the victim happened to be passive, while the offender happened to be active. Instead, one's passivity is the other's activity. The offender doesn't just commit, and the victim isn't just committed against. The offender's committing and the victim's being committed against are simply two ways of capturing the same event, the crime.

As we saw earlier, the essence of crime is the attempt by one person to deny the personhood of another by subjecting him, in the true sense of the word, to the harm of crime. The offender through her criminal act(ivity) renders the victim passive, or, more precisely, she treats him as essentially passive, that is, as incapable of autonomy and, therefore, of personhood.

It is the function of the criminal process to show the insignificance of this one distinction between offender and victim. The offender, through her crime, acted as though the victim differed from her in a fundamental respect: she, as a person, treated the victim as a nonperson. But the offender's criminal act, that is, her acting upon the victim, merely reflected her misperception of the victim as essentially passive. The offender might well have experienced the crime as a manifestation of her active personhood. The victim may even have experienced the crime, from the other side, as a manifestation of his passive nonpersonhood. The event of crime, however, remains one and the same, no matter how it might have been experienced by offender and victim. The criminal act does not *actually* manifest the offender's personhood any more than it manifests the victim's nonpersonhood.

The criminal process thus makes it clear that this pretended difference exists nowhere except in the offender's (and often enough also the victim's) imagination.[74] At the end of the criminal process, only persons remain. The "person who suffers personal physical injury as a direct result of a crime" and the "person who inflicts personal physical injury as a direct result of a crime" once again become persons, period. The criminal process thus manifests the very identity between offender and victim that the offender denied in her crime.

The function of the criminal process, understood broadly as a state response to crime through law, thus is to manifest the identity between offender and victim and to manifest that identity in the same way, by treating both as equal persons. Both the law of offenderhood and the law of victimhood contribute to this function by analyzing the phenomenon of crime from two complementary properties, the crime offender's and the crime victim's. It's the crime that creates offender and victim alike. Before the crime, there are only persons. During the crime, these persons become offender and victim. During the criminal process, offender and victim are returned to their original status as persons, or, more precisely, are shown to have retained that status all along, the offender's attempt at differentiation notwithstanding.

So much for the general relation between the law of victim compensation and the law of offender punishment, which together constitute a general law of crime, that is, the law's rebuttal of an assault on its core concept, personhood. More specific parallels emerge as we address each element of the inquiry into victim compensation in turn, moving from the question of eligibility to that of compensation.

We use the now familiar New York definition of victim as the conceptual backbone of our analysis of the law of compensation: "an innocent person who suffers personal physical injury as a direct result of a crime." Another structure, such as the definition of the victim at the heart of the victims' rights movement or the one found in the thoughtfully drafted Uniform Victims of Crime Act, would serve just as well. Other statutes are referred to throughout. It makes no difference for our purposes, for instance, whether compensability requires a showing that the victim suffered harm as "a result,"[75] as "the result,"[76] as "a direct result,"[77] or as "a direct or indirect result"[78] of the crime. (One compensation statute even requires that the harm be "a proximate result" of the criminal act.[79]) What matters is *that* the causal connection between crime and harm matters, not *how*, at least not yet. The point is to structure our analysis, not to predetermine its results.

Whenever we need to take the offender's viewpoint and to explore parallels in the law of punishment, we rely primarily on the Model Penal Code. Here, too, the Model Code's resolution of particular questions is not as important as its general approach to the nature of crime.

The offender law analogue to our general test of victim compensability, based on New York's compensation statute, appears in section 1.02 of the Model Penal Code, which identifies the Code's central purpose: "to forbid and prevent conduct that unjustifiably and inexcusably inflicts or threatens substantial harm to individual or public interests."[80] In other words, the criminal law punishes those who engage in "conduct that unjustifiably and inexcusably inflicts or threatens substantial harm to individual or public interests." (The equivalent section in the New York Penal Law, which is based on the Model Code, similarly provides that the criminal law concerns itself with "conduct which unjustifiably and inexcusably causes or threatens substantial harm to individual or public interests.")[81]

At first glance, these two nutshell provisions, one condensing the law of compensation and the other the law of punishment, appear not to have all that much in common. Most important, the compensation provision is about "persons," whereas the punishment provision is about "conduct." This is no accident. Traditional criminal law, as was pointed out earlier, has, at least on the doctrinal surface, shown little interest in offenders. It was the offense, the conduct, that mattered. The offender mattered only as the person who engaged in the conduct, which was described more or less meticulously in statutes or court opinions. This purported act focus, however, may provide a doctrinal cover for the sub rosa search for evil and otherwise undesirable characters (such as "vagrants" or "disorderly persons") and, second, even on its face may reflect a dangerous neglect of the person who, rather than her "offense," is the eventual object of criminal punishment, threatened and inflicted.

On the flip side, we see that the law of compensation has paid little attention to the question of precisely what *conduct* entitles the victim to compensation or precludes him from it. In its focus on the "victim" in "crime victim," it has implicitly left the question of the "crime" to traditional criminal law. In fact, by often speaking in terms of "victims" in general, rather than of "crime victims" in particular, victim law all too often obscures its connection to the law of crime. Moreover, it has shown little interest in specifying what conduct on the part of the ostensible *victim* disqualifies him from compensation for the harm he has suffered as a result of a crime to which he may have contributed. Here, once again, we have to turn to traditional criminal law for help.

Other discrepancies between the tests of compensability and of punishability appear on the face of the two nutshells. Take, for instance, the reference to innocence in the compensation provision. "Innocent" can be seen as the victim law analogue to the offender law requirement that the criminal harm be inflicted or threatened "inexcusably," where both innocence and excuse turn on the question of responsibility. A responsible victim is not "innocent"; a responsible offender is not "excused." The labels "innocent" and "excused" thus simply are the victim and the offender version of some more general designation, "nonresponsible."

But for an offender to be responsible means more than she be not excused. It also means that she has engaged in certain behavior that has caused a certain harm. The judgment of responsibility—or guilt—is based on each of these elements, not merely on a finding that the defense of nonresponsibility (say, infancy or insanity) did not succeed. These defenses ("excuses") are merely the last opportunity to check whether a person who has engaged in certain criminal and unlawful conduct really deserves to be punished, that is, whether she can be held responsible for this conduct.

Likewise, for a victim to be responsible means both that he has engaged in certain conduct that resulted in certain harm (in this case, against himself) *and* that he is responsible for that conduct. The second requirement has so far been ignored by the law of victim compensation. Instead, compensation law tends to assign "responsibility" exclusively on the basis of the victim's acts, in particular, his "contribution" to the crime. The question whether the victim is responsible for that conduct is generally not considered. It seems, however, that, in analogy with the criminal law, the question of responsibility in compensation law should turn not only on conduct and its result but also on the victim's responsibility for that conduct. A formulation in terms of "accountability," rather than merely in terms of "contribution," may make room for this insight. Under such a test, which appears in the Uniform Victims of Crime Act,[82] the question of responsibility could then turn on the victim's accountability not only for the crime but also for his contribution to the crime.

The distinction between the reference to "result," in the compensation provision, and to "inflicts," in the punishment provision, is similarly insignificant. The requirement of "infliction" can be read as the offender-based flip side of the victim-focused requirement of "result." This connection is made explicit in the New York Penal Law version of the Model Penal Code nutshell, which speaks in terms of "conduct which unjustifiably and inexcusably *causes* or threatens substantial harm to individual or public interests."[83]

That the victim suffers "personal physical injury," whereas the offender inflicts "substantial harm to individual or public interests," also is no reason to deny the connection between compensability and punishability. These formulations represent two attempts to capture the nature of criminal harm. They approach this problem in different ways and from different viewpoints, but approach it they do. That's not to say, of course, that it's clear what victim precisely is supposed to be suffering harm to "*public* interests," other than the elusive public, of course. We've seen earlier that it's the ultimate victim, the state, that tends to stand behind vague references to the "public," thereby protecting itself from harm. The formulation taken from the law of compensation, which restricts itself to "personal" injury, avoids this danger. It also specifies the similarly vague reference to "substantial" harm by requiring that the harm be "physical," thus eliminating notoriously malleable harm categories such as emotional, psychological, and financial harm or even the "mental anguish" that one finds in other victim statutes.[84]

Notice, also, that the victim "suffers," while the offender "inflicts." This distinction is significant. It captures the core of the distinction between victim and offender. That distinction is merely functional, however, and temporary, and so it merely represents two sides of the same coin, the criminal event, which is experienced by the offender as infliction and by the victim as suffering. Still, both experience one and the same thing, the crime.

Then there's the difference between "injury" "suffered" by the victim on the one hand and "harm" "inflicted or threatened" by the offender on the other. While the distinction between injury and harm deserves some attention, it doesn't distinguish compensability from punishability—victim compensation schemes refer to either. The more significant distinction is that between actual harm and threatened harm. The question here is whether a victim should be compensated for threatened harm or only for actually suffered harm. Threats can, of course, constitute harm in and of themselves. But what about threats of which their object is not aware? How, in general, should attempts be treated as a matter of victim compensation? The law of compensation is muddled on this question. Several statutes extend victimhood to any "person who suffers direct or threatened physical, emotional, or financial harm."[85] Just how a person is to suffer *threatened* harm—beyond the harm caused by the threat itself—remains unclear. The treatment of attempts and of threats, however, is unclear not only in the law of compensation. Their place in the law of punishment remains contested to this day. While it is a fact that criminal law punishes attempts as well as consummated crimes, there is no consensus on why this should be so. Upon closer analysis, it therefore turns out that the inclusion of threatened harm only in the punishment provision says less about the difference between punishment and compensation than about the contested status of threatened harm both in the law of punishment and of compensation.

And this is one of the greatest benefits of putting the law of compensation and the law of punishment side by side and reading them as complementary approaches to a common problem: it enables us to identify conceptual and doctrinal weaknesses and to suggest remedies, something comparative law so often tries and almost as often fails to do. Uncertainty on a given point in one area of law can suggest the need to reconsider it in the other. In addition to the problem of threatened but not inflicted harm, consider the question of the nature of criminal harm, the significance of personhood to the infliction *and* the suffering of typically criminal harm, even the difficulty of distinguishing victim status from innocence, and so on and so on. The advantage of this sort of intrajurisdictional comparative law is that the legal schemes subjected to comparison are actually about the same thing, which cannot always be said for interjurisdictional comparisons, the bread and butter of traditional comparative law.

The unsophisticated and haphazard law of victimhood has the additional advantage of being, well, unsophisticated and haphazard. This area of law, where the state deems it prudent to disperse benefits to needy victims "as a matter of grace,"[86] meaning not as a matter of right, is still shaped largely by missives that often read more like interoffice memos among bureaucrats than statutes crafted with an eye toward litigation. After all, no one is entitled to anything, unless the member of something like the New York State Crime Victims Board says so, as a matter of grace. These victim bureaucrats approach issues that have occupied the attention of criminal law judges and scholars for centuries, if not millennia, with refreshing directness. Where in the annals of criminal law would one find remarks such as this helpfully explicit note of caution taken from a Montana guideline for compensation commissioners on the question of reducing compensation awards for victim "contribution" to her harm?

> Contribution is not stupidity, but gross stupidity can be contribution, that is, no reasonable person would have done what the victim did. . . .
>   Beware of moral judgments. It is inappropriate to deny benefits on a moral issue and may be unconstitutional and illegal as well, since the decision maker is using an arbitrary standard.[87]

And what police department policy, never mind what statute, would come right out and say what Florida's victim contribution guidelines express so clearly and so vaguely at the same time?

> If the victim *was involved in drugs*, as verified by the police report or other official documents, a 100% contribution factor should be assessed and the claim denied.[88]

In other words, crime victims are to be denied any and all compensation whatsoever (because of a "100% contribution factor"), no matter how severe their injuries, how unbearable their suffering, physical, psychological, mental, emotional, financial, simply because they were "involved in drugs." Their plight simply does not matter. How many statute books, how many collections of judicial opinions, how many treatises, could be discarded if the various machinations of the war on crime could be reduced to this simple, straightforward formula!

So much for our preliminary glance at the definitions of victim and crime, placed side by side. The mentioned points of friction between the

tests of compensability and punishability require our careful consideration. For now, it's enough to recognize that they are also points of contact. That's why it's worth viewing the analyses of compensability and
punishability in tandem, or rather as one superimposed upon the other.
They deal with the same general issue: the need to capture the nature of
crime in its various components from the viewpoint of the victim, who
seeks compensation, and the offender, who faces punishment, and then
to define the law's response to the fact of crime in the form of compensation and punishment.

6

The Law of Victim- and Offenderhood

The structural similarity between the law of victim compensation and that of offender punishment makes their parallel treatment not only worthwhile but necessary, as well, if we are to prevent one from engulfing the other. In this chapter we home in on their similarities and differences in greater detail. We move through the various steps in the analysis of compensability and punishability, considering each step from both perspectives along the way. The end result is a complementary analysis of the phenomenon of crime from the standpoints of the two persons who constitute it, the victim and the offender, adding up to a two-pronged law of crime, one "legalizing" crime through compensation, the other through punishment.

Eligibility (Compensability)/Liability (Punishability)

Jurisdiction

The first question any analysis of compensability must address is whether the victim-claimant falls within the scope of the compensation statute in question. In other words, the claimant must establish that she falls within the *jurisdiction* of the commission to which she has applied for compensation. This preliminary inquiry is governed by a test that is both remarkably uniform throughout American jurisdictions and relatively well crafted, in stark contrast to many other aspects of the law of victimhood. Characteristically, this test resulted not from a lengthy and careful scholarly discourse about the nature of jurisdiction in victim compensation law but from a federal statute that forced states to adopt it if they were interested in receiving federal crime victim compensation funds.[1] Before the arrival of the uniform federal test, the approaches to the jurisdictional question were as haphazard and varied as those to other issues of victim compensability, if the question was addressed at all.

The federal test sets up the following three-pronged analysis of compensability jurisdiction:

> The victim compensation program
> (i) "as to compensable crimes occurring within the State, makes compensation awards to victims who are nonresidents of the State on the basis of the same criteria used to make awards to victims who are residents of such State";
> (ii) "provides compensation to victims of Federal crimes occurring within the State on the same basis that such program provides to victims of State crimes;"
> (iii) "provides compensation to residents of the State who are victims of crimes occurring outside the State if—
>> (a) the crimes would be compensable crimes had they occurred inside that State; and
>> (b) the places the crimes occurred in are States not having eligible crime victim compensation programs."[2]

And here is a typical statute drafted in compliance with this model (this one is from Arkansas):

> "Victim" means a person who suffers personal injury or death as a result of criminally injurious conduct committed either within the State of Arkansas of against any Arkansas resident who suffers personal injury as a result of criminally injurious conduct which occurs in states presently not having crime victims reparations programs for which the victim is eligible and further includes any Arkansas resident who is injured or killed by an act of terrorism committed outside of the United States as defined in § 2331, Title 18, United States Code.[3]

This test combines various traditional bases of jurisdiction, taking account of two factors, location and residency. First, there's location: the compensation commission of a particular state exercises jurisdiction over any harm resulting from "crimes occurring within the state." Notice here that it is the location of the crime (the *locus criminis*), not the location of the suffering, that determines jurisdiction. This is the territoriality principle of jurisdiction.[4]

Second, there's residency. If the crime that caused the harm occurred in the state, the victim's residency makes no difference. This was not so originally. Before the promulgation of the federal test, states frequently limited compensation to their residents.[5] Initially, victim compensation was viewed as a matter of welfare, rather than as a matter of victims' rights. Even today, the Virgin Islands' "criminal victims compensation act" appears in the code title dedicated to "welfare."[6] States have always been eager to restrict welfare benefits to their residents, and victim compensation benefits were no exception, at least until the widespread adoption of the federal test.

Even under the federal test, as well as its state versions, residency still makes a difference. A state's compensation commission has jurisdiction even over harm caused by crimes committed outside the state, but only if the person who suffered the harm is a resident of the state. This is the passive personality principle of jurisdiction.

Nonresidents are ineligible for compensation for harm suffered from extraterritorial crimes under any circumstances. Resident victims are eligible for compensation for this type of harm provided that "(a) the crimes would be compensable crimes had they occurred inside that State; and (b) the places the crimes occurred in are States not having eligible crime victim compensation programs."[7] These restrictions, too, are familiar features of jurisdiction based on the personality principle. The point of the first provision is obvious. The second provision is designed to avoid jurisdictional conflicts, since the state where the crime occurred would have jurisdiction based on the territoriality principle.

Many states, including Arkansas, treat the question of jurisdiction in their definition of "victim." Others, New York for instance, address it in their definition of "crime."[8] Both approaches make sense, at least initially, since the test of jurisdiction combines victim elements (residency) and offense elements (location). The first approach is more in keeping with the person-focus of victim compensation law. The second approach has the advantage of uncluttering victim definitions that already tend to be complex, if not convoluted, especially if they attempt, unlike the Arkansas statute, also to define the precise nature of the cause of the victim's harm. Jurisdictional and substantive elements of the victim definition should be carefully separated if one hopes to avoid the confused and confusing mishmash of the Illinois Crime Victims Compensation Act, which in passing extends the reach of the Illinois compensation commission via the passive personality principle from crimes, and not only acts of terrorism, committed in other states to those committed in other *countries*:

"Victim" means

(1) a person killed or injured in this State as a result of a crime of violence perpetrated or attempted against him or her,

(2) the parent of a child killed or injured in this State as a result of a crime of violence perpetrated or attempted against the child,

(3) a person killed or injured in this State while attempting to assist a person against whom a crime of violence is being perpetrated or attempted, if that attempt of assistance would be expected of a reasonable man under the circumstances,

(4) a person killed or injured in this State while assisting a law enforcement official apprehend a person who has perpetrated a crime of violence or prevent the perpetration of any such crime if that assistance was in response to the express request of the law enforcement official,

(5) a person under the age of 18 who personally witnessed a violent crime perpetrated or attempted against a relative and, solely for the purpose of compensating for pecuniary loss incurred for psychological treatment of a mental or emotional condition caused or aggravated by the crime, any other person under the age of 18 who is the brother, sister, half brother, or half sister of a person killed or injured in this State as a result of a crime of violence, or

(6) an Illinois resident who is a victim of a "crime of violence" as defined in this Act except, if the crime occurred outside this State, the resident has the same rights under this Act as if the crime had occurred in this State upon a showing that the state, territory, country, or political subdivision of a country in which the crime occurred does not have a compensation of victims of crimes law for which that Illinois resident is eligible.[9]

It is this focus on the victim, rather than on the act, that distinguishes compensation jurisdiction from punishment jurisdiction. The analysis of jurisdiction in American criminal law continues to be dominated by the territoriality principle. The *locus criminis* determines jurisdiction. So obvious is this proposition that the topic of criminal jurisdiction generally is deemed unworthy of attention either in American criminal codes or in American criminal law scholarship. Whatever jurisdictional questions may arise in particular cases from time to time deal with the application of the territoriality principle, not its applicability. So occasionally a court finds itself forced to determine whether a crime occurred in one state or another, say when a homicide victim is stabbed in Indiana but dies across the border in Pennsylvania, with the murderous plan having been forged in Illinois. These issues are then resolved on the basis of an analysis of the various elements of the crime in question, which are first identified, then classified as "essential" or "nonessential," which classification is then followed by a determination whether (and generally that) the "essential" elements were in fact committed in the state where the court making the determination happens to be located.

In other words, jurisdiction under the territoriality principle is a matter of the act alone. The only thing that matters is where the act "was committed," without regard to who did the committing.

Only recently has the passive personality principle begun to chip away at the uncontested dominance of territoriality. Federal criminal law has led the way, extending federal criminal jurisdiction to reach extraterritorial offenses against United States nationals, including not only acts of terrorism but also homicide and other crimes of serious physical violence.[10]

Nowhere has the passive personality principle and its focus on the person attained greater influence than in the law of compensation. This makes perfect sense, given that victim compensation, as an aspect of the victims' rights movement, is about protecting innocent victims against evil offenders. Whereas traditional criminal law still retains, if only in doctrine, its bloodless focus on the criminal act, the law of victim compensation can freely manifest the visceral, and very personal, core of the urge to punish. What matters to victim compensation laws is not some act, whose elements are abstractly defined in some statute, but the very real suffering of very real persons, and in particular persons with whose suffering we can identify for one reason or another. The requirement of fellow residency here appears as a pale representative of the connection the drafters and appliers of victim compensation statutes feel toward certain victims of crime.

What's at stake in victim compensation law isn't the classification of acts but nothing less, and nothing more, than "the government's duty to protect *its* people from the consequences of criminal acts," to quote the Hawaii Supreme Court once more.[11] Ironically, this vital connection between the victim and her compensator is obscured by the very federal statute that attempted to extend compensation to victims across the land by encouraging states to compensate nonresidents and residents alike.

To thus conflate nonresidents and residents is to dilute the friend-foe distinction at the bottom of victim compensation law as a plank in the platform of the victims' rights movement. That crucial distinction would manifest itself most clearly in a victim compensation law that limited compensation to resident victims harmed by nonresident offenders. By contrast, a victim compensation law that distinguishes between residents and nonresidents neither as victims nor as offenders feeds itself exclusively from the gulf of hostility that separates victims from offenders *as such*. That gulf, however, already is considerable, as the nationwide and prolonged success of the victims' rights movement demonstrates.

Compensability jurisdiction differs from punishability jurisdiction not only in its focus on the person, rather than on the act. As one might expect, it also differs in the person who receives the law's attention. The active personality, or nationality, principle of criminal jurisdiction has no counterpart in compensation law. The active personality principle bases jurisdiction not on the person of the victim but on that of the offender. So one state might punish one of its residents for having committed a crime in another state, solely on the basis of his residency or nationality.

This jurisdictional principle is unknown in domestic American criminal law. By contrast, its influence is growing in international federal criminal law, and it's alive and well in many other countries throughout the world, particularly in the so-called civil law countries, where the Roman law principle of personal jurisdiction retains considerable influence.[12] In Germany, for instance, courts have criminal jurisdiction over extraterritorial acts committed against Germans (passive personality), as well as acts committed by Germans (active personality):

> § 7. Applicability to acts outside the country in other cases.
> (I) German penal law is applicable to acts committed outside the country against a German, if the act is threatened with punishment at the place of the act or the place of the act is not subject to any penal power.
> (II) German penal law is applicable to other acts committed outside the country, if the act is threatened with punishment at the place of the act or the place of the act is not subject to any penal power and if the actor . . . was a German at the time of the act or became a German after the act. . . .[13]

Nowhere, however, is the active personality principle more significant than in the criminal law of the U.S. military. In fact, the active personality principle is more dominant in American military criminal law than the territoriality principle is in American "civilian" criminal law. The jurisdictional scope of the Uniform Code of Military Justice is defined by personal status alone, which is defined in a lengthy jurisdictional section at the outset of the Code, entitled "Persons subject to this chapter."[14]

By contrast, the territoriality principle in American military criminal law is disposed of in a single laconic sentence:

§ 805. Art. 5. Territorial applicability of this chapter
This chapter applies in all places.

The detailed attention American military criminal law lavishes on the definition of the offender who falls within its jurisdiction would be un-thinkable in a victim compensation statute. In the law of victim compen-sation, the focus is emphatically on the victim. The offender figures only as the nameless cause of the victim's harm. The victim is defined, not the offender. And if jurisdiction is to turn on a person, as opposed to a place, then it will turn on the victim, not the offender. Put another way, there is no place for the active personality principle in the law of victim compen-sation, because the law of victim compensation is about passivity, not ac-tivity, about victimhood, not offenderhood.

Compensability jurisdiction, however, differs from punishability juris-diction in more than substance. Also significant is the fact that the ques-tion of compensability jurisdiction, in sharp contrast to criminal law, has attracted much attention and legislative care. One reason that American legislatures have shown so little interest in the question of criminal juris-diction is that criminal jurisdiction has never been understood to be ex-clusive. Just because one state exercises criminal jurisdiction over a par-ticular act—since it is the act, not the person, that determines jurisdic-tion—doesn't mean that another state can't do the same. Thanks to the principle of dual sovereignty, a person might find himself prosecuted, and even punished, for the same conduct by several states. It's simply a matter of discretion, for example, that drug offenders don't find them-selves tried in federal court after serving their state prison sentence for one and the same "act" of possession, which turns out, without fail, to make out both a state and a federal crime. (Likewise, no principle of ju-risdiction would protect Rita Gluzman from facing a murder trial in state court, after her conviction of interstate domestic violence in violation of the federal Violence Against Women Act.)[15]

In contrast to criminal jurisdiction, compensation jurisdiction is ex-clusive. In fact, the national law of compensation is carefully constructed so as to avoid multiple compensation awards to the same victim. Double-dipping into two state treasuries is not tolerated, since it would constitute an unconscionable attempt to obtain a "windfall" by manipulating the law of compensation in a way unbecoming an innocent victim.

No similar concerns mitigate against two states' double-dipping into their punishment potential. If an act constitutes a violation of the criminal law of two states, then each of these states is entitled to punish it. And the person who has committed the act has no reason to complain; through her act she has subjected herself to whichever sovereign deems itself offended.

There are, then, at least three things that the law of criminal jurisdiction might learn from the law of compensation jurisdiction. First, the question of jurisdiction is of crucial importance. The temptation to treat the question of criminal jurisdiction as a quibble raised by impertinent criminals is as great as the need to counteract it. Lack of interest in the question of criminal jurisdiction stems from a time when crime was considered a violation of the king's peace and therefore a personal affront to the king himself. In this view of criminal law as a personal matter of royal dignity, even the exercise of criminal jurisdiction was within the discretion of the person offended. Any attempt to construct binding rules governing the exercise of that discretion would by itself constitute an insult to the wisdom of the offended sovereign.

This deeply hierarchical view of criminal law, however, is incompatible with the personal foundation of modern law. It must be abandoned in favor of an egalitarian approach that regards crime as a specific kind of conflict between persons. The state merely exercises the victim's delegated right to have the offender punished. As an apersonal entity, it has no rights whatsoever, nor does it have any interests that punishment could protect. The only sovereign who is affronted in crime is the victim as a person, not the state. Once applied to the true victim of crime, the person, the principle of one victim, one punishment thus mitigates *against* multiple punishment by multiple states, rather than for it. Put another way, the "dual sovereignty" principle thus justifies multiple punishments if, and only if, a crime against multiple personal victims has been committed. (Perhaps it should be renamed the "dual victimhood" principle.)

The cavalier attitude toward criminal jurisdiction, therefore, is a relic from the premodern English conception of criminal law as the sovereign's policing of his territory and must be rejected for that reason alone. What's more, whatever American law of criminal jurisdiction there is today turns on an act-based view of criminal law that ignores the basic fact that we punish persons, and not acts. The question of criminal jurisdiction is a question of whether a particular person may be subjected to the criminal laws of a particular state, not whether a particular act fits the definition of one or more crimes in the criminal codes of one or more states. Only a criminal law that disregards the offender in favor of the offense can countenance the multiple punishment of a single offender for multiple offenses, as they are defined in multiple criminal codes.

Once American legislatures begin to devote more attention to the question of criminal jurisdiction, the active personality principle, which turns on the offender's person, deserves serious consideration. Criminal law, after all, is no more a matter of places than it is a matter of acts. Neither the *locus* nor the *crimen* can, without more, provide a state with criminal jurisdiction over the person. Perhaps the territoriality principle can be connected to the personality principle by reframing it as a convenient shorthand presumption that a person subjects himself to the criminal jurisdiction of a political community by entering it, remaining within it for a certain period, or even engaging in certain acts. No matter how the connection between place and person is established, without it criminal jurisdiction based on territoriality justifies the condemnation, or else the purification, of the *locus criminis* (perhaps by performing various condemnatory and purifying rituals there in regular intervals), but not of the offender.

Our look at compensability jurisdiction, however, also points up the pitfalls of placing criminal jurisdiction on a personal footing. As always, to make the personal basis of crime and punishment explicit is to open the door to the unreflected manifestation of hostility toward those who inflict criminal harm and of empathy toward those who suffer it. Here American military criminal law may provide a useful corrective. There we find a recognition of the personal aspect of criminal law without the concomitant exclusion of the offender as the incarnation of evil. Instead, the offender is defined as an insider, rather than as an outsider. It is, after all, the alleged offender's membership in the political community that subjects him to the criminal jurisdiction of its courts. Whether military criminal law can be of use to a new theory of criminal jurisdiction beyond providing an example of a nonexclusionary system of personal jurisdiction is, of course, another question.

Capacity

Assuming jurisdiction, the analysis of compensability next turns to the question of capacity. Having determined that the claimant is justiciable, we now investigate whether he is capable of being a victim. If he is justiciable and capable, we can proceed to the question of whether he was in fact a victim. A justiciable, capable, and actual victim is compensable, assuming he is also innocent. A victim found to be compensable then moves on to the final step of the compensation inquiry, where the amount of compensation, if any, is determined.

A claimant is capable of being a victim if he qualifies as a person. Recall the definition of victim, taken from the New York victim compensation statute, that provides our analysis of compensability with occasional guideposts: a victim is "an innocent *person* who suffers personal physical injury as a direct result of a crime." Only if the claimant is a person and therefore capable of criminal victimhood do we consider whether he in fact is a victim, that is, whether he in fact "suffer[ed] personal physical injury as a direct result of a crime."

We've already had occasion to explore the significance of limiting victimhood to persons. This is no surprise. The concept of person permeates every layer of the project pursued in this book. The victims' rights movement is, ideally, about victims as persons and so is a system of criminal law in a modern state based on the concept of the equal worth of persons. Again, this book represents an extended attempt to tease out the implications of the notion of personhood for the two complementary systems of law that address the common phenomenon of crime, from the victim's and the offender's perspective, respectively.

Personhood is the most important point of identity between victim and offender, and therefore the central point of contact between the law of victimhood and the law of offenderhood, that is, between the law of victim compensation and the criminal law. This point should be reflected in any test of victimhood and offenderhood. In other words, both victim and offender should be defined as "a person."[16] Consider, for instance, the Uniform Victims of Crime Act, the best effort so far to systematize the law of victimhood. The Act defines victim as "a person against whom a crime has been committed, but does not include a person who is accountable for the crime or a crime arising from the same conduct, criminal episode, or plan and does not include a government or a governmental subdivision, agency, or instrumentality."[17] As a typical victims' rights document, the Uniform Act does not define offender. It does, however, define crime: "an act or omission committed by a person, whether or not competent or an adult, which, if committed by a competent adult, is punishable by [incarceration]."[18] This renders the following implicit definition of offender: "a person, whether or not competent or an adult, who has committed an act or omission, which, if committed by a competent adult, is punishable by [incarceration]."

These definitions are extraordinarily rich in that they expose all of the crucial features of the law of victimhood, as one might expect from a carefully drafted uniform statute. To begin with, the Act captures, if only indirectly, the identity of victim and offender as persons. An offender simply is the person who commits a crime against another person, the victim. Victim and offender differ only in their roles in the crime. These roles, however, do not affect their status as persons.

This sounds obvious enough. But, as we have seen, the limitation of the law of crime to interpersonal offenses is anything but self-evident.

Noteworthy is also the Act's explicit exclusion of the state from the scope of victimhood. No "government or a governmental subdivision, agency, or instrumentality" can claim victim status. One would think that this provision would have been unnecessary given the general limitation of victimhood to persons. Unfortunately, however, the Act also includes a very broad definition of person, which stretches the concept beyond recognition: "'Person' means an individual, corporation, business trust, estate, trust, partnership, association, joint venture, government, governmental subdivision, agency, or instrumentality, or any other legal or commercial entity."[19] The state, in other words, must be explicitly denied victimhood because it had previously been granted personhood, along with "any other legal or commercial entity."

Still, the drafters of the Act deserve credit for recognizing that the state has no business including itself among the victims of crime. This recognition is a result of the Act's comprehensive scope. Only if one considers the law of victimhood as a whole, including compensation, restitution, participation at trial, and even constitutional rights, can a comprehensive concept of the victim emerge. And, by attempting to distill a general definition of victim, this is precisely the task that the drafters of the Uniform Act faced. The plain absurdity of listing the state as a victim entitled to compensation from the state suggests that the state does not deserve the status of victim, generally speaking.

Without the Act's broad definition of "person," the explicit exclusion of the state from the definition of "victim," however," becomes superfluous. Discarding the Act's definition of person, we therefore get two very sensible preliminary definitions of victim and offender as "a person against whom a crime has been committed" and "a person who has committed a crime," respectively.

But the Act does not stop there. Having identified the person as the point of identity between victim and offender, it proceeds to expand the concept of person, now in a different direction but once again to a point where that concept loses any significance. Not only does the Act include apersonal "entities" among the *victims* as persons. On the other side of the nexus of crime, it also lists among *offenders* as persons individuals whose personhood is at least questionable. Following general practice among victim compensation statutes throughout the country, the Act includes among offenders any "person, whether or not competent or an adult." To remove any ambiguity on this point, the drafters' comment to this provision explains that "'crime' covers an offense even if it is (1) uncharged, (2) denominated as an act of juvenile delinquency rather than a crime because of the offender's age,[20] or (3) subject to a successful mental nonresponsibility (insanity) defense." Moreover, "[t]here is no requirement that a defendant be successfully prosecuted or even identified for a victim to be entitled to the rights under this Act."[21]

This sort of emphatic declaration of the offender's irrelevance is typical of victims' rights statutes. The law of victim compensation, in particular, is about compensating victims, in conscious contrast to the law of offender punishment, which is about punishing offenders. To uncouple punishment from compensation in this way makes sense. The experience of victimization, which compensation is designed to end, does not depend on the identification, apprehension, prosecution, conviction, or punishment of the offender.

Still, to say that it doesn't matter what happens to the offender is not to say that it doesn't matter whether there was an offender in the first place. The experience of victimization is the same, regardless of whether the offender is punished. It is not the same if there was no offender. The first is a distinction of procedure. The second is a distinction of substance. Without an offender, there was no crime. And, without an offender, there was no crime victim. And, without a crime victim, there is no need for crime victim compensation.

The Uniform Act sidesteps this issue by defining only victim and crime but not offender. But even victim compensation is not simply a matter between the state and the victim harmed by "crime" (rather than an offender). To cut out the offender, not merely as a matter of procedure but as a matter of substance, is to deny the realities of the experience of victimization through crime. As we pointed out already, that experience is unique in the same way that crime is unique: it does damage to the core of one's identity as a person. This sort of damage only a person can inflict on another. It's something that is not simply sustained or incurred but suffered, often literally, at the hands of another person.

From the victim's perspective, it matters whether her suffering was caused by a dog, a tree, a lunatic, a child, a drunk, or an adult person "in the full possession of her faculties," that is, acting as an autonomous person. There's nothing wrong with the state compensating persons for all sorts of injuries. But to treat all of them as qualitatively similar injuries simply because they all represent "loss" "incurred" by some entity is to dilute the categorical distinction between criminal and other victimization and therefore to ignore, rather than to vindicate, the rights of victims of crime in the true sense of the word.

The Uniform Act leaves "offender" undefined not only because any mention of the offender in a statute exclusively dedicated to the victim is to be studiously avoided. It doesn't define "offender" for a much simpler reason: it can't. There is no offender in "an act of juvenile delinquency." There is no offender in "an act or omission committed by a person . . . not competent or an adult." There is no offender in an act "subject to a successful mental nonresponsibility (insanity) defense."

Both insanity and infancy—and not merely insanity, as the Uniform Act implies—are defenses of "nonresponsibility." To say that someone is nonresponsible, however, is to say that she lacks certain characteristics of personhood, because it is to persons, and only to persons, that responsibility or guilt can attach. Individuals to whom the Uniform Act refers vaguely as "nonresponsible" don't just happen to be nonresponsible for their act. They are incapable of responsible behavior. Their fundamental capacity to govern themselves, that is, their capacity for autonomy, is abnormally stunted for one reason or another. In the case of children or "juveniles," they have not yet developed that capacity. The criminally insane either have never developed it or have lost it due to some catastrophic event or over time.

Children and the insane in this sense differ from normal adults who commit crimes. The latter are exercising their capacity for autonomy in the criminal act. The former may commit an act that meets the definition of a crime, but their doing so does not manifest their autonomy in any way. As persons incapable of autonomous action, they also are incapable of oppressing another individual. They can inflict harm, even serious harm, but they cannot cause criminal harm: they cannot substitute their autonomy for that of another person for the simple reason that they have none.

The failure to distinguish between criminal and noncriminal harm is also inconsistent with the concept of crime as an act, which underlies all victim legislation. According to traditional criminal law doctrine, a crime must be an act or an omission in violation of some clearly defined duty. Many victims' rights statutes even make this act requirement explicit. So the Uniform Act defines "crime" in "crime victim," quite correctly, as "an act or omission committed by a person."

The problem is that the requirement of an *act*—or a punishable omission, that is, a failure to act—already limits the commission of crime to persons. Only persons, defined as human beings endowed with the basic capacity for autonomy, can act. An act, understood as the exercise of one's capacity for autonomy, can be committed only by someone endowed with that capacity. Animals can't act. Trees can't act. "Entities," corporate or not, can't act.[22] Even orthodox criminal law recognizes that certain human beings can't act, or at least can't be said to act in certain cases, such as when they engage in certain behavior while sleepwalking, suffering from an epileptic attack, or engaging in some sort of reflex motion, perhaps to swat away an obnoxious fly. Only persons have a self that they can manifest through external behavior, and only they can attempt to form their environment, human or not, in their image.

The internal inconsistency of the concept of a crime victim suffering from the result of an offenderless offense becomes even clearer in statutes that, like the Uniform Act, define "victim" in "crime victim" as a person "against whom" a crime has been committed.[23] As any parent knows, even the smallest child is capable of engaging in behavior that results in considerable injury, even to full-grown adults. But whether that child is capable of taking action "against" anyone is another question altogether. A child is incapable of the self-direction required to engage in any purposive action, never mind purposive action "against" a particular person with the aim of inflicting harm. The same is true for the criminally insane, who are by definition incapable of conforming their behavior to whatever rules of conduct they may be able to make out from the confusing world around them, if any.

From the crime victim's perspective, then, both victim and offender must be persons. Nonhuman "entities," animals, and plants count neither as victims nor as offenders. All this seems clear enough. Yet one important problem remains. How can we account for the obvious and undisputed fact that certain individuals who count as victims do not count as offenders? How can one commit a crime against someone who cannot commit a crime?

These questions raise the important and difficult issue of the symmetry of victimhood and offenderhood. If we agree that both victim and offender must be persons, then precisely what attributes of personhood must they possess? How, in short, are we to define "person"?

The question of who counts as a person for victimhood is rarely discussed. Outside the context of victims' rights statutes, it arises most frequently in the law of homicide. Here one even finds definitions of "person." For instance, the New York Penal Law defines homicide as "caus[ing] the death of another person,"[24] where "person" in turn is defined as "a *human being* who has been born and is alive."[25] (The Penal Law also contains a definition of person, in its general part, which, however, is clearly intended to cover persons as offenders, rather than as victims. There "person" means "a *human being*, and where appropriate, a public or private corporation, an unincorporated association, a partnership, a government or a governmental instrumentality.")[26]

If we disregard, in the offender-focused definition of person, the reference to obviously apersonal entities and "instrumentalities" and, in the victim-focused definition, the abortion-related reference to birth and life, we are left with the following simple definition of the person, as victim and as offender: a human being. This definition is helpful not only in eliminating animals, trees, and apersonal entities. It's also helpful in exposing an important commonality of offender and victim: their humanity.

But humanity is not personhood. All persons are humans, but not all humans are persons. And humanity qualifies for victimhood but not for offenderhood. Offenderhood requires not only humanity but personhood, as well. How is it possible to commit a crime against a human who is not a person? How can we punish the offender for (mis)treating another as a nonperson if that other is in fact a nonperson? How can the criminal process vindicate the autonomy of a victim who had none to start with? How can the victim's experience of nonpersonhood be overcome through the criminal process if that experience never occurred? And, finally, how can a nonperson have victims' rights, in particular the right to *have* the offender punished, especially if that same individual would not have the right to be punished had she been on the other side of the crime, as the offender, rather than the victim?

For the relation between offenderhood and victimhood, this means that every potential offender is also a potential victim, but not vice versa. This relation is rarely explored, largely because the legal system operates on the general assumption that distinctions among human beings are irrelevant, or at least suspect. It was more likely to attract attention at a time when the law had fewer qualms of this sort.

So, for instance, the Mississippi Supreme Court concluded, in 1820, that the intentional killing *of* a black slave was murder on the ground that the intentional killing *by* a black slave also would be murder:[27] "By the provisions of our law, a slave can commit murder, and be punished with death; why then is it not murder to kill a slave?" In other words, the slave qualified as a murder victim because he qualified as a murderer. Every potential offender is also a potential victim; offenderhood implies victimhood. Or, once again in the inexorable logic of the Mississippi Supreme Court, if "[t]he law views them as capable of committing crimes," it must also view "them" as capable of having crimes committed against them.[28]

The connection between personhood and humanity is complex. Its detailed exploration would lead us too far afield into the outskirts of moral theory and the moral—and legal—rights of nonhuman animals, particularly but not exclusively primates.[29] (To my knowledge, no one has so far claimed rights for other life forms or even inanimate objects, though perhaps even these claims can be found if one looks hard enough at some theories of "environmental rights.") Perhaps it will turn out that we punish crimes against humans who cannot commit crimes because we identify with them as members of our species or because they can experience pain (which we then feel vicariously through intraspecies identification), or both. Perhaps we punish crimes against those human nonpersons and against human persons for different reasons. Perhaps it turns out that, for the former, punishment is a matter of mercy and for the latter, one of right.

Absent a comprehensive theory of the foundation of our motivations for and practices of punishment, we are better off sticking to the connection between punishment as a matter of the right to, and hence the capacity for, autonomy. In this vein, the connection between crimes against children and autonomy is clear enough. Child victims—that is, individuals who, as offenders, would qualify for the infancy defense—have the capacity for developing a capacity for autonomy. They are wired to develop a capacity for autonomy, which they will be free to exercise or not, according to their wishes. To commit a crime against a child, or anyone whose capacity for autonomy is not fully formed, is to interfere not merely—or at least so much—with the exercise of their capacity but with the development of that capacity itself. A crime committed against a child, therefore, can result in much greater damage than the same crime committed against an adult. The child may never develop her capacity for autonomy and therefore—a fortiori—never exercise it. The adult merely needs to rediscover that capacity to the point where he feels self-confident enough to exercise it.

To vindicate the right to autonomy of a child victim may require the intervention of an adult representative. That representative, however, should act only on behalf of the child victim, and only to the extent that his participation would help to minimize whatever damage the crime inflicted on the child's capacity for autonomy. In the case of child victims, it is particularly important to prevent literally self-defeating efforts to restore autonomy through fixation on the damage to that autonomy caused by another.

Now let's move from the victim version of the infancy defense to the victim version of the other "nonresponsibility" defense, insanity. Here, the case of an adult deprived by the offender of his capacity for autonomy poses no difficulties. An act that compromises, or even destroys, the victim's capacity for autonomy qualifies not only as a crime but as a more serious crime than one that interferes merely with the exercise of that capacity.

More difficult is the case of a crime committed against an adult—or a child, for that matter—who suffered at the time of the crime from a mental abnormality that is certain permanently to deny her the capacity for autonomy. Here the offender, by hypothesis, could have interfered with neither the capacity for autonomy nor its current or future exercise. In this case, the offender's treatment of the victim as a nonperson did not amount to *mis*treatment. Deprived of the capacity for autonomy and without hope to achieve it, the victim was in fact a nonperson at the time of the crime. Still, we cannot deny that the urge to punish the abusers of these victims is as strong as, if not stronger than, the urge to punish the oppressors of autonomous, or at least potentially autonomous, victims.

The ultimate explanation for our desire to punish the use of nonautonomous humans as mere tools for the self-aggrandizement of the offender's person, that is, their treatment not as persons but as constituents of the environment that a person is free to shape in his image, remains

262 | The Law of Victim- and Offenderhood

unclear, as we remarked earlier. Still, there's a general norm that nonautonomous humans are to be treated *as if* they were autonomous or, more broadly speaking, that abnormal humans are to be treated *as if* they were normal, at least as much as is consistent with their well-being and the well-being of those around them. Whether this norm enjoys the status of a right is another question. It, instead, may be a matter of mercy, rather than of right, which of course isn't saying much, since it leaves the foundation of this exercise of mercy in the dark. For our purposes, however, it's enough to notice the existence of the norm of putative autonomy without fully elucidating its origins.

On the basis of the norm that all humans, autonomous or not, are to be treated as autonomous, the distinction between crimes against autonomous and nonautonomous humans falls away. This makes sense of our urge to punish the instrumentalization of nonautonomous humans *as crimes* and, moreover, *as crimes against normal, autonomous humans*, in stark contrast to our attitude toward acts perpetrated upon human corpses, for instance. Necrophilia and various other offenses against corpses are in a completely different category from their analogues in the realm of live victims. If they are treated as crimes at all, they are viewed as offenses against public sensibility or, less honestly, against public health, rather than as "offenses against the person," the criminal code chapter where one would look for offenses against live human victims. By contrast, crimes against nonautonomous victims are not defined separately in our criminal codes. They are treated as instances of general offenses against the person, such as homicide, assault, or whatever.

There is another, less sophisticated explanation for the urge to punish crimes against those who cannot now, and never will be able to, commit crimes. It may simply reflect the general sense that anyone who looks like us—any member of the human species—possesses at least a spark of the capacity for the capacity for autonomy, no matter how faint. Perhaps this sense is based on intraspecies empathy. Perhaps it has some religious foundation. Perhaps it is crucial for the survival of human communities, even our species. Whatever its source, it is unlikely to be debunked by scientific proof, no matter what that proof might look like, or by medical evidence that a particular individual has no chance whatsoever of gaining or regaining autonomy.

So much for the doctrinal implications of the requirement that the victim be a person. As we have seen, the criminal law reaches harm inflicted upon humans as endowed with the capacity for autonomy; even actually nonautonomous humans are treated as putatively autonomous, that is, as though they were at least capable of developing a capacity for autonomy and, therefore, personhood.

Offenders must be persons in the same sense: they must possess the capacity for autonomy. Unlike victims, however, they must actually, and not merely putatively, possess that capacity. This makes sense because an individual who only putatively has the capacity for autonomy could not in fact exercise that capacity. Crime, however, is nothing but the exercise of that capacity against, or to the detriment of, another person. Without actual autonomy, *committing* a crime is impossible; *having a crime committed against oneself* is not.

This is not the place for an in-depth exploration of the ways in which criminal law manifests the personhood of offenders. Such an exploration would require a careful analysis of the entirety of so-called substantive criminal law and, in particular, its general part, which contains the general principles of criminal liability. For our present purposes, it suffices to have shown that the offender's personhood is not merely a matter for an offender-based law of punishment. It also matters to a victim-based law of compensation. The personal nature of the offender distinguishes the experience of criminal victimization from other types of harm that a person might suffer. It's the offender as a person who transforms an event that causes damage into a crime. Criminal law principles that capture the offender's personhood, including the act requirement and the mens rea requirement, as well as the defenses of infancy and insanity, do more than simply protect certain individuals from punishment: they preserve the unique pointedness of victimization through crime. By limiting crime to personal offenders, these principles also respect the personhood of *victims*, which can be threatened only through the intentional attack by another person. These principles of offender personhood, therefore, are a matter of right for offender and victim alike.

Having established the relevance of the offender's personhood in victim law, it's time to reverse viewpoints once again, to fix the victim's place in the offender-based law of punishment. So far we have focused on the question of what it means to say that the victim must be a person for the offender to face criminal liability. In particular, we considered what happens to the offender's criminal liability if a victim *lacked* actual autonomy at the time of the alleged crime. We saw that a capacity for autonomy was enough.

The more common question, however, concerns what happens if the victim not only has the capacity for autonomy but exercises it in a particular way. The victim's defensive assertion of his autonomy against the offender's attempt to subjugate him makes no difference to the offender' criminal liability. It simply serves as evidence that the offender is in fact committing a crime, that is, that the offender is in fact attempting to deny the victim's autonomy in the face of her own. The victim's resistance is relevant only as absence of consent, where consent is understood broadly as the victim's recognition that an apparent act of other-subjugation is in fact an act of self-manifestation.

By consenting, the apparent victim rebuts the presumption of victimhood. He indicates that another's act that facially satisfies the elements of a crime does no harm to his autonomy in fact. In the light of consent, an apparent act of heteronomy is revealed as an act of autonomy.

"Consent" is the doctrinal category in the offender-based law of punishment that functions as a placeholder for considerations of the victim's personhood, that is, his capacity for autonomy. American criminal law has yet to fully appreciate the central significance of the consent defense. That defense stands as a constant reminder that criminal law is about persons first. Consent as a reflection of the criminal law's basis in personal autonomy is less a defense than a general limitation, less an exception than the rule. Consent deprives the criminal process of its legitimacy, of its reason for being. It finds its broadest recognition in the Model Penal Code. According to the Code, consent is a defense if nonconsent is an element of the offense charged or if it "precludes the infliction of the harm or evil sought to be prevented by the law defining the offense."[30] That harm, however, is always the interference with the victim's autonomy. That interference is absent in the presence of consent.

One, therefore, would expect consent to be a defense to, or nonconsent an implicit element of, every offense. It isn't, not even in the Model Code. The Code instead preserves the traditional, and traditionally ill-supported, exception for serious bodily harm.

Attempts to justify exceptions to a general consent defense tend to consist of general references to the unique nature of criminal law. Criminal law, so it is said, is about not individual victims but about the state (or the king).[31] We already have dealt with this pre-Enlightenment theory of criminal law in the first part of this book. It reflects a hierarchical political community inconsistent with the ideal of equal personhood that underlies not only the political theory of American government in particular but also Enlightenment moral and political theory in general. Moreover, it proves too much. If it is correct that the state is the victim of every crime, then consent should be a defense to none.

A failure to recognize consent as a defense in the law of punishment amounts to a violation of victims' rights, particularly of the apparent victim's fundamental right to autonomy. It also violates the apparent *offender's* right to autonomy, assuming her facially criminal conduct manifested an agreement between her and the apparent victim (as opposed to her merely carrying out the "victim's" orders, say). Punishing the apparent offender, therefore, would do nothing to vindicate autonomy. On the contrary, it would deny the autonomy of offender and victim alike.

As we've seen, victims and offenders alike must qualify as "a person." Moreover, the offender's personhood matters to the victim as much as the victim's personhood matters to the offender. Without a personal offender, there is no victim. And without a personal victim, there is no offender. At the same time, the victim's personhood is not only a prerequisite for the offender's punishment (and for the victim's compensation). It can also work to exculpate the offender, provided he acted with the victim's consent.

Aside from particular points of doctrinal correspondence, taking the victim's point of view once again reaffirms the central place of personhood, not only in the law of victim compensation but also in the law of offender punishment. A criminal law that puts persons first, rather than acts, would do well to consider the question of personhood first. There is no point in considering the question of whether the offender has committed, or the victim has suffered from, behavior that matches the description of some criminal act unless it is clear that one is dealing with persons, that is, with beings capable of offenderhood or victimhood.

Contemporary criminal law, by contrast, tends to treat the question of capacity haphazardly at various points in the analysis of punishability, with a particular emphasis on the final step of this analysis, when the offender's responsibility for his unjustified criminal act is considered. This shotgun approach to personhood reflects the failure to recognize personhood not only as a single but as the single most important issue in the analysis of punishability (and compensability). Rather than investigate the offender's capacity for punishment as a matter of personhood, current analysis considers aspects of this question under the heading of actus reus (where sleepwalkers or epileptics are said either to be incapable of acting or, at least, of acting voluntarily) or mens rea (where certain offenders are said to possess insufficient mental capacity, or "diminished capacity," to form the required mental state). It then struggles to differentiate these forays into the question of personhood from others, most important, the inquiry into the offender's sanity, which functions as a sort of final personhood sieve after all is said and done.

Instead, one might consider adopting an analytic approach that asked about capacity first and about acts and the like later. Blackstone's treatment of criminal law, for example, began not with a discussion of the act requirement or the mens rea requirement but with a discussion of the capacity to commit crimes.[32] Blackstone covered far more under the heading of capacity than we might want to today. For instance, he treated mens rea as a personal character trait—in a way, as *the* capacity to commit crimes: an evil mind—rather than as a temporary mental state that does not mark the offender as degenerate. But that's not the point. The point is that Blackstone's approach assigns the question of capacity the firstness it deserves, even if he never worked out the concept of personhood that underlies his theory of punishability or the connection between that concept and the capacity for crime and for punishment.

This approach would bundle the dispersed considerations of aspects of personhood into a single inquiry and assign that inquiry the firstness it deserves. It thereby would highlight the person not only as the common denominator within the law of compensation and within the law of punishment but as the common denominator across the law of crime generally speaking, which encompasses both the law of victimhood and the law of offenderhood.

Crime

Now that we have addressed the preliminary, and abstract, issue of capacity (for victimhood and offenderhood), it's time to move on to the factual aspect of our inquiry into compensability (and punishability). Assuming that the claimant (or defendant) qualifies as a person and is therefore generally *capable* of victimhood (or offenderhood), the question now is whether she was *in fact* the victim (or the perpetrator) of a crime. In terms of our definitional guidepost provided by the New York victim compensation statute, we have determined that the claimant is a "person." Now we need to find out whether she is a person "who suffers personal physical injury as a direct result of a crime." Each component of this definition receives our attention, one after the other. Finally, we must check whether she is also "innocent."

An Innocent Person Who Suffers . . . Given the systematic significance of the common ground between victims and offenders, personhood, which we explored in some detailed in the previous section, one might expect the law of victimhood and of offenderhood to revolve around the concept of the person, defining victims and offenders as persons first. That's not so, however. The Uniform Victims of Crime Act is the exception, not the rule, and even it is far from highlighting the fundamental similarity of victims and offenders as persons. Instead, it follows the general practice of victims' rights legislation of mentioning the offender as little as possible, and preferably not at all.

The offender is as invisible in the law of victim compensation as the victim is, and always has been, in the law of offender punishment. Our look at the two legal schemes in tandem, or more precisely as mirror images, is designed to drag out into the open what so far has remained covered by thick layers of ignorance and rhetoric: the victim in the law of offenderhood and the offender in the law of victimhood.

The traditional offender-based law of punishment so far has simply ignored the victim. In fact, it hasn't paid much attention to the offender, either. It has, instead, focused on the description of acts and the ascription of criminal liability based on those acts. At any rate, it has seen no need to define "offender." It has on occasion found it expedient to define "person," mostly as a matter of drafting convenience. These definitions generally had nothing to do with victims. They simply clarified that the "person" or the "whoever" one might find in the definitions of particular offenses included not only individuals but also various apersonal entities. Although this expansion of personhood to include nonpersons has considerable substantive significance, it has attracted little attention in American law. The criminal liability of apersonal entities has for some time been the generally accepted rule in American criminal law.

Rarely did the definition of "person" concern itself with victims. The exception that proves the rule is the law of homicide, which occasionally had to address the question of whether fetuses qualified as homicide victims. This question was crucial for purposes of distinguishing homicide from abortion: they were thought to differ only in the nature of their victim. The need for a definition of "person" is particularly acute in criminal codes that define homicide and abortion in the same chapter and that define homicide in terms of acts committed against a "person," rather than "another human being" or simply "another." The New York Penal Law does both. As we noted earlier, it defines homicide as "caus[ing] the death of another person"[33] and then treats abortion alongside homicide in an article on "homicide, abortion, and related offenses,"[34] which in turn appears in the code title devoted to "offenses against the person involving physical injury, sexual conduct, restraint and intimidation."[35]

Small wonder, then, that the New York legislature took the rather unusual step of defining "person," at least for purposes of the article on "homicide, abortion, and related offenses." There we learn that a person is "a human being who has been born and is alive."[36] By implication, a fetus isn't a person, and, therefore, abortion isn't homicide. This clarification is helpful but doesn't quite solve the problem. If the fetus isn't a person, then abortion isn't homicide, but it also isn't an offense against a person, which means it has no place in a title containing "offenses against the *person* involving physical injury, sexual conduct, restraint and intimidation."

Other codes avoid the issue of personhood altogether, by simply fudging the distinction between homicide and abortion. In the Model Penal Code's definition of homicide, for instance, the victim isn't a "person" after all but a "human being."[37] (Still, it can't cut the person out of homicide altogether, for it then turns around and defines "human being" as "a person who has been born and is alive,"[38] the reverse of the New York definition.) It also places abortion not alongside homicide, and not even among its "offenses involving danger to the person," but among the "offenses against the family," which also include bigamy, incest, endangering the welfare of children, and persistent nonsupport.[39] Abortion in the Model Code, in fact, has no victim of any kind. Abortion simply means "terminating a pregnancy."[40]

The law of victimhood doesn't just *ignore* offenders. It is, as we've seen, consumed by the desire to excise them, not only from the community of potential and actual victims (i.e., of all upstanding citizens) but also from its doctrinal vocabulary. But, unlike the law of punishment, which showed little interest in the offender apart from his connection to an offense, the law of victims' rights pays considerable attention to the victim. Whereas the law of punishment sees no need to define offender, the law of compensation has taken to construct detailed, if not always clear, definitions of victim.

Moreover, all definitions of victim in victims' rights legislation have one thing in common: their emphasis on the irreconcilable and unmistakable difference between victim and offender, between friend and foe. That distinction defines the victims' rights movement, and we will encounter it again and again as we find our way through the doctrinal maze of compensation law. By definition, the victim is the sufferer, and only the sufferer.

That offenders have nothing to do with victimhood—and its benefits—isn't quite so obvious when the offender is a child. (This is the flip side of the infancy question discussed in the previous section; there the question was whether the (adult) *victim* is entitled to compensation for harm suffered at the hands of a child offender.) "Juvenile offenders" or "youthful offenders" still aren't entitled to victim compensation. But it takes a statute to make it clear that they aren't.

One of the most straightforward exclusions of offenders from victimhood thus appears in a juvenile justice code. In the world of juvenile justice, offenders are not quite so easily demonized as incarnations of evil, preying upon victims as the incarnations of good. In this world, offenders aren't even called offenders but are referred to as "delinquents," and crimes aren't crimes but "acts of delinquency." This would make victims not crime victims but act of delinquency victims, which is not only a mouthful but also an oxymoron. An act of delinquency, after all, is a victimless event. It's a manifestation of a condition, delinquency, which happens to have affected another person. As a victimless symptom, the delinquent act isn't punished, nor is the delinquent who committed it. Instead, the delinquent is treated so as to remove the delinquency. None of this has anything to do with the victim, and everything with the juvenile.

Still, the attempt has been made to treat juvenile delinquents as adult offenders, and correspondingly to treat act of delinquency victims as crime victims. The result has been oxymoronic definitions of the victim as, for instance, "a person against whom a delinquent act has been committed,"[41] where the very idea of a delinquent act precludes its commission "against" anyone or anything. Again, the delinquent act manifests delinquency, period. While it may affect others, it is irrelevant whether it is directed "against" them, since the distinguishing feature of juveniles precisely is their inability to commit acts "against" others, at least in the sense that adults do.

The oddity of victims' rights in the law of juvenile delinquency manifests itself not only in the difficulty of defining victims but also in the difficulty of denying delinquents victim status. So the same juvenile justice code that defines victim as "a person against whom a delinquent act has been committed" finds it necessary to clarify that "'victim' does not include a juvenile alleged to have committed the delinquent act."[42]

The problem with juvenile delinquency is that it straddles, and transcends, the line between offender- and victimhood. The question whether a juvenile is an offender is as irrelevant as that whether whoever happens to be affected by her behavior is a victim. The juvenile delinquent is treated not because she is an offender but because she is a delinquent. Similarly, it doesn't matter whether the delinquent is a *victim*. What triggers her need for treatment is her delinquency, regardless of its cause. The cause of the juvenile's delinquency affects not her need for treatment but the kind of treatment she needs.

The radical distinction between offender and victim is politically expedient because it fits the victims' rights movement into the friend-foe dynamic that characterizes the political realm.[43] The victims' rights movement ceases to be a political movement without it, at least in the way it has defined itself until now. Unfortunately, that distinction breaks down as a matter of moral and political theory, as well as a matter of fact. We have already seen that the categorical distinction between victims and offenders violates the fundamental principle of the enlightened modern state, that all persons are equal as persons. Any system of law built on this distinction is therefore illegitimate.

Moreover, as we have begun to see, the distinction between offender and victim cannot be maintained in its politically necessary rigidity in the face of the undeniable existence of certain individuals who resist classification as one or the other. It is not only illegitimate but also impossible to divide the sociolegal realm of crime into offenders and victims.

The relevant distinction is not between victims and offenders but between persons, victims and offenders alike, and the state. The victims' rights movement may lose its political significance with the collapse of the artificial distinction between victims and offenders. Expanded and resurrected as a persons' rights movement, however, it merely replaces one friend-foe relation with another. The new enemy is the state.

But let's step back and take a look at the way in which the crucial attempt to draw a categorical line between victim and offender manifests itself at that level of compensability analysis, *suffering*, which currently has our attention. Here the distinction between offenders and victims results from their different role in the criminal event that defines them. In the terms of our backbone definition of compensability, the victim "suffers" the harm that the offender inflicts. The offender acts upon the victim; the victim is acted upon by the offender. So the law of victimhood conditions eligibility on the offender's "act"[44] (or omission),[45] "conduct,"[46] or "activities."[47]

We find the same requirement in the law of offenderhood. There the so-called act requirement, which we have encountered several times already, provides that punishability, as opposed to compensability, hinges on the ostensible offender's conduct.

By contrast, *victim* conduct is not required for compensability. On the contrary, it is prohibited. The offender's act(ivity) requirement is matched by the victim's passivity requirement. An active victim risks being denied victim compensation, and even victimhood itself. As might be expected, the line between offender and victim turns out to be as difficult to maintain as that between activity and passivity.

Whether activity on the part of the victim precludes general eligibility or affects only the amount of compensation (though possibly to the point of denying compensation altogether) depends on where the question of the victim's "innocence" is considered in the analysis of compensability. In a two-part analytic scheme (such as the one that underlies our overview), this question is considered after the question of general eligibility. In a one-part scheme, the innocence question is part and parcel of the eligibility question, so only an innocent victim can be considered a victim in the first place.

Wherever it might be considered in the analysis, one type of activity prevents the victim's compensability altogether, either by denying her victimhood or by denying her compensation: participation in the offender's activity. As the Alabama victims restitution statute puts it: "'Victim' shall not include any participant in the defendant's criminal activities,"[48] no matter how much "direct or indirect pecuniary damage" that person might have suffered "as a result of the defendant's criminal activities."

Participation in the offender's activity categorically precludes compensability because that sort of activity is simply incompatible with the image of the victim as a passive sufferer of harm. A victim who participates in the *offender's* activity is no longer a victim. Whatever harm she suffers she will have inflicted upon herself. Here "participation" denies the very distinction between offender and victim that underlies the inquiry into victim compensability. Victim compensation is to compensate the victim for harm suffered at the hand of the offender, and not merely harm suffered as a result of some criminal act, no matter by whom.

Activity of any kind removes the victim from the pure passivity end of the victimhood spectrum. The farther she moves toward the other end, the weaker her case for compensation as a victim becomes. At some point, she falls off the spectrum altogether and becomes a nonvictim. Thus removed from the realm of victim compensability, she enters the nether regions of offender punishability. She has left the confines of the law of victimhood for those of the law of offenderhood. She is no longer of interest to the vehemently victim-focused law of victim compensation. Whether she has joined the ranks of offenderdom is now a question for the offender-focused law of punishment.

Victim activity thus is the first step on a slippery slope toward offenderhood. Some types of activity disqualify the crime sufferer from victimhood altogether. Others simply mitigate her victimhood and therefore reduce her compensation. The initially categorical but eventually gradual nature of this transformation from victimhood to offenderhood is captured by the Uniform Victims of Crime Act. The initial eligibility question is addressed at the outset of the Act, as a matter of definition. There the Act declares that "'[v]ictim' . . . does not include a person who is accountable for the crime or a crime arising from the same conduct, criminal episode, or plan."[49]

The Uniform Act thus measures the distance between victimhood and offenderhood in terms not of participation but of accountability. Once the victim clears the initial hurdle of eligibility and escapes the somewhat awkward label of "a person who is accountable" (analogous to that of "coparticipant" in other statutes), she may nonetheless see her compensation award reduced or even denied entirely, depending on her "conduct." As the Act explains in a section entitled "limit on compensation because of claimant's conduct," the state "may reduce or deny compensation to the extent that the victim or claimant engaged in a violation of law, misconduct, or unreasonably dangerous behavior that contributed to the claimant's loss."[50]

The Uniform Act is silent on the initial question of what activity renders a "claimant"—that is, a potential victim—ineligible for victimhood on account of her "accountability." Other victim statutes are similarly unclear on the question of when a claimant is considered a coparticipant in the "defendant's criminal activities" and therefore likewise ineligible for victimhood. The latter statutes appear to maintain a distinction between the victim's conduct and the offender's. Otherwise it would make no sense to speak of the ostensible victim as a coparticipant in what, for some reason, remain the *defendant's* criminal activities. It's not clear whether the Uniform Act would maintain this distinction. The offender certainly would qualify as someone who "is accountable for the crime," as would any of her coparticipants.

These questions of participation and accountability are familiar from traditional offender-focused criminal law. In the law of offenderhood, they are handled under the rubric of accomplice liability. There, who is accountable for a particular crime, or who deserves to be treated as a participant in it, depends on to whom the criminal act can be imputed. The person who actually engages in the criminal act can be held accountable for it. That person is called the principal. The interesting, and difficult, question is who other than the principal can be punished for the principal's act, or, to quote the Model Penal Code, under what circumstances one person "is legally accountable for the conduct of another person. . . ."[51]

Perhaps the analysis of accountability and coparticipation in the law of victimhood is meant to be informed by the analysis of accomplice liability in the law of offenderhood. The New York compensation statute, in fact, makes the link between victim accountability and accomplice liability explicit: "A person who is criminally responsible for the crime upon which a claim is based or an *accomplice* of such person shall not be eligible to receive an award with respect to such claim."[52]

If so, we would have found an instance of how the law of compensation might learn from the law of punishment. As we remarked earlier on, looking at the two systems of law side by side has the benefit of exposing and then remedying the shortcomings of either. The traditional offender-focused criminal law can learn a great deal about victims from the new law of victim compensation. Conversely, the law of compensation might learn a thing or two about the offender from the criminal law. And the question of victim accountability for crime is about as close as the law of *victimhood* can come to the question of *offender* liability.

Let's assume then that there is an analogy between the victim (of compensation law) and the accomplice (of criminal law) on the one hand and between the offender and the principal on the other. In that case a claimant is ineligible for victimhood based on victim activity (as opposed to other factors, such as the nature of the crime or her injury or the connection between her injury and the crime)—or "claimant's conduct," in the formulation of the Uniform Act—if she would be punishable as an accomplice. An accomplice is punishable if, and now I'm again quoting from the Model Penal Code,

with the purpose of promoting or facilitating the commission of the offense, he
  (i) solicits such other person to commit it; or
  (ii) aids or agrees or attempts to aid such other person in planning or committing it; or
  (iii) having a legal duty to prevent the commission of the offense, fails to make proper effort so to do . . .[53]

This test of victim accountability, however, is not complete. The victim can be accountable, or responsible, for the crime even if she doesn't qualify as an accomplice. That's why the New York compensation statute distinguishes between a person "criminally responsible for the crime upon which a claim is based" and "an accomplice of such person."[54]

The most obvious example of a claimant who is "criminally responsible for the crime upon which a claim is based" and yet doesn't qualify as an accomplice is the person who commits the crime all by herself or as the principal. This person is not only denied victimhood but qualifies for outright offenderhood. No matter what "personal physical injury" a person labeled "offender" might "suffer[] . . . as a direct result of a crime," *his* crime, he will not receive *victim* compensation for it.

But there are other, less obvious, instances of nonaccomplice victims who nonetheless bear responsibility for a (their?) crime. To see why, another quick glance at the criminal law might be helpful. There, as a general matter, the victim's conduct is as irrelevant to the offender's punishability as the offender's conduct is required. There are two exceptions to this rule, however. We've already encountered the first one earlier. The victim's conduct may be relevant to the question of *consent*. (Whether cases of consent would be covered by the complicity provision just quoted is another question.)

Second, the victim's conduct may give rise to a different type of accountability altogether, not *with* the offender, so to speak, but *against* him. Put another way, the complicity-consent test covers only situations in which the victim is accountable for the crime as a coparticipant. It doesn't cover cases in which the victim is also an offender, without being a co-offender.

In traditional criminal law, this type of victim conduct can prevent, or at least reduce, the punishment of the ostensible offender in two ways. The most drastic example is provided by the defense of person or property. Here the eventual victim is the original offender. The eventual offender, in rebuffing an unlawful attack on herself, another, or her property, transforms the original offender into the eventual victim. The eventual victim, through his original conduct, is held accountable for the crime against him. As a result, the eventual offender escapes punishment.

For the same reason, the victim-claimant in the law of compensation is ineligible for victimhood. His accountability for the crime thus not only deprives the offender-defendant of offenderhood for purposes of punishability but also deprives him of victimhood for purposes of compensability.

The defense of provocation (or "extreme mental or emotional disturbance") also may reduce, if not eliminate, the offender's punishability on the basis of victim conduct. This defense applies only in homicide cases and reduces the offender's criminal liability from murder to manslaughter if his homicidal act was provoked by the victim's conduct.[55] The idea here is that the offender would not have killed the victim *but for* the victim's prior provocation. In that sense, the victim, through his conduct, contributed to the crime (as a "but for" cause), even if his contribution did not rise to the level of full-fledged accountability.

Unlike self-defense, provocation does not shield the offender from punishability entirely. Analogously, it does not deprive the victim-claimant of victim status and, therefore, of general eligibility for victim compensation. Victim conduct amounting to provocation may, however, result in a reduction, or even a complete denial, of compensation.[56] We have an opportunity to explore questions of degree when we turn our attention to the final step in the analysis of compensability, where we address the question of actual compensation.[57]

At the current level of analysis, we are concerned with one particular reason that a claimant might find herself declared noncompensable, namely that she engaged in an act of some sort, thereby testing the limits of victimhood by doing more than merely "suffering." By acting, the victim may have violated the passivity requirement of compensation law, which is the complementary opposite of the act(ivity) requirement of criminal law.

Active provocation may even be used to deny the status of victimhood, and thus compensability, altogether. At least, that's what happened in a recent federal appellate case. There the First Circuit Court of Appeals decided that the federal government, in particular the U.S. Department of Agriculture, doesn't qualify as a victim for purposes of receiving restitution (not compensation) under the federal Victim and Witness Protection Act "when it *provokes* the commission of a crime that, by design, directly results in depletion of public coffers," to wit a sting operation.[58] As the court put it, "calling the organization that sets up a sting and carries it out a victim is like calling the rabbit who lurks in Houdini's hat a magician."[59]

Admittedly, it's quite a stretch to get from a sting operation to provocation in a *nonhomicide* case to a complete denial of victimhood. Presumably, the court undertook this exercise to give weight to the well-founded sense that the state cannot be permitted to qualify itself as a victim. The general incompatibility between active provocation and victimhood, where a "victim is commonly considered to be a passive sufferer of harm,"[60] thus may have helped to manifest the more blatant incompatibility between statehood and victimhood.

Still, the opinion is noteworthy in its (innovative) use of the passivity presumption. Whatever rhetorical appeal it has derives from the general acceptance of that presumption.[61]

Another way of reading the opinion is to recognize the victim flip side of another offender excuse defense: entrapment. Under this interpretation, the problem with sting operations isn't that they are inconsistent with the image of the passive victim. They are relevant for victim compensation for the same reason that entrapment is relevant for offender punishment. They shift "responsibility" from the offender to the victim. The entrapper's conduct, like the provoker's, is a "but for" cause of the transformation of a person into an offender.

We've now seen how cases of active victims (as principals, as accomplices, as initial attackers or provokers) undermine the victims' rights movement's attempt to categorically separate active (inflicting) offenders from passive (suffering) victims. The problem with this attempt is not simply that activity and passivity are not essential characteristics of a particular interpersonal relationship, never mind of the persons who constitute it. The underlying problem resides in the goal of categorically differentiating offenders from victims itself.

Instead, activity and passivity, and offenderhood and victimhood, are best regarded as opposite sides of the same coin, as complementary attempts to capture a single phenomenon from the standpoint of those who experience it. While these standpoints differ, as do the experiences connected with them, the "offender" and the "victim" who occupy them remain the same. "Offender" and "victim" are but labels attached to persons.

This recognition of identity in the face of difference, however, runs counter to the friend-foe rhetoric of the victims' rights movement. For that movement, the distinction between active offender and passive victim is not a theoretical, or even a doctrinal, matter. It's a political question. The distinction is not between persons who happen to be active and those who happen to be passive but between qualitatively different beings. Ultimately, it's the distinction between good and evil.

To maintain its political nature, the victims' rights movement cannot acknowledge that victims and offenders are alike, not merely as a matter of moral and political theory, or even of legal doctrine, but as a matter of fact. It is a fact that victims and offenders have a lot more in common with each other than the victims' rights movement would have us believe. (They also have far more in common with each other than with the state official in charge of handling their interpersonal conflict.) This is particularly true of crimes of violence, the very crimes that have fueled the anti-offender hatred underlying the victims' rights movement. Victims of violent crimes are disproportionately poor. So are offenders.[62] Victims of violent crimes are disproportionately black. So are offenders.[63] Most murders, for instance, are intraracial: between 1976 and 1998, 94 percent of black victims were killed by blacks, and 86 percent of white victims by whites.[64]

But the similarity between victim and offender is not only a sociological fact and a moral principle. It's also a recurring problem in the doctrinal treatment of criminal cases and, by analogy, of compensation cases, as well. It is difficult to maintain a categorical distinction between offender and victim as a political matter if that distinction collapses regularly in actual cases.

No matter how much contemporary criminal law likes to reduce itself into a mechanism for the identification and incapacitation of essentially evil predators, it's simply not the case that all crimes are committed by a group of categorical criminals. Not everyone who commits a crime will commit another or will commit as many crimes as he can.

Moreover, and for our purposes most relevant, not everyone who commits a crime, even a compulsive continuous criminal, will never be a victim. On the contrary, most offenders have been victims, and many victims have been offenders, as well. For this reason alone, any attempt to divide the world into offenders and victims must fail, no matter how politically expedient it might be.

The nonexclusivity of offender- and victimhood is illustrated most clearly in cases where a single person appears to vacillate between the two, even to the point where he is both victim and offender at the same time. These ambiguous cases cannot be ignored in a system of law that distributes benefits based on the classification as "victim." That's why, if not the victim compensation statutes themselves, then their implementation guidelines are forced to deal with cases where the victimhood is less than pure, such as the provocation cases we mentioned earlier.[65]

Narratives of offenders who are also victims, and victims who are also offenders, however, do not, and cannot, appear in the stump speeches of victims' rights advocates for one obvious reason: they explode the simplistic dichotomy of victim and offender, and of friend and foe, that drives this political movement. In them, it's not clear whom to hate and whom to pity, whom to punish and whom to compensate.

Take, for example, the celebrated California case of Alex Cabarga.[66] Cabarga's parents turned their son over to the care of Luis "Tree Frog" Johnson when he was nine years old. For the next eight years, Johnson beat and sexually abused the boy. Eventually, when Cabarga was seventeen, he helped Johnson abduct a two-year-old girl, Tara Burke, and then to sexually abuse her for nearly ten months. He was sentenced to 208 years in prison, for the crimes he inflicted upon Burke. (Johnson got 527 years.)

At the same time, however, Cabarga received *victim compensation* under California's Victims of Crime Program for the crimes inflicted upon him by Johnson. In the words of the Program's chief administrator at the time, "[t]he fact that he was found guilty of child molestation does not preclude Mr. Cabarga from being a victim of the same crime."[67] What's more, an appellate court eventually overturned Cabarga's sentence (i.e., his classification under the law of *offenderhood*) on the ground that he, too, had been a victim. One of the judges on the panel remarked that "[i]f the record makes anything clear it is that Alex Cabarga is as tragic a victim as [Tara Burke]; a victim not just of Tree Frog Johnson but of the misguided parents who delivered him to that monstrous pedophile at the age of about 10."[68] Victim or offender?

In another well-known case, from North Dakota, Janice Leidholm killed her husband, Chester.[69] Chester had been beating his wife for years, including the night of his death. That night, the couple had been out drinking. Chester's abuse began on their drive home. At one point, he tried to throw Janice out of their moving pickup truck. After they got home around midnight, he continued to assault her, pushing her down whenever she tried to get up and preventing her from calling the police for help. Later that night, they went to bed. After Chester had fallen asleep, Janice went into the kitchen, got a knife, and stabbed him to death. Who is the victim here, and who the offender?

Note that, in this case, the ostensible offender was not only a victim. The ostensible victim was the offender responsible for the ostensible offender's victimization. When Janice Leidholm killed her husband, an offender inflicted criminal harm on a victim who had, as an offender, inflicted criminal harm upon her, as a victim. An offender-victim committed a crime against a victim-offender. In fact, on the face of it, Ms. Leidholm was entitled to victim compensation for the harm she had suffered at the hands of her husband, just as her husband, had he survived, would have been entitled to victim compensation for the harm he suffered at the hands of his wife. (Better still, Ms. Leidholm could, at least in theory, be compensated twice—directly, as her offender-husband's victim and, indirectly, as her victim-husband's wife.)

This sort of back-and-forth, and even hand-in-hand, of victimhood and offenderhood is characteristic of cases in which the defense of self-defense is raised. In self-defense cases, the victim hat might pass from one person to the other and back again several times throughout a conflict. Consider the classic nineteenth-century Ohio case of *Stoffer v. State*. The defendant Stoffer, armed with a knife (and, more important, the intent to kill), had assaulted a man named Webb in the street. At that time, Stoffer was the offender, and Webb the victim. In fact, Webb had every right to defend himself against Stoffer's attack. But Stoffer backed off, literally, and soon found himself pursued not only by Webb but by two other men "in concert with him," namely Webb's brother and "one Dingman." This threesome, throwing stones and yelling "Kill him!," chased Stoffer down the street. Stoffer then ducked into a house to escape his pursuers, shutting the door behind him. Webb and his posse were not to be denied, however: "forcibly opening the door, they entered the house and assaulted [Stoffer], and in the conflict which immediately ensued, Webb was killed."[70]

The question addressed by the court was who counted as the victim and who the offender at the time of the homicide. In other words, the court had to determine whether the initial assignment of "victim" and "offender" labels on the basis of the original "conflict," Stoffer's assault on Webb, was still appropriate at the time of the second "conflict," which left Webb dead.

It wasn't. So short-lived was Stoffer's offender status that it had vanished within minutes. Simply by "retreating to a place of supposed security," Stoffer had shed his offenderhood. In the concise words of the court, "[a] *conflict* is the work of at least two persons, and when one has wholly withdrawn from it, *that* conflict is ended; and it cannot be prolonged by the efforts of him who remains to bring on another."[71]

In the new conflict, the roles were reversed, with the aggressor-offender in the one being the defender-victim in the other, and vice versa. In the end, Stoffer was punished as the offender in the first conflict (the assault with intent to kill Webb), but not in the second. In fact, had Webb succeeded in killing Stoffer, *he* would have been punished for homicide. Stoffer then would have been the assault-offender one minute and the homicide-victim the next, with Webb playing the respective, and shifting, complementary roles.

The categorical distinction between victims and offenders, and between good and evil, that motivates the victims' rights movement therefore is factually baseless, doctrinally impossible, politically dangerous, and theoretically unjustifiable. On top of all this, it's bad for victims. Victimological essentialism is as demeaning to victims as criminological essentialism is to offenders. The label "victim" may prove useful to capture the distinction between victims and offenders in relation to their shared experience of the moment when their lives intersect, labeled "crime." But to forget that "victim," "offender," and "crime" alike are not essential categories is to lock persons who happened to experience crime from the victim's perspective into a passivity and dependence on their victimizer that runs counter to the central autonomy-enhancing function of criminal law and the law of compensation. So, for instance, to recognize Ms. Leidholm as a victim, even at the moment when she thrust the kitchen knife into her sleeping husband, is not to identify her as a categorical victim who always was and always will be a sufferer.

This essentialist danger is particularly acute in cases where the victim belongs to a group whose members are perceived as sharing the passivity characteristic of victimhood. Here the "victim" diagnosis in a particular case merely confirms a prior general, stereotypical diagnosis based on membership in some group. This compounding effect is the victim analogue of the practice of viewing criminal behavior by members of certain groups as confirmation of a general diagnosis of criminal dangerousness for all members of some group.

But, in both cases, essentialism need not confirm prior discriminatory judgments. A victim may be marked as a victim for life simply because he happens to have been the victim of a crime. And an offender may be marked as an offender for life simply because she happens to have committed a crime. The labels "offender" and "victim" stigmatize by themselves, without the help of preexisting stereotypes.

Either way, victimological and criminological essentialism flies in the face of the commitment to personhood that provides the modern state with whatever legitimacy it can claim. To claim that victims are congenitally needy and permanently passive may guarantee eternal life to the victims' rights movement and those activists, lobbyists, and politicians whose professional lives depend on it. But it does nothing for victims.

An Innocent Person Who Suffers. Personal Physical Injury . . . Having explored the implications of requiring that a victim-claimant "suffer" criminal injury, rather than contribute to its infliction, let's turn to the nature of that injury itself. Each element of the limitation of criminal harm to *personal physical injury* is noteworthy. We consider each in turn.

PERSONAL PHYSICAL INJURY

The restriction of criminal harm for purposes of compensating victims of crime to "personal" harm is consistent with the restriction of victimhood to persons. Since only persons can be victims, the only harm that matters for compensation is personal. We have already discussed the significance of personhood as a precondition of victimhood (and, it turns out, offenderhood) in the section on the capacity for victimhood (and offenderhood).[72] There's no need to repeat that discussion here.

PERSONAL *PHYSICAL* INJURY

That only victims who have suffered "physical" harm should be entitled to victim compensation is consistent with the victim icon animating the victims' rights movement. It's victims of *serious* crime whose suffering cries out for state help. And much of the serious harm of crime surely is physical. Other victim compensation statutes achieve a similar effect by limiting compensation to victims of "violent" crimes, which generally include acts causing physical harm.[73] Hawaii, for instance, defines a victim as a person "injured or killed by any act or omission of any other person . . . which act or omission is within the description of the crimes enumerated in section 351–32,"[74] entitled "violent crimes," which lists the following offenses:

(1) Murder in the first degree;
(2) Murder in the second degree;

(3) Manslaughter;
(4) Negligent homicide in the first degree;
(5) Negligent homicide in the second degree;
(6) Negligent injury in the first degree;
(7) Negligent injury in the second degree;
(8) Assault in the first degree;
(9) Assault in the second degree;
(10) Assault in the third degree;
(11) Kidnapping;
(12) Sexual assault in the first degree;
(13) Sexual assault in the second degree;
(14) Sexual assault in the third degree;
(15) Sexual assault in the fourth degree;
(16) Abuse of family and household member; and
(17) Terrorism, as defined in title 18 United States Code section 2331.[75]

Each of these crimes inflicts physical harm. The one exception is kidnapping, which often does, but need not, include physical harm to the victim. As you may recall, the New York compensation statute, which guides our analysis of compensability, also includes a special provision on kidnapping that entitles kidnapping victims to compensation even if they didn't suffer physical harm:

"Victim" shall mean
  (a) a person who suffers personal physical injury as a direct result of a crime; [or]
  (b) a person who is the victim of either the crime of
      (1) unlawful imprisonment in the first degree,
      (2) kidnapping in the second degree, or
      (3) kidnapping in the first degree.

Kidnapping and unlawful imprisonment, according to their fairly typical definitions in the New York Penal Law, may be committed without inflicting any physical harm on the victim. In fact, they may be committed without even *threatening* the infliction of physical harm. The core of unlawful imprisonment is not to inflict, or even to threaten, physical harm but to *restrain* the victim, "to interfere substantially with his liberty by moving him from one place to another, or by confining him either in the place where the restriction commences or in a place to which he has been moved, without consent. . . ."[76] Kidnapping similarly is about "abducting," a sort of aggravated "restraining": "'Abduct' means to restrain a person with intent to prevent his liberation by either (a) secreting or holding him in a place where he is not likely to be found, or (b) using or threatening to use deadly physical force."[77]

By definition, then, unlawful imprisonment and kidnapping do not require the infliction of physical harm. Any harm the victim suffers in the course of the kidnapping may expose the offender to other criminal liability—say, for assault, sexual assault, or homicide. But the offense of kidnapping is independent of, and additional to, these offenses of physical violence and therefore captures some harm other than physical harm.

This nonphysical harm of kidnapping might result either from the experience of abduction or confinement itself or from any threats of physical harm the offender might communicate in the course of the kidnapping. Both varieties of harm raise important questions about the nature of criminal harm in general, and of nonphysical criminal harm in particular. Ultimately, these questions can only be resolved by a comprehensive theory of criminal harm.

ABDUCTION AND CONFINEMENT. As accounts by former kidnap victims and hostages, along with those by other involuntarily confined persons, including penal prisoners and prisoners of war, make clear, the mere fact of confinement inflicts considerable psychological harm.[78] As criminal law reformers have pointed out for centuries, prison is punishment. Although the psychological pain of "imprisonment" is qualitatively different from the physical pain of corporal punishment, this qualitative difference does not imply a difference in degree. From the sufferer's perspective, the psychological pain of confinement may be just as intense as physical pain, or even more so.

The psychological pain of kidnapping derives from a sense of powerlessness, a complete and utter dependence on the will of another. The subjugation begins with the abduction, a radical interference with one's self-determination, particularly one's freedom of movement. That subjugation, and its accompanying feeling of powerlessness, is often further aggravated by physically restraining the victim and by disorienting her in space and time. Beginning with the abduction, the kidnapping victim is entirely at the mercy of her captors, left without any means of controlling her fate.

The psychological experience of kidnapping, in other words, is the extended experience of victimization common to all crime. In this sense, kidnapping is a typical crime. The subjugation of a robbery is brief and intense, often followed by a lingering sense of insecurity, that is, of distrust in one's ability to live free from oppressive interference by others for their own sake.[79] By contrast, the subjugation of kidnapping often is protracted and complex, moving through a series of violations of one's autonomy over an extended period of time, an experience of powerlessness so complete the victim literally remains in the dark about when, or even if or how, it will end. And so profound is the experience of victimization that kidnapping victims often struggle to regain their sense of autonomy long after the immediate victimization at the hands of the captor has stopped.

Kidnapping therefore makes clear that psychological harm may not be physical harm but that it may constitute serious harm nonetheless. And, if victim compensation is to be limited to victims who suffer serious harm, there is no need to deny compensation to those who suffer serious psychological harm.

As we know from the law of torts, however, psychological harm is difficult to measure and varies widely among different persons. Still, there may be some crimes that, as a rule, inflict such serious psychological harm on their victims that an inquiry into the actual harm suffered is not necessary in each particular case, at least when it comes to determining general eligibility for compensation. This is the sort of abstract judgment that a legislature may have to make to draw the line between compensable and noncompensable harm, and between punishable and nonpunishable harm. And to draw the line between "serious crime" and other crime at kidnapping appears reasonable enough.

The important point here is that seriousness is what matters, not the type of harm. As long as it's serious, it doesn't matter whether the harm is physical or psychological, or even financial. Unlike the New York statute, some compensation schemes do not even implicitly distinguish between serious and other harm. Instead, they include among compensable victims anyone "who suffers direct or threatened physical, emotional, or financial harm as the result of an act by someone, else, which is a crime."[80] In such a scheme, the limitation to seriousness could be maintained only by limiting the scope of "crime" to acts that inflict serious harm on another person.

The restriction to serious harm that one finds in crime victim compensation statutes may reflect a basic truth about the nature of crime. One way to stem the tide of criminalization that has swept Western societies over the past one hundred years or so is to carefully redefine the concept of crime and, thereby, the borders of the criminal law.

Perhaps our look at the law of crime *victims* can trigger a fundamental reconsideration of what makes them *crime* victims, rather than sufferers of harm. For the law of compensation to have provided this general impetus would count for more than any number of specific doctrinal lessons it might pass on to the law of punishment. This is not to suggest that the victims' rights movement set out to limit the reach of criminal law. It's enough that the victims' rights movement, and the victims legislation it has spawned, *could* be read as reducing the criminal law to its serious core. It's this core, after all, that makes the emotions run high and that generates the political call for state action on behalf of victims.

The concept of "seriousness" could be the beginning of such a theory of specifically criminal harm. The other half of such a theory would have to work out not what degree of harm but what type of harm deserves to be recognized as criminal. In other words, we need to figure out *what* needs to be harmed, not only *how* or *how much*. We have already answered the primary question of *who* (or what) needs to be harmed, namely the person. The answer to the other two questions are related to our answer to the first, I think. The answer to the *what* of criminal harm is the personhood of its victim, understood here as the capacity for autonomy. We get back to this question when we check what's behind the definition of compensable criminal harm as "personal physical *injury*."[81] What we need is an account of what is criminal about criminal injury.

The answer to the *how* question is: a serious interference with the capacity for autonomy or its exercise. What is or isn't serious depends on such questions as whether the capacity for autonomy is harmed or only its exercise, how much the capacity or the exercise has been interfered with, and for how long. Harm would run from the permanent destruction of the capacity, to a temporary minor interference with its exercise.[82]

But this is not the place to develop a comprehensive account of personal criminal law. These remarks are meant simply to suggest how one might use the law of victim compensation, and particularly its attempt to capture the essence of crime, to start building such an account.

THREATS. If we continue in the same spirit of exploration, the inclusion of kidnapping among the compensable "serious" crimes turns out to raise another central issue any victim sensitive account of criminal law must address. As we noted earlier, a kidnapping victim may experience not only the psychological harm of abduction and confinement but also that caused by *threats* of physical violence.

Can a threat constitute criminal harm? It can, in two senses: as the threat of harm or as the harm of threat. The threat of harm is potential, but not actual, harm. In this sense, threat is synonymous with risk or danger. By contrast, the harm of threat *is* a kind of actual harm. It's the psychological harm one suffers as a result of being threatened with some other, usually physical, harm. A threat of serious bodily injury may put me in fear. That immediate fear may translate into an inability to function as an autonomous being.

The distinction between the two senses of threat becomes clear when we assume the victim's perspective. That perspective is irrelevant for purposes of the threat of harm. In the traditional law of attempt, for example, it makes no difference whether or not the "victim" of a failed homicide attempt was aware of that attempt. In particular, it makes no difference whether or not she felt threatened by the attempt.

By contrast, that experience makes all the difference in the case of threats understood not as potential physical harm but as actual psychological harm. The harm of threat is the short-term and the long-term psychological effects of the experience of fear that are triggered by a threat. An attempt, in this sense of threat, does not constitute a threat unless the "victim" was aware of it.

Victim compensation statutes are inconsistent on the question of whether and, if so, which threats are compensable. Some explicitly treat "threatened harm" as compensable. The South Carolina statute defines victims as anyone "who suffers direct or threatened" harm.[83] Others don't refer to threats at all. The New York statute, as we know, limits compensable victims to those who "suffer[] personal physical injury." Still others don't mention threats but do mention attempts, as in Delaware, where a victim is a "natural person against whom any crime . . . has been attempted, is being perpetrated or has been perpetrated."[84] Missouri mentions both.[85]

No matter which of the two senses of threat these statutes try to capture, one thing is clear. If taking victims seriously means taking the victim's point of view, threats that do not inflict harm on an actual personal victim are beyond the scope of our inquiry. There is no such thing as objective victimization. Victimization is the subjective experience of a particular person. Without that experience, there is no victim, and without a victim, there is no victim compensation.

Simply because a person doesn't immediately perceive a threat or perceives it after it has been defused doesn't mean that this threat cannot be criminal and therefore compensable or even punishable. In general, just because a person isn't aware that another is committing a crime against her doesn't mean that the crime didn't happen. When I come home from work to find my house vandalized, my experience of victimization may differ—and in generally will be less intense—from what I would have experienced had I been home during the crime, but victimized I will certainly feel. (Ditto for my belated discovery that my wallet has been lifted from my pants pocket.) The later vicarious (re)experience of the harm suffered amounts to victimization and therefore qualifies the victim for compensation and the offender for punishment.

In the case of threats, as in the case of all other harm, what matters in the end is the victim's experience. The decisive question is whether the threat caused the victim to suffer, regardless of whether this suffering occurred at the moment of the criminal act (such as in crimes that criminalize threatening another person, including kidnapping) or later (such as in crimes that criminalize endangerment, whether or not the victim was aware of the danger).[86]

Still, in each case, compensation ought to be limited to the actual experience of victimization, that is, to the actual psychological harm suffered by the victim. If a victim learns that her neighbor, unbeknownst to her, was about to gun her down through the living room window, her compensation should be limited to emotional harm (perhaps fear) she actually suffered as a result, not the harm (namely death) she would have suffered in the event her neighbor's homicidal attempt had not been thwarted at the last minute by an observant police officer who happened to cruise by.

As a rule, compensation for *the fear of* suffering an injury lies significantly below that for suffering it. In some cases, compensation may be entirely inappropriate. Take, for instance, the case of an assault "victim" who is not impressed by her assailant's attempt to threaten her.[87] Without an "apprehension of immediate bodily harm,"[88] there's no harm, and without harm, there's no need to compensate.

Threats, then, may be criminal. As with any harm, threats are criminal insofar as they affect a person's capacity for autonomy or its exercise. Compensation, like punishment, should strive to restore and reaffirm the autonomy thus compromised. As with any harm, however, threats must also be subject to the seriousness limitation. By themselves, the apprehension of physical harm, especially if experienced only vicariously after the fact, may not interfere sufficiently with a person's autonomy to warrant state intervention, in the form of either criminal punishment or of victim compensation.

The paradigmatic threat offense is assault, or menacing, as it is called in some modern American codes. To menace, in the New York Penal Law, means to "intentionally place[] . . . another person in fear of death, imminent serious physical injury or physical injury."[89] The *what* of assault thus includes the quality most central to the victim's autonomy, namely life. Moreover, the *how* of assault requires intention and the selection of a particular person as the target of the threat, as opposed to some undefined group of persons or some interest (such as "public safety"). Finally, "fear" is the explicit result of assault. It is not a byproduct of some other act directed at some other result. To compensate an assault victim for his fear therefore simply is to compensate him for having suffered the harm specified in the definition of the offense.

The reference in victim compensation statutes to "threatened harm" therefore makes sense, at least for crimes involving physical injury. To compensate a person for a death threat is to compensate her as an assault victim. The compensability of other threatened harm can't rely on this construction, however, because threats of nonphysical harm aren't criminalized as assaults (or "menacings"). In fact, they aren't criminalized at all. To compensate someone for having suffered threatened nonphysical harm therefore amounts to compensating her for noncriminal harm. If a state wishes to compensate victims of threatened property crimes, say, it should do so outside the scope of compensation statutes intended for victims of crime.

The threat of nonphysical harm may not be criminal, but the attempt to inflict it certainly is. And, as we saw earlier, several victim compensation statutes explicitly include attempts among the compensable crimes. But the compensability of attempts, be they of physical or nonphysical crimes, is a complicated matter. There is no doubt that a person who has been the target of an unsuccessful murder attempt may be paralyzed with fear, if not at the moment of the attempt, then later when she learns about it (presumably while also feeling considerable relief). But, in this case, the victim's fear is not the result specified in the definition of the offense. The resulting harm of murder is death. And the resulting harm of *attempted* murder is, well, attempted death. The point of attempts is that they fail to bring about the intended result. Fear is at best a byproduct of attempts; unlike in assaults, it's not an element.

Strictly speaking, therefore, to compensate an attempt victim is to compensate a crime victim, but not for the harm specified in the definition of the crime. As we noted earlier, the victim of an attempted murder is not entitled to the same compensation as a murder victim. Instead, she presumably is entitled to compensation for whatever emotional harm she has suffered as a result of the unpleasant realization that someone tried to kill her. This compensation in turn might resemble the compensation she would have received for an assault, that is, if the offender, instead of trying to murder her, had "intentionally place[d] [her] in fear of death, imminent serious physical injury or physical injury."

The problem with compensating attempt victims stems from the problem with *punishing* attempt *offenders*. While virtually everyone today agrees that attempts should be punishable, it's far from clear what the harm of attempts is supposed to be. After all, attempts differ from so-called consummated offenses precisely in that they do not consummate, or inflict, the harm specified in the definition of the consummated offense. Attempted murder differs from murder in, and only in, the absence of a dead body. But that corpse, that corpus delicti, is precisely what makes murder a delict.

Punishing attempts raises no problems for a treatmentist theory of criminal law that assigns punitive treatment on the basis of symptoms of an abnormal disposition to commit crimes. And an unsuccessful attempt to commit a crime is as good a symptom as a successful one. This theory of criminal attempts underlies the Model Penal Code and today remains the dominant theory in American criminal law generally speaking, not only in the case law but also in the treatise literature.[90]

A theory of punishment, rather than of treatment, finds it more difficult to justify the punishment of attempts. And switching to the victim's point of view doesn't make things easier. On their face, attempts are crimes without victims. That's why justifications of attempt tend to focus on the offender, stressing that, from the offender's point of view, there's no difference between an attempt and a consummated offense. The offender, after all, has done everything she could to commit the crime. From the victim's standpoint, however, attempts differ dramatically from consummated crimes. Victims of attempt do not experience the sort of harm that led to the criminalization of the consummated crime in the first place.

Still, taking the victim's point of view suggests a parallel to assaults that otherwise might not be obvious.[91] Attempts differ from assaults in that attemptors, unlike assailants, need not set out to frighten their victims. But, from the victim's perspective, that difference is imperceptible.

As far as he can tell, the offender in both cases plans to make good on her threat. If he didn't think so, he wouldn't have been frightened in the first place. Idle threats aren't assaults.

Considering the phenomenon of attempted crime from the victim's perspective, however, also elucidates just why it is so difficult to justify punishing attempts as crimes. There is no victim's perspective in the law of attempts, because there are no victims. To treat attempts on a par with consummated crimes, as the Model Penal Code does, therefore, is misguided. In particular, to disregard the distinction between attempted and consummated crime is to disregard the victim in favor of an exclusive focus on the offender.

The victim (or, rather, its absence) marks the Achilles tendon of the criminal law of attempt. The fixation on the offender emerges most clearly in the dominant treatmentist theory of attempts. Attempts are punished because they reveal the *offender's* abnormal criminal disposition (or his "moral defect," another name for this condition used by the drafters of the Model Penal Code).[92] Having diagnosed abnormal dangerousness on the basis of this telltale symptom, the *state* (represented by the police) interferes to subject the deviant to the proper penal treatment. The *victim* has no place in this doctor-patient relationship between the state and the offender.

The law of compensation can make a contribution to the criminal law of attempts simply by highlighting the need to make room for the victim. By including persons who have suffered harm as a result of an attempted crime, victim statutes encourage us to acknowledge and explore the harm of attempt in general. What's more, compensation statutes force us to specify the harm of attempt in particular cases in order to set the appropriate compensation award. While this determination is, of course, fact specific, there can be no doubt that the harm of a completed crime tends to be greater than the harm of an attempted one. In fact, the relevant comparison may well turn out to be not between the attempted and the completed crime but between attempts and assaults, and more specifically assaults as threats to various aspects of the victim's personhood.

PERSONAL PHYSICAL *INJURY*

The difficulty in justifying compensation for harm suffered as a result of attempted, rather than only consummated, crimes is symptomatic of the general failure of American criminal law to develop a general theory of criminal harm. If we're not clear on why we punish people for causing certain harm, we can't expect to be clear on why we compensate those who suffer it.

Both the law of compensation and the law of punishment reflect this ambiguity about what makes harm criminal. Victim-focused statutes have struggled to capture the essence of criminal harm, and therefore of victimhood. Our New York statute defines the compensable result of the crime as "injury."[93] Other statutes refer to it as "loss,"[94] "damage,"[95] or "harm."[96] Most simply mix and match: "loss or injury,"[97] "loss or harm,"[98] "personal injury, death or economic loss,"[99] "personal injury . . . , property damage or property loss,"[100] "property damage or loss, monetary expense, or physical injury or death,"[101] and so on.

In this cornucopia of compensable suffering, one thing is clear. Injury, loss, damage, and harm are not synonymous. Otherwise, it would make no sense to mix and match. The shotgun approach suggests that the drafters were groping for some notion of criminal harm that they had difficulty defining but that appears to have various aspects some or all of which they tried to capture. So, instead of defining compensable criminal harm generally speaking, they fell back on the drafter's default, the laundry list. Since the items on the list, however, likewise remain undefined, it's difficult to determine which aspect of criminal harm each was designed to cover.

To get a better handle on the definition of these elusive concepts, we might once again want to turn to the criminal law, which is centuries, if not millennia, older—and perhaps wiser—than the law of crime victim compensation. Here we find little help, however. The theory of criminal harm in traditional criminal law consists roughly of two parts. In the first part, we learn that criminal harm is somehow special because it harms the state (or the king), rather than persons. We have dealt with, and rejected, this antiquated view of criminal law in some detail above and won't dwell on it here. In the second part, there are laundry lists. The special parts of criminal codes are lists of particular kinds of criminal harm, without any attempt to explain what makes a particular kind of harm punishment worthy. In the special part of the Model Penal Code, we find the following offense categories: offenses against the existence or stability of the state, offenses involving danger to the person, offenses against property, offenses against the family, offenses against public administration, and offenses against public order and decency.[102] As we noted earlier, most of these offense categories are of no interest to us because they do not involve victims as persons. Most of the offenses in the Code are directed "against" other sorts of "victims": the state, property, family, public administration, and public order and decency. The offenses against the person are further divided into homicide, assault, kidnapping, and sexual offenses.[103]

The Code makes no attempt is made to explain why a particular offense is included among the offenses involving danger to the person, or what harm the various included offenses are designed to capture. The harm of homicide is obvious enough: death. The same goes for that of assault: physical injury short of death. But as we saw earlier, the harm of kidnapping is more difficult to specify. Even more difficult to define is the harm of sexual offenses, as the protracted debate about this very issue illustrates.

Perhaps the Model Code's general part, famous for its all-inclusiveness, will help us figure out the theory of criminal harm that underlies the offenses defined in its special part. There we do find the now familiar general provision announcing the Code's primary purpose: "to forbid and prevent conduct that unjustifiably and inexcusably inflicts or threatens substantial harm to individual or public interests."[104] Apparently, then, the offenses in the Code's special part are meant to protect certain "individual or public interests" against "substantial harm." But what is an interest? And what distinguishes an individual interest from a public one? And why should the criminal law concern itself with individual interests? Why with public interests? And what is harm?

Answers to these fundamental questions are not forthcoming. Instead of defining the all-important concepts of "interest" or "harm," the Code dedicates an entire section to the definition of "substantial." There we learn that

> [t]he Court shall dismiss a prosecution if, having regard to the nature of the conduct charged to constitute an offense and the nature of the attendant circumstances, it finds that the defendant's conduct:
> (1) was within a customary license or tolerance, neither expressly negatived by the person whose interest was infringed nor inconsistent with the purpose of the law defining the offense; or
> (2) did not actually cause or threaten the *harm or evil* sought to be prevented by the law defining the offense or did so only to an extent too trivial to warrant the condemnation of conviction . . .[105]

This section, however, deals only with the question of how to apply criminal offense definitions in particular cases. It says nothing about what makes an offense criminal in the first place. It's addressed to courts, not legislatures. References to the elusive "harm or evil" appear throughout the Code, so also in the provisions on double jeopardy,[106] material elements,[107] mens rea,[108] consent,[109] and justification.[110] They, too, remain silent about what sort of "harm or evil" a legislature may wish to "prevent[] by the law defining the offense" or, for that matter, how a court might go about determining which "harm or evil" a particular offense is meant to prevent.

The "harm or evil" to be prevented by a particular criminal offense now appears to be the "substantial harm" to the "individual or public" interest or interests that the offense was included in the criminal code to prevent. But this means that we're back where we started. Simply to speak of "harm" to "interests" defines neither. Three of the Code's offense categories can be said to refer to interests: "existence and stability of the state," "property," and "public order and decency." Neither "the person," nor "the family," nor "public administration" is an interest. Yet it is obviously possible to commit offenses against them; the Code says so itself.

Without a clear understanding of evil, of harm or interest, or of individual or public, to say that criminal law concerns itself with certain evils called harms to individual or public interests is to say nothing much. It's no surprise, then, that one searches the Model Penal Code and its Commentaries in vain for an explanation of why the criminal law is supposed to be about interests in the first place. At least one obvious alternative candidate for criminal protection suggests itself: rights. Rights are not interests. Most important, rights are personal. As we saw earlier, this means two things, both of which are important for criminal law. First and foremost, only persons have rights. There may be public interests, but there are no public rights. Second, all rights are ultimately derived from the notion of personhood. Unlike interests, they are not free-floating preferences but entitlements grounded in the nature of persons as autonomous. Both features of rights recommend them as foundations of criminal law because they mitigate against the state's turning the power to punish into an unlimited license to pursue its interests to the detriment of persons.

Occasionally, rights managed to infiltrate the Model Code despite its professed concern with interests, and interests only. So, for example, the Code defines false imprisonment as "restrain[ing] another unlawfully so as to interfere substantially with his *liberty*."[111] (Recall that the New York

Penal Law, which also dedicates itself to the prevention of harm to "individual or public interests," likewise defines kidnapping as "restrict[ing] a person's movements intentionally and unlawfully in such manner as to interfere substantially with his *liberty* by moving him from one place to another. . . .")[112]

One could, of course, construct an interest in one's liberty and thereby bring rights within the realm of interests. All that would do, however, would be to illustrate the dangerous malleability of the concept of interest, which can be stretched to encompass anything and molded to attach to anything and anyone, individual, public, natural, abstract, institutional, communal, and so on.

Instead, one would do better to acknowledge that the "liberty" in question is simply an aspect of the victim's personal autonomy. To be restrained against one's will is to experience a blatant interference with one's autonomy. If you prevent me from going where I want to go, you prevent me from exercising my capacity for self-determination. If you do so intentionally, you may have committed a crime.

If one looks long and hard, one can even make out the core offense of such an autonomy-based theory of criminal law in the Model Penal Code. "Criminal coercion" in the Code is defined as "with purpose unlawfully [restricting] another's freedom of action to his detriment, . . . threaten[ing] to . . . commit any criminal offense."[113] This reference to restricting another's freedom of action points toward, or at least is consistent with, a theory of criminal harm that looks to a person's freedom, broadly understood as self-government or autonomy, as that which deserves the criminal law's protection.

The "harm or evil" of all crimes could similarly be expressed in terms of interference with the victim's autonomy. Let's take the Model Code's offenses "involving danger to the person." Homicide is the permanent elimination of the victim's capacity for autonomy.[114] Depending on its severity, an assault compromises the victim's autonomy, by interfering either with her capacity for autonomy or merely with its exercise.[115] The infliction of bodily injury probably leaves the victim's capacity for autonomy intact, though it may temporarily interfere with its exercise. The infliction of serious bodily injury, by contrast, may inflict severe enough damage on the victim's mental capacities to temporarily or even permanently affect her capacity for autonomy. Kidnapping we have already discussed.[116] Finally, sexual offenses compromise the victim's sexual autonomy, that is, her right to determine if, when, and how she exercises her sexual capacity.[117] It's unclear how much the law of compensation could contribute to a theory of criminal harm. Still, the very fact that victim statutes define *crime* victims in terms of the *criminal* harm they have suffered attracts attention to the need for a better understanding of that special kind of harm. So far, the criminal law has been content with listing criminal offenses. But, as the heap of crimes continues to grow, it becomes increasingly difficult to discern the concept of criminal harm that motivates its expansion.

A theory of the nature of criminal harm is critical to any account of criminal law that hopes to draw and police the boundaries of the state's power to punish. It's also important in matters of application. A court can't be expected to pick its way through today's pile of overlapping and poorly drafted offenses of all shapes and sizes without any guide as to what each of these offenses is designed to do. The alternative to a right-based theory of harm is a target-based approach that applies (or doesn't apply) criminal offenses to particular persons, depending on whether these persons were the offense's intended target. So, for instance, a judge would decide whether to apply federal RICO and conspiracy laws against the coordinators of nationwide anti-abortion protests by comparing her image of these organizers with whatever image of the criminal (most?) legislators might have had in mind when passing the laws in question.[118] The discriminatory potential of this approach is obvious, as obvious as the reasons that legislators in fact do not publish their statutes with a photo gallery of their intended target types, though perhaps they should, for honesty's sake.

An Innocent Person Who Suffers Personal Physical Injury as a Direct Result. . . . In the law of victim compensation, it's a good idea to keep separate two kinds of causation. First, there is the causal relationship between the offender's act and the primary harm, as specified in the definition of the crime. This type of causation is familiar from traditional criminal law. Second, there is the causal relationship between this primary harm and secondary harm. The victim's "bodily injury," say a broken arm, is the result that turns the offender's attack into the crime of "assault" (here defined as "caus[ing] bodily injury to another").[119] That's primary harm. The victim then incurs medical expenses in connection with the treatment of her fracture. That's secondary harm.

In contrast to traditional criminal law, which focuses on the primary statutory harm caused by a criminal act, compensation statutes devote a lot of attention to defining categories of compensable *secondary* harm. Under the Uniform Victims of Crime Act, for instance, a victim is eligible for compensation from the state (as well as restitution from the offender) for:

(1) reasonable expenses related to medical care, including prosthetic or auditory devices; ophthalmic care, including eye glasses; dental care, including orthodontic or other therapeutic devices; mental-health care; and rehabilitation;

(2) loss of income;

(3) expenses reasonably incurred in obtaining ordinary and necessary services instead of those the victim, if not injured, would have performed, not for income but for the benefit of the victim or a member of the victim's family;

(4) loss of care and support; and

(5) reasonable expenses related to funeral and burial or crematory services.[120]

So, instead of being compensated for the broken arm caused by her assailant's criminal act, the victim, instead, is reimbursed for the economic loss caused by the broken arm.

Compensation for secondary harm presupposes the suffering of primary harm. But that doesn't mean that a victim can be compensated only for secondary harm caused by the primary harm, as defined in the statute. It's enough if the claimant has had *some* crime committed against herself and, as a result of the commission of that crime, has suffered some injury. For instance, an Oklahoma court held that a victim could be compensated for injuries sustained as a result of having his "hands and feet tied with wire during the course of events which resulted in [the offender's] burglary conviction," even though the tying of hands and feet is not primary harm that appears anywhere in the definition of burglary, though it might appear in other offense definitions, such as those for battery and even kidnapping, of which the offender was not convicted. (In Oklahoma, burglary is defined as "break[ing] into and enter[ing] the dwelling house of another, in which there is at the time some human being, with intent to commit some crime therein."[121] Battery is "any willful and unlawful use of force or violence upon the person of another,"[122] kidnapping "without lawful authority, forcibly seiz[ing] and confin[ing] another, or inveigl[ing] or kidnap[ping] another, with intent, . . . [t]o cause such other person to be secretly confined or imprisoned in this state against his will."[123]) As the court explained:

[T]he Crime Victims Compensation Act [does not] apply only to those personal injuries or deaths which arise solely through the commission of a specific element of a crime. It is the commission of a criminal act which results in injury or death of the victim, not the commission of the elements that constitute a particular crime, which falls within the purview of the statute. Stated otherwise, to be compensable under this Act, the injury or death must only have been inflicted during the course of criminal conduct set afoot by appellant and be causally related to such conduct. The injury or death need not be directly related to the commission of a particular essential element of a crime which is committed during the course of the criminal conduct and it is not necessary that the injury or death precede the performance of an act which constitutes the last essential element necessary to establish a crime.[124]

Her primary victimization of some kind thus qualifies the victim for compensation for her secondary victimization. Many victim compensation statutes limit the definition of "victim" to direct victims, that is, to persons who have suffered primary harm. The Uniform Act defines victim as "a person against whom a crime has been committed."[125] And, as we know, the New York compensation statute limits victimhood to "a person who suffers personal physical injury as a direct result of a crime."[126]

Other statutes, however, take a broader view of victimhood. They include not only direct but also indirect victims. By definition, these indirect victims suffer only secondary harm. (Direct victims always suffer primary harm, whatever other harm they may also suffer.) An indirect victim's compensation claim depends on *someone else's* (a direct victim) having suffered primary harm (the broken arm). That's why an indirect victim is also called a *derivative* victim.[127] An indirect victim might include a "health care provider who has provided medical treatment to a directly injured victim if such treatment is for an injury resulting from the defendant's criminal conduct. . . ."[128] That way the (indirect) victim can directly apply for victim compensation, instead of the (direct) victim's applying for reimbursement for her medical expenses. The compensation scheme acts as the insurer's insurer.

The failure to distinguish between direct and indirect victims tends to be accompanied by a failure to distinguish between primary and secondary harm, as well as by a failure to distinguish between personal and apersonal victims.[129] The personal, direct victim who suffers a physical injury, the "good samaritan" who requires medical treatment for a groin injury sustained while coming to her aid and as a result incurs an economic loss, and "any person or entity who suffers economic loss because such person or entity has made payments to or on behalf of a directly injured victim pursuant to a contract including, but not limited to, an insurance contract"[130]—all are thrown into a single pot.

With all these essential distinctions blurred, the actual crime victim may get lost in the list of entities clamoring for compensation. There is nothing distinctive about her suffering, nothing distinctive about her claim to compensation, nothing distinctive about her as a person, as the only true victim of crime, whose plight ostensibly lies at the heart of every compensation scheme for victims of crime and at the bottom of any derivative compensation claim.

Mixing up direct and derivative victimhood and primary and secondary harm also makes it difficult, if not impossible, to distill a single standard of causation. It's often unclear whether the statutes, when they define some causal relationship, are referring to the connection between the offender's conduct and the direct victim's *primary* harm (the act of hitting her and the broken arm), to the link between the offender's conduct and the direct victim's *secondary* harm (the assault and the medical bills), or perhaps to the connection between the direct victim's primary and secondary harm (the broken arm and the medical bills), or to the nexus between the offender's conduct and the *indirect* victim's secondary harm (the assault and the insurance company's liability), or to the link between the victim's primary harm and the indirect victim's secondary harm (the broken arm and the insurer's liability).

It doesn't help matters that different statutes differ on what *kind* of causal connection they require, never mind between what and what. This vagueness is to be expected in statutes that commingle primary and secondary harm and direct and indirect victims, all of which and whom stand in a different causal relationship to the crime (or whatever other cause might be relevant). So some statutes include harm that is merely "a result" or "the result" of or is "caused"[131] by a crime. Some, like the New York statute, are stricter and limit compensability to a "direct result," while others explicitly encompass any "direct or indirect result." The Uniform Victims of Crime Act requires that the harm be "*directly caused* by death or physical, emotional, or psychological injury or impairment" for purposes of compensation but only that it "be *caused* to a person by the crime" for purposes of restitution.[132]

And these interwoven and criss-crossing causal chains, evaluated under varying standards, are only those that emanate from the *offender*, or, rather, the offense. There's an entirely separate causation inquiry that focuses on the *victim* and his connection to the harm for which he seeks compensation from the state. In traditional criminal law, as we've seen, this inquiry is folded into the (offender-focused) causation analysis or appears, if only implicitly, in the analysis of defenses, particularly provocation. So victim conduct may (or may not) "break the chain of causation" between the offender's act and some result, say by ripping off a bandage and thereby "causing" his death through loss of blood.[133] Or the victim might have "caused" his injuries through provocation "but for" which the offender would have left him alone or at least wouldn't have inflicted the injuries she did.[134] Other excuses also locate the cause of the offender's conduct, and therefore the harm that conduct inflicts, outside the offender. But they either don't locate it in another person (as insanity) or don't locate it in the person of the victim (duress).

As one might expect, the law of victim compensation pays particular attention to injuries caused, or also caused, by the victim. It arguably shouldn't make a difference, from the victim's standpoint, whether his injury can be traced back to one person or another (duress) or to one person's mental illness (insanity). But it's a different matter entirely when the very person who asks for compensation caused the injury that created the need for the compensation in the first place.

Compensation law, in fact, takes great care to limit compensation to "innocent" victims, as we shall see. And, as in traditional criminal law, courts have had a difficult time separating the inquiry into causation from that into blameworthiness. As one court put it in a marvelous conflation of proximate causation and blameworthiness, an innocent person is "a person without proximate fault."[135] One way of not being innocent, in other words, is to have contributed the proximate cause of one's injuries. If the victim's conduct is the proximate cause, the offender's can't be.[136]

This proximate cause problem tripped up an Ohio police officer who filed a claim for victim compensation on the basis of injuries sustained "when he exited his vehicle and slipped on ice" while "assisting with the execution of a warrant."[137] A colleague who "had exited his vehicle and was securing the back of the residence in an attempt to serve a warrant for felony rape when he stepped in a hole and injured his foot" later suffered the same fate and for the same reason. Pointing out that "[t]he alleged felon was not at the residence, and there was no confrontation with any alleged offenders," the court denied the compensation claim in light of "traditional proximate cause standards."[138]

Precisely what "traditional proximate cause standards" compensation tribunals have in mind is unclear. At least two traditions suggest themselves: criminal law and tort law. Another Ohio court, which also invoked the aforementioned "traditional proximate cause standards," clearly was thinking of tort law: "The trier of the fact, at a minimum, must be provided with evidence that a result is more likely to have been caused by an act, in the absence of any intervening cause. The quantum of evidence required is a preponderance of competent, material and relevant evidence of record on that issue."[139]

Tort law also seemed to be on the mind of a Michigan court when it announced that

> [t]he determination of whether a victim 'contributed to the infliction of his injury' involves an assessment of the particular factual situation similar to that used in determining whether a defendant's *negligent acts* were a proximate cause of a plaintiff's injuries. The test used in determining proximate cause involves assessing the foreseeability that the injury would result from the defendant's acts. If the injury which resulted from the defendant's acts is deemed too remote or unforeseeable, the defendant's acts are not held to be a proximate cause of the injury and the plaintiff cannot recover damages from defendant.[140]

But why should *tort* law supply the causation standard in *crime* victim compensation law? It seems that criminal law might be more relevant here. What's at stake, after all, isn't compensation for victims (as in tort) but compensation for victims of *crime*. Moreover, as the courts never tire of pointing out, the ultimate issue in the *victim* causation analysis is one of *blameworthiness*, that is, whether the victim is to be blamed for her injuries and therefore is not innocent, in which case she can't turn around and ask the state to compensate her for having suffered them. The victim's (or, for that matter, the offender's) blameworthiness, or actual blame, is largely irrelevant for purposes of the law of torts. By contrast, the notion of blame is central to criminal law, and to criminal law only.

Moreover, even if one chooses a tort causation standard for the analysis of the *victim's* causal relationship to her injuries, which causation standard is appropriate for the *offender*? Here a court might be less willing to identify "traditional proximate cause standards" with tort law, if only because the offender's causal relationship to the primary harm of the crime would have to be evaluated by the *criminal law's* "traditional proximate cause standards," since otherwise no crime would have taken place. But, without a crime, there could hardly be compensation for its victim (any more than there could be punishment for its offender).

The real danger, however, of turning to the law of torts for guidance on causation lies in the sub rosa infiltration of tort causation standards into the criminal law. Whatever precisely distinguishes tort causation from criminal causation, one thing is clear: what counts as a cause in tort law doesn't necessarily count as one in criminal law. While criminal law surely can learn a great deal from tort law on the subject of causation—if only in the sophistication with which this issue is analyzed—nothing is to be gained from the unconsidered adoption of tort causation in the law of crime. Compensation law should not be permitted to reinforce criminal courts' often cavalier disregard for questions of causation in general, and for the distinction between causation in criminal law and tort law in particular.

But not only the invocation of "traditional proximate cause standards" from the law of torts threatens to transform the compensation of crime victims for their criminal harm into a general insurance scheme for all who are somehow negatively affected by crime; so does the failure to separate primary from secondary harm, and direct from derivative victims. The distinction between primary and secondary harm is not merely a distinction between two causal links, one longer than the other, but, more important, a distinction between criminal and noncriminal harm. The primary victim is not only the person harmed immediately by the offender. She is also the person harmed immediately by the offender, *as specified in the definition of the offense.* Otherwise, she may have suffered harm as a result of the crime, but not criminal harm. She is a victim, but not a victim of crime.

Limiting crime victim compensation to primary, criminal harm—that is, primary harm specified in the definition of the crime—eliminates all victimless, or *harm*less, offenses from the realm of compensation law. Harmless offenses, in this sense, are offenses that do not require that the offender inflict harm on another person. Consider speeding for example. The offense of speeding is consummated simply by one's operating a motor vehicle at a speed in excess of the speed limit. Whether one's speeding results in any harm is irrelevant in determining whether one has committed the offense. In particular, it makes no difference whether one's speeding caused an accident, which, in turn, resulted in damage to a car and perhaps even in harm to its occupants.

Keeping speeding off the list of compensable offenses seems uncontroversial enough. But this means that DWI isn't a compensable offense, either. Thanks to the concerted efforts of MADD, DWI now regularly appears among the list of compensable offenses. Even the statute that sets minimum requirements for federal support of state victim compensation programs explicitly requires that these programs "offer[] compensation to victims and survivors of victims of criminal violence, including drunk driving."[141]

"Drunk driving," however, is exactly like speeding. Just calling it "criminal violence" doesn't make it so. Like speeding (and gun possession), DWI is an abstract endangerment offense. It requires the operation of a motor vehicle in a certain condition, namely while intoxicated or under the influence of alcohol or some other intoxicant. That's all. It does not require the infliction, or even the threat of infliction, of harm upon anyone. The person who drives down a deserted country road at night is as guilty of it as the person who hits and kills three people in downtown Buffalo. "Drunk driving" is just that, drunk driving. By definition, then, it has no more victims than, say, "propelling a bicycle . . . other than upon or astride a permanent and regular seat attached thereto [or] with [one's] feet removed from the pedals."[142]

There may, of course, be particular persons who suffer as a result of someone's drunk driving. But they are not victims of drunk driving in the criminal sense. They cannot be victims of the crime of drunk driving for the simple reason that the crime of drunk driving does not include within its definition any reference to a victim. That's why we call it an *accident* when someone who commits the offense of speeding or of driving while intoxicated or some other "moving violation" causes harm to another or to himself. Victims of drunk driving are victims of tragic accidents, not victims of crime.

Here it makes no difference whether DWI is classified as a "crime" or perhaps as a "traffic violation," or whether it is defined in the criminal code or in the vehicle and traffic code. The only thing that matters is how it is defined and, specifically, whether its definition includes a reference to another person. If it doesn't, and it never does, then it can have no crime victims.

It's easy to miss this point if one refers to victims of drunk driving as victims of "drunk drivers," as is commonly the case. MADD is a misnomer in that it isn't a movement against "drunk driving" as much as it is a movement against "drunk drivers." It gets its political punch by portraying drunk drivers as uncontrollable and incurable sources of extreme danger who must be incapacitated. In other words, it blurs the distinction between drunk driving and homicide and thereby transforms a harmless offense into the most serious offense of all. However effective, this political strategy cannot change the simple fact that drunk driving is merely driving drunk, and not driving by an incurable alcoholic or even driving drunk by a terrible driver.

A person who engages in the offense of drunk driving and, as a result, causes harm to another may, of course, be liable for crimes other than drunk driving. In particular, she may be liable for every variety of homicide and assault, as well as the modern crimes of vehicular manslaughter and vehicular assault,[143] depending on what harm she has caused. The victims of these crimes are then entitled to crime victim compensation for their harm. They have suffered the harm specified in the definition of the crime, that is, they have been victims of crime, rather than of an accident.

This distinction between harm suffered as a result of some conduct that happens to be criminal (like drunk driving) and harm suffered as specified in the definition of a crime is crucial. In the first case, the harm is not criminal; in the second, it is. Those who suffer the first type of harm surely deserve compensation, but they deserve it as victims of an accident, a tragedy, or perhaps a tort, but not as victims of crime.

In general, the treatment of causation in the law of criminal compensation, as well as in the law of criminal restitution, therefore leaves much to be desired. One cannot help feeling that, the various standards of causation notwithstanding, the question of causation is largely a matter of unguided discretion. It would, therefore, be a mistake to read too much into the distinctions among different types of compensation causation, and that between "direct" and "indirect" results in particular. The general sloppiness on the causation question affects even the otherwise carefully drafted Uniform Victims of Crime Act, which uses different causation standards in otherwise substantially identical compensation and restitution provisions ("direct result" in one, "result" in the other) not only without explaining this difference but also apparently without noticing it. (The drafter's comment on the restitution section speaks of it as "providing for a finding of the economic loss *directly caused* to any person by the crime," while the section in fact refers to "economic loss *caused* to a person by the crime.")[144]

This vagueness on causation means that the criminal law stands to derive little immediate benefit from the law of compensation on this point.
In fact, the approaches to causation in compensation and criminal law
are remarkably similar. Despite valiant efforts, particularly by the drafters
of the Model Penal Code, American criminal law has not developed a coherent approach to the question of causation. And even the Code drafters
had to admit that, in the end, causation often is a matter of the notoriously ill-defined "sense of justice."[145]

It may well be that fine distinctions among standards of causation,
types of harm, and categories of victims collapse in the face of the often
catastrophic phenomenon of crime. Courts are particularly impatient
with questions of causation in cases of serious crime, specifically in murder cases. Causation questions in the criminal law arise only in cases that
involve result offenses (since it's the causation of the result that's at issue),
and homicide is the paradigmatic result offense. The criminal law's jurisprudence of causation is dominated by homicide cases. This means
that the inquiry begins with the undeniable and undeniably catastrophic
fact of a dead victim, the corpus delicti. Death is universally acknowl-
edged to be the most serious harm one person can inflict on another, and
the court now faces the unenviable task of connecting this harm to a particular person. And, since the jurisprudence is made almost exclusively by
appellate courts (and criminal appeals, in American law, can be brought
only by the defendant and therefore presume a conviction), the particular
person before the court has already been convicted of having caused it. In
these circumstances, appellate courts tend to show little patience for attempts to sever the proven causal link on the basis of some fancy doctrinal distinction or other.

One of these distinctions is that between primary and secondary
harm, and in particular between primary *criminal* and secondary harm.
Disregard for this distinction underlies one of the harshest doctrines in
American criminal law, the felony murder rule. Under this rule, persons
are held criminally liable for murder for any death that occurs while
they're committing a felony (e.g., robbery), even if the death was entirely
accidental. Under different versions of the rule, it may also make no difference whether they pulled the trigger, who was killed, or even who did
the killing. So, for instance, an unarmed burglar was convicted of murder
when one police officer killed another while investigating the burglary.[146]

Felony murder cases often raise causation questions. It seems a stretch
to say that one robber has "caused" the death of another when the latter

was in fact shot by the robbery victim. Yet courts have had remarkably little difficulty dismissing these questions as quibbles, even at the cost of dismantling well-established principles of criminal liability, in particular the requirement that (proximate) causation presumes foreseeability.[147]

But even the most straightforward felony murder case, where the perpetrator of the felony accidentally kills her victim, requires that we differentiate two kinds of harm and, therefore, their causation. To hold a robber criminally liable for the accidental death of his victim is to hold her liable not only for the primary harm of the robbery but also for the secondary harm of the victim's death. In felony murder, the "felon" is held liable for harm not specified in the definition of her offense. The victim's death did result from the robbery, but it's not the criminal result of the robber's actions, as specified in the definition of robbery.

The dynamic of felony murder in criminal law closely resembles that of drunk driving in the law of compensation. In one case, the "drunk driver" has engaged in some criminal conduct—"drunk driving." As a result of that offense—though not as specified in its definition—something terrible happens, in fact the most terrible thing known to law: the death of another person. *Therefore*, the drunk driver's victim is entitled to compensation.

In felony murder, the felon commits a crime. While committing it, she causes the catastrophic harm of death. Having revealed herself as a felon—that is, a being possessed of a malignant heart or of an abnormal criminal disposition, depending on one's point of view—she is held liable for this secondary harm as well, even though it is not specified in the definition of the offense she has actually committed. The felon murderer is thus punished not for murder but for her felony, as well as for the harm resulting from it. While she can be said to have caused the secondary harm of death, that harm is not criminal harm.

Similar causation questions also arise in the context of compensation law, though causation rules are now manipulated not to punish disagreeable offenders ("felons") but to deny compensation to disagreeable victims. Compensation boards similarly are tempted to jettison the *proximate* cause requirement of foreseeability to deny victimhood to anyone whose conduct amounted to a factual cause of his injuries, especially if that conduct constituted a crime. For instance, the Michigan Crime Victims Compensation Board denied a compensation claim by an assault victim partly on the ground that he was in the midst of committing a crime when he suffered his injury:

> The claimant was a customer of an unlicensed establishment that was sell-
> ing liquor after two o'clock in the morning. . . . The injury occurred within
> the establishment.
>
> The above facts render the claimant ineligible to receive compensation
> for injuries incurred, as his presence at and participation in the activities of
> that establishment constitute a substantial contribution on his part to the
> infliction of injuries incurred there.[148]

In overturning the board's decision, the appellate court insisted that
the commission of *some* offense (in this case a misdemeanor) combined
with *factual* cause (*but for* the claimant's commission of the offense, his
presence in an unlicensed bar, he wouldn't have gotten shot) wasn't
enough to render the claimant noncompensable. Proximate cause was
needed, and there was none to be found: "[t]he risk of being shot while
merely present in an unlicensed bar is too remote and unforeseeable to
hold him blameworthy in any way for his injuries."[149]

Not that the presence of a causation requirement, and even a proximate causation requirement, has prevented courts and compensation
boards from exercising their discretion to deny compensation to those
they deem unfit for victimhood. Consider the following case.

> On the morning of [October 27, 1978], Robert DeCerbo entered his vehi-
> cle parked in the vicinity of his residence, started the engine, and was in the
> process of engaging the gears when sound and fury erupted. It is inferable
> that murder and not mayhem was intended. The victim was supine on a
> couch in his living room at 10:45 p.m. on February 13, 1980 watching a
> videotape when pellets from two shotgun shots came through the picture
> window causing his demise within an hour.[150]

Apparently, DeCerbo had engaged in "illegal gambling activities" before the first attempt upon on his life. On the issue of causation, the Ohio
attorney general argued that "the shotgunning was merely an extension
of the earlier bombing assault, and that the victim's contributory misconduct of the first carried over and was thus causally related to the shooting." The court agreed and reversed an order granting compensation in
the amount of $500 for burial expenses, finding that "the *anti-social ac-
tivity* prior to the bombing was the same *proximate cause* of the victim's
subsequent demise."[151]

In other words, DeCerbo wasn't entitled to compensation because he
had only himself to blame for whatever might happen to him whenever
and however, be it a car bomb one day and what the court referred to as

"the powder and pellet treatment" another. Living—or at least having once lived—in a mysterious gambling underworld, DeCerbo was removed from the realm of "innocent victims" entitled to compensation as victims of crime. In the case of an antisocial claimant so palpably ineligible for victimhood, there was no need to dirty one's hands by investigating the question of what exactly caused, factually and proximately, the inevitable:

> It is not persuasive to suggest that the powder and pellet treatment occurred because of jealousy over an unidentified female, or that DeCerbo became an informer (for the general good or his salvation) or because he had "welshed" on an obligation (the record indicating a financial reverse prior to the bombing) or that it was not connected with an ongoing rival organizational confrontation for control of territory or activity. For, if those situations existed, or to the extent they existed, they may as reasonably apply to the bombing injury as to the shooting injury. If in fact they were continuing, most, if not all of them, would be sufficient for a finding that the death was a result of the victim's contributory misconduct.

The proximate cause inquiry was over as soon as the claimant's antisocial activity was revealed. Antisocial people aren't victims, and can't become victims, since their suffering always is proximately caused by their sociopathology. When they fall victim to crime, criminals only get what's coming to them.

Doctrinally speaking, any harm that befalls a criminal is *foreseeable* because he is a criminal and therefore is proximately caused by that criminal status. Put another way, entering or belonging to a criminal "milieu" of one type or another means not only foreseeing but also assuming a certain risk of suffering harm, even death.[152]

In the end, therefore, a look at causation in compensation is more revealing than it is helpful for the treatment of causation in criminal law. In both aspects of the law of crime, causation provides a doctrinal haven for discretionary, and often arbitrary, judgments about the compensability and punishability of claimants and defendants, respectively. Compensation law simply is more open about this fact than is the far more formalized law of punishment.

An Innocent Person Who Suffers Personal Physical Injury as a Direct Result of a Crime. By including within the scope of victimhood any "innocent person who suffers personal physical injury as a direct result of a crime," the New York compensation statute embraces a particular group of indirect victims: "good samaritans." Other indirect victims, such as family members, may receive compensation as well, but only good samaritans can hope to be compensated as "victims," right alongside the person "against whom" the crime was committed, because only they stand any chance of having suffered personal *physical* injury, except for the real victim, of course. The parent of a direct victim may suffer economic loss in the form of medical expenses. Only the good samaritan might receive a blow to the head while rushing to the victim's aid.

These good samaritans crop up in one victim compensation statute after another.[153] They require special treatment because they fall somewhere between the victim and her relatives or representatives because they have no relation to the victim other than the crime itself. As a result, if they are going to be compensated for their harm, they must establish a connection not to the victim (as the victim's relatives or representatives can) but to the crime itself. But, unlike the victim, they haven't suffered *criminal* harm, that is, the harm specified by the result element in the definition of the crime. Instead, they have suffered harm "as a direct result of [the] crime." If they had suffered criminal harm, they would be entitled to compensation as a direct victim, rather than as a good samaritan.

In this way, the New York statute equates the criminal harm suffered by the direct, true crime victim and the noncriminal harm suffered by an indirect victim. Once again, the decision to compensate good samaritans is laudable and bespeaks a generous heart (and perhaps even an effort to encourage citizens to assist one another in times of need, something to which they are not legally obligated). And, once again, this beneficence comes at the cost of blurring the line between criminal and noncriminal harm and between criminal and noncriminal victims.

What's more, defining victimhood in terms of harm suffered "as a result of a crime" may shift the focus of victim compensation from direct to indirect victim and even turn the good samaritan into the paradigmatic victim. For it is the good samaritan who suffers harm as a result, and only as a result, of a *crime*. The direct victim may also suffer secondary harm, but it's the experience of primary harm, the harm specified in the definition of the offense, that sets her apart from all other pretenders to victimhood. The criminal harm lies in the crime itself, not some secondary effect of its commission. So a robbery victim may acquire a fear of going out alone at night as a result of the robbery, but it's not this secondary harm but the primary harm of the immediate experience of being robbed that makes her a victim of crime. Depending on the robbery, that harm consists of experiencing a "forcible stealing," defined as having someone take something from you by "us[ing] or threaten[ing] the immediate use of physical force."[154] After all, her fear could also have other, noncriminal causes, such as persistent news reports about nighttime robberies or some deep-seated paranoia of unknown origin.

Other compensation statutes, intentionally or not, sidestep this pitfall by defining victims not as those who suffer harm as a result of "a crime"—which encompasses both primary and secondary harm—but as a result of someone's "criminally injurious conduct,"[155] "criminal conduct,"[156] or simply "criminal act."[157] Definitions of this sort highlight the fact that the harm of a crime may also be one of its elements. A result offense consists of two basic elements: conduct (or act) and result. The connection between conduct and result is governed by the rules of causation. In criminal law, causation requires both actual (or but-for) and legal (or proximate) cause, though both of these elements are often lumped together under the heading of proximate cause. So, *but for* the offender's conduct, the victim's statutorily defined harm (e.g., death) would not have occurred. In addition, the victim's harm must have been foreseeable—though jurisdictions differ on what precise standard of proximate cause they prefer.

So a direct victim suffers primary harm not as "a result of a crime," as the New York statute puts it, but as a particular result of some particular conduct, both as defined in the crime. The crime includes the harm, instead of causing it. Harm included in the crime is primary, statutory harm. Harm caused by the crime is secondary harm. The direct victim suffers the first kind, and possibly also the second. By definition, the indirect victim, including a good samaritan, suffers only the second kind.

In contrast to its New York analogue, Washington's compensation statute is fairly clear on this point. It defines victim as "a person who suffers bodily injury or death as a proximate result of a criminal act of another person...." That statute also accords good samaritans victim status but correctly differentiates between them and true crime victims by differentiating between the cause of their respective harm. The good samaritan, in contrast to a crime victim, is "a person who suffers bodily injury or death as a proximate result of . . . his good faith and reasonable effort to prevent a criminal act, or his good faith effort to apprehend a person reasonably suspected of engaging in a criminal act."[158] (What's not so clear is what "proximate cause" might mean in this context, other than "something more than but-for cause." It's unlikely that the Washington legislature meant to limit compensation to injuries foreseeable to the offender, or to the good samaritan, for that matter. Presumably it was looking for some way to allow compensation boards to deny compensation for remote injuries.)

So a person who suffers only secondary harm as the result of someone else suffering primary harm doesn't deserve compensation as a *crime* victim. At the same time, it's not the case that *anyone* who suffers primary criminal harm, as it is captured in a criminal statute, qualifies as a crime victim and, therefore, for crime victim compensation. As we'll see, suffering statutory harm is a necessary, but not a sufficient, condition of compensability as a *crime* victim.

Let's say arson is defined as intentionally destroying a house by fire. I intentionally burn down a house. Is the owner entitled to compensation as a crime victim?

That depends on our definition of "crime." Technically speaking, I have committed a crime, and a serious one at that. Technically speaking, the owner is entitled to crime victim compensation.

But what if I can claim that my burning down the house was *justified*? The point—or at least the effect—of the justification inquiry in traditional criminal law, as distinct from the inquiry into whether a crime has been committed, is to shield certain persons from criminal liability who don't deserve to be punished despite the fact that they have engaged in conduct that, on the face of it, qualifies as a crime. There are generally two ways of thinking of justification, depending on whether one thinks a justified crime is an oxymoron. Under one approach, to say that a particular action was justified is to say that it wasn't criminal in the first place. In the formulation of the New York Penal Law, to accept a justification defense is to find that "conduct which would otherwise constitute an offense is justifiable and *not criminal*."[159] I'm not punished because, under the circumstances, intentionally burning down a house wasn't arson.

Under another approach to justification, a justified act remains a crime. I'm not punished because, under the circumstances, I was justified in resorting to arson.

Either way, the actor escapes punishment altogether. In the first case, punishment is not an issue, since no crime was committed. In the second, punishment is inappropriate because, even though a crime was committed, the law, generally speaking, wasn't broken: the act was criminal but not unlawful.

Under the first version of the justification inquiry, victims of crime do not receive compensation for harm suffered as a result of justified, though facially criminal, acts. Justified acts by definition are not "crimes." But without a crime, there is no victim of crime, and no criminal offender, for that matter. Take the standard example of a justified, though facially criminal, act: the house I burnt down was in the path of an oncoming firestorm. I set fire to it in order to prevent the blaze from engulfing the entire town. Assuming that this act of arson—intentional destruction of a house by fire—was justified, the owner of the house cannot be compensated for his loss because, though a crime on its face, the arson in this particular case was not a crime in fact. I didn't commit a crime, and so the owner isn't a victim of crime.

Under the second view of justification, compensation is not barred simply through a finding of justification. The owner of the house can be compensated as a crime victim because my act amounted to a crime—arson—even though it didn't amount to a violation of the law generally speaking. The basic idea here is that the law, generally speaking, protects the rights of persons, generally speaking. Particular statutes, including particular criminal statutes such as that on arson, must be seen in the context of the broader function of law. Typically, to violate a criminal statute means also to violate the law. (If this weren't so, then the criminal statute would be null and void because it didn't advance the function of law.) To intentionally burn down a house typically does nothing to protect the rights of persons and, in fact, does a great deal to violate the rights of all persons attached to, never mind in, the house.

In certain cases, however, the presumption of unlawfulness that attaches to a violation of a criminal statute can be rebutted. In those cases. it's violating the criminal statute, as opposed to complying with it, that furthers the goal of law. By burning down the house, I sacrificed the rights of the one to protect those of the many. In the end, I wouldn't be punished, and yet the owner would be compensated.

The compensation statutes are silent on the question of justification.[160] In contrast, they often make it clear that the presence of an *excuse* does not preclude compensation, particularly if that excuse is based on a claim of irresponsibility due to infancy or insanity.[161] As we've seen, the Uniform Act explicitly provides that an offense is a crime for purposes of *crime* victim compensation even if it has been "denominated as an act of juvenile delinquency rather than a crime because of the offender's age."[162]

But, at least under the first conception of justification discussed, justified acts raise the same problem as acts of delinquency. They, too, are facially criminal acts that are "denominated" something other than a crime. Insanity is a little different. While it also results in an acquittal, it's not so clear that traditional criminal law considers a facially criminally act something other than a "crime" merely because it was committed by someone found to be criminally insane, or, in the similarly awkward formulation of the Uniform Act, because it was "subject to a successful mental nonresponsibility (insanity) defense." Such an act is not "denominated" as an "act of criminal insanity," for example.

Some statutes are careful not to condition compensation on the commission of "a crime," perhaps to avoid having to deal with harm suffered as a result of an act that is not labeled a crime by the law of punishment, for one reason or another. These relabeling exercises, however, do little to address the problem. So Alabama victim laws employ no fewer than three pseudonyms for "crime." For purposes of court attendance, the victim is the "victim of the defendant's criminal offense."[163] In the restitution statute, we find a reference to "the defendant's criminal *activities*."[164] The compensation statute even features a neologism, with a hint of tort: "criminally injurious conduct."[165] Other states' statutes speak of "criminal conduct,"[166] "criminal act,"[167] or, more vaguely, "any act or omission . . . coming within the criminal jurisdiction of the State."[168]

At least one statute conditions crime victim *restitution* neither on a crime nor on any obvious pseudonym thereof. In Georgia, a victim is entitled to restitution from the offender for any damages caused by the offender's "unlawful act."[169] As we just saw, a facially criminal act committed by someone found to be criminally insane or a juvenile delinquent may not qualify as a crime, but it is generally thought to constitute an unlawful act. Excuses have nothing to do with unlawfulness.

Justifications, however, do. A facially criminal but justified act may be a crime, depending on one's view of justification, but it is not unlawful. Conditioning compensation on an *unlawful* act therefore can result in preventing compensation for harm suffered as a result of facially criminal but justified conduct, no matter which view of justification one adopts. Even under the second conception of justification, which retains the label of "crime" even for justified acts, no compensation is forthcoming, since the justified crime does not amount to an unlawful act.

It's unlikely the Georgia legislature had justification in mind when it opted for the label of "unlawful act" over that of "crime." Rather than intending to deny compensation to victims of justified but facially criminal acts, it probably was intent on *extending* compensation to victims of criminal acts that nonetheless weren't labeled as such because of a particular incapacity excuse, infancy. The same statute defines the "offender" whose "unlawful act" triggers the victim's right to restitution as "any natural person who has been placed on probation . . . or sentenced for any crime or *any juvenile who has been adjudged delinquent or unruly*."[170] It's these "unruly" juveniles who can't commit crimes, strictly speaking, and therefore fall outside the scope of a statute that provides for restitution for crimes, rather than for unlawful acts, which these delinquents are very capable of committing, or so it seems.

Most important, the Georgia statute deals with restitution, not compensation. And the justification question doesn't arise in the law of restitution. Restitution, as a sanction, presumes a conviction. A conviction, however, presumes a finding that no justification defense rebutted the presumption that committing an act that's defined as a crime (such as intentionally burning down a house) makes one guilty of that crime. Restitution for justified acts, therefore, is by definition impossible.

The confusion in the law of compensation about how to treat facially criminal but justified acts suggests that we should take a look at the treatment of this subject in the law of punishment. There, however, we don't find much clarification. From the standpoint of criminal law, the question whether justified acts count as crimes is generally considered irrelevant because the result in particular cases is the same either way: acquittal.

From the law of crime, we are referred to the law of tort. In the words of the Model Penal Code, "[t]he fact that conduct is justifiable . . . does not abolish or impair any remedy for such conduct which is available in any civil action."[171] So the owner of the house that I set ablaze to shield the rest of the town from the oncoming flames may sue me in tort, even if I can't be punished for arson.

Unfortunately for him, however, the general rule that the absence of criminal liability because of justification doesn't imply the absence of tort liability won't do him much good. The law of torts boasts its very own, separate theory of justification, under the confusing heading of "excuses."[172] In particular, tort law happens to recognize a privilege of "public necessity" that closely resembles the justification of necessity, or choice of evils, of the law of crimes: "One is privileged to commit an act which would otherwise be a trespass to a chattel . . . if the act is or is reasonably believed to be necessary for the purpose of avoiding a public disaster."[173]

Compare this to the analogous Model Penal Code section on necessity, which provides that "[c]onduct which the actor believes to be necessary to avoid a harm or evil to himself or to another is justifiable, provided that . . . the harm or evil sought to be avoided by such conduct is greater than that sought to be prevented by the law defining the offense charged."[174] There may well be situations that are covered by the criminal necessity defense and not by its tort analogue, but the destruction of an entire town—a good candidate for public disasterhood—isn't among them.

We're right back where we started, with the question of whether justified though facially criminal acts constitute a crime for purposes of compensation law. The criminal law doesn't tell us. Tort law doesn't tell us, either, not only because it too recognizes justifications (even if it calls them excuses) but also because the question of whether a given act constituted a crime is of secondary importance for purposes of determining tort liability.

Luckily, we've encountered a similar question before when considering the compensability of persons who suffer harm as a result of a nonintentional, or negligent, act.[175] To compensate these persons as victims of *crime* seems inappropriate, since nonintentional acts are not crimes in the relevant sense, namely from the victim's perspective. This discussion isn't directly applicable here because there's no doubt that I intentionally set fire to the house. In fact, had I unintentionally set fire to the house, I wouldn't have qualified for the justification in the first place.[176]

As intentional, justified acts "which would otherwise constitute an offense" are very criminal indeed. But it's another ingredient of crime that may be missing in cases of justification. The intentional commission of a facially criminal act here is not directed "against" another person. From the perspective of the victim, it makes a difference whether she, as a person, is the target of the criminal act. The point of my burning down the house, however, is not to impose my will on that of its owner, to subjugate him by treating him as a being incapable of autonomy and unworthy of respect as a person. The point, instead, is to save the town. And this ultimate purpose is not criminal. In fact, it is not even unlawful.

What appears to be a crime thus turns out not to have been one because it was committed for a not unlawful purpose. The presumption of criminality that attaches to conduct that facially matches the definition of a crime has been rebutted. In this exceptional case, the appearance of criminality proved deceiving.

If we adopt this view of justification, under which justified acts are only apparently but not actually criminal, it's clear that the owner of the burnt-down house is not entitled to crime victim compensation because he's not the victim of a *crime*. The state, of course, may decide, in its mercy, to compensate him, nonetheless. He certainly is no less entitled to compensation than other victims of the blaze, or whatever the public disaster might be.

Once again, as in the case of nonintentional "crimes," we have taken the victim's perspective to try to elucidate a murky area in the law of offenderhood. Nonintentional acts differ from intentional ones, and justified acts differ from nonjustified ones, in their effect on the victim. They do not victimize in the way that intentional unjustified acts do. They may create victims, but not victims of crime.

By thinking about the compensation of victims of justified facially criminal acts as victims of *crime*, we have identified a problem that tends to receive insufficient attention in the law of crimes: what's the relation between justification and criminality? Having identified the problem, we also have come upon a solution—or at least an approach: justification precludes criminality. Whether this solution fits with the rest of the law of crimes, as well as with other areas of law that deal with the same issue, such as the law of torts, remains to be seen. But our consideration of the law of victim compensation proved useful, if only by forcing us to regard the issue from a new, the victim's, perspective.

Responsibility (Innocence/Guilt)

Before we address this, the final issue in the parallel analysis of victim compensability (and offender punishability), let's review what we have covered so far. A victim-claimant (offender-defendant) who has reached this point of the inquiry has been found to be "a person who suffers (inflicts) personal physical injury as a direct result of a crime." He has been found to be a person, and therefore capable of victimhood (offenderhood). Moreover, he has been determined to have in fact suffered (inflicted) personal physical injury as a direct result of a crime.

To be compensable (punishable), only one question remains. He must be innocent (guilty). He must, in fact, have not been (have been) responsible for the crime. He must not only have been capable of innocence (guilt), but he must also actually be innocent (guilty). He must not just be "a person who suffers (inflicts) personal physical injury as a direct result of a crime." He must be "an *innocent (guilty)* person who suffers (inflicts) personal physical injury as a direct result of a crime."

The question of innocence is of central importance to the compensability inquiry and, in fact, to the very idea of victim compensation. So important is the question of innocence that the entire analysis of compensability can be reduced to it. In the words of an Ohio court, "the 'innocent victim' concept constitutes the soul of the [compensation] statute and the solid basis on which it is anchored."[177] To find that a person is compensable as a victim is to find that she is innocent; to find her not innocent is tantamount to declaring her noncompensable.

Analogously, the finding of guilt (the "verdict") is the central moment in the criminal process. Everything else that goes on before, every other question that must be addressed on the way, is merely a preparation for this climactic moment of the criminal trial, when the jury (or the court, in a bench trial) chooses between the two verdicts: guilty or not guilty.

In traditional criminal law, this is the place where all so-called excuse defenses are considered. These include defenses of *incapacity*, most important of which are insanity and infancy, and defenses of *inability*, such as duress and entrapment. The former type of excuses we have already addressed in our discussion of the capacity for victimhood (and offenderhood).[178] They go to the basic question of the offender's personhood, no matter what harm she might have inflicted.

Defenses of inability, by contrast, assume the offender's personhood, that is, his general capacity to govern himself. They claim, instead, that the offender's ability to exercise that capacity was temporarily compromised. The defense of duress suggests that the defendant was prevented from behaving as she normally would have because someone (or something) else forced her to behave otherwise. She should not be held responsible for this abnormal interlude of nonautonomy, this momentary suspension of self-control, precisely because it is abnormal. The bank teller was "not herself" when she tied up her boss, the branch manager, as commanded by the bank robber. In this situation, she was not only not herself but was someone else, namely the bank robber, who turned her into a mere tool of his own will, a means for the manifestation of his autonomy.

In other words, she was the bank robber's victim, not his co-offender. Even doctrinally speaking, she was the victim of the crime of "criminal coercion," in addition to whatever other crimes the bank robber might have committed against her (false imprisonment, robbery, assault, and so on). Under the Model Penal Code definition of this offense, by pointing a loaded gun at her, the bank robber "threaten[ed] to . . . commit any criminal offense," in this case murder or at least assault, "with purpose unlawfully to restrict another's freedom of action to his detriment."[179]

Victim compensation statutes generally ignore the question of inability excuses. By contrast, they often explicitly provide that *incapacity* excuses, infancy and insanity, have no bearing on the compensability question. As we noted, they tend to go out of their way to characterize the acts of juvenile delinquents and the criminally insane as "crimes," no matter what the criminal law (or family law or "mental hygiene law") might say.[180]

It's unclear whether the irrelevance of incapacity excuses is also meant to apply to inability excuses, such as duress. Perhaps not. Impatience with excuses during the current war on crime has focused on incapacity excuses, in particular the "special treatment" accorded juveniles and the insane, who are perceived as evading the punishment they deserve. There's been no similar concerted attack on inability excuses. Intoxication is the possible exception here; it's been made abundantly clear, again and again, that "voluntary" intoxication is not an excuse, no matter how debilitating the influence of alcohol might have been on the offender at the time of the offense.[181]

The politics of the war on crime aside, it would be difficult to maintain that a crime committed under duress wouldn't be a "crime" for purposes of compensation. Even in the law of punishment, the offender-defendant who raises the duress defense claims not that he didn't commit a crime but that he isn't responsible—or at least not fully responsible—for the crime he concedes he committed.

Still, there is the question whether this crime, assuming it can be described as such, can be said to have been committed by one person *against* another. The purpose of the act committed under duress, after all, was not to oppress the victim but to protect the actor (or her family, and so on). Justified though facially criminal acts don't constitute a crime for the same reason; the only difference is that the purpose of a justified act is to advance, on balance, the law's general function of protecting the rights of persons, as opposed to the decidedly less heroic one of saving one's skin by sacrificing that of another.

Even if the person under duress shouldn't have committed a crime in the strict sense, we may still decide that a crime *was* committed. The only question is who will be viewed as having committed it. If the person under duress really was reduced to a mere tool of the person exerting the duress, then the latter emerges as the one who committed the crime. While the question of "who did it" is of great significance for the law of punishment (and of restitution), it matters little from the victim's perspective that underlies the law of compensation. As long as the claimant was a victim of "a crime"—no matter who committed it, alone or in tandem—she is entitled to compensation.

But to qualify for victimhood, and therefore for compensation, a victim-claimant needs not only some offender who is guilty of, and responsible for, a crime but also to establish that she is innocent of, and *not* responsible for, that crime.

The only difference between a victim-claimant and an offender-defendant when it comes to the final, all-encompassing, issue of guilt and innocence, or ultimate responsibility when all is said and done, is this: one pursues the label of "victim," and the other seeks to avoid that of "offender." The inquiries into victim innocence and offender guilt are two sides of the same coin.

To prove innocence is at least as tricky as to disprove guilt, it turns out. The victim-claimant must affirmatively establish her innocence. She must show herself to be an "innocent person," to fit the image of that innocent needy person who triggers the empathy of her fellows (in this case the members of the victim compensation board). If, and only if, she matches this ideal victim type will the state find itself moved to extend its beneficently helpful hand in the form of a compensation award. Since victim compensation is a matter of mercy, or "grace," as the New York statute puts it,[182] it's up to the state to decide who's worthy of it and who isn't.

The innocence inquiry thus makes explicit what implicitly motivates the entire project of victim compensation and offender punishment: the struggle between good and evil. Victims deserve compensation because they are pure, innocent, and good. Offenders deserve punishment because they are pure, guilty, and evil. No matter how entitled a victim may be to compensation as "a person who suffers personal physical injury as a direct result of a crime," she will not actually receive compensation if she doesn't instantiate innocence. On the flip side, an offender may escape punishment even if he is "a person who inflicts personal physical injury as a direct result of a crime" if he doesn't match the image of the criminal, or guilt personified. (At least that's the hope of defense attorneys who tell their clients to dress up for court.)

The innocence inquiry is the last chance to home in on the victim as a person, in the bad sense. It's the last chance to take a close look at the *type of person* that the compensation board has before it, claiming victimhood and requesting compensation. This sort of character scrutiny also occurs in criminal law. There, however, the professed act-focus of traditional criminal law prevents it from bubbling to the surface, at least until the conviction has occurred and it's time to move on to the assessment of punishment.[183]

In the explicitly person-focused law of victim compensation, however, these constraints do not exist. Here the victim-claimant is before the state—typically, an organ of the state bureaucracy—not as a person insisting on her rights, as the offender-defendant is in a criminal trial, but as a claimant appealing for the mercy of the state.

The language of victim compensation thus is full of moral and religious images. The availability of compensation is a matter of the state's "grace." Only "innocent" victims will be considered even compensable. Among those lucky few who may find themselves blessed with a compensation award, there are the "good samaritans"[184] or, less profanely, the "good Samaritans,"[185] who not only combine moral and religious imagery but also make "good faith" efforts to do various good deeds, including preventing a crime against another person and assisting in the apprehension of criminals if the effort at prevention is unsuccessful. These embodiments of human kindness, who selflessly risk their lives to help others, are joined among the forces of good by police officers, who have dedicated their professional lives "to serve and protect" their fellow humans.[186]

On the other side are the forces of evil. There we find the guilty offenders, the criminals, and the predators, the felons, the murderers, the convicts, the recidivists. So evil are they that their names are rarely, if ever, mentioned, in statutes celebrating the innocence of victims and their helpers.

Once a person has slipped, revealing himself as an evil one, he finds himself marked for quite some time, perhaps forever. Often innocence and guilt turn out to be personal traits that are diagnosed and rarely if ever lost. The Arizona victims' rights statute comes right out and says it: "'Victim' means a person against whom the criminal offense has been committed . . . except if the person is in custody for *an* offense or is the accused."[187] Offenders thus are categorically precluded from victim status, but so are prison inmates. It appears that a prison inmate is by definition (or rather by trait) incapable of innocence, no matter how much he might fit the bill as "a person who suffers personal physical injury as a direct result of a crime" and even if he might appear to someone unfamiliar with his criminal record to have been entirely innocent of—or nonresponsible for—the crime in question.

In 1996, the state of Ohio went so far as to disqualify from victimhood anyone who, "within ten years prior to the criminally injurious conduct that gave rise to the claim, was convicted of a felony or who is proved by a preponderance of the evidence . . . to have engaged, within ten years prior to the criminally injurious conduct that gave rise to the claim, in conduct that, if proven by proof beyond a reasonable doubt, would constitute a felony."[188] To remove any doubts about its essentialist and differentiating motivation, this provision recently has been applied retroactively on the ground that "felons have no reasonable right to expect that their conduct will never thereafter be made the subject of legislation."[189]

Thanks to the proliferation of felonies in modern criminal law,[190] supplemented by a low burden of proof, this felon (or rather suspected felon) exclusion clause has proved a powerful device for denying victimhood to compensation claimants deemed unworthy. Any felony will do, whether or not it was serious or violent or would have qualified as "criminally injurious conduct" for purposes of compensation.[191] Its use against drug felons has proved particularly popular. Since drug possession is a felony in Ohio (as it is everywhere else), merely finding drugs on (or in) the claimant is enough to dispose of the victimhood question.[192] So, for example, the hospital medical records that document the treatment of injuries sustained as a result of the crime that gave rise to the compensation claim may reveal that the ostensible victim possessed cocaine, either because he said he did[193] or, even more convenient, because a toxicology report showed that he did.[194]

It is simply unthinkable to have "criminals" apply for victim compensation. Criminals can never be victims, and victims are never criminals. And apparently one *is* either one or the other, no matter what one *does* or *has done to* oneself.

Moral taints can spread from one thing to another, provided the two carriers are in close enough contact. It's no surprise, then, that many victim compensation statutes categorically exclude not only the offender but also anyone in the offender's family or, even more broadly, his household from the realm of victimhood.[195] This "family exclusion" has embroiled legislatures, courts, and agencies in the predictably distasteful task of determining just who counts as belonging to the family of the tainted man, resulting in unsavory definitions such as this:

4. "Family", when used with reference to a person, shall mean (a) any person related to such person within the third degree of consanguinity or affinity, (b) any person maintaining a sexual relationship with such person, or (c) any person residing in the same household with such person.[196]

Victims boards and courts that face definitions of this sort, rendered in terms of "degrees of consanguinity" and "affinity," are not to be envied. Is the "illegitimate son" of the man who murdered his mother eligible for victim compensation? No.[197] A presumably "legitimate" child whose father murdered her mother? No.[198] A child whose *stepfather* murdered her mother? Yes.[199] A husband who was shot by his wife? No.[200] A wife who was attacked by her husband? Yes.[201] What about the widow and children of a man beaten to death during a family altercation by his brother-in-law and nephew? No.[202]

Note that association with the offender is enough. Once contracted, the taint of derivative offenderhood cannot be neutralized, not even by one's association with the victim. Derivative victimhood is no antidote for derivative offenderhood. It makes no difference that the offender's child is also the victim's, that the offender's sister is also the victim's husband, that the offender's cousins are also the victim's children. All are categorically disqualified from victimhood by their "involvement" with the offender.

While criminal law has prided itself in limiting, if not abandoning, the imposition of criminal liability merely on the basis of association, vicarious noncompensability thus is alive and well. (That's not to say that there is no vicarious liability in criminal law *in fact*, as in the law of corporate crime and of conspiracy.)[203] Being related to a criminal may no longer expose you to punishment, but the state can decide to deny you victim compensation, as a matter of grace. This euphemistically named "household exclusion" began to disappear only after the federal government conditioned assistance for state victims programs on its removal.[204]

But not only evil offenderhood is communicable; so is the positive mark of good victimhood. As the criminal passes on her evilness, so the victim passes on his goodness, to the same people and in the same way. So we find among the compensable the members of the victim's family and household. The victim even transfers his compensability onto people outside his clan. Good samaritans derive their goodness from the victim's.

Imagine someone coming to the aid of a prison inmate who is being beaten to a pulp by a fellow inmate or perhaps a prison guard. The samaritan is good only if the victim is. Put another way, if the victim isn't compensable, neither is her helper.

But before a victim can pass her victimhood onto others, she must first attain it for herself. This is no easy task, and not only because she bears the burden of proof. Even if she isn't the offender, or a prison inmate, or related or otherwise associated with either, the badge of victimhood may be elusive if she suffers from other character defects. If, for instance, she has violated victimhood's iron rule against any sort of activity and did something that might be interpreted as a provocation or a threat directed at the offender, she will be ill advised to excuse her conduct by explaining that she wasn't herself because she was under the influence of alcohol, or even of drugs. These sorts of excuse fall on deaf ears in the law of punishment. They are even less welcome in the law of compensation.

It's not just that being drunk or otherwise intoxicated doesn't excuse conduct that otherwise would preclude a finding of victimization. Drunkenness and intoxication, by themselves, are incompatible with victimhood. Hence, in Florida, the mere fact that "the victim was involved in drugs," without more, is enough to disqualify an otherwise eligible victim from compensation altogether.[205] In Minnesota, the compensation may be reduced or denied if the victim "consumed alcohol or other mood-altering substances."[206] In the law of punishment, vague and sweeping "guidelines" of this sort would be unthinkable, and even unconstitutional. In the law of compensation, they are neither one nor the other. Compensation, after all, is a matter of grace, not of right, and the source of grace may be dispensed by its source, the state (or, rather, a state bureaucrat), as it (or he) sees fit.

Looking at how the law of compensation deals with the victim side of the question of responsibility for crime is both refreshing and troubling. It is refreshing because here we find an open, unembarrassed exploration of the question whether a particular individual fits a profile, in particular whether she is the type of person who deserves to be treated like a victim, notwithstanding what might have happened to her in a particular case of crime. Here the phenomenon of crime is significant only as an occasion for a general evaluation of the person's character and, more specifically, her goodness. Only good people are entitled to victim treatment. Therefore, the analysis of compensability is not complete without a close analysis of a claimant's moral stature. Is she ready to receive the grace of victim compensation?

At the same time, this exploration of a person's fundamental goodness or innocence, no matter how refreshingly brazen, is also frightening, unfettered as it is by concerns about injustice and arbitrariness, prejudice and discrimination, and the proper limits of state intrusion into the affairs and habits of its constituents. It exposes a serious danger of any legal scheme that focuses on the persons before it, rather than their acts. Such a system does well to heed the warning that the only relevant immutable characteristic of a person is personhood itself. All other characteristics are either temporary or, if they are immutable, irrelevant to the question of how a person deserves to be treated. A person-based system of law, whether it distributes compensation or punishment, that forgets its foundation in the concept of a person runs the risk of facilitating the sort of blatant and arbitrary differentiation *among* persons that characterizes the law of victim compensation. The approach to the question of responsibility in the law of compensation thus is more of a warning for the law of punishment than a model.

Compensation/Punishment

Now we are ready to proceed to the second, and final, stage of the compensation analysis. At this point, the victim-claimant has successfully completed the obstacle course of compensability, with its various and sundry hurdles. She is a person (and therefore has the capacity of being a victim). She has in fact suffered the relevant harm (and therefore not only was capable of being a victim but was actually victimized). And, finally, she is innocent (and therefore has been cleared for compensation).

The only question that remains is just how much compensation is appropriate in her case. At this point in the compensation inquiry, the victim (she's no longer merely a victim-claimant, because she's been granted victimhood) occupies the same position that the offender (who likewise has shed his preliminary classification as "defendant") does in the punishment inquiry. Having been found compensable, the victim awaits the assessment of compensation (the "award"). Having been found punishable, the offender awaits the assessment of punishment (the "sentence").

At this stage of the inquiry, the similarities between the law of compensation and the law of punishment are more obvious than were those at the previous stage of compensability and punishability. This is to be expected because the law of punishment traditionally has relaxed its focus on the offense, rather than on the offender, at the point of conviction. Once a person has been labeled an offender, by being found guilty of a criminal offense, he himself becomes the focus of the inquiry as the sentencer (almost always a judge, rather than a jury) decides his fate.

Only recently has judicial sentencing discretion been curtailed by so-called determinate and mandatory sentencing laws that set narrow penalty ranges or even specific penalties for particular offenses and offenders. In these sentencing regimes, the gap between the offense-based law of *punishability* and the offender-based law of *punishment* has been closed by turning the latter into an appendage of the former. In other words, the law of punishment, too, has become offense based in the sense that the sentence to be imposed reflects the offense, or at least more of the offense than it once did.

Still, the offender focus of traditional criminal law remains alive and well even today, and even in determinate sentencing jurisdictions. Some of the best-known, and most devastating, mandatory sentencing laws apply to particular offenders, not particular offenses. The infamous three-strikes-and-you're-out statutes now in place throughout the country target certain offender types, variously characterized as recidivists, repeat offenders, persistent felony offenders, and so on.[207] Similarly, the federal sentencing guidelines, the most influential, harshest, and—despite their innocuous title—most restrictive of determinate sentencing schemes, provide for stiffer penalties for offenders labeled "career criminals."[208]

Other recent innovations in the law of sentencing are more open about their offender focus. They provide for the indefinite detention of offenders labeled "sexual predators." Their relation to the criminal law, however, is contested. Legislatures that have passed these laws have stressed that they deal not with punishment and, therefore, criminal law, but with commitment and, therefore, noncriminal law. (This bit of window dressing succeeded in insulating these statutes against constitutional scrutiny.)[209]

The most obvious example of offender focus in the contemporary law of sentencing is capital punishment. At the same time that determinate sentencing schemes called for reducing the offender's significance, the U.S. Supreme Court constructed a system of "individualized" capital punishment that culminates in an elaborate sentencing trial after the trial, which is focused entirely and explicitly on the person of the offender, rather than his offense. When the Court in 1991 endorsed victim impact testimony at the sentencing trial, it merely expanded (some might say shifted) this person focus from the offender to the victim.[210]

In sum, the new law of sentencing is *offense* focused when it comes to denying sentence reductions for minor offenders but *offender* focused when it comes to justifying sentence enhancements for major offenders. In other words, it's about longer sentences, first and foremost. It doesn't amount to a paradigm shift from offender to offense in the law of punishment.

That the law of compensation focuses on persons shouldn't be a surprise. The same is true of the law of compensability. It's the law of punishment that shifts focus from offense to offender, from act to person, once punishability has been determined. With no need to shift its focus from one stage of the analysis to the next, the law of *compensation* simply spells out the application of the general principles of the law of *compensability* to particular victims.

Given this continuity between the first and the second stage of analysis in compensation law, there's little need for a detailed treatment of the latter. In fact, the distinction between compensability and compensation is often difficult to draw. Take, for example, the question of "victim contribution." This question can be divided in two. First, it must be decided whether the victim contributed so much to the crime that she doesn't qualify as a victim, or at least as an innocent victim. This is a question of compensability. It's a yes-no question. If the answer is no, then we must ask ourselves, second, if the victim contributed enough to the crime to have her compensation award reduced. This is a question of actual compensation. It's not a yes-no question but allows for a wide range of answers.

To separate the question of responsibility, or "accountability" or "contribution," in two, however, is easier said than done. Take the Uniform Victims of Crime Act. In its general definitional section, it precludes from compensability anyone who "is accountable for the crime or a crime arising from the same conduct, criminal episode, or plan."[211] Later on, in its compensation section, it provides that "[t]he [agency] may reduce *or deny* compensation to the extent that the victim or claimant engaged in a violation of law, misconduct, or unreasonably dangerous behavior that contributed to the claimant's loss."[212] So a claimant who contributed to the crime in some way can find herself compensable at the first stage, only to learn that, at the second stage, she is denied any and all compensation on account of her contribution to the crime.

Some statutes make no attempt to maintain the distinction between compensability and compensation in this context. For example, Florida doesn't limit the definition of victim to innocent or nonresponsible claimants. Instead, it entitles the relevant agency to "determine whether, because of his conduct, the victim of such crime or the intervenor contributed to the infliction of his injury or to his death," and to "reduce the amount of the award or *reject the claim altogether*, in accordance with such determination."[213] The accompanying agency guidelines set up a sliding scale of contribution, from 0 to 100 percent, parts of which we have already encountered.

> Contribution is determined by the actions portrayed by the victim at the time of or immediately preceding the crime. While there is no set formula for calculating the percentage of contribution to be assessed, the following factors should serve as a guideline:
>
> (1) If it appears that the victim was provoked by the defendant in a manner threatening bodily harm to the victim, and the victim acted in self defense, no contribution should be assessed.
>
> (2) If it appears that the victim was provoked by the defendant in a manner where bodily harm to the victim appeared unlikely, and the victim used poor judgment because of intoxication or other drug involvement, a 25% contribution factor should be assessed.
>
> (3) If it appears that the defendant was provoked by the victim in a manner where bodily harm appeared unlikely, a 50% contribution factor should be assessed.
>
> (4) If the victim is injured as a result of his conduct not being that of a prudent person, a 50% contribution factor should also be assessed.
>
> (5) If it appears that the defendant was provoked by the victim in a manner where bodily harm to the defendant appears intentional, a 75% contribution factor should be assessed.
>
> (6) If it appears that the defendant was provoked by the victim in a manner where bodily harm to the defendant is unquestionable, a 100% contribution factor shall be assessed and the claim denied.
>
> (7) If the victim is not wearing protective equipment as prescribed by law, a 25% contribution factor shall be assessed. This includes helmets, seat belts, etc.
>
> (8) If the victim was involved in drugs, as verified by the police report or other official documents, a 100% contribution factor should be assessed and the claim denied.[214]

This set of compensation guidelines is noteworthy, first, because it makes no effort to distinguish between compensable victims and victims who, though compensable, are not entitled to any compensation. In this sense, it turns the law of compensation into an assessment of compensation awards, burying the question of innocence in a calculus of contribution percentages and denying the significance of the question of who qualifies as a victim in the first place and in general. As a result, the law of victim compensation looks nothing like the law of offender punishment. Instead, it looks like a species of insurance law, or perhaps the law of workers' compensation.

At the same time, however, this scheme looks very much like criminal law. The question of contribution is said to turn on conduct, specifically the victim's "actions . . . at the time of or immediately preceding the crime."[215] (The only concession to the fact that this is compensation, and not criminal, law is that these actions are considered as "portrayed by the victim.")

From the perspective of criminal law, this catalogue of victim contributory conduct looks like a list of criminal defenses, such as provocation and self-defense. The references to provocation are clear enough. But when is self-defense justified if not in the following situation: "the defendant was provoked by the victim in a manner where bodily harm to the defendant is unquestionable . . ."?

More specifically, this list of victim contributory conduct closely resembles similar lists familiar from the law of sentencing. For example, the federal sentencing guidelines provide that "victim misconduct" may reduce the sentence even if that misconduct did not rise to the level of a justification or excuse such as self-defense or provocation.

§5K2.10. Victim's Conduct (Policy Statement)
If the victim's wrongful conduct *contributed* significantly to provoking the offense behavior, the court may reduce the sentence below the guideline range to reflect the nature and circumstances of the offense. In deciding the extent of a sentence reduction, the court should consider:
(a) the size and strength of the victim, or other relevant physical characteristics, in comparison with those of the defendant;
(b) the persistence of the victim's conduct and any efforts by the defendant to prevent confrontation;
(c) the danger reasonably perceived by the defendant, including the victim's reputation for violence;
(d) the danger actually presented to the defendant by the victim; and
(e) any other relevant conduct by the victim that substantially contributed to the danger presented. [216]

So the same conduct that reduces the victim's compensation also reduces the offender's punishment. The connection between compensation law and criminal law is obvious. Both speak in terms of conduct, and both ascribe analogously identical significance to it. Now the law of compensation looks very much like the law of punishment.

This pocket of criminal law doctrine in the middle of victim compensation law makes sense as soon as we recognize that the contributing victim here is treated like an offender. By engaging in "actions," the victim has removed himself from the heartland of passive victimhood and now, paradoxically, must turn to rules from the law of offenderhood to retain his status as a victim. By invoking self-defense (as in guideline no. 1), he can claim victimhood despite his "actions," much as the offender-defendant would raise self-defense to ward off offenderhood. At the same time, the rules of criminal law may work to the victim-offender's disadvantage. Without recourse to self-defense, he will find himself compensated less if he engaged in "provocative" conduct, where it remains unclear what standard of provocation is to be applied (nos. 5 & 6). To say that the "defendant was provoked by the victim in a manner where bodily harm appeared unlikely" says nothing about whether the presence of provocation or the "appearance" of the risk of bodily harm is to be determined from the defendant's standpoint, from the victim's, or perhaps from that of some "reasonable person" familiar from criminal law.

As we saw earlier, the active victim faces an uphill battle for compensation. Besides these criminal law- and conduct-based hurdles, he also faces other impediments that are drawn from other sources and that are primarily concerned not with his conduct but with his shortcomings as a person. To establish one's award-worthiness takes more than merely convincing the compensation board of one's criminal innocence. Refraining from unvictimlike conduct helps rebut the suspicion that one doesn't have what it takes to be a victim. But it's not enough to establish affirmatively that one is entitled to victim compensation in fact. Being a victim means not being an offender, and a whole lot more.

That "whole lot more" is difficult to specify. Hence the warning at the outset of the Florida list that "there is no set formula for calculating the percentage of contribution to be assessed." The victim compensation bureaucrats just have to know a victim when they see one. All the law (or rather the intraoffice directive from one victim bureaucrat to another) can hope to do is to enumerate some factors that "should serve as a guideline." "[P]oor judgment" (or, in Montana, "gross stupidity")[217] can do him in, especially when related to drug or alcohol use (no. 2). So can not being a "prudent person" (no. 4) or simply "not wearing protective equipment as prescribed by law" (no. 7). And those "involved in drugs" (no. 8) need not apply. They, and only they, face the same categorical (100 percent) denial of compensation as do victims who provoked the defendant "in a manner where bodily harm to the defendant is unquestionable. ..." Drug "involvement," in other words, is as fatal to victimhood as is violent criminal conduct. This is the law of victimhood, after all. Conduct matters, but only as a symptom of victimhood.

The question now is whether any of these factors should affect not only the victim's compensation but also the offender's punishment. No one has suggested that an offender who commits a crime against a person of "gross stupidity" should be punished more leniently than if her victim had been a person of higher intelligence. Likewise, a blanket reduction in punishment for crimes committed against anyone "involved in drugs" hardly seems appropriate, no matter how much it might reflect the actual attitudes of state combatants in the "war on drugs."

To remove certain persons labeled "criminals," "felons," "robbers," "inmates," or simply "guilty" from the protection of the criminal law by letting their victimizers mistreat them with impunity (and thus turning them into "outlaws" in the historical sense of the word) is similarly unthinkable, if not undoable. A thief, for instance, deserves the same protection against theft as any other person.[218] As a person, she is as capable of victimhood as any other. For the same reason, a thief also deserves the same compensation as any other person. The temporary label "thief" doesn't remove her from the realm of the criminal law, *either as offender or as victim*, any more than it removes her from the realm of the law of compensation. The categorical denial of compensation to prison inmates, regardless of their crime of conviction, is as illegitimate as a categorical immunity from punishment for anyone who steals from a thief—or commits any other crime against her.

Despite the freewheeling consideration of victim conduct in the law of compensation, the criminal law ought to take a more expansive view toward victim conduct. There is no reason to consider victim conduct in the law of guilt (or punishability) only if it amounts to "criminal activity [that] give[s] rise to circumstances whereby another may act with justification for the purpose of thwarting or terminating the criminal actions," that is, if it triggers full-blown justification defenses of "self-defense, defense of another, defense of property, and law enforcement."[219] Nor should victim conduct be relevant in the law of sentencing (or punishment) only if it "contributed significantly to provoking the offense behavior," that is, if it made out a partial excuse defense for the offender.[220] Instead, victim conduct should be considered, both for punishment and for compensation, whenever it manifests the victim's autonomy, whether or not it was directed against the offender. Anything else would fly in the face of the victim's right to be treated as a person.

One final feature of the law of compensation deserves our attention. It is the possibility of denying compensation altogether to otherwise compensable victims. One cynical way of looking at the denial of benefits to victims who generally fit the definition of a compensable victim is to see the finding of compensability as a an irrelevant farce at best and an insult at worst. In a different, more positive light, it suggests that the finding of compensability may be significant in and of itself. Even a victim who does not receive compensation or who sees her compensation reduced for one reason or another (say because she wasn't sufficiently "needy") may see her identification as a victim as an acknowledgment of her experience of victimization. To be found compensable implies that one is respected as a person (because only a person is capable of victimhood), that one is seen as someone who has "suffer[ed] personal physical injury as a direct result of a crime" and who was "innocent," at least in the sense of not being accountable for the crime.

In this way, victim compensation schemes can contribute to the project of reaffirming the victim's autonomy following the criminal attack on that autonomy in two ways. First, they can acknowledge the victim as a person who has suffered criminal harm and therefore requires the state's attention as someone who may need help in rediscovering and reasserting her autonomy. Second, they can provide victims who do need this help with additional assistance, beyond the recognition of their victimization inherent in the finding of compensability.

The distinction between punishability (guilt) and punishment (sentence) in the traditional criminal law allows for a similar, and analogous, distinction between acknowledgment and assistance. The distinction is *similar* from the victim's perspective in that the finding of guilt may be enough to set the victim on the road to recovery from the trauma of crime. A finding of offender guilt, in the law of punishment, may be appropriate *in addition to* a finding of victim innocence, in the law of compensation, because the trauma of crime consists not only in the suffering of harm but also in the suffering of harm at the hands of another person. The crime is not just an assault on one's autonomy but an assault on one's autonomy for the sake of that of another. The finding of guilt identifies the person who inflicted the harm. The finding of compensability identifies the person who suffered it.

The process is the punishment, and no part of the process is more punishment than the verdict. The ceremonial finding of guilt marks the culmination of an often lengthy process during which the offender-defendant may experience a sense of powerlessness not unlike that experienced by his victim. That feeling is particular intense among offenders who distrust the criminal justice system, and particularly its commitment to them as persons, that is, exactly as they should have treated but did not treat their victim.

Still, in certain cases, merely identifying the offender as responsible for the threat to the victim's autonomy isn't enough. The victim who has suffered severe injuries and struggles to regain his sense of self in the wake of a serious crime will regard a finding of criminal responsibility without subsequent punishment as an insufficient acknowledgment of his experience of victimization, and rightly so.

The distinction between punishability and punishment is also *analogous* to that between compensability and compensation because it allows the state, as the delegated punisher, to differentiate among offenders much as it does among victims. Since the criminal law seeks to affirm the autonomy of victims and offenders alike, it must avoid any damage to the offender's autonomy through the infliction of gratuitous punishment that serves to affirm neither the victim's nor the offender's autonomy. And every punishment that goes beyond a public finding of guilt represents a presumptive interference with the offender's autonomy. Only its lawfulness separates imprisonment from "unlawful imprisonment." The state therefore bears a heavy burden of justifying the use of actual punishment beyond a public verdict of criminal guilt.

In many cases, the process of investigation and imposition itself, culminating in the verdict of guilty, is enough to manifest to the offender (and to the victim, as well as to anyone else) the significance of the victim as a person and the inviolability of her personhood. This communication comes not only, and not even primarily, in the defendant-offender's painful experience of what he perceives as oppression by the state apparatus in cahoots with the victim. More important, it is achieved by the respect that this very apparatus accords the victim's and the offender's personhood in the course of the proceedings. Nothing is more devastating to an offender's worldview than the recognition that he is accorded the respect that he denied the victim. In many cases, the "award" of punishment in the narrow sense thus is gratuitous and, therefore, illegitimate. The offender already has suffered sufficient punishment.

But the offender and her victim are not the only addressees of modern criminal law. Just as the criminal code addresses all persons, so the criminal process generally speaking addresses not only victims and offenders but judges and onlookers, as well. To vindicate the victim's rights is to affirm her right to personal autonomy *to all*. To eradicate the effects of crime, to rebuff the offender's attempt to deny the victim's autonomy by reducing her self to a means for the aggrandizement of his own, the state must extinguish every hint of the perception that the victim is in fact not a person and that the offender could thus have succeeded, no matter who might harbor it, victim, offender, or anyone else.

Through interpersonal identification, any threat to the personhood of any person is experienced vicariously by every other person, to a greater or lesser degree. That threat therefore must be neutralized not only for the sake of the person directly affected but also for the sake of all those who experience her victimization vicariously. This experience can trigger not only sympathy for the direct victim and a desire to help her reassert her sense of autonomy but may also constitute a separate experience of victimization. In this way, the onlooker may experience the crime as an indirect threat against her own autonomy. Thus, even in cases where the offender has eliminated the victim as an addressee, as in homicides, punishment is addressed not only to the offender himself but also to others.

Whether viewed from the offender's or from the victim's perspective, the distinction between guilt (or punishability) and sentence (or punishment) helps us recognize the significance of a finding of guilt in and of itself, even if it isn't followed by the imposition of a particular measure of punishment. This nominal punishment in the law of offenderhood mirrors the nominal compensation in the law of victimhood. Just as a finding of compensability acknowledges the claimant as an innocent victim, so the finding of punishability acknowledges the defendant as a guilty offender. Nominal punishment, and nominal compensation, minimizes the threat that the process of punishment, and of compensation, will harm, rather than affirm, the autonomy of offender and victim alike. Just as excessive punishment, inflicted under oppressive conditions, may well do permanent damage to the offender's sense of autonomy, so excessive compensation, paid out in a way that overemphasizes the victim's "neediness," may cement the victim's perception of herself as a perpetual victim, incapable of managing her own affairs.

Conclusion

As a matter of fact, the vindication of victims' rights has everything to do with the war on crime. As a matter of principle, the vindication of victims' rights has *nothing* to do with the war on crime.

If we disentangle victims' rights from the war on crime, what's left of victims' rights? Every right the victim has she enjoys as a person. What rights, then, does a victim have, qua person? As a person, she deserves to be treated as someone capable of self-determination, of managing her own affairs, and of overcoming crises, including the traumatic crisis of crime during which she sees her personhood challenged by another person intent on imposing his will upon her and transforming her into an environmental resource for the manifestation of his own personhood. But, as a person, the victim also has the right not to be treated as a nuisance or an afterthought or a fig leaf for brute state power. As a person, then, the victim deserves respect from the offender and the state alike.

This basic right of autonomy, or self-determination, gives rise to a number of subordinate rights, including the right to participate in the decision whether, and, if so, how, the state should invoke the law in response to a criminal assault on the victim's autonomy. From the victim's perspective, the principle of *ultima ratio*, which provides that the state may use the criminal law only as a last resort, applies not only to criminal law but to any kind of legal intervention on the part of the state. Faced with the occurrence of a "crime," the state's first choice—and the one, in fact, most often taken—is to do nothing. The next option is to intervene by law, through the law of victim compensation. Only the third, and final, option is to turn to the law of offender punishment.

Some nominal victims of crime have no need for state assistance in regaining their sense of autonomy after the experience of crime, either because that sense was never damaged or because they have the wherewithal to repair whatever damage the offender managed to inflict. Others may require state intervention in the form of compensation law so that they can recover their sense of autonomy by undergoing medical treatment of one form or another or, perhaps more directly, by regaining their fiscal health.

Finally, some crime victims may have sustained such severe damage to their all-important sense of autonomy that the most serious form of state intervention through law is called for: the criminal law. Invocation of the criminal law is obligatory, for example, in cases of intentional homicide, for two reasons. First, restoring the autonomy of a murder victim through financial assistance or any other means is impossible, by definition. (Providing financial assistance to surviving relatives of homicide victims is praiseworthy but has nothing to do with crime victim compensation.) Second, permitting one person to intentionally and permanently destroy another's personhood with impunity would reflect a deep disrespect for the victim as the person she once was.

In case a state response in the form of criminal law is necessary, the victim is, at least prima facie, entitled to whatever rights are consistent with the vindication of her right to autonomy, since that's why the criminal process was set in motion in the first place. There is no need to detail the various and sundry ways in which a victim might be included in the criminal process to reempower her. One of these rights certainly is the right "to reasonable notice of, and not to be excluded from, any public proceedings relating to the crime," as contained in the proposed federal victims' bill of rights and many other similar documents. Whether that right should be *constitutionally* enshrined is, of course, another question. The very notion of a *victims'* bill of rights flies in the face of the fact that victims enjoy rights as persons, not as victims. Rather than cement the rights of victims, a victims' bill of rights cements their essential victimhood.

In granting victims participation rights in the criminal process, however, one must exercise extreme caution. To begin with, not every opportunity for participation translates into an opportunity for self-assertion. Take, for instance, the most controversial of procedural victims' rights, the right to give victim impact evidence. A victim's testimony at the sentencing hearing (orally or in writing) may strengthen the victim's sense of self after the traumatic experience of crime. Then, again, it may discourage the victim from reassembling herself as a person, instead of continuing to conceive of herself as a victim, and thus prolong the experience of criminal victimhood, rather than help overcome it.

Furthermore, and this is a related point, victim participation may fly in the face of the *offender's* right to personal autonomy. The state must use its power, including the power of criminal law, to safeguard the autonomy of all persons within its jurisdiction. The victim is not the only person whose autonomy is at stake in a criminal case. So is the offender's. Acting out anti-offender hostility under the cover of a victim impact statement not only does nothing for, and may even damage, the victim's sense of self-control. It also treats the offender as a nonperson and, perhaps more important, may prompt the legal decision makers (judge or jury) to do likewise.

In setting the criminal process in motion, the state invokes law, and the criminal law in particular, to fulfill its basic function: manifesting and preserving the autonomy of the persons who constitute it. Before the law, however, each and every one of these persons is equal, and equally entitled to respect for his autonomy. This is the essence of state neutrality, even and especially in a criminal trial—to treat all persons equally as persons.

The great threat to the legitimacy of the criminal process is its transformation into a system of danger control. As the war on crime powerfully illustrates, such a system reduces persons to apersonal sources of danger that are to be extinguished. Victim participation in the criminal process, in particular through victim impact statements at sentencing, is a common way of achieving this transformation. Victims who communicate their contempt for the offender as a worthless subhuman creature or ahuman object characterized by an inherent dangerousness may well influence a sympathetic decision maker similarly to view the criminal sanction as pest control or hazardous waste management.

This blatant and unjustifiable assault on the offender's personhood also does not translate into an affirmation of the victim's personhood. A victim consumed with hatred of "her" offender continues to define herself in terms of her victimization and therefore reaffirms the offender's control over her. What's more, in acting out on the witness stand, the victim reveals herself not only as under the continued spell of the offender but also as the tool of another person, the prosecutor, who uses her to convince the decision makers, particularly in capital cases, that they are dealing with anyone, or rather anything, other than a fellow person. In the end, the victim contributes to a criminal process that denies the offender's personhood, as he denied hers in the criminal act. The trial thus *reenacts* the crime, rather than *processing* it.

Still, victim impact evidence may well help some victims regain their sense of self. The victim may experience the very opportunity to detail his experience of the crime and his struggle to recover his ability to function autonomously, as a person rather than as a victim, as a recognition that his suffering is significant, so significant, in fact, that the state initiated the process of punishment.

At the same time, victim impact evidence can serve as a constant reminder to the *state officials* who operate the criminal justice system that the state's (and therefore their) punitive power springs from the victimization of one person at the hands of another, rather than from the violation of some state norm or other that the state, in its wisdom, has decided to back up with a criminal sanction. Criminal law is an intensely personal affair and cannot be legitimated on any other basis, a crucial fact all too often forgotten by the state officials who make and apply it.

Moreover, victim impact evidence lays out before the *offender* the precise nature of her act, ideally in such a way as to permit and encourage her to identify with the victim's suffering as a person. In this way, victim impact evidence can help legitimize the process of her punishment in the eyes of the offender and perhaps even contribute to her recognition of herself as one person among others entitled to mutual respect and, in this sense, to her "rehabilitation."

And, finally, the victim's participation in the sentencing decision after the ascription of guilt to the offender in the form of a conviction or a guilty plea provides an opportunity for the victim to reevaluate the need for further punishment. Victims, therefore, should be encouraged, in their victim impact statements, to reflect on the extent to which the criminal process, culminating in the ascription of offenderhood to the defendant and of victimhood to himself, has contributed to his rediscovery of himself as a person. Perhaps the process was punishment enough. Why should victim impact evidence always be an aggravating factor, a call for maximum incapacitation?

Simply asking this question illustrates why, at a time when victims' rights and the war on crime are joined at the hip, the question of victim impact evidence must be approached with much trepidation. As long as the war on crime sets the tone of American criminal law and American prosecutors cannot be trusted not to use victims to dehumanize offenders in the hope of winning more convictions and harsher sentences, victim impact evidence all too quickly turns the criminal process into a spectacle of hate that strips both victim and offender of their dignity as persons. Perhaps the danger of its abuse is so great that victim impact evidence should be excluded altogether.

Alternatively, one might limit victim impact evidence to *direct* victims of crime. The point of victim impact evidence, after all, is to contribute to the victim's "repersonalization" by permitting her to describe her depersonalization by the offender. This restriction to direct victims would also exclude such testimony from death penalty cases, where the potential for its abuse is particularly great because of the nature of the crime and of the threatened punishment, as well as the jury's unique role in capital sentencing.

Moreover, victim impact evidence might be restricted to written statements, as opposed to live testimony before the sentencer, and submitted as part of the presentence report. (The statement could be composed by the victim herself or written by an official on the basis of a conversation with the victim; this would allow the victim to speak about her experience to a state official other than the eventual decision maker.) This procedure would help minimize the possibility of ad hoc communal scapegoating of the offender through identification between victim and sentencer in the courtroom. It might also prove more conducive to the sort of reflection on the victim's part that facilitates, rather than hinders, the victim's rediscovery of herself as a person.

But taking victims seriously means not only respecting their autonomy in the criminal process. It also requires a drastic reduction in the scope of criminal law, that is, in the class of cases that might qualify for criminal processing. Even "victim impact statements" presume a *victim*, a victim who has suffered a certain kind of *impact*, and finally a victim who can make a *statement* about that impact.

More generally, taking victims seriously requires us to narrow our conception of crime, no matter what form the state's legal response to this sociolegal phenomenon might take. The law of victimhood already proceeds from a notion of crime as an act of violence perpetrated by one person against another; the law of offenderhood should do the same. Only the attempt by one person to negate the autonomy of another, ostensibly equal person results in the sort of victimhood that warrants state intervention through law of one kind or another. Other types of victimhood don't require the manifestation or restoration of autonomy in the face of an attack and therefore don't involve either the state or its law.

Taking victims seriously also means taking the victim's perspective. And, from that perspective, the experience of criminal victimhood differs qualitatively from any other suffering precisely because it doesn't come out of nowhere but originates in the will of another person. Criminal victimhood is no accident, no strike of fate. It is the result of a deliberate attempt by one person to subjugate another. In this sense, crime is not a conflict, which presumes rough equality of the parties involved, but an assault, which presumes the opposite.

Private law can handle interpersonal conflict, with the state merely setting the background conditions for the two parties to resolve their differences, preferably through settlement. But for the state to deny victims of intentional interpersonal violence the assistance of public law would be to abdicate its responsibility to safeguard the autonomy of its constituents, given that the distinctive harm of crime lies precisely in damage to that autonomy, including its complete and permanent destruction in the case of homicide. That is not to say, however, that crime victims should not have the opportunity to challenge their offenders as plaintiffs in the less structured environs of civil law. On the contrary, they should be encouraged to do just that, thus manifesting their reemergence as autonomous persons who can manage their own affairs, even if that includes bringing a tort claim against their one-time oppressor.

The state's direct, public law response to crime, however, need not take the form of criminal law. Only an offender-focused system of law would confuse law with the law of offenderhood and ignore the law of victimhood. In the mid-1960s, the law of crime victim compensation grew out of concern for the plight of persons transformed by others into needy victims of crime. Focusing on the victim, compensation law was conceived as an alternative to criminal law, which punished persons for offenses against the state or the "public" or "society" and therefore showed little interest in personal victims.

From the victim's perspective, compensation law, not criminal law, is the most immediately appropriate state response to crime. The victim's immediate, and legitimate, interest—the victim's *right* as a person—is to regain his ability to function as an autonomous person, that is, to stop being a victim and to start being a person again. The punishment of the person responsible for damaging his autonomy is only indirectly related to this interest. Assuming the victim needs any state assistance in overcoming the effects of crime at all, he may well be able to achieve this without seeing the offender punished. Compensation may be enough. In fact, compensation without punishment is possible, because, unlike restitution, compensation doesn't presuppose a conviction, or even a prosecution.

Compensation law still has a long way to go before it can stand next to criminal law as an alternative public law response to crime. Although it has made great strides over the thirty-five years or so of its existence in this country, it cannot match the sophistication or the sheer bulk of traditional criminal law. It has attracted little attention among commentators, who tend to focus on offender-paid restitution as a form of offender punishment, rather than on state-paid compensation as a form of victim assistance (if they distinguish between restitution and compensation at all). And the victims' rights movement has had no use for it, either, since compensation law's concern with victims for their own sake is inconsistent with the nexus between victims' rights and offender incapacitation that defines the victims' rights movement in its current punitive incarnation.

One of the goals of this book is to rescue compensation law from a remote corner of American administrative law and assign it its rightful place as the victim-focused half of a general law of crime, which so far has been identified with the offender-focused law of punishment. Compensation law and criminal law address the same sociolegal phenomenon, crime, in complementary ways. They are mirror images of each other, as they analyze the legal significance of a crime from the viewpoints of the victim and the offender, respectively.

Our extended exploration of victim compensation law, however, also is meant to illustrate a larger point, namely that vindicating victims' rights requires a basic revision of the way in which American law deals with crime. Looking at the criminal law through victims' eyes, we notice that much of contemporary American criminal law is inconsistent with victims' rights. Most obviously, so-called victimless crimes, such as possession offenses, don't fit into a victim-based system of criminal law. But neither do *offenderless* crimes, such as so-called crimes of strict liability and negligence, and those committed by nonpersonal entities, such as corporations.

In general, we come to better appreciate the nature and varieties of criminal harm, as opposed to other forms of injury. From the victim's perspective that underlies the law of victimhood, crime appears as one person's attack on the autonomy of another, with some attacks inflicting greater harm than others, depending on the nature and permanence of the interference. This focus on the victim's autonomy allows us to see more clearly the failure of American criminal law fully to give victims their due in the law of attempt, consent, and causation and raises doubts about such statist doctrines as the "dual sovereignty" exception to the prohibition against multiple punishments for the same crime (double jeopardy). It becomes clear that not only the general principles of American criminal law but also the law of particular crimes, such as assault, teems with doctrines that reflect the irrelevance of the victim's perspective on the ground that the true victim of criminal law is the state, rather than any particular person.

We must ask ourselves, always also from the victim's standpoint, *whether* the criminal law is the proper response to crime and, in cases where it is, *how* the criminal law can do justice to the victim's experience during and after the crime. Taking the victim's standpoint means that our answers to these questions should not, in the first instance, consider how they might affect the offender's criminal liability, assuming we need to turn to the criminal law at all. Increased criminal liability for the offender is no reason either to fight for, or against, the recognition of a victim's right. The offender doesn't have a right to less punishment, nor does the victim have a right to more. The only right the offender has is the right she shares with the victim: to be treated in accordance with her status as a person.

The challenge of the criminal process, and of the criminal law in general, is to find a way to respect the rights of victims and offenders as persons, rather than to protect "victims' rights"—or "offenders' rights," for that matter. Victims' rights will be vindicated only after we abandon the concept of victims' rights and reform our law to vindicate instead the rights of persons.

Notes

Notes to the Introduction

1. Cal. const. art. I, § 28.

2. See Markus Dirk Dubber, The Unprincipled Punishment of Repeat Offenders: A Critique of California's Habitual Criminal Statute, 43 Stan. L. Rev. 193
(1990); Candace McCoy, Politics and Plea Bargaining: Victims' Rights in California (1993).

3. See, e.g., Lynne Henderson, The Wrongs of Victim's Rights, 37 Stan. L. Rev.
937 (1985). Henderson's article remains the best critical analysis of the American
victims' rights movement.

4. See Carl Schmitt, The Concept of the Political (George Schwab trans.
1996).

5. Charles H. Whitebread & Christopher Slobogin, Criminal Procedure: An
Analysis of Cases and Concepts 355 (4th ed. 2000).

6. See, e.g., Murder Victims' Families for Reconciliation (founded in 1976),
<http://www.mvfr.org>. Thanks to Sam Gross for bringing this group to my at-
tention.

7. See generally Robert Elias, The Politics of Victimization: Victims, Victimology, and Human Rights (1986); Andrew Karmen, Crime Victims: An Introduction to Victimology (2d ed. 1990).

8. Gesetz über die Entschädigung für Opfer von Gewalttaten ("Law Regarding the Compensation of Victims of Violent Acts") (OEG). Since throughout this
book we occasionally glance at this statute and its judicial interpretation, here is a
translation of the relevant provisions:

§ 1 Entitlement to Assistance.
(1) Whoever . . . has sustained damage to his health caused by an intentional
     unlawful physical attack against his or another person or by his lawful de-
     fense against such an attack, shall upon application receive compensation
     . . . for health-related and economic harm. . . .
§2 Grounds for Denial of Compensation.

(1) Compensation shall be denied when the claimant caused the harm or when it would be inappropriate for other reasons, specifically those related to the claimant's behavior, to grant compensation. . . .

9. See, e.g., Dieter Rössner, Mediation as a Basic Element of Crime Control: Theoretical and Empirical Comments, 3 Buff. Crim. L. Rev. 211 (1999); Detlev Frehsee, Restitution and Offender-Victim Arrangement in German Criminal Law: Development and Theoretical Implications, 3 Buff. Crim. L. Rev. 235 (1999).

10. This is the crucial insight that underlies the victim-based analysis of criminal liability (Viktimodogmatik) developed by Bernd Schünemann. See Bernd Schünemann, The Role of the Victim within the Criminal Justice System: A Three-Tiered Concept, 3 Buff. Crim. L. Rev. 33, 38–40 (1999).

NOTES TO CHAPTER 1

1. See Ronald L. Goldfarb, Perfect Villains, Imperfect Heroes: Robert Kennedy's War against Organized Crime (1995).

2. See Richard Nixon, Toward Freedom from Fear (position paper on crime) (New York, May 8, 1968), reprinted in 114 Cong. Rec. 12936, 12936 (May 13, 1968) ("The war on poverty which I started—is a war against crime and a war against disorder.") (quoting Lyndon Johnson, Oct. 16, 1964); see also President Lyndon B. Johnson's Annual Message to the Congress on the State of the Union, Jan. 17, 1968 (federal government should "help the cities and the States in their war on crime to the full extent of its resources and its constitutional authority").

3. See Nixon, supra note 2, at 12936, 12937; see also Todd R. Clear, Societal Responses to the President's Crime Commission: A Thirty-Year Retrospective, in Research Forum, The Challenge of Crime in a Free Society: Looking Back, Looking Forward, at 131 (U.S. Dep't of Justice, Office of Justice Programs 1997); James Vorenberg, The War on Crime: The First Five Years, Atlantic Monthly, May 1972, at 63.

4. On the distinction between wars—which require an open "declaration" and are bound by the law of war—and police actions—which are often carried out clandestinely and arguably are beyond the constraints of the law of war, see Geoffrey S. Corn, "To Be or Not to Be, That Is the Question": Contemporary Military Operations and the Status of Captured Personnel, 1999 Army Law. 1; Robert O. Weiner & Fionnuala Ni Aolain, Beyond the Laws of War: Peacekeeping in Search of a Legal Framework, 27 Colum. Hum. Rts L. Rev. 293 (1996); Benedetto Conforti, Non-Coercive Sanctions in the United Nations Charter: Some Lessons from the Gulf War, 2 Eur. J. Int'l L. 110 (1991).

5. U.S. Dep't of Justice, Office of Justice Programs, Bureau of Justice Statistics, Bureau of Justice Statistics 2000: At a Glance 19 (Aug. 2000, NCJ 183014); Fox Butterfield, Number in Prison Grows Despite Crime Reduction, N.Y. Times,

Aug. 10, 2000, at A10; The Sentencing Project, Facts about Prisons and Prisoners, http://www.sentencingproject.org/brief/facts–pp.pdf; Justice Policy Institute, The Punishing Decade: Prison and Jail Estimates at the Millennium, http://www.cjcj .org/punishingdecade/.

6. See generally Markus Dirk Dubber, Recidivist Statutes as Arational Punishment, 43 Buff. L. Rev. 689 (1995).

7. Here I'm invoking police in the broad sense, as in "police power," rather than in the limited institutional sense, as in "police department." The police power of the state is the power to order its constituents so as to maximize the "public welfare" according to rules of expediency. Ernst Freund, The Police Power: Public Policy and Constitutional Rights 4 (1904); see Adam Smith, Juris Prudence or Notes from the Lectures on Jurisprudence 396, 398 (R. L. Meed, D. D. Raphael, and P. G. Stein eds. 1978). In Blackstone's oft-quoted definition, to police is the "due regulation and domestic order of the kingdom: whereby the individuals of the state, like members of a well-governed family, are bound to conform their general behaviour to the rules of propriety, good neighbourhood, and good manners: and to be decent, industrious, and inoffensive in their respective stations." 4 William Blackstone, Commentaries on the Laws of England 162 (1769). Law, by contrast, is concerned with the "maintenance of right and the redress of wrong" according to principles of justice. Freund, supra; see Smith, supra. For more recent accounts of the distinction between police and law, see Christopher L. Tomlins, Law, Labor, and Ideology in the Early American Republic (1993); William J. Novak, The People's Welfare: Law & Regulation in Nineteenth-Century America (1996). See also Michel Foucault, Governmentality, in The Foucault Effect: Studies in Governmentality 87 (Graham Burchell, Colin Gordon, and Peter Miller eds. 1991); Mark Neocleous, The Fabrication of Social Order: A Critical Theory of Police Power (2000).

8. See infra text accompanying notes 55–67.

9. Cf. Paul H. Robinson, Punishing Dangerousness: Cloaking Preventive Detention as Criminal Justice, 114 Harv. L. Rev. 1429, 1432 (2001) (exploring "the wish to keep the old criminal 'punishment' façade" in a prevention system).

10. For suggestive remarks on the problem of punishing possession, see George P. Fletcher, Rethinking Criminal Law 197–205 (1978); see also Michael S. Moore, Act and Crime: The Philosophy of Action and Its Implications for Criminal Law 20–22 (1993); Charles H. Whitebread & Ronald Stevens, Constructive Possession in Narcotics Cases: To Have and Have Not, 58 Va. L. Rev. 751 (1972); Cornelius Nestler, Rechtsgüterschutz und Strafbarkeit des Besitzes von Schußwaffen und Betäubungsmitteln, in Vom unmöglichen Zustand des Strafrechts 65 (1995); Eberhard Struensee, Besitzdelikte, in Festschrift für Gerald Grünwald 713 (Erich Samson et al. eds. 1999).

11. State of New York, Division of Criminal Justice Services, Possession-Related Offenses New York State (Feb. 4, 2000).

12. U.S. Dep't of Justice, Bureau of Justice Statistics, Estimated Number of Arrests, by Type of Drug Law Violation, 1982–99.

13. 392 U.S. 1 (1968).

14. 528 U.S. 119 (2000).

15. Pinkerton v. United States, 328 U.S. 640 (1946) (possession of liquor).

16. United States v. Bass, 404 U.S. 336 (1971) (gun possession).

17. Stone v. Powell, 428 U.S. 465 (1976) (gun possession).

18. McMillan v. Pennsylvania, 477 U.S. 79 (1986) (gun possession).

19. Harmelin v. Michigan, 501 U.S. 957 (1991) (drug possession).

20. United States v. Lopez, 514 U.S. 549 (1995) (gun possession).

21. Apprendi v. New Jersey, 530 U.S. 466 (2000) (gun & bomb possession).

22. This also distinguishes possession from minor offenses the more rigorous, though still far from universal, enforcement of which is often referred to as "zero tolerance."

23. But see The Real War on Crime: The Report of the National Criminal Justice Commission (1996); see also Robert M. Cipes, The Crime War (1968). Though not explicitly about the war on crime as such, there is an excellent, and growing, criminological literature on modern criminal law as social control. See, e.g., David Garland, The Culture of Control: Crime and Social Order in Contemporary Society (2001); Criminology and Social Theory (David Garland & Richard Sparks eds., 2000); Malcolm M. Feeley & Jonathan Simon, The New Penology: Notes on the Emerging Strategy of Corrections and Its Implications, 30 Criminology 449 (1992).

24. For more on Project Exile, see infra text accompanying note 67.

25. For years, crime rates have been on the decline. See Fox Butterfield, Number in Prison Grows Despite Crime Reduction, N.Y. Times, Aug. 10, 2000, at A10.

26. On the connection between rehabilitation and incapacitation, see already Herbert L. Packer, The Limits of the Criminal Sanction 55 (1968).

27. This is not to say, of course, that Communitarians with a capital C have endorsed, or would endorse, this function of criminal law.

28. See generally Carol S. Steiker, Foreword, The Limits of the Preventive State, 88 J. Crim. L. & Criminology 771 (1998); Robinson, supra note 9.

29. Model Penal Code § 1.02(1)(b).

30. The crime war prevents by incapacitation, not deterrence. There can be no deterrence, general or special, of undeterrable predators.

31. United v. Lopez, 514 U.S. 549, 602, 603 (1995) (Stevens. J., dissenting).

32. United States v. Dillard, 214 F.3d 88 (2d Cir. 2000); but see United States v. Singleton, 182 F.3d 7 (D.C. Cir. 1999).

33. Harmelin v. Michigan, 501 U.S. 957, 1002 (1991) (Kennedy, J., concurring) (emphasis added).

34. See, e.g., Peter W. Greenwood & Allan Abrahamse, Selective Incapacita-

tion (1982); John Monahan, Predicting Violent Behavior: An Assessment of Clinical Techniques (1981); Joan Petersilia, Peter W. Greenwood, & Marvin Lavin, Criminal Careers of Habitual Felons (1978); see also Franklin E. Zimring & Gordon Hawkins, Incapacitation: Penal Confinement and the Restraint of Crime (1995); Markus Dirk Dubber, The Unprincipled Punishment of Repeat Offenders: A Critique of California's Habitual Criminal Statute, 43 Stan. L. Rev. 193 (1990).

35. See, e.g., Model Penal Code § 5.06 (Instruments of Crime; Weapons).

36. See id. § 5.01.

37. See infra texts accompanying notes 48–50 & 198–205 in ch. 2.

38. Cf. Arthur P. Scott, Criminal Law in Colonial Virginia 54 (1930) (discussing old law on vagrancy authorizing arrest of "such Persons as they have probable Cause to suspect, as Idlers and Vagrants or suspicious Characters, and who can give no satisfactory account of themselves").

39. See, e.g., N.Y. Veh. & Traf. Law § 1800(b) (penalty for first traffic infraction "fine of not more than one hundred dollars or . . . imprisonment for not more than fifteen days or . . . both").

40. N.Y. Penal Law §§ 120.13–15.

41. See infra text accompanying notes 107–147 in ch. 2.

42. For similar scenarios, taken from U.S. Supreme Court opinions, see infra text accompany notes 108–148 in ch. 2.

43. Cf. Florida v. J. L., 529 U.S. 266 (2000) (anonymous informer's tip regarding illegal gun possession); Alabama v. White, 496 U.S. 325 (1990) (anonymous informer's tip regarding drug possession; drugs found during consensual car search); Adams v. Williams, 407 U.S. 143 (1972) (known informer's tip regarding illegal gun and drug possession; drugs found during search incident to gun possession arrest).

44. See, e.g., David Barstow & David Kocieniewski, Records Show New Jersey Police Knew of Racial Profiling in '96, N.Y. Times, Oct. 12, 2000, at A1, col. 1; John Kifner, Van Shooting Revives Charges of Racial 'Profiling' by New Jersey State Police, N.Y. Times, May 10, 1998, at 33, col. 1; see also Katheryn K. Russell, The Color of Crime (1998) ("driving while black").

45. Max Radin, Enemies of Society, 27 J. Crim. L. & Criminology 308 (1936).

46. Cf. Emile Durkheim, The Division of Labor in Society (George Simpson trans. 1933); George Herbert Mead, The Psychology of Punitive Justice, 23 Am. J. Sociology 577 (1918); Sigmund Freud, Civilization and Its Discontents (Joan Riviere & James Strachey trans. 1963).

47. See Mead, supra note 46.

48. Heinrich Brunner, Abspaltungen der Friedlosigkeit, in Forschungen zur Geschichte des deutschen und französischen Rechtes 444, 458 (1894).

49. John Rawls, The Sense of Justice, 72 Phil. Rev. 281, 302 (1963).

50. Model Penal Code § 1.02(1)(b).

51. See, e.g., Randall Kennedy, The State, Criminal Law, and Racial Discrimination, 107 Harv. L. Rev. 1255, 1255 (1994).

52. See Bureau of Justice Statistics, U.S. Dep't of Justice, Pub. No. NCJ–147005, Crime and Neighborhoods (1994); Bureau of Justice Statistics, U.S. Dep't of Justice, Pub. No. NCJ–147004, Young Black Male Victims: National Crime Victimization Survey (1994).

53. Nixon, supra note 2, at 12936; see also U.S. Dep't of Justice, Bureau of Justice Statistics, Crime and Neighborhoods (June 1994, NCJ 147005); U.S. Dep't of Justice, Bureau of Justice Statistics, Young Black Male Victims: National Crime Victimization Survey (June 1994, NCJ 147004). Nixon, of course, didn't invent freedom from fear as a political concept; Roosevelt did, in 1941. See David M. Kennedy, Freedom From Fear: The American People in Depression and War, 1929–1945 (1999). Nixon, however, turned the ideal inward, by locating the threat within. And so freedom from fear was transformed from a goal of foreign policy, and war, into one of domestic policy, and police.

54. See Dubber, supra note 6 (three-strikes as symbolic policy).

55. Thad H. Westbrook, At Least Treat Us Like Criminals!: South Carolina Responds to Victims' Pleas for Equal Rights, 49 S.C. L. Rev. 575 (1998).

56. Roscoe Pound, Introduction, in Francis Bowes Sayre, A Selection of Cases on Criminal Law xxix, xxxv (1927). For an excellent extended discussion of Pound's views on criminal administration, see Thomas A. Green, Freedom and Criminal Responsibility in the Age of Pound: An Essay on Criminal Justice, 93 Mich. L. Rev. 1915 (1995).

57. Pound, supra note 56, at xxxii.

58. Id. at xxxiv.

59. Francis A. Allen, The Decline of the Rehabilitative Ideal: Penal Policy and Social Purpose (1981); Herbert Morris, Persons and Punishment, 53 The Monist, No. 4, at 475 (1968).

60. Francis Bowes Sayre, Public Welfare Offenses, 33 Colum. L. Rev. 55, 67 (1933).

61. Francis Bowes Sayre, Mens Rea, 45 Harv. L. Rev. 974, 1018 (1932).

62. Sayre, supra note 60, at 68 (emphasis added).

63. Id. at 55.

64. Id. at 78.

65. Id. at 69.

66. Id. at 78.

67. Eric Westervelt, Philadelphia's Crackdown on Criminals Who Possess Illegal Guns, Morning Edition, Nat'l Pub. Radio, Mar. 23, 2000; see also William Clauss & Jay S. Ovsiovitch, "Project Exile" Effort on Gun Crimes Increases Need for Attorneys to Give Clear Advice on Possible Sentences, N.Y.B.J., June 2000, at 35.

N OTES TO C HAPTER 2

1. N.Y. Penal Law §§ 265.01–.05; Model Penal Code §§ 5.06 (Instruments of Crime; Weapons); 5.07 (offensive weapons).

2. New York, N.Y., Admin. Code § 10–131(g).

3. Id. § 10–131(e).

4. Id. § 10–131(h).

5. Id. § 10–131(i).

6. N.Y. Penal Law §§ 270.20, 400.05.

7. Id. § 170.47.

8. Id. § 140.35.

9. Id. §§ 165.40–.65; see also 625 Ill. Comp. Stat. § 5/4–103(a)(1) (possession of stolen vehicle).

10. N.Y. Penal Law arts. 220 & 221.

11. Id. § 220.50.

12. Id. § 220.60.

13. Model Penal Code § 5.06 ("Instruments of Crime; Weapons"); Com. v. Donton, 439 Pa. Super. 406, 654 A.2d 580 (1995).

14. N.Y. Penal Law § 145.65.

15. Id. § 156.35.

16. Id. §§ 165.71–.73.

17. Id. §§ 275.15–.45.

18. Id. § 158.40.

19. Id. §§ 170.20–.30.

20. Id. §§ 170.40–.50.

21. State v. Saiez, 489 So. 2d 1125 (Fla. 1986)

22. N.Y. Penal Law §§ 170.55–.60.

23. Id. § 170.70.

24. 625 Ill. Comp. Stat. § 5/4–104(a)(2).

25. N.Y. Penal Law §§ 225.30–.35.

26. Id. §§ 225.00–.35, 415.00.

27. Id. § 190.45.

28. United States v. Teicher, 987 F.2d 112, 119–21 (2d Cir. 1993); see generally Alan Strudler & Eric W. Orts, Moral Principle in the Law of Insider Trading, 78 Tex. L. Rev. 375, 385 n. 36 (1999) (possession vs. use of inside information).

29. N.Y. Penal Law § 205.25.

30. Stanley v. Georgia, 394 U.S. 557 (1969); N.Y. Penal Law §§ 235.05–.07.

31. N.Y. Penal Law § 263.11; see also Osborne v. Ohio, 495 U.S. 103 (1990) (upholding Ohio Rev. Code § 2907.323(A)(3), criminalizing possession of "material or performance that shows a minor . . . in a state of nudity").

32. N.Y. Penal Law § 230.40.

33. Id. § 250.10.

34. Id. § 270.00.

35. Id. § 270.05.

36. Id. § 145.70.

37. Delmonico v. State, 155 So. 2d 368 (Fla. 1963).

38. La. Rev. Stat. Ann. § 56:326(A)(7)(b) (State v. Wingate, 668 So.2d 1324 (La. App. 1996)).

39. People v. Young, 94 N.Y.2d 171 (1999).

40. State of New York, Division of Criminal Justice Services, Possession Related Offenses New York State (Feb. 4, 2000); State of New York, Division of Criminal Justice Services, Criminal Justice Indicators New York State: 1994–1998 (Dec. 13, 1999).

41. Harmelin v. Michigan, 501 U.S. 957, 1022, 1024 (1991) (White, J., dissenting) (quoting Tr. of Oral Arg. 30–31).

42. State v. Cleppe, 96 Wn. 2d 373 (1981).

43. People v. Almodovar, 62 N.Y.2d 126 (1984). There is such a thing as a defense of "innocent" or "temporary" possession, but this is not a justification defense. The idea behind this awkward defense is not that you didn't possess the gun unlawfully, or with justification, but that you didn't "really" possess the gun at all, say because you had just discovered it and were about to surrender it to the police. Id. at 130.

44. People v. Sierra, 45 N.Y.2d 56 (1978).

45. See, e.g., N.Y. Penal Law § 221.05 (unlawful, as opposed to criminal, possession of marihuana).

45. See Sierra, 45 N.Y.2d at 56.

47. N.Y. Penal Law § 10.00(8).

48. Id. §§ 220.25 (drugs; "knowing"), 265.15 (guns; "unlawful").

49. Id. § 220.25.

50. 2 Frederick Pollock & Frederic William Maitland, The History of English Law before the Time of Edward I 152 (2d ed. 1898; reissued 1968).

51. N.Y. Penal Law §§ 10.00(8), 15.00(2).

52. Heinrich Brunner, Ueber absichtslose Missethat im altdeutschen Strafrechte, in Forschungen zur Geschichte des deutschen und französischen Rechtes 487, 507, 522 (1894).

53. People v. Carter, 53 N.Y.2d 113 (1981) (emphasis added). For an interesting discussion of the differentiated analysis of dangerousness in tort law, see Edward J. Levi, An Introduction to Legal Reasoning 9–27 (1949) (distinguishing among "inherently dangerous," "imminently dangerous," "eminently dangerous," and "latently dangerous").

54. On the notion of criminal law as waste management, see Malcolm M. Feeley & Jonathan Simon, The New Penology: Notes on the Emerging Strategy of Corrections and Its Implications, 30 Criminology 449 (1992).

55. See, e.g., Toxic Substances Control Act, 15 U.S.C. §§ 2601 et seq.

56. N.Y. Envtl. Conserv. Law art. 37.

57. See, e.g., Wash. Rev. Code Ann. § 16.08.080.

58. See, e.g., N.Y. Agric. & Mkts. Law art. 7.

59. See, e.g., Wash. Rev. Code Ann. §§ 16.08.070–.100.

60. N.Y. Penal Code of 1829, ti. 2, art. 1, § 14 (third-degree manslaughter); N.Y. Penal Code of 1881, § 196 (second-degree manslaughter).

61. See, e.g., N.Y. Penal Law ch. 40, pt. 4 ("administrative provisions").

62. N.Y. Penal Law § 400.05.

63. N.Y. Pub. Health Law § 3387.

64. See 21 U.S.C. § 881; Bennis v. Michigan, 516 U.S. 442 (1996).

65. See, e.g., N.Y. Pub. Health Law § 3387 (declaring illegally possessed drugs public nuisances); N.Y. Penal Law § 400.05 (declaring illegally possessed guns public nuisances).

66. See, e.g., Mich. Comp. Laws Ann. § 600.3801, the statute at issue in *Bennis*.

67. See, e.g., Miller v. Schoene, 276 U.S. 272 (1928)

68. See, e.g., N.Y. Pub. Health Law § 3387 (drugs; public nuisances); N.Y. Penal Law § 400.05 (guns; public nuisances); N.Y. Agric. & Mkts. Law § 121 (dogs; dangerous); Wash. Rev. Code Ann. § 16.08.090 (dogs; dangerous).

69. N.Y. Penal Law § 415.00.

70. Mich. Comp. Laws Ann. § 600.3801 ("[a]ny building, vehicle, boat, aircraft, or place used for the purpose of lewdness, assignation or prostitution or gambling, or used by, or kept for the use of prostitutes or other disorderly persons").

71. 21 U.S.C. § 881(4) ("[a]ll conveyances, including aircraft, vehicles, or vessels, which are used, or are intended for use, to transport, or in any manner to facilitate the transportation, sale, receipt, possession, or concealment of [controlled substances]").

72. N.Y. Penal Law § 415.00(7); 21 U.S.C. § 881(e).

73. N.Y. Penal Law § 415.00(7).

74. Id. § 400.05(2); see also 21 U.S.C. § 881(f) (destruction of drugs); N.Y. Pub. Health Law § 3387 (same).

75. N.Y. Agric. & Mkts. Law § 121(4).

76. N.Y. Penal Law § 400.05(3) (emphasis added).

77. 1934 N.J. Laws ch. 155, N.J. Rev. Stat. § 2:136(1) (1937).

78. N.Y. Penal Law § 400.05(1) (guns).

79. See State v. Bash, 130 Wn.2d 594, 607 (1996) (possession of dangerous dog).

80. N.Y. Agric. & Mkts. Law § 108(24).

81. Model Penal Code § 1.02(1)(a).

82. Id. § 1.02(1)(b).

83. N.Y. Agric. & Mkts. Law § 106.

84. Model Penal Code § 1.02(1)(b).

85. U.S. Const. amend. xiii, sec. 1.
86. Cesare Beccaria, Of Crimes and Punishments §§ 16 & 30 (1764).
87. N.Y. Agric. & Mkts. Law § 108(8).
88. See, e.g., Bailey v. Lally, 481 F. Supp. 203, 220–21 (D. Md. 1979).
89. N.Y. Agric. & Mkts. Law art. 7.
90. Id. § 106.
91. Id. § 121(1).
92. Id. § 121(2); cf. Wash. Rev. Code Ann. § 16.08.070(1) & (2) (defining "potentially dangerous dog" and "dangerous dog").
93. N.Y. Agric. & Mkts. Law § 121(5).
94. Id. § 121(1).
95. Id. § 121(2) (emphasis added).
96. Model Penal Code § 3.02(1)(a).
97. Id. § 3.05.
98. Id. § 3.06.
99. Id. § 3.04.
100. Id. § 210.3(1)(b).
101. See also Wash. Rev. Code Ann. § 16.08.070(2) (defining "dangerous dog" as "any dog that . . . has inflicted severe injury on a human being without provocation").
102. See generally Christopher Slobogin, Dangerousness as a Criterion in the Criminal Process, in Law, Mental Health, and Mental Disorder 360, 372 (Bruce D. Sales & Daniel W. Shuman eds. 1996); see also Julia A. Houston, Sex Offender Registration Acts: An Added Dimension to the War on Crime, 28 Ga. L. Rev. 729 (1994).
103. See, e.g., N.Y. Veh. & Traf. Law § 1800(b) (penalty for first traffic infraction "fine of not more than one hundred dollars or by imprisonment for not more than fifteen days or . . . both").
104. See, e.g., United States v. Martinez-Salazar, 528 U.S. 304 (2000).
105. United States v. Rabinowitz, 339 U.S. 56 (1950).
106. Id.
107. 395 U.S. 752 (1969).
108. Chimel v. California, 395 U.S. 752 (1969).
109. 494 U.S. 325 (1990).
110. Id. at 342 (Brennan, J., dissenting).
111. 453 U.S. 454 (1981).
112. 392 U.S. 1 (1968).
113. People v. Atmore, 13 Cal. App. 3d 244 (2d Dist. 1970) (marijuana cigarette); Taylor v. Superior Court, 27 Cal. App. 2d 145 (4th Dist. 1969) (cigarette lighter containing hashish); People v. Watson, 12 Cal. App. 3d 130 (3d Dist. 1970) (bag of marijuana cigarettes).
114. State v. Campbell, 53 N.J. 230 (1969) (lottery slips); see also United

States v. Peep, 490 F.2d 903 (8th Cir. 1974); see generally Charles H. Whitebread & Christopher Slobogin, Criminal Procedure: An Analysis of Cases and Concepts 269–70 (4th ed. 2000).

115. 434 U.S. 106 (1977); Commonwealth v. Mimms, 232 Pa. Super. 486 (1975).

116. 434 U.S. at 107 (emphasis added).

117. 463 U.S. 1032 (1983).

118. Id. at 1035–36 (emphasis added).

119. People v. Long, 94 Mich. App. 338 (1979).

120. U.S.S.G. § 2D1.1 (offense level 20 (18 for 75 pounds, plus two for possession of a dangerous weapon, the knife).

121. Mich. Stat. Ann. § 333.7401(d)(ii) (possessing with intent to deliver controlled substance).

122. Harmelin v. Michigan, 501 U.S. 957 (1991).

123. 267 U.S. 132 (1925).

124. United States v. Martinez-Fuerte, 428 U.S. 543 (1976).

125. Texas v. Brown, 460 U.S. 730 (1983); Merrett v. Moore, 58 F.3d 1547 (11th Cir. 1995); but see Delaware v. Prouse, 440 U.S. 648 (1979).

126. United States v. Lopez, 777 F.2d 543 (10th Cir. 1985).

127. Michigan Dept. of State Police v. Sitz, 496 U.S. 444 (1990).

128. Minnesota v. Dickerson, 508 U.S. 366 (1993).

129. Cf. United States v. Kahn, 41 U.S. 143 (1974).

130. Cf. United States v. Place, 462 U.S. 696 (1983) (dog sniff); United States v. Villamonte-Marquez, 462 U.S. 579 (1983).

131. Coolidge v. New Hampshire, 403 U.S. 443 (1971).

132. 460 U.S. 730 (1983) (drug possession).

133. See already United States v. Lee, 274 U.S. 559, 563 (1927) ("[The] use of a searchlight is comparable to the use of a marine glass or a field glass. It is not prohibited by the Constitution.").

134. Brown v. State, 617 S.W.2d 196, 197 (Tex. Ct. Crim. App. 1981).

135. 517 U.S. 806 (1996).

136. 528 U.S. 119 (2000).

137. 720 Ill. Comp. Stat. § 5/24–1.1.

138. Donald B. Kates, Why Handgun Bans Can't Work 43 (1982).

139. 412 U.S. 218 (1973).

140. Ohio v. Robinette, 519 U.S. 33 (1996) (possession of a controlled substance); United States v. Mendenhall, 446 U.S. 544 (1980) (possession with intent to distribute heroin); Illinois v. Rodriguez, 497 U.S. 177 (1990) (possession of a controlled substance with intent to deliver); Florida v. Jimeno, 500 U.S. 248 (1991) (possession with intent to distribute cocaine).

141. United States v. Watson, 423 U.S. 411 (1976).

142. 427 U.S. 38 (1976).

143. 120 S. Ct. 1375, 1377 (2000).

144. 407 U.S. 143, 145 (1972).

145. State v. Williams, 157 Conn. 114, 115–16 (1968).

146. 528 U.S. 119 (2000).

147. See Harris v. United States, 331 U.S. 145, 175 (1947) (Frankfurter, J., dissenting) (Appendix: Analysis of Decisions Involving Searches and Seizures, from Weeks v. United States, 232 U.S. 383, up to Davis v. United States, 328 U.S. 582).

148. Davis v. United States, 328 U.S. 582 (1946).

149. E.g., Harris v. United States, 331 U.S. 145 (1947).

150. E.g., United States v. Rabinowitz, 339 U.S. 56 (1950).

151. E.g., Henry v. United States, 361 U.S. 98 (1959).

152. E.g., Smith v. California, 361 U.S. 147 (1959).

153. E.g., Beck v. Ohio, 379 U.S. 89 (1964).

154. E.g., Stanford v. Texas, 379 U.S. 476 (1965).

155. E.g., Liparota v. United States, 471 U.S. 419 (1985).

156. E.g., United States v. Alvarez-Sanchez, 511 U.S. 350 (1994).

157. Lanzetta v. New Jersey, 306 U.S. 451 (1939).

158. 1934 N.J. Laws ch. 155, N.J. Rev. Stat. § 2:136 (1937) (some emphases added).

159. See, e.g., Jacksonville, Fla., Ordinance Code § 26–57 (quoted in Papachristou v. City of Jacksonville, 405 U.S. 156, 158 (1972)) ("disorderly persons . . . shall be deemed vagrants").

160. Pinkerton v. United States, 328 U.S. 640 (1946).

161. See infra text accompanying notes 223–264.

162. See supra text accompanying notes 48–50.

163. 379 U.S. 476 (1965).

164. Reid v. Georgia, 448 U.S. 438 (1980); Florida v. Royer, 460 U.S. 491 (1983); United States v. Sokolow, 490 U.S. 1 (1989).

165. United States v. Freed, 401 U.S. 601 (1971) (guns); Liparota v. United States, 471 U.S. 419 (1985) (foodstamps); Staples v. United States, 511 U.S. 600 (1994) (guns); Rogers v. United States, 522 U.S. 252 (1998) (guns).

166. United States v. Bass, 404 U.S. 336 (1971).

167. United States v. Lopez, 514 U.S. 549 (1995).

168. Harmelin v. Michigan, 501 U.S. 957 (1991).

169. United States v. Gonzales, 520 U.S. 1 (1997) (emphasis added).

170. 18 U.S.C. § 924(c).

171. United States v. Gonzales, 65 F.3d 814 (10th Cir. 1995), rev'd, 520 U.S. 1 (1997).

172. 18 U.S.C. § 924(c)(1)(C).

173. See William Clauss & Jay S. Ovsiovitch, "Project Exile" Effort on Gun Crimes Increases Need for Attorneys to Give Clear Advice on Possible Sentences, N.Y.B.J., June 2000, at 35, 38.

174. Bailey v. United States, 516 U.S. 137 (1995).

175. Mandatory Minimum Prison Sentences for Firearms Violations, 105 P.L. 386, 112 Stat. 3469, 105th Cong., 2d Sess., Nov. 13, 1998 (emphasis added).

176. U.S.S.G. §§ 2D1.1(b)(1), 2D2.1(b)(1).

177. See Mistretta v. United States, 488 U.S. 361 (1989); Williams v. United States, 503 U.S. 193 (1992) (policy statement); Stinson v. United States, 508 U.S. 36 (1993) (commentary).

178. Jones v. United States, 526 U.S. 227, 229 (1999) (quoting old 18 U.S.C. § 2119).

179. N.Y. Penal Law § 140.17(1).

180. People v. Cantarella, 160 Misc. 2d 8 (N.Y. Sup. Ct. 1993).

181. U.S.S.G. § 2A2.3(a)(1).

182. U.S.S.G. § 2A6.2(b)(1)(C).

183. McMillan v. Pennsylvania, 477 U.S. 79 (1986) (sentence enhancement for "visible possession of a firearm").

184. 18 U.S.C. § 3583(g); see also Spencer v. Kemna, 523 U.S. 1 (1998).

185. Ted Conover, Newjack: Guarding Sing Sing 97 (2000).

186. Id. at 104–05 (emphasis added).

187. Id. at 104.

188. Id.

189. Id.

190. Id.

191. Id. at 105.

192. Id. at 106.

193. N.Y. Penal Law § 265.20(2).

194. See U.S.S.G. § 2P1.2 (Providing or Possessing Contraband in Prison); 18 U.S.C. § 1791.

195. In one of the more bizarre possession cases that made it before the Supreme Court, the defendant was convicted under the federal felon-in-possession statute after using a gun to try to kill himself:

> At about 4 a.m. on August 25, 1990, a police officer stopped petitioner Terry Lee Shannon, a convicted felon, on a street in Tupelo, Mississippi. For reasons not explained in the record before us, the officer asked Shannon to accompany him to the station house to speak with a detective. After telling the officer that he did not want to live anymore, Shannon walked across the street, pulled a pistol from his coat, and shot himself in the chest. Shannon survived his suicide attempt and was indicted for unlawful possession of a firearm by a felon in violation of 18 U.S.C. § 922(g)(1).

Shannon v. United States, 512 U.S. 573, 578 (1994). Shannon was sentenced to "fifteen years without the possibility of probation or parole." He raised an insanity defense, without success.

196. 18 U.S.C. § 922(g); 18 U.S.C. § 924(e)(1) (15 year minimum); U.S.S.G. § 2K2.1.

197. Robert J. McCarthy, Gun-Toting Criminals Faced with Disarming Sign, Buffalo News, July 11, 2000, at 1B.

198. See, e.g., County Court of Ulster Co. v. Allen, 442 U.S. 140 (1979).

199. See, e.g., Wright v. West, 505 U.S. 277 (1992) (possession of stolen property as presumptive evidence of larceny); see generally Richard J. Bonnie & Charles H. Whitebread, II, The Forbidden Fruit and the Tree of Knowledge: An Inquiry into the Legal History of American Marijuana Prohibition, 56 Va. L. Rev. 971, 1086 (1970); see also Charles H. Whitebread & Ronald Stevens, Constructive Possession in Narcotics Cases: To Have and Have Not, 58 Va. L. Rev. 751, 754 (1972) (possession of stolen property as presumptive evidence of larceny).

200. Barnes v. United States, 412 U.S. 837 (1973) (possession of stolen property as presumptive evidence of knowledge that property was stolen); N.Y. Penal Law §§ 165.55, 170.71, 225.35; see also id. § 265.15(6) (defacement).

201. See, e.g., N.Y. Penal Law §§ 158.00 (possession of five or more public benefit cards presumptive evidence of intent to use them for fraudulent purposes), 265.15(4) (unlawful use of explosive substance), 270.00(2)(c) (sale of fireworks), 270.05(3) (use of noxious material); Model Penal Code § 5.06 ("purpose to employ [weapon] criminally").

202. See, e.g., N.Y. Penal Law §§ 170.27, 235.10.

203. Leary v. United States, 395 U.S. 6, 36 n.63 (1969).

204. People v. Saunders, 85 N.Y.2d 339 (1995) (attempted weapon possession); see also State v. Clark, 527 S.E.2d 319 (N.C. App. 2001) (attempted *constructive* drug possession).

205. United States v. Peoni, 100 F.2d 401 (1938) (Hand, J.) (conspiracy to possess counterfeit money); see also Pinkerton v. United States, 328 U.S. 640 (1946) (conspiracy to possess liquor).

206. See supra text accompanying notes 184–194.

207. Stanley v. Georgia, 394 U.S. 557, 568 n.11 (1969).

208. 478 U.S. 186, 195 (1986) (citing *Stanley*).

209. 2 & 3 Vict. c. 71, § 30.

210. Id. § 36.

211. Id. §§ 24, 25.

212. See infra text accompanying notes 270–274.

213. See William J. Novak, The People's Welfare: Law & Regulation in Nineteenth-Century America 178–81 (1996) (discussing Maine's 1851 Act for the Suppression of Drinking Houses and Tippling Shops and its progeny).

214. Nancy Cohen, New Law in Connecticut Allows Police to Seize Guns from People They Believe to Be Dangerous, Even When No Crime Has Been Committed, All Things Considered, Nat'l Pub. Radio, Jan. 18, 2000.

215. Arthur P. Scott, Criminal Law in Colonial Virginia 273–74 (1930).

216. Christopher G. Tiedeman, A Treatise on the Limitations of Police Power in the United States Considered from Both a Civil and Criminal Standpoint 124 (1886).

217. See supra text accompanying notes 1–51.

218. Eric Foner, Nothing but Freedom: Emancipation and Its Legacy 51–52 (1983).

219. Jacksonville, Fla., Ordinance Code § 26–57 (quoted in Papachristou v. City of Jacksonville, 405 U.S. 156, 158 (1972)).

220. Scott, supra note 215, at 273–74.

221. State v. Hogan, 63 Ohio St. 202, 211 (Ohio 1900) (last emphasis added).

222. Papachristou, 405 U.S. at 164.

223. E.g., Regina v. Dugdale, 1 El. & Bl. 435, 439 (1853) (Coleridge, J.).

224. See, e.g., Rex v. Lennard, 1 Leach 90 (1772) (applying 8 & 9 Will. 3 c. 26 (1697)).

225. See Regina v. Prince, 2 L.R. Cr. Cas. Res. 154 (1875).

226. Robinson v. California, 370 U.S. 660 (1962).

227. Id. at 667.

228. Id. at 664 (emphasis added).

229. See, e.g., Model Penal Code § 2.01(4); N.Y. Penal Law § 15.00(2).

230. See, e.g., State v. Cleppe, 96 Wn. 2d 373 (1981).

231. State v. Smyth, 14 R.I. 100, 101 (1883).

232. N.Y. Penal Law §§ 265.01, 265.20; 18 U.S.C. § 922(g)(1)–(11).

233. 18 U.S.C. § 922(g)(1)–(11).

234. N.Y. Penal Law § 265.20.

235. Id. § 265.01(4) (convicted of a felony or serious offense).

236. Id. § 265.01(5).

237. 114 Cong. Rec. 14,773 (1968) (statement of Sen. Long). But see Tennessee v. Garner, 471 U.S. 1, 14 (1985) ("the assumption that a 'felon' is more dangerous than a misdemeanant [is] untenable" given the proliferation of felonies in modern criminal law).

238. State v. Hogan, 63 Ohio St. 202 (Ohio 1900) (applying Ohio law prohibiting any "tramp" from "carrying a firearm, or other dangerous weapon").

239. Tiedeman, supra note 216, at 124.

240. United States v. Leviner, 31 F. Supp. 2d 23, 26–27 (D. Mass. 1998).

241. N.Y. Elec. Law §§ 5–102, 5–106(2)–(5). See generally Patricia Allard & Marc Mauer, Regaining the Vote, An Assessment of Activity Relating to Felon Disenfranchisement Laws (2000); Note, The Disenfranchisement of Ex-Felons: Citizenship, Criminality and 'The Purity of the Ballot Box,' 102 Harv. L. Rev. 1300 (1989).

242. See Ambach v. Norwick, 441 U.S. 68 (1979); Sugarman v. Dougall, 413 U.S. 634 (1973).

243. N.Y. Jud. Law § 510; cf. Ambach v. Norwick, 441 U.S. 68 (1979).

244. N.Y. Exec. Law § 513(3) (citizen & good moral character); see Foley v. Connelie, 435 U.S. 291 (1978).

245. 4 William Blackstone, Commentaries on the Laws of England 249 (1769).

246. Id. at 250.

247. Id. at 253.

248. Id. at 169–70; Vagrancy Act, 1744, 17 Geo 2 c. 5.

249. Id. at 170.

250. N.Y. Penal Law § 265.01 ("a person is guilty of criminal possession of a weapon in the fourth degree when . . . [h]e possesses any firearm").

251. Shapiro v. New York City Police Dep't (License Division), 157 Misc. 2d 28 (N.Y. 1993).

252. Id.

253. N.Y. Penal Law § 400.00(1)(a).

254. Shapiro, 157 Misc. 2d at 28.

255. 8 U.S.C. § 1427(a)(3).

256. See supra texts accompanying notes 48–50 & 198–205.

257. 17 Geo. 3 c. 56, § 14 (1777) (emphasis added).

258. 14 & 15 Vict. c. 19, § 1 (1851) (emphasis added).

259. See also N.Y. Agric. & Mkts. Law art. 7 (dog licensing).

260. New York, N.Y., Admin. Code § 10–131(a)(1).

261. 331 U.S. 145, 183, 187–88 (1947).

262. People v. Almodovar, 62 N.Y.2d 126, 129 (1984).

263. See supra text accompanying note 43.

264. N.Y. Penal Law art. 405.

265. Blackstone, supra note 245, at 176.

266. Id. at 127.

267. Id. at 162.

268. John Locke, Second Treatise of Government: An Essay Concerning the True Original, Extent and End of Civil Government § 52 (1690).

269. See supra text accompanying note 219.

270. For an interpretation of American slave law as "boundary law" and police measure, see Jonathan A. Bush, Free to Enslave: The Foundations of Colonial American Slave Law, 5 Yale J.L. & Humanities 417 (1993).

271. See generally Robert Cottrol & Raymond Diamond, The Second Amendment: Toward an Afro-Americanist Reconsideration, 80 Geo. L.J. 331 (1991).

272. See, e.g., An Act for preventing Negroes [sic] Insurrections, 1680, 2 Va. Stat. 481 (William Waller Hening ed. 1810) ("it shall not be lawfull for any negroe or other slave to carry or arme himselfe with any club, staffe, gunn, sword or any other weapon of defence or offence"); An Act for the better ordering and governing of Negroes and Slaves, 1712, 7 S.C. Stat. 352, 353 (David J. McCord ed.

1840) ("negro houses to be searched diligently and effectually, once every four-teen days, for fugitive and runaway slaves, guns, swords, clubs, and any other mischievous weapons"); Black Code, ch. 33, § 19, 1806 La. Acts 150, 160 (1807) ("no slave shall by day or by night, carry any visible or hidden arms, not even with a permission for so doing"); An Act to provide for the more effectual performance of Patrol Duty, 1819 S.C. Acts 29, 31 ("it shall not be lawful for any slave, except in the company and presence of some white person, to carry or make use of any fire arms, or other offensive weapon, unless such slave shall have a ticket or license in writing from his owner or overseer, or be employed to hunt . . . , or shall be a watchman"); N.C. Rev. Code of 1854, ch. 107, § 26 ("[n]o slave shall go armed with gun, sword, or other weapon, or shall keep any such weapon, or shall hunt or range with a gun in the woods").

273. An Act to Govern Patrols, § 8, 1825 Fla. Acts 52, 55.

274. Act of Feb. 17, 1833, ch. 671, §§ 15, 17, 1833 Fla. Acts 26, 29–30.

275. See, e.g., An Act to punish certain offences [sic] therein named, and for other purposes, § 1, 1865 Miss. Laws 165 (approved Nov. 29, 1865) ("no freedman, free negro or mulatto, not in the military service of the United States Government, and not licensed so to do by the board of police of his or her county, shall keep or carry firearms of any kind, or any ammunition, dirk or bowie knife"). In legislative debate, proponents of the Civil Rights Act, 14 Stat. 27 (1866), cited racist gun possession statutes as evidence that federal intervention was necessary. See, e.g., Cong. Globe, 39th Cong., 1st Sess., pt. 1, 474 (Jan. 29, 1866) (statement of Sen. Trumbull); see also Freedmen's Bureau Act, 14 Stat. 173 (1866) (guaranteeing "full and equal benefit of all laws and proceedings concerning personal liberty, personal security, . . . including the constitutional right to bear arms"); see generally Stephen P. Halbrook, Personal Security, Personal Liberty, and "The Constitutional Right to Bear Arms": Visions of the Framers of the Fourteenth Amendment, 5 Seton Hall Const. L.J. 341 (1995) (discussing legislative history).

276. Watson v. Stone, 148 Fla. 516, 524, 4 So. 2d 700, 703 (1941) (Buford, J., concurring) (emphasis added) (discussing Florida gun possession law).

277. Cf. Wash. Rev. Code Ann. § 16.08.080 (police dogs exempted from prohibition of possession of unregistered dangerous dog).

278. See Stefan B. Tahmassebi, Gun Control and Racism, 2 Geo. Mason U. Civ. Rts. L.J. 67 (1991).

279. U.S. Dep't of Justice, Office of Justice Programs, Bureau of Justice Statistics,, Weapons Offenses and Offenders 2 (Nov. 1995, NCJ 155284).

NOTES TO CHAPTER 3

1. On the distinction between use and abuse in the context of possession, see already Beebe v. State, 6 Ind. 401, 419–20 (1855).

2. Elizabeth Anne Stanko, The Impact of Victim Assessment on Prosecutors' Screening Decisions: The Case of the New York County's District Attorney's Office, 16 L. & Soc'y Rev. 225 (1981); see generally Towards a Critical Victimology (Ezzat A. Fattah ed. 1992).

3. See generally Markus Dirk Dubber, The Victim in American Penal Law: A Systematic Overview, 3 Buff. Crim. L. Rev. 3 (1999).

4. 2 Frederick Pollock & Frederic William Maitland, The History of English Law before the Time of Edward I 54 (2d ed. 1898; reissued 1968).

5. Id. at 42.

6. See, e.g., Wayne R. LaFave & Austin W. Scott, Jr., Criminal Law 703–04 (2d ed. 1986).

7. Commonwealth v. Crow, 303 Pa. 91 (1931); People v. Otis, 235 N.Y. 421 (1923); Ellis v. Commonwealth, 186 Ky. 494 (1920); State v. May, 20 Iowa 305 (1866).

8. Smith v. State, 187 Ind. 253 (1918).

9. Damaging property of another person. See, e.g., N.Y. Penal Law § 145.00; Model Penal Code § 220.3.

10. Inflicting minor or serious physical harm on another person. See, e.g., N.Y. Penal Law §§ 120.00, 120.05; Model Penal Code § 211.1(1) & (2).

11. Restraining another person so as to interfere substantially with his liberty. See, e.g., N.Y. Penal Law § 135.05; Model Penal Code § 212.3.

12. Entering any building without permission. See, e.g., N.Y. Penal Law § 140.05; Model Penal Code § 221.2.

13. Intentionally causing the death of another person. See, e.g., N.Y. Penal Law § 125.25; Model Penal Code § 210.2.

14. See, e.g., Oystead v. Shed, 13 Mass. 520 (1816).

15. N.Y. Penal Law § 145.00 (criminal mischief).

16. Model Penal Code § 221.2 (criminal trespass).

17. N.Y. Penal Law § 135.05 (unlawful imprisonment).

18. Model Penal Code § 212.3 (false imprisonment).

19. Cf. N.Y. Penal Law § 265.20.

20. Analogously, in tax law, claiming an exemption is different from claiming a deduction. A deduction reduces tax liability; an exemption denies it altogether. To claim an exemption is not to explain one's failure to pay taxes but to assert that one had no obligation to pay any in the first place.

21. It goes without saying that state officials today also enjoy all manner of broad and explicit immunity, qualified and absolute, from all manner of civil liability, even for constitutional violations. See Harlow v. Fitzgerald, 457 U.S. 800, 818 (1982); see also Imbler v. Pachtman, 424 U.S. 409, 431 (1976) (prosecutors entitled to absolute immunity); Pierson v. Ray, 386 U.S. 547, 553–55 (1967) (so are judges).

22. See, e.g., Smith v. State, 187 Ind. 253, 256 (1918) (quoting Commonwealth v. Rourke, 10 Cush. (Mass.) 397, 399 (1852)).

23. People v. Otis, 235 N.Y. 421, 423 (1923). For an analogous provision in

current law, see 21 U.S.C. § 881(a) (drug-related forfeiture; "[t]he following shall be subject to forfeiture to the United States and no property right shall exist in them").

24. Id. at 423–24.

25. Wynehamer v. People, 13 N.Y. 378 (1856) (applying Act for the prevention of intemperance, pauperism, and crime, of Apr. 9, 1855); see also Beebe v. State, 6 Ind. 401, 419–20 (1855).

26. William J. Novak, The People's Welfare: Law & Regulation in Nineteenth-Century America 173 (1996).

27. Id.

28. Id. at 179.

29. Fisher v. McGirr, 67 Gray 1 (Mass. 1854).

30. Beebe v. State, 6 Ind. 401 (1855).

31. Id. at 416.

32. Id. at 415.

33. Wynehamer v. People, 13 N.Y. 378 (1856).

34. Id. at 388–89.

35. Id. at 385.

36. Christopher G. Tiedeman, A Treatise on the Limitations of Police Power in the United States Considered from Both a Civil and Criminal Standpoint 499–500 (1886).

37. State v. Gilman, 33 W. Va. 146, 149 (1889).

38. State v. Smyth, 14 R.I. 100, 101 (1883).

39. Wynehamer, 13 N.Y. at 415.

40. 1 Joel Prentiss Bishop, New Commentaries on the Criminal Law upon a New System of Legal Exposition 111 (1892).

41. Regina v. Dugdale, 1 El. & Bl. 435, 439 (1853) (Coleridge, J.).

42. 8 & 9 Will. 3 c. 26 (1697) (quoted in Rex v. Lennard, 1 Leach 90 (1772)).

43. Ex parte Mon Luck, 29 Ore. 421 (1896).

44. Id. at 428.

45. Id.

46. Id. at 427.

47. Ex parte Yung Jon, 28 F. 308 (D. Ore. 1886).

48. Id. at 312.

49. Id. For an extended exploration of this question a century later, see John Hart Ely, Legislative and Administrative Motivation in Constitutional Law, 79 Yale L.J. 1205 (1970).

50. Lucy E. Salyer, Laws Harsh as Tigers: Chinese Immigrants and the Shaping of the Modern Immigration Laws (1995).

51. 163 U.S. 537, 561 (1896) (Harlan, J., dissenting).

52. United States v. Hing Quong Chow, 53 F. 233, 234 (C.C.E.D. La. 1892) (citations omitted).

53. Id.

54. Id. at 235.

55. New York v. Miln, 36 U.S. (11 Pet.) 102, 142–43 (1837).

56. Richard J. Bonnie & Charles H. Whitebread, II, The Forbidden Fruit and the Tree of Knowledge: An Inquiry into the Legal History of American Marijuana Prohibition, 56 Va. L. Rev. 971, 1035 (1970).

57. Id. at 1096.

58. Id. at 1100–01; see also People v. Valot, 33 Mich. App. 49, 51 (1971) ("hippie-type people").

59. 2 Frederick Pollock & Frederic William Maitland, The History of English Law before the Time of Edward I 463 (2d ed. 1898; reissued 1968).

60. Id. at 45.

61. Laws of William the Conqueror § 3.

62. United States v. Smith, 27 F. Cas. 1147 (C.C.D. Mass. 1792).

63. 4 William Blackstone, Commentaries on the Laws of England 284 (1769).

64. N.Y. Penal Law § 120.08.

65. Id. § 120.11.

66. Id. § 120.05(3).

67. Id. § 125.27(1)(a)(i), (ii), (iii).

68. Id. § 195.06 (emphasis added).

69. Id. § 240.20(6).

70. Riot Act, 1714, 1 Geo c. 5.

71. N.Y. Penal Law § 205.30.

72. Id. § 195.10.

73. Id. § 215.58.

74. Id. § 270.15.

75. Id. §§ 215.50 & 215.51.

76. Id. § 215.50(1).

77. Id. § 215.50(3).

78. Id. § 215.50(4).

79. Id. § 215.50(6).

80. Id. § 215.51(a).

81. Id. § 215.51(d).

82. Id. § 215.60.

83. Id. § 215.65.

84. Id. § 215.66.

85. Id. § 265.01(6).

86. Id. § 265.20(1)(f).

87. Id. §§ 190.25 & .26.

88. See generally Markus Dirk Dubber, Recividist Statutes as Arational Punishment, 43 Buff. L. Rev. 689 (1995).

89. See, e.g., N.Y. Penal Law § 125.27(1)(a)(9).

90. See, e.g., Strickland v. Washington, 466 U.S. 668 (1984); Agan v. Singletary, 12 F.2d 1012 (11th Cir. 1994); see also Welsh S. White, The Death Penalty in the Nineties: An Examination of the Modern System of Capital Punishment 53–72 (1991).

91. Klaus Lüderssen, Strafrecht als schwarzer Mann, in Abschaffen des Strafens? 17, 18 (1995); Markus Dirk Dubber, American Plea Bargains, German Lay Judges, and the Crisis of Criminal Procedure, 49 Stan. L. Rev. 547, 604 (1997).

92. U.S.S.G. § 3E1.1.

93. Id. § 5K1.1.

94. N.Y. Penal Law § 400.05(3).

95. See generally Ted Conover, Newjack: Guarding Sing Sing (2000).

96. United States v. Helmsley, 941 F.2d 71, 101 (2d Cir. 1991), cert. denied, 502 U.S. 1091 (1992).

97. Cal. Penal Code § 1202.4.

98. See supra text accompanying notes 56–66 in ch. 1.

99. People v. Robinson, G99 N.E.2d 1086, 1093 (Ill. App. Ct. 1998), vacated, 719 N.E.2d 662 (Ill. 1999).

100. Francis Bowes Sayre, Public Welfare Offenses, 33 Colum. L. Rev. 55, 79 (1933).

101. Id. at 79 n.87.

102. 258 U.S. 250 (1922).

103. Id. at 251.

104. Id. at 252 (quoting Shevlin-Carpenter Co. v. Minnesota, 218 U. S. 57, 69, 70 (1910)).

105. Sayre, supra note 100, at 80.

106. 218 U. S. 57 (1910).

107. United States v. Dotterweich, 320 U.S. 277, 285 (1943).

108. See generally Markus Dirk Dubber, Penal Panopticon: The Idea of a Modern Model Penal Code, 4 Buff. Crim. L. Rev. 53 (2000).

109. See, e.g., Model Penal Code §§ 1.02(3), 1.13(9)–(10), 2.20(3)–(5) (interpretive guidelines).

110. See Gerard E. Lynch, Toward a Model Penal Code, Second (Federal?): The Challenge of the Special Part, 2 Buff. Crim. L. Rev. 297 (2000).

111. Model Penal Code § 7.08.

112. See, e.g., id. § 303.1(1)(a).

113. See, e.g., id. § 303.6(1).

114. See id. §§ 3.01 to 5.07 cmt. at 186–201 (Official Draft and Revised Comments 1985).

115. Model Penal Code § 4.08.

116. See Markus Dirk Dubber, Reforming American Penal Law, 90 J. Crim. L. & Criminology 49, 73–74 (1999).

117. See, e.g., Model Penal Code §§ 1.01 to 2.03 cmt. 240–41 (negligence), 262 (causation) (Official Draft and Revised Comments 1985).

118. See Christopher Waldrep, Due Process for Slaves in Mississippi (unpublished manuscript 1995).

119. See Markus Dirk Dubber, The German Jury and the Metaphysical *Volk*: From Romantic Idealism to Nazi Ideology, 43 Am. J. Comp. L. 227, 263–67 (1995).

120. Herbert Wechsler, The Challenge of a Model Penal Code, 65 Harv. L. Rev. 1097 (1952).

121. Jerome Michael & Herbert Wechsler, A Rationale of the Law of Homicide I & II, 37 Colum. L. Rev. 701, 1261 (1937).

122. Sayre, supra note 100, at 65 n.33, 75, 79.

123. Id. at 75.

124. Model Penal Code §§ 1.04(5)., 2.05

125. Model Penal Code 241 (Proposed Official Draft 1962).

126. Model Penal Code §§ 1.04(5), 6.03(6).

127. See, e.g., N.Y. Penal Law § 10.00(3).

128. Sayre, supra note 100, at 79.

129. Model Penal Code (Official Draft and Explanatory Notes) § 1.02, at 3 (explanatory note) (1985).

130. Model Penal Code § 1.02(1)(a).

131. Wechsler, supra note 120, at 1123.

132. See Henry M. Hart, Jr., The Aims of the Criminal Law, 23 Law & Contemp. Problems 401, 425 (1958).

133. See generally Dubber, supra note 108, at 66–73.

134. See, e.g., Model Penal Code (Official Draft and Explanatory Notes) § 1.02, at 3 (explanatory note) (1985) ("[t]he major goal is to forbid and prevent conduct that threatens substantial harm to individual or public interests").

135. Model Penal Code § 1.02(1)(a).

136. Id. § 1.01(1).

137. Model Penal Code and Commentaries: Part II (Definition of Specific Crimes) §§ 220.1 to 230.5, at 157 n.99 (Official Draft and Revised Comments 1980).

138. Model Penal Code arts. 210–213.

139. Id. § 211.2.

140. Model Penal Code (Official Draft and Explanatory Notes) art. 211, at 125 (explanatory note) (1985).

141. Model Penal Code § 211.2 (emphasis added).

142. Model Penal Code and Commentaries (Official Draft and Revised Comments): Part I (General Provisions) §§ 3.01 to 5.07, at 323 (1985); see also id. at 325.

143. Model Penal Code § 5.01(2).

144. Id.

145. Id. §§ 5.06 & .07.

146. Id. § 5.06.

147. 14 & 15 Vict. c. 19, § 1 (1851).

148. Model Penal Code § 5.06(2).

149. Id.

150. Id. § 5.06(3).

151. Model Penal Code § 2.01(1).

152. Id. § 1.02(1)(b) (emphasis added).

153. Id. § 2.01(4).

154. Model Penal Code and Commentaries (Official Draft and Revised Comments): Part II (Definition of Specific Crimes) §§ 220.1 to 230.5, at 157 (1980) (emphasis added).

155. N.Y. Agric. & Mkts. Law § 108(24).

156. Section 1.02(1)(a) originally referred to "individual and public interests." See Model Penal Code § 1.02(1)(a) (Tentative Draft No. 4, 1955) (emphasis added). The crucial change from "and" to "or" was made shortly before the completion of the Model Code to "eliminate an ambiguity" mentioned in the proceedings of a 1960 conference on "law and electronics." See Model Penal Code and Commentaries (Official Draft and Revised Comments) § 1.02, n.3 (1985) (citing Layman E. Allen, Logic and Law, in Law and Electronics: The Challenge of a New Era—A Pioneer Analysis of the Implications of the New Computer Technology for the Improvement of the Administration of Justice 187–98 (Edgar A. Jones Jr. ed. 1962)).

157. Model Penal Code 241 (Proposed Official Draft 1962).

158. Id.

159. Model Penal Code § 1.13(8).

160. Model Penal Code and Commentaries (Official Draft and Revised Comments): Part II (Definition of Specific Crimes) §§ 220.1 to 230.5, at 157 (1980).

161. Model Penal Code § 4.02. See, e.g., McGautha v. California, 402 U.S. 183, 202 (1971); Gregg v. Georgia, 428 U.S. 153, 158, 190–91, 194 (1976); Proffitt v. Florida, 428 U.S. 242, 247 (1976); California v. Ramos, 463 U.S. 992, 1009 (1983).

162. Model Penal Code 241 (Proposed Official Draft 1962).

NOTES TO CHAPTER 4

1. 4 William Blackstone, Commentaries on the Laws of England 176 (1769).

2. Id. at 162.

3. Thomas M. Cooley, A Treatise on the Constitutional Limitations Which Rest upon the Legislative Power of the States of the American Union 704 n.1 (6th ed. 1890); Christopher G. Tiedeman, A Treatise on the Limitations of Police Power in the United States Considered from Both a Civil and Criminal

Standpoint 2 (1886); Ernst Freund, The Police Power: Public Policy and Constitutional Rights 2 (1904).

4. Commonwealth v. Steinberg, 362 A.2d 379, 391 (Pa. Super. 1976) (quoting Commonwealth v. McHale, 97 Pa. 397, 408 (1881)).

5. See, e.g., Wayne R. LaFave & Austin W. Scott, Jr., Criminal Law 128 (2d ed. 1986).

6. This is how Blackstone identified himself on the title pages of the Commentaries. The office was a sinecure that Blackstone accepted after turning down the position of solicitor general. Stanley N. Katz, Introduction to Book I, in 1 William Blackstone, Commentaries on the Laws of England iii, iv (1979) (1763); see also Bernard Baylin, The Ideological Origins of the American Revolution 171 (enlarged ed. 1992) (1967) (revolutionary pamphleteer referring to Blackstone as a "*court* lawyer" and adding "*Mr. Blackstone is solicitor to the Queen.*").

7. 1 William Blackstone, Commentaries on the Laws of England 239 (1763).

8. On autonomy and personhood, see, e.g., S. I. Benn, "Freedom, Autonomy and the Concept of a Person," 76 Proceedings of the Aristotelian Society (new series) 109 (1975/76).

9. See, e.g., Andrew C. McLaughlin, The Foundations of American Constitutionalism 83–84 (1932).

10. John Rawls, A Theory of Justice (1971); Jürgen Habermas, Faktizität und Geltung: Beiträge zur Diskurstheorie des Rechts und des demokratischen Rechtsstaats (1992; enlarged ed. 1998). That's not to say that the basic view of criminal law that underlies this book qualifies as either "Rawlsian" or "Habermasian," whatever that might mean. For one thing, both Rawls and Habermas studiously avoided questions of criminal law, for different reasons. For a summary of Rawls's occasional remarks on the subject, see Jutta Wittig, Die Aufrechterhaltung gesellschaftlicher Stabilität bei John Rawls, 107 Zeitschrift für die gesamte Strafrechtswissenschaft 251 (1995). The closest thing to a Habermasian account of criminal law can be found in Klaus Günther, Möglichkeiten einer diskursethischen Begründung des Strafrechts, in Recht und Moral: Beiträge zu einer Standortbestimmung 205 (Heike Jung, Heinz Müller-Dietz & Ulfrid Neumann eds. 1991).

11. In American criminal law scholarship, the notion of autonomy has received particular attention in the literature on sex offenses (where criminalization is said to *protect* the *victim's* autonomy) and on so-called victimless crimes (where criminalization is said to *violate* the *offender's* autonomy). See, e.g., Note, Feminist Legal Analysis and Sexual Autonomy: Using Statutory Rape Laws as an Illustration, 112 Harv. L. Rev. 1065 (1999); Dorothy E. Roberts, Rape, Violence, and Women's Autonomy, 69 Chi.–Kent L. Rev. 359 (1993); Stephen J. Schulhofer, Taking Sexual Autonomy Seriously: Rape Law and Beyond, 11 L. & Phil. 35 (1992); Gerald Dworkin, Devlin Was Right: Law and the Enforcement of Morality, 40 Wm. & Mary L. Rev. 927 (1999); Lawrence C. Becker, Crimes against Au-

tonomy: Gerald Dworkin on the Enforcement of Morality, 40 Wm. & Mary L. Rev. 959 (1999).

12. Cf. Jean Hampton, Correcting Harms Versus Righting Wrongs: The Goal of Retribution, 39 UCLA L. Rev. 1659 (1992); see also Stephen Paul Brown, Punishment and the Restoration of Rights, 3 Punishment & Soc'y 485 (2001).

13. See infra text accompanying notes 62–71 in ch. 6.

14. On the latter point, see, e.g., Herbert Morris, Persons and Punishment, 53 The Monist, No. 4, at 475 (1968); Francis A. Allen, The Decline of the Rehabilitative Ideal: Penal Policy and Social Purpose (1981).

15. Thad H. Westbrook, Note, At Least Treat Us Like Criminals!: South Carolina Responds to Victims' Pleas for Equal Rights, 49 S.C. L. Rev. 575 (1998).

16. Elizabeth Anne Stanko, The Impact of Victim Assessment on Prosecutors' Screening Decisions: The Case of the New York County's District Attorney's Office, 16 L. & Soc'y Rev. 225 (1981); see generally Towards a Critical Victimology (Ezzat A. Fattah ed. 1992).

17. Randall Kennedy, Race, Crime and the Law (1997).

18. Uniform Victims of Crime Act (National Conference of Commissioners on Uniform State Laws) 4 (1992) (Prefatory Note).

19. See Jan Phillip Reemtsma, Das Recht des Opfers auf die Bestrafung des Täters—als Problem (1999).

20. See Markus Dirk Dubber, The Right to Be Punished: Autonomy and Its Demise in Modern Penal Thought, 16 L. & Hist. Rev. 113 (1998); Herbert Morris, Persons and Punishment, 53 The Monist, No. 4, at 475 (1968).

21. Harold Garfinkel, Conditions of Successful Degradation Ceremonies, 61 Am. J. Soc. 420 (1956).

22. For recent treatments of the role of the victim in the general part of other criminal law systems, see Manuel Cancio Meliá, Opferverhalten und objektive Zurechnung, 111 ZStW 357 (1999) (focusing on Spanish and German criminal law); Manuel Cancio Meliá, Conducta de la víctima e imputación objetiva (1998) (also discussing Swiss, Italian, and Anglo-American law); Knut Amelung, Über Freiheit und Freiwilligkeit auf der Opferseite der Strafnorm, 1999 GA 182 (German criminal law) (with particular emphasis on the victim's autonomy).

23. See Christopher L. Blakesley, A Conceptual Framework for Extradition and Jurisdiction over Extraterritorial Crimes, 1984 Utah L. Rev. 685, 715.

24. 18 U.S.C. § 2332(a)–(e) (1994); see Brandon S. Chabner, The Omnibus Diplomatic Security and Antiterrorism Act of 1986, 37 UCLA L. Rev. 985 (1990).

25. See Manuel Cancio Meliá, Opferverhalten und objektive Zurechnung, 111 ZStW 357, 359, 362 (1999); Wayne R. LaFave & Austin W. Scott, Jr., Criminal Law 289 (2d ed. 1986).

26. See, e.g., Model Penal Code § 3.08(4).

27. Washington v. Glucksberg, 521 U.S. 702 (1997); Vacco v. Quill, 521 U.S. 793 (1997).

28. Anne M. Coughlin, Excusing Women, 82 Cal. L. Rev. 1 (1994); Shelby A.D. Moore, Battered Women Syndrome: Selling the Shadow to Support the Substance, 38 How. L.J. 297 (1995).

29. See, e.g., Model Penal Code § 210.3(1)(b).

30. See generally Tatjana Hörnle, Distribution of Punishment: The Role of a Victim's Perspective, 3 Buff. Crim. L. Rev. 175 (1999).

31. U.S.S.G. §§ 3A1.1 & 3A1.2.

32. Id. § 5K2.10.

33. N.Y. Penal Law § 125.27 (1997).

34. See supra text accompanying notes 59–97 in ch.3.

35. See generally, James B. Jacobs & Kimberly Potter, Hate Crimes: Criminal Law & Identity Politics (1998).

36. N.Y. Penal Law §§ 240.30 & 240.31 (1997); see also N.Y. Civ. Rights Law §§ 40–c & 40–d (1992) (defining crime of "discrimination").

37. Ill. Crim. Code § 12–7.1 (1998).

38. In re B.C., 680 N.E.2d 1355 (Ill. 1997).

39. The classic treatment of this topic is Lynne N. Henderson, The Wrongs of Victim's Rights, 37 Stan. L. Rev. 937 (1985). For a useful collection of materials, see Douglas E. Beloof, Victims in Criminal Procedure (1999); see also Douglas Evan Beloof, The Third Model of Criminal Process: The Victim Participation Model, 1999 Utah L. Rev. 289 (1999). An earlier account appears in Donald J. Hall, The Role of the Victim in the Prosecution and Disposition of a Criminal Case, 28 Vand. L. Rev. 931 (1975); see also William F. McDonald, Towards a Bicentennial Revolution in Criminal Justice: The Return of the Victim, 13 Am. Crim. L. Rev. 649 (1976).

40. Cheryl Hanna, No Right to Choose: Mandated Victim Participation in Domestic Violence Prosecutions, 109 Harv. L. Rev. 1849, 1860 n.36 (1996); Angela Corsilles, No-Drop Policies in the Prosecution of Domestic Violence Cases, 63 Fordham L. Rev. 853 (1994).

41. Ala. Code § 15–23–64 (1998); Ariz. Rev. Stat. § 13–4408 (1996); Miss. Code. Ann. § 99–43–11 (1998); N.C. Gen. Stat. § 15A–832 (1998); 18 U.S.C. § 1512 (1996).

42. Ascherman v. Bales, 78 Cal. Rptr. 445, 446 (1969) (emphasis added).

43. Linda R.S. v. Richard D., 410 U.S. 614 (1973).

44. Inmates of Attica Correctional Facility v. Rockefeller, 477 F.2d 375 (2d Cir. 1973) (interpreting 42 U.S.C. § 1987).

45. See, e.g., Ariz. Const. art. II, § 2.1; Ill. Const. art. I, § 8.1.

46. People v. Eubanks, 927 P.2d 310 (Cal. 1996).

47. Young v. United States ex rel. Vuitton, 481 U.S. 787 (1986).

48. See, e.g., New Jersey v. Kinder, 701 F. Supp. 486 (D.N.J. 1988).

49. As citizens, victims enjoy the right indirectly and directly to influence criminal lawmaking through their right to vote, as well as their right to be voted for. Many convicted offenders do not, even after they have served their time. See

Note, The Disenfranchisement of Ex-Felons, 102 Harv. L. Rev. 1300 (1989). Occasionally, legislators have been elected not only as victims' representatives but also as victims themselves. See, e.g., Libby Quaid, Execution Turns Tables for Lawmaker, Memphis Commercial Appeal, Aug. 8, 1996 at 2A; see also Sara Faherty, Victims and Victims' Rights 41–49 (1998).

50. See, e.g., Stockton v. Commonwealth, 402 S.E.2d 196 (Va. 1991).

51. U.S. Const. amend. VI; see generally Drew L. Kershen, Vicinage, 29 Okla. L. Rev. 801 (1976) (pt. I), 30 Okla. L. Rev. 3 (1977) (pt. II).

52. Or. Const. art. 1.

53. Burdeau v. McDowell, 256 U.S. 465 (1921). But see N.Y. Crim. Proc. Law § 4506 (1993) (state law providing for exclusion of evidence obtained in violation of criminal eavesdropping statute).

54. See, e.g., Ala. Code. § 15–23–66 (1998); Ariz. Rev. Stat. § 13–4419 (1998); Miss. Code. Ann. § 99–43–17 (1998).

55. See, e.g., Ariz. Rev. Stat. § 8–290.09 (1998).

56. See United States v. Cowan, 524 F. 2d 504 (5th Cir. 1975); United States v. Biddings, 416 F. Supp. 673 (N.D. Ill. 1976); City of Lakewood v. Pfeifer, 583 N.E.2d 1133 (Ohio Mun. 1991).

57. See, e.g., N.Y. Crim. Proc. Law § 170.40 (1993).

58. See, e.g., Jennifer Gerarda Brown, The Use of Mediation to Resolve Criminal Cases: A Procedural Critique, 43 Emory L.J. 1247 (1994).

59. See Bill Blum & Gina Lobaco, The Prop. 8 Puzzle, 5 Cal. Law., Feb. 1985, at 29, 32 (California); Josh Getlin, Plea Bargain Issue: The Jury's Still Out, L.A. Times, Aug. 30, 1987, § 2, at 1, col. 4 (same); People v. Tung, 30 Cal. App. 4th 1607 (1994) (same); see also Albert W. Alschuler, Implementing the Criminal Defendant's Right to Trial: Alternatives to the Plea Bargaining System, 50 U. Chi. L. Rev. 931, 943 (1983) (Alaska)

60. See, e.g., 42 U.S.C. § 10606 (1994) (advisory); Mich. Comp. Laws § 780.756(6)(3) (1998) (mandatory).

61. George P. Fletcher, With Justice for Some: Protecting Victims' Rights in Criminal Trials 247–48 (1995).

62. See State v. McDonnell, 794 P. 2d 780 (Or. 1990); Ala. Code. § 15–23–66 (1998); Ariz. Rev. Stat. § 13–4419 (1998); Miss. Code. Ann. § 99–43–17 (1998).

63. See, e.g., Knutson v. County of Maricopa ex rel. Romley, 857 P. 2d 1299 (Ariz. Ct. App. 1993); State of California: Commission on Judicial Performance, 1996 Annual Report 24 (1996).

64. E.g., Ariz. Rev. Stat. § 13–4434 (1998); Minn. Stat. § 611A.033 (1998); Miss. Code. Ann. § 99–43–19 (1998); Mo. Const. art. I, § 32; Or. Rev. Stat. § 42 (1998); Wis. Stat. § 950.04 (1997).

65. Ala. Code § 15–23–70 (1998); Ariz. Rev. Stat. § 13–4433–4 (1998); Minn. Stat. § 611A.035 (1998); Miss. Code. Ann. § 99–43–25 (1998); Or. Rev. Stat. § 42 (1998); Tex. Crim. Proc. Code Ann. § 56.09 (1997).

66. E.g., Ill. Const. art. 1, § 8.1.

67. E.g., Ala. Code § 15–23–61 (1998); Ariz. Rev. Stat. § 13–4430 (1998); Cal. Penal Code § 679.04 (1998); Colo. Rev. Stat. § 16–10–401 (1998); Wis. Stat. § 950.04 (1997).

68. E.g., 16 Pa. Cons. Stat. Ann. § 1409 (1999); Tenn. Code Ann. § 8–7–401 (1999).

69. For an interesting discussion of similar devices in the German criminal process, see William T. Pizzi & Walter Perron, Crime Victims in German Courtrooms: A Comparative Perspective on American Problems, 32 Stan. J. Int'l L. 37 (1996); see generally Symposium, Victims and the Criminal Law: American and German Perspectives, 3 Buff. Crim. L. Rev. 1 (1999).

70. George P. Fletcher, With Justice for Some: Protecting Victims' Rights in Criminal Trials 194 (1995).

71. Id. at 180, 246.

72. See Markus Dirk Dubber, Regulating the Tender Heart When the Axe Is Ready to Strike, 41 Buff. L. Rev. 85 (1993).

73. See infra text accompanying notes 154–158.

74. State v. Harris, 934 P. 2d 882, 883 (Colo. Ct. App. 1997).

75. Linda Satter, 'Conscience' to Cost Kidnapper $1 a Month, Ark. Democrat-Gazette, Aug. 23, 1995, at 1A (the victim was abducted on Dec. 19).

76. See United States v. McVeigh, 106 F.3d 325 (10th Cir. 1997); 18 U.S.C. § 3510 (1998).

77. On the federal restitution scheme, see, e.g., Jennifer Gerarda Brown, Robbing the Rich to Feed the Poor?, 3 Buff. Crim. L. Rev. 261 (1999).

78. National Victim Center, 1996 Victims' Rights Sourcebook: The Right to Restitution from the Offender 299–301 (1996).

79. Many victim compensation programs are funded in part through various "surcharges," "assessments," "administrative fees," and "restitution fines" imposed upon convicted offenders. Other funding sources include wages of prison inmates, "supervision fees" and "administrative fees" imposed on prison inmates (e.g., in Kansas), and punitive damage awards in civil cases (e.g., in Oregon). Alaskan felons forfeit their annual check from the state's permanent oil fund to the compensation fund. See generally Directory of State Crime Victim Compensation Programs, <http://www.mailbag.com/users/derene/progdir.html> (accessed July 23, 2001).

80. See Henderson, supra note 39; see also Markus Dirk Dubber, The Unprincipled Punishment of Repeat Offenders: A Critique of California's Habitual Criminal Statute, 43 Stan. L. Rev. 193 (1990).

81. People v. Robinson, 699 N.E.2d 1086 (Ill. App. Ct. 1998), vacated, 706 N.E.2d 502 (Ill. 1999).

82. Id. at 1089.

83. Id (emphasis added).

84. Id. at 1092, 1093 (Quinn, J., concurring).

85. Id.

86. State v. Roberts, 894 P.2d 1340 (Wash. 1995).

87. Michael Sangiacomo, Banished to an Island Instead of Imprisoned, Minneapolis Star Trib., Dec. 27, 1994, at 1A.

88. Kristen Delguzzi, Judge Voids Order to Wed; Critics Line Up, Cincinnati Enquirer, July 21, 1995, at A1.

89. But see the case of the prison inmate who was forced to watch videos of his crimes, discussed in text accompanying note 74 supra.

90. Treason, the most serious offense against the state, remains a capital offense. See, e.g., 18 U.S.C. § 2381; see also 18 U.S.C. § 794 (espionage); James Risen, Ex-Agent Pleads Guilty in Spy Case, N.Y. Times, July 7, 2001, at A1, col. 5 (guilty plea in exchange for agreement not to pursue death penalty for espionage).

91. McVeigh Victims' Kin Will Get to See Execution, N.Y. Times, Apr. 12, 2001, at A27, col. 1. On the execution's actual effect on observers, see Jim Yardley, Execution on TV Brings Little Solace, N.Y. Times, June 12, 2001, at A26, col. 4.

92. Bomb Case Telecast Is Rejected by Court, N.Y. Times, Apr. 9, 1998, at A21, col. 1.

93. Mark W. May, Victims' Rights and the Parole Hearing, 15 J. Contemp. L. 71 (1989).

94. President's Task Force on Victims of Crime, Final Report vi (1982) (emphasis added).

95. Id. at 2 (emphasis added).

96. Congressional findings and declaration of purpose § (a)(2), Act Oct. 12, 1982, P.L. 97–291, § 2, 96 Stat. 1248, effective upon Oct. 12, 1982, as provided by § 9(a) of such Act, which appears as 18 U.S.C. § 1512 note (emphasis added).

97. Senate Joint Resolution 3, 106th Congress, 1st Sess., § 1.

98. Katharine Q. Seelye, Gore Seeks Constitutional Guards for Crime Victims, N.Y. Times, July 19, 2000, at 23A, col.1.

99. Paul G. Cassell, Balancing the Scales of Justice: The Case for and the Effects of Utah's Victims' Rights Amendment, 1994 Utah L. Rev. 1373, 1377–78 (citations omitted; emphasis added).

100. Congressional findings and declaration of purpose § (a)(1), Act Oct. 12, 1982, P.L. 97–291, § 2, 96 Stat. 1248, effective upon Oct. 12, 1982, as provided by § 9(a) of such Act, which appears as 18 U.S.C. § 1512 note.

101. Lucy N. Friedman, Executive Director, Victim Services, Letter to the Editor, Victims Should Have Their Day in Court, Too; Coming to Terms, N.Y. Times, Sept. 28, 1997, § 4, at 14, col. 6.

102. Terry A. Maroney, Note, The Struggle against Hate Crime: Movement at a Crossroads, 73 N.Y.U.L. Rev. 564, 577 (1998).

103. See Michael Tonry, Malign Neglect: Race, Crime, and Punishment in America 10 (1995).

104. Id.

105. United States v. Morrison, 120 S. Ct. 1740, 1747 (2000) (discussing 42 U.S.C. § 13981(b), Violence Against Women Act of 1994, § 40302, 108 Stat. 1941–1942) (emphasis added).

106. E.g., Susan Estrich, Real Rape (1986); see generally Henderson, supra not 39, at 949. For a recent attempt to reassert the significance of these narratives in the context of victims' rights, see Lynne Henderson, Revisiting Victim's Rights, 1999 Utah L. Rev. 383.

107. United States v. Gluzman, 953 F. Supp. 84 (S.D.N.Y. 1997).

108. Id. at 91 n.4 (citing S. Rep. 103–138 (1993), at 54).

109. Joseph Berger, Woman Sentenced to Life for Ax Killing of Husband, N.Y. Times, May 1, 1997, at B4, col. 5.

110. See supra text accompanying notes 24 and 67 in ch. 1.

111. Scientist's Wife, on Trial in His Killing, Is Said to Have Been Desperate to Keep Him, N.Y. Times, Jan. 7, 1997, at B4, col. 1.

112. See infra text accompanying notes 24–33 in ch. 5.

113. See Richard Epstein, Torts § 17.11, at 453–57 (1999).

114. Restatement of the Law, Second, Torts § 925 (comment a).

115. To recover for the experience of dying, that is, for pain suffered prior to death, there's another tort action, that survives the death of the victim and therefore is brought by others *on the victim's behalf.* See Restatement of the Law, Second, Torts § 926.

116. Congressional findings and declaration of purpose (a)(7), Act Oct. 12, 1982, P.L. 97–291, § 2, 96 Stat. 1248, effective upon Oct. 12, 1982, as provided by § 9(a) of such Act, which appears as 18 U.S.C. § 1512 note.

117. Booth v. Maryland, 482 U.S. 496 (1987); Payne v. Tennessee, 501 U.S. 808 (1991).

118. The Polly Klaas Story, <http://www.klaaskids.org/pg–stry.htm> (accessed Oct. 18, 2000).

119. Governor Pataki Signs Landmark Law to Require Community Notification for Convicted Sex Offenders, July 25, 1995, <http://www.state.ny.us/governor/press/megan.htm> (accessed July 12, 2001).

120. Id.

121. Id.

122. Governor Signs Jenna's Law; Ends Parole for Violent Felons; Grieshabers Join Governor to Sign Historic Parole Legislation into Law, August 6, 1998, <http://www.state.ny.us/governor/press/aug6_98.htm> (accessed July 12, 2001) (emphasis added).

123. Id.

124. Id.

125. Governor's "Kendra's Law" to Protect Public; Mentally Ill Measure Designed to Ensure Potentially Dangerous Mentally Ill Receive Treatment, May 19, 1999, <http://www.state.ny.us/governor/press/year99/may19_99.htm> (accessed July 12, 2001).

126. Brent Staples, Editorial Observer, When Grieving 'Victims' Can Sway the Courts, N.Y. Times, Sept. 22, 1997, at A26, col. 1.

127. On co-victims and their victims' rights, see Deborah Spungen, Homicide: The Hidden Victims (1998) (defining co-victims as "families and friends of a homicide victim").

128. The Serial/Sexual Predator, East Lansing, Mich., Mich. State Univ., Apr. 1–3, 1998, Conference Speakers, <http://www.newslinkassociates.com/predator/speakers.html> (accessed Oct. 18, 2000).

129. Id.

130. The Polly Klaas Story, <http://www.klaaskids.org/pg–stry.htm> (accessed Oct. 18, 2000).

131. KlaasKids Foundation Accomplishments, <http://www.klaaskids.org/pg–acc.htm> (accessed Oct. 18, 2000).

132. Libby Quaid, Execution Turns Tables for Lawmaker, Memphis Commercial Appeal, Aug. 8, 1996 at 2A; see also Faherty, supra note 49, at 41–49. Douglass and his sister were also *direct* victims of the same criminal episode but, unlike their parents, they escaped death. Nonetheless, Douglass acted as an indirect victim of his parents' homicide, rather than as the direct victim of the assault upon himself.

133. John Greiner, Senator Ready for New Life: Seeing Parents' Killer Die Pivotal for Douglass, Sunday Oklahoman, Nov. 2, 1997, at 1.

134. Id.

135. Cal. Gov't Code § 13960 (distinguishing "victim" from "derivative victim"); see also California Board of Control, "Who Is Eligible to Receive Assistance," <http://www.boc.cahwnet.gov/victims.htm> (accessed Oct. 20, 2000) (distinguishing "direct victim" from "derivative victim").

136. Ralph Winingham, Texas Massacre Spurs Concealed Handgun Law, Times Union (Albany, N.Y.), Oct. 27, 1997, at A8; see also Victim Influential in Passage of Texas Concealed Carry Legislation, <http://www.seedship.com./politics/guns1.html> (accessed May 15, 2000) (Suzanna Gratia Hupp, Jan. 18, 1996 (CBS This Morning)).

137. Carol Morello, Massacre Survivor Speaks for Gun Rights, Post & Courier (Charleston, S.C.), May 14, 2000, at A5.

138. Norman Berkowitz, Letter to the Editor, Victims Should Have Their Day in Court, Too, N.Y. Times, Sept. 28, 1997, § 4, at 14, col. 4.

139. President's Task Force on Victims of Crime, Final Report 114 (1982).

140. Ky. Rev. Stat. § 346–020(6)(a) (1998) ("compensation of crime victims") ("needy person who suffers personal physical or psychological injury or death from a criminal act").

141. See Cornelius Prittwitz, The Resurrection of the Victim in Penal Theory, 3 Buff. Crim. L. Rev. 109 (1999).

142. Jan Phillip Reemtsma, Im Keller (1997). It's also available in English translation, which, however, fails to capture much of the power of the German original. Jan Phillip Reemtsma, In the Cellar (Carol Brown Janeway trans. 1999).

143. See Jan Phillip Reemtsma, Das Recht des Opfers auf die Bestrafung des Täters—als Problem (1999).

144. Id. at 5, 8, 18.

145. Id. at 26–27.

146. Id. at 27.

147. See text accompanying notes 105–06 supra.

148. See, e.g., Donna Coker, Enhancing Autonomy for Battered Women: Lessons from Navajo Peacemaking, 47 UCLA L. Rev. 1 (1999).

149. Staples, supra note 126.

150. Id.

151. See, e.g., Robison v. Maynard, 943 F.2d 1216 (10th Cir. 1991); Barbour v. State, 673 So. 2d 461 (Ala. Crim. App. 1994).

152. Campbell v. State, 679 So. 2d 720, 725 (Fla. 1996); State v. Barone, 328 Ore. 68, 96, 969 P.2d 1013, 1031 (1998).

153. Campbell, 679 So. 2d at 725.

154. Conover v. State, 933 P.2d 904, 920–21 (Okla. Crim. App. 1997).

155. See Wayne A. Logan, Through the Past Darkly: A Survey of the Uses and Abuses of Victim Impact Evidence in Capital Trials, 41 Ariz. L. Rev. 143, 167 (1999).

156. Willingham v. State, 947 P.2d 1074, 1085–86 (Okla. Crim. App. 1997).

157. Witter v. State, 921 P.2d 886 (Nev. 1996).

158. People v. Williams, 692 N.E.2d 1109, 1124 (Ill. 1998).

159. See, e.g., Payne v. Tennessee, 501 U.S. 808 (1991) (overturning Booth v. Maryland, 482 U.S. 496 (1987)); see especially id. at 834 (Scalia, J., concurring) (invoking "public sense of justice keen enough that it has found voice in a nationwide 'victims' rights' movement"); Booth, 482 U.S. at 520 (Scalia, J., dissenting) ("outpouring of popular concern for what has come to be known as 'victims' rights'").

160. Logan, supra note 155, at 151.

161. KlaasKids Foundation Accomplishments, <http://www.klaaskids.org/pg–acc.htm> (accessed Oct. 18, 2000).

162. While race is the main, if only implicit, point of political identification, kinship also plays a central role in the victims' rights movement. The testimonials of surviving family members often manifest a reflexive identification among members of the same family. The emotions triggered by this empathic response are as powerful as they are morally and legally irrelevant; that's why victims' (or offenders') relatives don't serve on juries, or as judges, or—ordinarily—as en-

forcement officials at either end of the criminal process (i.e., police officers and prison guards).

163. See, e.g., Coker, supra note 148. On autonomy in psychotherapy, see Cornelius Castoriadis, The Imaginary Institution of Society (1987).

164. N.Y. Exec. Law § 631(6)(a).

165. See, e.g., Model Penal Code § 2.12.

166. See Markus Dirk Dubber, American Plea Bargains, German Lay Judges, and the Crisis of Criminal Procedure, 49 Stan. L. Rev. 547, 597–601 (1997).

167. Randall Kennedy, Race, Crime and the Law (1997).

168. For more on the right to be punished, see Markus Dirk Dubber, The Right to Be Punished: Autonomy and Its Demise in Modern Penal Thought, 16 L. & Hist. Rev. 113 (1998); Herbert Morris, Persons and Punishment, 53 The Monist, No. 4, at 475 (1968).

169. N.Y. Penal Law § 5.10(1).

170. N.Y. Correct. Law § 662(2).

171. John Sullivan, Beating Victim Testifies in Murder Case, N.Y. Times, Feb. 3, 1998, at B3, col. 4.

172. Restatement of the Law, Second, Torts § 924.

173. Cf. Logan, supra note 155.

174. Payne v. Tennessee, 501 U.S. 808 (1991) (victim); Saffle v. Parks, 494 U.S. 484 (1990) (offender); see Markus Dirk Dubber, Regulating the Tender Heart When the Axe Is Ready to Strike, 41 Buff. L. Rev. 85 (1993).

175. See Cornelius Castoriadis, The Imaginary Institution of Society (1987).

176. Model Penal Code § 210.6(3)(h).

Notes to Chapter 5

1. Conflating victims and witnesses threatens to merge the victims' rights movement into a general campaign for improving government services. The bureaucratization of criminal justice is a serious problem, but it's important not to confuse vindicating the rights of crime victims with cutting lines at the local DMV.

2. See, e.g., California Board of Control, "Authority," <http://www.boc.cah-wnet.gov/victims.htm> (accessed Oct. 20, 2000); Wash. Rev. Code § 7.68.120; see also Jennifer Gerarda Brown, Robbing the Rich to Feed the Poor?, 3 Buff. Crim. L. Rev. 261 (1999) (federal funding for state compensation programs). For a very useful overview of state victim compensation programs, see Directory of State Crime Victim Compensation Programs, <http://www.mailbag.com/users/derene /progdir.html> (accessed Oct. 20, 2000).

3. Senate Joint Resolution 3, 106th Congress, 1st Sess., § 2.

4. N.Y. Exec. Law § 649.

5. Senate Joint Resolution 3, 106th Congress, 1st Sess., § 2.

6. Victims' Rights Constitutional Amendment Implementation Act of 1997, H.R. 1322, 105th Cong. 1st Sess., 2, 5, at § 2(c)(4) (1997).

7. Wayne A. Logan, Through the Past Darkly: A Survey of the Uses and Abuses of Victim Impact Evidence in Capital Trials, 41 Ariz. L. Rev. 143, 155 (1999).

8. Beck v. Commonwealth, 484 S.E.2d 898, 906 (Va. 1997).

9. See Mosley v. State, 983 S.W.2d 249, 262 (Tex. Crim. App. 1998) (en banc).

10. Va. Code Ann. § 19.211.01(B).

11. N.Y. Exec. Law § 621(5).

12. D.C. Code § 3–421 (1999).

13. Ala. Code ti. 1, ch. 23, art. 1(3).

14. N.Y. Penal Law § 60.27(4)(b).

15. Cal. Penal Code § 1202.4.

16. Mass. Ann. Laws. ch. 127, § 1 (1999).

17. H.R. 1322, 105th Cong. 2, 5 (1997), at § 5(2)(a) (emphasis added).

18. Idaho Code, ti. 19, ch. 53.

19. Ga. Code Ann. § 17–14–2 (1999) (emphasis added).

20. See Francis Bowes Sayre, Criminal Conspiracy, 35 Harv. L. Rev. 393 (1922).

21. See, e.g., United States v. Dotterweich, 320 U.S. 277 (1943).

22. Id. at 285.

23. United States v. Park, 421 U.S. 658, 673 (1975).

24. Minn. Stat. § 611A.01(b) (1998).

25. 17–A Me. Rev. Stat. Ann. § 1322 (1998).

26. Nev. Rev. Stat. § 213.005.

27. 18 U.S.C. §§ 3363–3364.

28. Congressional findings and declaration of purpose § (a)(2), Act Oct. 12, 1982, P.L. 97–291, § 2, 96 Stat. 1248, effective upon Oct. 12, 1982, as provided by § 9(a) of such Act, which appears as 18 U.S.C. § 1512 note.

29. See, e.g., Gall v. United States, 21 F.3d 107 (6th Cir. 1994); United States v. Daddato, 996 F.2d 903, 905 (7th Cir. 1993).

30. See, e.g., United States v. Salcedo-Lopez, 907 F.2d 97, 98 (9th Cir. 1990).

31. See United States v. Gibbens, 25 F.3d 28, 32–33 (1st Cir. 1994).

32. See, e.g., Gall v. United States, 21 F.3d 107 (6th Cir. 1994).

33. Cal. Penal Code § 1202.4.

34. N.Y. Crim. Proc. Law § 215.20; 13 Vt. Stat. Ann. § 5301(4).

35. Minn. Stat. § 611A.01(b) (1998).

36. See, e.g., Idaho Code, ti. 19, ch. 53; Ala. Code ti. 15, ch. 18, art. 4A(4); Ala. Code ti. 1, ch. 23, art. 1(3); Ark. Code Ann. § 16–90–703(2) (1997); Texas Crim. Proc. Law § 56.01(3); Va. Code Ann. § 19.2–368.2 (1999); D.C. Code § 3–421 (1999); Fla. Stat. § 775.089 (1998); Ga. Code Ann. § 17–14–2 (1999); Kan. Stat. Ann. § 19–4802; Ky. Rev. Stat. § 346–020(6)(a) (1998); 17–A Me. Rev. Stat. § 1322

(1998); Md. Ann. Code. art. 27, § 770 (1998); Mass. Ann. Laws. ch. 127, § 1; Mich. Comp. Laws § 18.351 (1999); Mich. Stat. Ann. § 28.1274(101) (1999); Ore. Rev. Stat. § 137.103 (1997); Ind. Code Ann. § 35–35–3–1 (1998); Mo. Rev. Stat. § 595.200 (1999); N.H. Rev. Stat. Ann. § 651:62(VI) (1999); N.D. Cent. Code § 12.1–34–01 (1999); Utah Code Ann. § 76–3–201(i) (1999); W. Va. Code § 14–2A–3(k) (1999); Wyo. Stat. § 1–40–102(ix) (1999); Wyo. Stat. § 1–40–202(ii) (1999); Wyo. Stat. § 7–9–101 (1999); Wyo. Stat. § 7–21–101 (1999); see also N.J. Stat. § 52:4B–39 (1999).

37. Nev. Rev. Stat. § 213.005.

38. Rhode Island ti. 12, ch. 25; Haw. Rev. Stat. § 351–2(1)–(3) (1999); Conn. Gen. stat. § 54–201 (1999); V.I. Code ti. 34, ch. 7, subch. 1, § 153; 740 Ill. Comp. Stat. 45/2 (1999); N.J. Stat. § 52:4B–27 (1999).

39. Uniform Victims of Crime Act (National Conference of Commissioners on Uniform State Laws) § 101(6) (1992); Ariz. Crim. Code ti. 13, ch. 40(18); 4 P.R. Laws Ann. § 1503d(1995); S.C. Code Ann. § 16–3–1110(8) (1998); N.C. Gen. Stat. § 15A–830(7) (1999); 11 Del. Code § 3531(2) (1998); Md. Ann. Code. art. 27, § 760 (1998); N.M. Stat. Ann. § 31–26–3 (1999); Wash. Rev. Code § 7.69.020 (1999); Mo. Rev. Stat. § 575.010 (1999); Nev. Rev. Stat. § 213.005; 21 Okla. Stat. § 142A–1 (1998); Pa. Stat. tit. 18, pt. II, art. E, ch. 49, subch. B; Utah Code Ann. § 77–38–2(9)(a) (2000); Utah Code Ann. § 77–27–1(13) (1999); Wis. Stat. § 938.02 (1998); W. Va. Rules Crim. Proc. 32 (1998); see also N.J. Stat. § 52:4B–39 (1999); cf. Gesetz über die Entschädigung für Opfer von Gewalttaten (OEG) § 1 ("intentional unlawful physical attack against his or another person").

40. Alaska Stat. ti. 11, ch. 41, § 270(4).

41. Miss. Code Ann. § 97–17–103 (1998).

42. 720 Ill. Comp. Stat. 5/12–12.

43. Idaho Code, ti. 19, ch. 53; Ala. Code ti. 15, ch. 18, art. 4A(4); Fla. Stat. § 775.089 (1998); Ore. Rev. Stat. § 137.103 (1997); N.H. Rev. Stat. Ann. § 651:62(VI) (1999); Utah Code Ann. § 76–3–201(i) (1999); Utah Code Ann. § 77–27–1(13) (1999).

44. Wyo. Stat. § 7–9–101 (1999) (emphasis added).

45. Ga. Code Ann. § 17–14–2 (1999).

46. R.I. Gen. Laws ti. 12, ch. 25 (emphasis added); see also N.J. Stat. § 52:4B–27 (1999).

47. Miss. Code Ann. § 97–17–103 (1998); see also S.C. Code Ann. § 16–3–1110(8) (1998).

48. S.C. Code Ann. § 16–3–1110(8) (1998) (emphasis added).

49. See infra text accompanying notes 183–204 in ch. 6.

50. 17–A Me. Rev. Stat. § 1322 (1998).

51. 13 Vt. Stat. Ann. § 5301(4) (emphasis added).

52. See, e.g., Uniform Victims of Crime Act § 101(1) (comment).

53. By contrast, the German Victim Compensation Law limits compensation

to the victim of an "intentional unlawful physical attack on his or another person." Gesetz über die Entschädigung für Opfer von Gewalttaten (OEG) § 1.

54. Ohio Rev. Code § 2743.51(C)(1) (emphasis added).

55. In re Petition of Oakgrove, 371 N.W.2d 69 (Minn. App. 1985).

56. In re Turner, 44 Pa. Commw. 326 (1979).

57. Id. at 330.

58. N.Y. Penal Law § 125.10.

59. See, e.g., Haw. Rev. Stat. § 351–32.

60. Paul G. Cassell, Balancing the Scales of Justice: The Case for and the Effects of Utah's Victims' Rights Amendment, 1994 Utah L. Rev. 1373, 1416–17 (quoting Black's Law Dictionary 1567 (6th ed. 1990)).

61. N.Y. Exec. Law § 621(5).

62. Id.

63. On the distinction, see, e.g., Cal. Gov't Code § 13960; see also California Board of Control, "Who Is Eligible to Receive Assistance," <http://www.boc.cahwnet.gov/victims.htm> (accessed Oct. 20, 2000) (distinguishing "direct victim" from "derivative victim").

64. N.Y. Exec. Law § 621(5).

65. Cf. Judith Lewis Herman, Trauma and Recovery 57 (1992). For further discussion of this point, see infra text accompanying notes 75–92 in ch. 6.

66. N.Y. Exec. Law § 621(12) (emphasis added).

67. President's Task Force on Victims of Crime, Final Report 2 (1982) (emphasis added).

68. N.Y. Exec. Law § 620 (emphasis added).

69. Cf. Gesetz über die Entschädigung für Opfer von Gewalttaten (OEG) § 1 ("intentional unlawful *physical* attack against his or another person").

70. See, e.g., Uniform Victims of Crime Act § 307 ("To receive compensation, the claimant must prove by a preponderance of the evidence that the requirements for compensation have been met."). Cf. Re Saferstein, 160 N.J. Super. 393 (1978) (standard is preponderance of the evidence, not beyond a reasonable doubt).

71. N.Y. Exec. Law. § 624(2) ("criminally responsible").

72. Ala. Code. ti. 15, ch. 18, art. 4A(4) ("restitution to victims of crimes").

73. See chapter 4.

74. Cf. G. W. F. Hegel, Elements of the Philosophy of Right § 99 (Allen W. Wood ed., H. B. Nisbet trans., Cambridge 1991).

75. E.g., Ala. Code ti. 15, ch. 18, art. 4A(4).

76. Wyo. Stat. § 1–40–202(ii) (1999).

77. Md. Ann. Code art. 27, § 770 (1998).

78. Fla. Stat. § 775.089 (1998).

79. Wash. Rev. Code § 7.68.020 (1999).

80. Model Penal Code § 1.02(1)(a).

81. N.Y. Penal Law § 1.05(1).

82. Uniform Victims of Crime Act § 101(6).

83. N.Y. Penal Law § 1.05(1) (emphasis added).

84. Mass. Ann. Laws. ch. 127, § 1.

85. S.C. Code Ann. § 16–3–1110(8) (1998); see also Md. Ann. Code. art. 27, § 770 (1998); Mich. Stat. Ann. § 28.1274(101) (1999); Wyo. Stat. § 1–40–202(ii) (1999); Mo. Rev. Stat. § 595.200 (1999); N.D. Cent. Code § 12.1–34–01 (1999).

86. N.Y. Exec. Law § 620.

87. Mont. Pol'y & Proc. Manual, quoted in Uniform Victims of Crime Act § 309 cmt.

88. Fla. Guideline 10L–4.02(8), quoted in Uniform Victims of Crime Act § 309 cmt. (emphasis added).

Notes to Chapter 6

1. 42 U.S.C. § 10602(b).

2. 42 U.S.C. § 10602(b)(4)–(6).

3. Ark. Stat. Ann. § 16–90–703(2) (1997).

4. See generally Wayne R. LaFave & Austin W. Scott, Jr., Criminal Law 129 (2d ed. 1986).

5. See, e.g., Ostrager v. State Board of Control, 99 Cal. App. 3d 1, 160 Cal. Rptr 317 (1st Dist. 1979) (rejecting various constitutional challenges against California residency requirement); In re Allen, 61 Ohio Misc. 2d 361, 579 N.E.2d 309 (1989) (applying residency requirement to derivative victim). But see Sailer v. Tonkin, 356 F. Supp. 72 (D.V.I. 1973) (residency requirement violates equal protection).

6. 34 V.I. Code Ann. § 153 (1998).

7. 42 U.S.C. § 10602(b)(4)–(6).

8. N.Y. Exec. Law § 621(3).

9. 740 Ill. Comp. Stat. § 45/2 (1999).

10. 18 U.S.C. § 233(a)–(e) (1998); see Brandon S. Chabner, The Omnibus Diplomatic Security and Antiterrorism Act of 1986, 37 UCLA L. Rev. 985 (1990).

11. In re Horner, 55 Haw. 514, 523 P.2d 311 (1974) (emphasis added).

12. See, e.g., Keith Loken, The OECD Anti-Bribery Convention: Coverage of Foreign Subsidiaries, 33 Geo. Wash. Int'l L. Rev. 325 (2001) (Foreign Corrupt Practices Act). Thanks to Mathias Reimann for bringing this legislation to my attention.

13. StGB § 7.

14. § 802. Art. 2. Persons subject to this chapter

   (a) The following persons are subject to this chapter:

      (1) Members of a regular component of the armed forces, including those awaiting discharge after expiration of their terms of enlist-

ment; volunteers from the time of their muster or acceptance into the armed forces; inductees from the time of their actual induction into the armed forces; and other persons lawfully called or ordered into, or to duty in or for training in, the armed forces, from the dates when they are required by the terms of the call or order to obey it.

(2) Cadets, aviation cadets, and midshipmen.

(3) Members of a reserve component while on inactive-duty training, but in the case of members of the Army National Guard of the United States or the Air National Guard of the United States only when in Federal service.

(4) Retired members of a regular component of the armed forces who are entitled to pay.

(5) Retired members of a reserve component who are receiving hospitalization from an armed force.

(6) Members of the Fleet Reserve and Fleet Marine Corps Reserve.

(7) Persons in custody of the armed forces serving a sentence imposed by a court-martial.

(8) Members of the National Oceanic and Atmospheric Administration, Public Health Service, and other organizations, when assigned to and serving with the armed forces.

(9) Prisoners of war in custody of the armed forces.

(10) In time of war, persons serving with or accompanying an armed force in the field.

(11) Subject to any treaty or agreement to which the United States is or may be a party or to any accepted rule of international law, persons serving with, employed by, or accompanying the armed forces outside the United States and outside the Commonwealth of Puerto Rico, Guam, and the Virgin Islands.

(12) Subject to any treaty or agreement to which the United States is or may be a party or to any accepted rule of international law, persons within an area leased by or otherwise reserved or acquired for the use of the United States which is under the control of the Secretary concerned and which is outside the United States and outside the Commonwealth of Puerto Rico, Guam, and the Virgin Islands.

15. See supra text accompanying notes 107–11 in ch. 4.

16. Cf. Gesetz über die Entschädigung für Opfer von Gewalttaten (OEG) § 1 ("intentional unlawful physical attack against *his or another person*").

17. Uniform Victims of Crime Act § 101(6).

18. Id. § 101(1).

19. Id. § 101(3).

20. See also Md. Ann. Code. art. 27, § 760 (1998); Wis. Stat. § 938.02 (1998).

21. Uniform Victims of Crime Act § 101, cmt.

22. See supra text accompanying notes 20–23 in ch. 5.

23. See supra text accompanying notes 34–42 in ch. 5.

24. N.Y. Penal Law § 125.10.

25. Id. § 125.05(1) (emphasis added).

26. Id. § 10.00(7) (emphasis added).

27. State v. Jones, 1 Miss. 83 (1820).

28. Id. at 84.

29. For a recent exploration of related questions, see Mary Anne Warren, Moral Status: Obligations to Persons and Other Living Things (1997).

30. Model Penal Code § 2.11(1).

31. See, e.g., Wayne R. LaFave & Austin W. Scott, Jr., Criminal Law 481 (2d ed. 1986).

32. 4 William Blackstone, Commentaries on the Laws of England ch. ii (1769) ("Of the Persons Capable of committing Crimes").

33. N.Y. Penal Law § 125.10.

34. Id. art. 125.

35. Id. tit. H.

36. Id. § 125.05(1).

37. Model Penal Code § 210.1(1).

38. Id. § 210.0(1).

39. Id. art. 230.

40. Id. § 230.3(2).

41. Wis. Stat. § 938.02(a)(1) (1998).

42. Wis. Stat. § 938.02(b) (1998).

43. Carl Schmitt, The Concept of the Political (George Schwab trans. 1996).

44. E.g., Wash. Rev. Code § 7.68.020 (1999).

45. E.g., N.J. Stat. § 52:4B–27 (1999).

46. E.g., Texas Crim. Proc. Law § 56.01(3).

47. E.g., Ala. Code tit. 15, ch. 18, art. 4A(4).

48. Id.; see also Ore. Rev. Stat. § 137.103 (1997); Utah Code Ann. § 76–3–201(ii) (1999).

49. Uniform Victims of Crime Act § 101(6).

50. Id. § 309(c).

51. Model Penal Code § 2.06(2).

52. N.Y. Exec. Law. § 624(2) (emphasis added).

53. Model Penal Code § 2.06(3).

54. N.Y. Exec. Law. § 624(2).

55. See, e.g., Model Penal Code § 210.3.

56. See, e.g., Fla. Guideline 10L–4.02(3), quoted in Uniform Victims of Crime Act § 309 cmt. (50% reduction if "defendant was provoked by the victim in a manner where bodily harm appeared unlikely"), (5) (75% reduction if "defen-

dant was provoked by the victim in a manner where bodily harm to the defendant appears intentional), (6) (complete denial of compensation if "defendant was provoked by the victim in a manner where bodily harm to the defendant is unquestionable"); Minn. R. 7505.2900 (minimum 25% reduction if victim "engaged in any of the following acts or behavior that contributed to the injury for which the claim is filed: . . . used fighting words, obscene or threatening gestures, or other provocation").

57. See infra text accompanying notes 207–20.

58. United States v. Gibbens, 25 F.3d 28, 35 (1st Cir. 1994) (interpreting 18 U.S.C. § 3663(b)(1)) (emphasis added). Contra United States v. Dougherty, 810 F.2d 763 (8th Cir. 1987).

59. Gibbens, 25 F.3d at 34.

60. Id.

61. In its style and rhetorical sophistication, the opinion also illustrates another significant difference between restitution and compensation. Restitution is determined by a court, compensation by a board, though a claimant may seek judicial review of an adverse compensation ruling. See, e.g., Criminal Injuries Compensation Board v. Gould, 273 Md. 486, 331 A.2d 55 (1975); Hughes v. North Dakota Crime Victims Reparations Board, 246 N.W.2d 774 (N.D. 1976).

62. U.S. Dep't of Justice, Bureau of Justice Statistics, Victims Characteristics: Annual Household Income <http://www.ojp.usdoj.gov/bjs/cvict_v.htm#income> (accessed Nov. 3, 2000).

63. U.S. Dep't of Justice, Bureau of Justice Statistics, Bureau of Justice Statistics, Homicide Trends in the U.S: Trends by Race, <http://www.ojp.usdoj.gov/bjs /homicide/race.htm> (accessed Nov. 3, 2000) ("Blacks were 6 times more likely than whites to be murdered in 1998."); id. ("Blacks were 7 times more likely than whites to commit homicide in 1998."); see also U.S. Dep't of Justice, Bureau of Justice Statistics, Violent Crime Rates by Race of Victim, <http://www.ojp.usdoj .gov/bjs/glance/race.htm> (accessed Nov. 3, 2000) (blacks twice as likely as whites to be victim of homicide, rape, robbery, or aggravated assault).

64. U.S. Dep't of Justice, Bureau of Justice Statistics, Homicide Trends in the U.S: Trends by Race, <http://www.ojp.usdoj.gov/bjs/homicide/race.htm> (accessed Nov. 3, 2000).

65. See supra text accompanying notes 55–57.

66. See John Kaplan, Robert Weisberg & Guyora Binder, Criminal Law: Cases and Materials 81–81 (3d ed. 1996); see also Paul Robinson, Criminal Law Case Studies 129 (2000).

67. Carl Ingram, Victims' Aid Funds for Convict Protested, L.A. Times, July 11, 1987, at 29, col. 1.

68. Philip Hager, 208–Year Term in 1982 Child Molestation Case Rejected, L.A. Times, Sept. 3, 1988, at 29, col. 1.

69. State v. Leidholm, 334 N.W.2d 811 (N.D. 1983); see also Paul Robinson, supra note 66, at 110.

70. Stoffer v. State, 15 Ohio St. 47, 49 (1864).

71. Id. at 52.

72. See supra text accompanying notes 16–32.

73. See, e.g., D.C. Code § 3–421 (1999).

74. Haw. Rev. Stat. § 351–31.

75. Id. § 351–32.

76. N.Y. Penal Law § 135.00(1).

77. Id. § 135.00(2).

78. See, e.g., Jan Phillip Reemtsma, In the Cellar (Carol Brown Janeway trans. 1999).

79. See supra text accompanying note 171, in ch. 4 (mugging victim's narrative).

80. S.C. Code Ann. § 16–3–1110(8) (1998).

81. See infra text accompanying notes 93–118 infra.

82. For an interesting attempt to categorize criminal harm, see Andrew von Hirsch & Nils Jareborg, Gauging Criminal Harm: A Living–Standard Analysis, in Principled Sentencing 220 (Andrew von Hirsch & Andrew Ashworth eds. 1992).

83. See also Md. Ann. Code. art 27, § 770 (1998); Mich. Stat. Ann. § 28.1274(101) (1999); Mo. Rev. Stat. § 595.200 (1999); N.D. Cent. Code § 12.1–34–01 (1999); Wyo. Stat. § 1–40–202(ii) (1999).

84. 11 Del. Code § 3531(2) (1998); see also 13 Vt. Stat. Ann. § 5301(4); Rev. Stat. Mo. § 595.200 (1999); 4 P.R. Laws Ann. § 1503d (1995); Md. Ann. Code. art. 27, § 760 (1998); Mo. Rev. Stat. § 575.010 (1999); Pa. Stat. Ann. tit. 18, pt. II, art. E, ch. 49, subch. B; Utah Code Ann. § 77–38–2(9)(a) (2000).

85. Mo. Rev. Stat. § 595.200 (1999).

86. The statute of limitations, as well as the causation requirement, places a time limit on the compensability of the latter type of harm. For more on the question of causation, see infra text accompanying notes 119–52.

87. Cf. Commonwealth v. Slaney, 185 N.E.2d 919 (Mass. 1962). American courts and textbook writers nonetheless often stress the irrelevance of the victim's perspective in assault cases, on the ground that the "criminal law is designed primarily to preserve the public peace." Id. at 922 (quoting Perkins on Criminal Law 89 (1957)).

88. E.g., Kan. Stat. Ann. § 21–3408; see also Model Penal Code § 211.1(c) ("fear of imminent serious bodily injury")

89. N.Y. Penal Law § 120.15.

90. See Model Penal Code and Commentaries (Official Draft and Revised Comments): Part I (General Provisions §§ 3.01 to 5.07, at 323, 325, 490 (1985).

91. Cf. R. A. Duff, Criminal Attempts (1996). See also Restatement of the Law

of Torts (Second) § 22 ("An attempt to inflict a harmful or offensive contact or to cause apprehension of such contact does not make the actor liable for an assault if the other does not become aware of the attempt before it is terminated.")

92. See Model Penal Code and Commentaries (Official Draft and Revised Comments): Part I (General Provisions §§ 1.01 to 2.13, at 243 (1985).

93. Idaho Code tit. 19, ch. 53; Fla. Stat. § 775.089 (1998); Ky. Rev. Stat. § 346–020(6)(a) (1998); 13 Vt. Stat. Ann. § 5301(4); Ala. Code tit. 1, ch. 23, art. 1(3); Ark. Stat. Ann. § 16–90–703(2) (1997); Texas Crim. Proc. Law § 56.01(3); Va. Code Ann. § 19.2–368.2 (1999); D.C. Code § 3–421 (1999); Fla. Stat. § 775.089 (1998); 17–A Me. Rev. Stat. § 1322 (1998); Mass. Ann. Laws. ch. 127, § 1; Mich. Comp. Laws § 18.351 (1999).

94. Idaho Code, tit. 19, ch. 53; Minn. Stat. § 611A.01(b) (1998); Fla. Stat. § 775.089 (1998); Kan. Stat. Ann. § 19–4802; 17–A Me. Rev. Stat. § 1322 (1998); Mass. Ann. Laws. ch. 127, § 1; N.H. Rev. Stat. Ann. § 651:62(VI) (1999); N.J. Stat. § 52:4B–39 (1999).

95. Ala. Code tit. 15, ch. 18, art. 4A(4); Fla. Stat. § 775.089 (1998); Ga. Code Ann. § 17–14–2 (1999); Mass. Ann. Laws. ch. 127, § 1; Ore. Rev. Stat. § 137.103 (1997); Utah Code Ann. § 76–3–201(i) (1999); Wyo. Stat. § 7–9–101 (1999).

96. S.C. Code Ann. § 16–3–1110(8) (1998); Minn. Stat. § 611A.01(b) (1998); Md. Ann. Code. art. 27, § 770 (1998); Mich. Stat. Ann. § 28.1274(101) (1999); Ind. Code Ann. § 35–35–3–1 (1998); Mo. Rev. Stat. § 595.200 (1999); N.D. Cent. Code § 12.1–34–01 (1999); Wyo. Stat. § 1–40–202(ii) (1999); id. § 7–21–101 (1999).

97. Idaho Code tit. 19, ch. 53.

98. Minn. Stat. § 611A.01(b) (1998).

99. 17–A Me. Rev. Stat. § 1322 (1998).

100. Mass. Ann. Laws. ch. 127, § 1.

101. Fla. Stat. § 775.089 (1998).

102. Model Penal Code pt. II ("Definition of Specific Crimes").

103. Id. arts. 210–213.

104. Id. § 1.02(1)(a).

105. Id. § 2.12 (emphasis added).

106. Id. §§ 1.09(1)(c), 1.10.

107. Id. § 1.12(10)(i).

108. Id. § 2.02(6).

109. Id. § 2.11.

110. Id. § 3.02(1).

111. Id. § 212.3 (emphasis added).

112. N.Y. Penal Law § 135.00(1) (emphasis added).

113. Model Penal Code § 212.5.

114. Id. art. 210.

115. Id. art. 211.

116. Id. art. 212; see supra text accompanying notes 63–65, in ch. 5.

117. Id. art. 213; see Stephen J. Schulhofer, Taking Sexual Autonomy Seriously: Rape Law and Beyond, 11 L. & Phil. 35 (1992)

118. See, e.g., NOW v. Scheidler, 968 F.2d 612 (7th Cir. 1992), rev'd, 510 U.S. 249 (1994).

119. Model Penal Code § 211.1(a).

120. Uniform Victims of Crime Act §§ 401 (restitution) & 305 (compensation).

121. 21 Okla. Stat. § 1431 (first degree burglary).

122. Id. § 642.

123. Id. § 741.

124. Pack v. State, 819 P.2d 280, 285 (Ok. Crim. App. 1991).

125. Uniform Victims of Crime Act § 101(6).

126. N.Y. Exec. Law § 621(5).

127. Cal. Gov't Code § 13960 (distinguishing "victim" from "derivative victim"); see also California Board of Control, "Who Is Eligible to Receive Assistance," <http://www.boc.cahwnet.gov/victims.htm> (accessed Oct. 20, 2000) (distinguishing "direct victim" from "derivative victim").

128. Idaho Code tit. 19, ch. 53.

129. See, e.g., State v. Coronado, 922 P.2d 927 (Ariz. App. 1996) (direct causation requirement as applied to indirect victims; right of surviving victim relatives not to submit to interview by defense counsel).

130. Idaho Code tit. 19, ch. 53.

131. Ga. Code Ann. § 17–14–2 (1999); N.D. Cent. Code § 12.1–34–01 (1999).

132. Uniform Victims of Crime Act §§ 401 (restitution) & 305 (compensation) (emphases added).

133. See supra text accompanying note 25 in ch. 4.

134. See supra text accompanying notes 55–57.

135. In re DeCerbo, 449 N.E.2d 526, 528 (Ohio Ct. Cl. 1982).

136. Wash. § 7.68.020 (1999).

137. In re May, No. V94–43540jud (Ohio Ct. Cl. Feb. 29, 1996) (cited in In re Kallay, 698 N.E.2d 132, 133–34 (Ohio Ct. Cl. 1997)).

138. Kallay, 698 N.E.2d at 134.

139. In re Thorpe, 593 N.E.2d 499 (Ohio Ct. Cl. 1990) (quoting In re Jones, No. V79–3029jud (Ohio Ct. Cl. Sept. 9, 1981) and Negligence § 43, 70 Ohio Jurisprudence 3d 108–09 (1986)).

140. McMillan v. Crime Victims Comp. Bd., 399 N.W.2d 515, 519 (Mich. App. 1986) (emphasis added).

141. 42 U.S.C.A. § 10602(b)(1) (West Supp. 1992).

142. N.Y. Veh. & Traf. Law § 1232(a).

143. N.Y. Penal Law §§ 120.03–.04 (vehicular assault), 125.12–.13 (vehicular manslaughter).

144. Uniform Victims of Crime Act § 401 (restitution) (emphases added).

145. Model Penal Code § 2.03, Comment at 261 n. 17 (1985); see also id. § 2.03(2)(b), (3)(b). For a vagueness challenge against this approach, see State v. Maldonado, 137 N.J. 536, 645 A.2d 1165 (1994).

146. People v. Hickman, 12 Ill. App. 3d 412, 297 N.E.2d 582 (1973).

147. See, e.g., People v. Stamp, 82 Cal. Rptr. 598 (Cal. App. 1969).

148. McMillan v. Crime Victims Comp. Bd., 399 N.W.2d 515, 517–18 (Mich. App. 1986).

149. McMillan, 399 N.W.2d at 519.

150. In re DeCerbo, 449 N.E.2d 526, 527 (Ohio Ct. Cl. 1982).

151. DeCerbo, 449 N.E.2d at 528 (emphases added).

152. See, e.g., Landessozialgericht Nordrhein-Westfalen (L 10 V 10/96; Mar. 5, 1998) (denying compensation to assault victim because of association with "pimp milieu" since "ca. 1970").

153. N.Y. Exec. Law § 621(7); D.C. Code § 3–421(C) (1999); 740 Ill. Comp. Stat. § 45/2(3); Miss. Code Ann. § 97–17–103(b); Minn. Stat. § 611A.01(b); N.H. Rev. Stat. Ann. § 651:62(vi); W. Va. Code § 14–2A–3(k); Wyo. Stat. § 1–40–102(ix)(A).

154. N.Y. Penal Law § 160.00.

155. E.g., Ala. Code tit. 1, ch. 23, art. 1(3).

156. E.g., Idaho Code tit. 19, ch. 53.

157. E.g., Ky. Rev. Stat. § 346–020(6)(a) (1998).

158. Wash. Rev. Code § 7.68.020 (1999).

159. N.Y. Penal Law § 35.05.

160. The German Victim Compensation Law isn't. It limits compensation to someone injured by an "intentional *unlawful* physical attack against his or another person." Gesetz über die Entschädigung für Opfer von Gewalttaten (OEG) § 1. Justified attacks, in other words, are not compensable. See, e.g., Landessozialgericht Nordrhein-Westfalen (L 6 VG 76/96; Jan. 25, 2000).

161. That's also the case under the German Victim Compensation Law. Unlike justifications, excuses do not stand in the way of compensation. See Gesetz über die Entschädigung für Opfer von Gewalttaten (OEG) § 1. See, e.g., Landessozialgericht Nordrhein-Westfalen (L 10 VG 43/96; Dec. 16, 1998). Unlawfulness is enough for victim compensation; the offender's guilt, or responsibility, isn't required.

162. Uniform Victims of Crime Act § 101, cmt.

163. Ala. Code § 15–14–52(3) (1999) ("crime victims' court attendance").

164. Ala. Code tit. 15, ch. 18, art. 4A(4) ("restitution to victims of crimes") (emphasis added); see also Ore. Rev. Stat. § 137.103 (1997) ("restitution"); Utah Code Ann. § 76–3–201(i) ("sentencing"); Wyo. Stat. § 7–9–101(v) (1999) ("restitution").

165. Ala. Code tit. 23, ch. 18, art. 1(3) ("crime victims' compensation"); see also Ark. Stat. Ann. § 16–90–703 (1997) ("crime victims reparations"); W. Va. Code § 14–2A–3 (1999) ("compensation").

166. Idaho Code tit. 19, ch. 53 ("compensation"); Texas Crim. Proc. Law § 56.01(3) ("crime victims' rights"); see also N.H. Rev. Stat. Ann. § 651:62(IV) ("restitution").

167. Wash. Rev. Code § 7.68.020 (1999) ("victims of crime—compensation, assistance"); see also N.D. Cent. Code § 12.1–34–01 (1999) ("fair treatment of victims and witnesses"); Wyo. Stat. § 1–40–102(ix) (1999) ("compensation"); id. § 1–40–202(ii) ("victim and witness bill of rights").

168. Haw. Rev. Stat. § 351–2(1) ("compensation").

169. Ga. Code Ann. § 17–14–2 (1999) ("restitution").

170. Id. § 17–14–2(4) (1999) (emphasis added).

171. Model Penal Code § 3.01(2).

172. See, e.g., Restatement of the Law of Torts (Second) § 288A ("excused violations").

173. Id. § 262.

174. Model Penal Code § 3.02(1).

175. See supra text accompanying notes 58–60 in ch. 5.

176. Model Penal Code § 3.02(2).

177. In re DeCerbo, 449 N.E.2d 526, 528 (Ohio Ct. Cl. 1982).

178. See supra text accompanying notes 16–32.

179. Model Penal Code § 212.5.

180. Uniform Victims of Crime Act § 101(1), cmt.

181. See, e.g., Montana v. Egelhoff, 518 U.S. 37 (1996).

182. N.Y. Exec. Law § 620.

183. See the distinction between *Täterstrafrecht* and *Tatstrafrecht*, or offender criminal law and offense criminal law, in the German literature. See Claus Roxin, Strafrecht Allgemeiner Teil (Band I) § 6 (3d ed. 1997).

184. N.Y. Exec. Law § 621(7).

185. Uniform Victims of Crime Act § 309(c), cmt.

186. Id.

187. Ariz. Crim. Code ti. 13, ch. 40(18) (emphasis added); see also Utah Code Ann. § 77–38–2(b).

188. Ohio Rev. Code § 2743.60(E).

189. In re Vaughn, 698 N.E.2d 148, 150 (Ohio Ct. Cl. 1997) (quoting State v. Brown, 525 N.E.2d 805, 808 (Ohio 1988)).

190. Cf. Tennessee v. Garner, 471 U.S. 1, 14 (1985); United States v. Watson, 423 U.S. 411, 440 (1976) (Marshall, J., dissenting).

191. In re Bradley, 706 N.E.2d 1278 (Ohio Ct. Cl. 1998) (receiving stolen property).

192. In re Paige, 643 N.E.2d 629 (Ohio Ct. Cl. 1994).

193. In re Porter, 684 N.E.2d 107 (Ohio Ct. Cl. 1994).

194. In re Ford, 698 N.E.2d 157 (Ohio Ct. Cl. 1997).

195. See, e.g., Hollis v. State, 468 N.E.2d 553 (Ind. App. 1984) (rejecting equal protection attack on "family exclusion" provision).

196. N.Y. Exec. Law § 621(4).

197. Gossard v. Criminal Injuries Compensation Board, 279 Md. 309, 368 A.2d 443 (1977).

198. Hollis v. State, 468 N.E.2d 553 (Ind. App. 1984).

199. In re Franck, 585 N.E.2d 589 (Ohio Ct. Cl. 1990).

200. Weisinger v. Van Rensselaer, 362 N.Y.S.2d 126 (Sup. Ct. 1974).

201. Ocasio v. Bureau of Crimes Compensation Div. of Workers' Compensation, 408 So. 2d 751 (Fla. App. 1982).

202. Criminal Injuries Compensation Board v. Remson, 384 A.2d 58 (1978).

203. See supra text accompanying note 21 in ch. 5.

204. Uniform Victims of Crime Act § 309(b).

205. Florida Guideline 10L–4.02(8).

206. Minn. R. 7505.2900(c).

207. See Markus Dirk Dubber, The Unprincipled Punishment of Repeat Offenders: A Critique of California's Habitual Criminal Statute, 43 Stan. L. Rev. 193, 193 (1990).

208. U.S.S.G. § 4B1.1; see also 28 U.S.C. § 994(d) ("categories of defendants").

209. Kansas v. Hendricks, 521 U.S. 346 (1997).

210. Payne v. Tennessee, 501 U.S. 808 (1991).

211. Uniform Victims of Crime Act § 101(2).

212. Id. § 309(c) (emphasis added).

213. Fla. Stat. Ann. § 960.13(6) (West Supp. 1992) (emphasis added).

214. Fla. Guideline 10L–4.02, quoted in Uniform Victims of Crme Act § 309 cmt.

215. Uniform Victims of Crime Act § 309 ("limit on compensation because of claimant's *conduct*") (emphasis added).

216. U.S.S.G. § 5K2.10 (emphasis added).

217. Mont. Pol'y & Proc. Manual, quoted in Uniform Victims of Crime Act § 309 cmt.

218. See, e.g., King v. State, 43 Tex. 351 (1875).

219. Wayne R. LaFave & Austin W. Scott, Jr., Criminal Law 480 (2d ed. 1986).

220. U.S.S.G. § 5K2.10.

Index

About the Author

Markus Dirk Dubber is Professor of Law and Director of the Buffalo Criminal Law Center at the State University of New York, Buffalo.